Praise for

THE SEVEN SINS
OF MEMORY

"You could hardly ask for a more knowledgeable interpreter of the scientific literature . . . The exposition is solid, the advice measured."
— Stephen S. Hall, *New York Times Book Review*

"Endlessly intriguing . . . [a] provocative examination of memory's seven deadly sins."
— David Kipen, *San Francisco Chronicle*

"Beyond the curious and amazing elements of memory, the technical, neurological, and legal issues, Schacter's work goes to the heart of what it means to be human."
— David Mehegan, *Boston Globe*

"A fascinating journey through paths of memory, its open avenues and blind alleys. Rarely have I received such a lucid, engaging, and enjoyable book about science."
— Jerome Groopman, M.D., author of
How Doctors Think

"This book brings together an enormous amount of material in a form that is entertaining, informative, and credible."
— Larry Squire, *Nature*

"Bravo: a tour de force. No one can better explain for the general reader the new insights on memory and its distortion than Daniel Schacter, one of the most exciting and original students of the biology of memory."
— Eric R. Kandel, M.D., Nobel laureate

THE SEVEN SINS
OF MEMORY

BOOKS BY

DANIEL L. SCHACTER

Stranger Behind the Engram: Theories of Memory
    and the Psychology of Science

Sleep and Cognition (*edited with Richard R. Bootzin and
    John F Kihlstrom*)

Awareness of Deficit After Brain Injury: Theoretical and
    Clinical Aspects (*edited with G. P. Prigatano*)

Memory Systems 1994 (*edited with Endel Tulving*)

Memory Distortion: How Minds, Brains, and Societies
    Reconstruct the Past

Searching for Memory: The Brain, the Mind, and the Past

The Cognitive Neuropsychology of False Memories

Memory, Brain, and Belief (*edited with Elaine Scarry*)

The Seven Sins of Memory: How the Mind Forgets and Remembers

Neuropsychology of Memory (*edited with Larry R. Squire*)

Forgotten Ideas, Neglected Pioneers: Richard Semon and
    the Story of Memory

Psychology (*authored with Daniel T. Gilbert, Matthew K. Nock,
    and Daniel M. Wegner*)

Introducing Psychology (*authored with Daniel T. Gilbert,
    Matthew K. Nock, and Daniel M. Wegner*)

The Seven Sins
of
Memory

HOW THE MIND FORGETS
AND REMEMBERS

Updated Edition

DANIEL L. SCHACTER

Mariner Books

Houghton Mifflin Harcourt

BOSTON   NEW YORK

Second Mariner Books Edition 2021

For information about permission to reproduce selections from this book,
write to trade.permissions@hmhco.com or to Permissions,
Houghton Mifflin Harcourt Publishing Company,
3 Park Avenue, 19th Floor, New York, New York 10016.

hmhbooks.com

Library of Congress Cataloging-in-Publication Data
Names: Schacter, Daniel L., author.
Title: The seven sins of memory : how the mind forgets and remembers /
Daniel L. Schacter.
Description: Updated edition. | Boston : Mariner Books ; Houghton Mifflin
Harcourt, 2021. | Includes bibliographical references and index.
Identifiers: LCCN 2021014679 (print) | LCCN 2021014680 (ebook) |
ISBN 9780358325680 (trade paperback) | ISBN 9780358296997 | ISBN 9780358297055 |
ISBN 9780618219193 | ISBN 9780547347455 (ebook)
Subjects: LCSH: Memory disorders. | Memory. | Recollection (Psychology)
Classification: LCC BF376 .S33 2021 (print) | LCC BF376 (ebook) |
DDC 153.1/2—dc23
LC record available at https://lccn.loc.gov/2021014679
LC ebook record available at https://lccn.loc.gov/2021014680

Printed in the United States of America
1 2021
4500831948

For my family:

SUSAN, HANNAH, AND EMILY

Contents

Acknowledgments

It sometimes seems unfair that a book bears only an author's name, because a number of people are responsible, directly or indirectly, for its conception, development, and production. This book is no exception. I've had the good fortune to consult with many colleagues and students about the topics in these pages — too many to thank individually. I hope that you know who you are and realize that I greatly value your input. I am especially thankful to the members of my laboratory during the past few years; your feedback and ideas have been invaluable for this book and all of my other scientific endeavors.

I owe a special debt to those who have taken the time to read and comment on the manuscript. Moshe Bar, Chad Dodson, Marc Hauser, Lael Schooler, David Sherry, and Gabriella Vigliocco provided incisive feedback on specific chapters, which helped me to rethink some important issues and saved me from a variety of oversights and errors. Randy Buckner, Wilma Koutstaal, Richard McNally, and Anthony Wagner read the entire manuscript, coming up with many helpful suggestions and constructive criticisms that have improved the final product considerably. Several of my research assistants — Steve Prince, Carrie Racine, and Danielle Unger — have helped me in ways too numerous to list; I want them to know how much I value their time and effort.

Laura van Dam, my editor at Houghton Mifflin, supported the book enthusiastically and provided insightful comments on several drafts of the evolving manuscript. Her keen eye for both style and substance helped me to improve the final product immensely. My agent, Susan Rabiner, lent her wisdom and energy to this project, and I appreciate both.

I began *The Seven Sins of Memory* during a sabbatical year that was supported by a John Simon Guggenheim Memorial Fellowship and an award from the James McKeen Cattell Fund; without them, I could not have completed it. I spent several months of my sabbatical at the Institute for Cognitive Neuroscience at University College London, where I wrote parts of the book. I am indebted to Professor Tim Shallice for making my stay possible, and to colleagues and staff at the institute for making my visit both enjoyable and productive. I am also thankful to the funding agencies that have supported my ongoing research: Human Frontiers Science Program, National Institute on Aging, National Institute of Mental Health, and National Institute on Neurological Disorders and Stroke. I describe significant portions of the work they have supported in these pages.

Finally, I owe so much to my wife, Susan McGlynn, and my daughters, Hannah and Emily Schacter, that I hardly know how to begin to say thanks. As a start, I dedicate this book to them.

Preface to the Updated Edition

I AM AMAZED THAT two decades have passed since I wrote the first edition of *The Seven Sins of Memory*, but the calendar doesn't lie. More than once during that time, I've come across an exciting new research finding or intriguing idea that is relevant to one of the sins and immediately thought: "I wish I had been able to talk about *that* in the book!" So, when my agent, Susan Rabiner, let me know that Houghton Mifflin Harcourt would be interested in publishing an updated version of *Seven Sins*, I embraced the opportunity to incorporate some of the important new developments regarding the sins that have emerged since 2001. I've done so by building on the contents of the 2001 edition with updates at the end of each chapter that discuss two noteworthy developments that are relevant to that chapter. Much has happened in memory research since 2001, and because I couldn't do justice to all of it without writing an entirely new book, I have included updates about ideas and findings that I think either illuminate the nature of the memory sins or highlight their impact on our day-to-day lives in a compelling way. I very much hope that the updates are as interesting for you to read as they have been for me to write.

The updates have been improved by feedback from students and colleagues who have taken the time to read them: thanks to Nadia Brashier, Adam Bulley, Alexis Carpenter, Ethan Harris, Catherine Ho, Sarah Kalinowski, Kevin Madore, Johannes Mahr, Paul Seli, Preston Thakral, Ruben van Genugten, John Wixted, and Jordana Wynn for their valuable input and insights. I'm also greatly appreciative for many stimulating discussions with students in my freshman seminar at Harvard concerning the seven sins of memory, which I've offered every few years since 2001 and will hopefully benefit from an updated course text. I also thank Susan Rabiner for planting the idea of a new edition and my editor at Houghton Mifflin Harcourt, Nicole Angeloro, for her interest and support throughout the revision process.

Finally, I dedicated the 2001 edition of this book to my wife, Susan, and my (now very impressive adult) daughters, Hannah and Emily, and with great satisfaction I do so again twenty years later.

— DANIEL SCHACTER
April 2021

THE SEVEN SINS
OF MEMORY

A Blessing Bestowed
by the Gods

IN YASUNARI KAWABATA'S UNSETTLING short story "Yumiura," a novelist receives an unexpected visit from a woman who says she knew him thirty years earlier. They met when he visited the town of Yumiura during a harbor festival, the woman explains. But the novelist cannot remember her. Plagued recently by other troublesome memory lapses, he sees this latest incident as a further sign of mental decline. His discomfort turns to alarm when the woman offers more revelations about what happened one day when he visited her room. "You asked me to marry you," she recalls wistfully. The novelist reels while contemplating the magnitude of what he has forgotten. The woman explains that she has never forgotten their time together and feels continually burdened by her memories of him.

After she leaves, the shaken novelist searches maps for the town of Yumiura with the hope of triggering recall of the place and the reasons why he had gone there. But no maps or books list such a town. The novelist then realizes that he could not have been in the part of the country the woman described at the time she remembered. Though the woman believed that her detailed and heartfelt memories were accurate, they were entirely false.

Kawabata's story dramatically illustrates different ways in which memory can get us into trouble.

Sometimes we forget the past, and at other times we distort it; some disturbing memories haunt us for years. Yet we also rely on memory to perform an astonishing variety of tasks in our everyday lives. Recalling conversations with friends or recollecting family vacations, remembering appointments and errands we need to run, calling up words that allow us to speak and understand others, remembering foods we like and dislike, acquiring the knowledge needed for a new job — all depend, in one way or another, on memory. Memory plays such a pervasive role in our daily lives that we often take it for granted until an incident of forgetting or distortion demands our attention.

Memory's errors have long fascinated scientists and have come to occupy a prominent place in our society. With the aging of our society, memory problems are increasingly common among this large sector of the population. Seemingly endless numbers of articles, books, and blogs remind us that memory has become a principal health concern of busy, stressed-out, and forgetful adults — and many others. Forgotten encounters, misplaced eyeglasses, and failures to recall the names of familiar faces are regular occurrences for many adults who are busily trying to juggle the demands of work and family and to cope with the bewildering array of new communication technologies. How many passwords and PINs do you have to remember just to manage your affairs on the Internet, not to mention your voice mail at the office or your cell phone? How often have you had to seek a new password at a website because you've forgotten your current one? I've lost track of how many times I've had to work through that annoying experience.

In addition to dealing with the frustrations of memory failures in daily life, the awful specter of Alzheimer's disease looms large. As the general public becomes ever more aware of its horrors through such high-profile cases as singer Glen Campbell's battle with the disorder before his death in 2017, the prospects of a life dominated by catastrophic forgetting further increase our preoccupations with memory.

Although the magnitude of the woman's memory distortion in "Yumiura" seems to stretch the bounds of credulity, it has been equaled and even exceeded in everyday life. Consider the story of Binjimin Wilkomirski, whose 1996 Holocaust memoir, *Fragments*, won worldwide acclaim for portraying life in a concentration camp from the perspective of a child. Wilkomirski presented readers with raw, vivid recollections of the unspeakable terrors he witnessed as a young boy. His prose achieved such power and eloquence that one reviewer proclaimed that *Fragments* is "so morally important and so free from literary artifice of any kind at all that I wonder if I even have the right to try to offer praise." Even more remarkable, Wilkomirski had spent much of his adult life unaware of these traumatic childhood memories, coming to terms with them only in therapy. Because his story and memories inspired countless others, Wilkomirski became a sought-after international figure and a hero to Holocaust survivors.

The story began to unravel, however, in late August 1998, when Daniel Ganzfried, a Swiss journalist and himself the son of a Holocaust survivor, published a stunning article in a Zurich newspaper. Ganzfried revealed that Wilkomirski was actually Bruno Dossekker, born in 1941 to a young woman named Yvonne Berthe Grosjean, who later gave him up for adoption to an orphanage. Young Bruno spent all of the war years with his foster parents, the Dossekkers, in the safe confines of his native Switzerland. Whatever the basis for his traumatic "memories" of Nazi horrors, they did not come from childhood experiences in a concentration camp. Was Dossekker/Wilkomirski simply a liar? Probably not: he still strongly believed that his recollections were real.

We're all capable of distorting our pasts. Think back to your first year in high school and try to answer the following questions: Did your parents encourage you to be active in sports? Was religion helpful to you? Did you receive physical punishment as discipline? The Northwestern University psychiatrist Daniel Offer and his collaborators put these and related questions to sixty-seven men in their late forties. Their answers are especially interesting because Offer had asked the same men the same questions during freshman year in high school, thirty-four years earlier.

The men's memories of their adolescent lives bore little relationship to what they had reported as high school freshmen. Fewer than

40 percent of the men recalled parental encouragement to be active in sports; some 60 percent had reported such encouragement as adolescents. Barely one-quarter recalled that religion was helpful, but nearly 70 percent had said that it was when they were adolescents. And though only one-third of the adults recalled receiving physical punishment decades earlier, as adolescents nearly 90 percent had answered the question affirmatively.

Memory's errors are as fascinating as they are important. What sort of system permits the kinds of distortions described in Kawabata's fiction and the Wilkomirski case, or the inaccuracies documented in Offer's study? Why do we sometimes fail to recall the names of people whose faces are perfectly familiar to us? What accounts for episodes of misplaced keys, wallets, or similar lapses? Why do some experiences seem to disappear from our minds without a trace? Why do we repeatedly remember painful experiences we'd rather forget? And what can we do to avoid, prevent, or minimize these troublesome features of our memory systems?

Psychologists and neuroscientists have written numerous articles on specific aspects of forgetting or memory distortions, but back in the late 1990s, I realized that no unified framework had conceptualized the various ways in which memory sometimes leads us astray. My main goal in the first edition of *The Seven Sins of Memory* was to provide such a framework by exploring the nature of memory's imperfections, presenting a new way to think about them, and considering how we can reduce or avoid their harmful effects. Yet twenty years have now passed since the publication of that 2001 edition. The field of memory research has moved forward during those two decades, and issues related to memory errors have continued to impact society, sometimes in new and even startling ways.

In February 2015, *NBC Nightly News* anchor Brian Williams reluctantly admitted that a story he often told about being shot at in a helicopter approaching Baghdad while covering a story on the Iraq War in 2003 was wrong — he had actually been in a helicopter behind the one that was hit by a rocket-propelled grenade. Williams was widely criticized for telling an outright lie despite his apology on national television and his assertion that he was not trying to deceive anyone. Could Williams have developed a false recollection of his helicopter experience that he came to believe was true? Memory researchers such as myself were interviewed about the case and pointed to scientific evidence that supports the possibility that Williams might have been a victim of memory rather than a knowing perpetrator of a lie. (Consistent with that perspective, Williams had, strangely, maintained an accurate memory of the event through at least 2008 and related the accurate version in public. It doesn't make sense that he would deliberately lie if he knew there was a public record that contradicted the lie.)

In September 2018, the national spotlight focused on the testimony of Dr. Christine Blasey Ford, a PhD research psychologist who testified before the Senate committee charged with assessing Brett Kavanaugh's fitness for a seat on the US Supreme Court. Blasey Ford recounted a terrifying sexual assault in high school at the hands of Kavanaugh, stating with 100 percent confidence that Kavanaugh was her assailant. Kavanaugh asserted emphatically that the event never happened. Politicians, sexual assault victims, psychologists, and others weighed in on one side or the other of the debate. But what struck me most clearly was that yet again, claimed or actual imperfections of memory were central to an event of great national importance.

Even during the unfolding of the COVID-19 pandemic in 2020, as fears of physical illness and death pervaded our lives, worries about post-COVID memory problems also grew, fueled by increasingly frequent accounts of a debilitating "brain fog" in COVID survivors: patients reported jarring and distressing episodes of memory loss, ranging from forgetting conversations that just happened to failing to recall anything about a recent twelve-day vacation in Paris. Though little is yet known about the basis for these memory problems, neuroscientists have begun to suggest possible explanations for how COVID-19 could impact the brain to produce memory loss.

Given the continuing relevance of memory to our society and the many new developments in the field since 2001, the time seemed right to update *The Seven Sins of Memory*. Back in the late 1990s, I brought together everything I knew about memory's imperfections and attempted to impose some order on a vast array of lapses, mistakes, and distortions. I generated a variety of unsatisfactory schemes for conceptualizing these diverse observations, but eventually hit on a way of thinking that helped to make everything fall into place.

I proposed that memory's malfunctions can be divided into seven fundamental transgressions, or "sins," which I call *transience, absent-mindedness, blocking, misattribution, suggestibility, bias,* and *persistence.* Just like the ancient seven deadly sins, the memory sins occur frequently in everyday life and can have serious consequences for all of us.

Transience, absent-mindedness, and blocking are sins of omission: we fail to bring to mind a desired fact, event, or idea. Transience refers to a weakening or loss of memory over time. It's probably not difficult for you to remember now what you have been doing for the past several hours. But if I ask you about the same activities six weeks, six months, or six years from now, chances are you'll remember less and less. Transience is a basic feature of memory, and the culprit in many memory problems.

Absent-mindedness involves a breakdown at the interface between attention and memory. Absent-minded memory errors—misplacing keys or eyeglasses, or forgetting a lunch appointment—typically occur because we are preoccupied with distracting issues or concerns and don't focus attention on what we need to remember. The desired information isn't lost over time; it is either never registered in memory to begin with or not sought after at the moment it is needed, because attention is focused elsewhere.

The third sin, blocking, entails a thwarted search for information that we may be desperately trying to retrieve. We've all failed to produce a name to accompany a familiar face. This frustrating experience happens even though we are attending carefully to the task at hand, and even though the desired name has not faded from our minds — as we become acutely aware when we unexpectedly retrieve the blocked name hours or days later.

In contrast to these three sins of omission, the next four sins of misattribution, suggestibility, bias, and persistence are all sins of commission: some form of memory is present, but it is either incorrect or unwanted. The sin of misattribution involves assigning a memory to the wrong source: mistaking fantasy for reality, or incorrectly remembering that a friend told you a bit of trivia that you actually read about in a newspaper. Misattribution is far more common than most people realize and has potentially profound implications in legal settings. The related sin of suggestibility refers to memories that are implanted as a result of leading questions, comments, or suggestions when a person is trying to call up a past experience. Like misattribution, suggestibility is especially relevant to — and sometimes can wreak havoc within — the legal system.

The sin of bias reflects the powerful influences of our current knowledge and beliefs on how we remember our pasts. We often edit or entirely rewrite our previous experiences — unknowingly and unconsciously — in light of what we now know or believe. The result can be a skewed rendering of a specific incident, or even of an extended period in our lives, which says more about how we feel *now* than about what happened *then*.

The seventh sin — persistence — entails repeated recall of disturbing information or events that we would prefer to banish from our minds altogether: remembering what we cannot forget, even though we wish that we could. Everyone is familiar with persistence to some degree: recall the last time that you suddenly awoke at 3:00 a.m., unable to keep out of your mind a painful blunder on the job or a disappointing result on an important exam. In more extreme cases of serious depression or traumatic experience, persistence can be disabling and even life-threatening.

This new edition retains nearly all the material from the first edition, including discoveries based on breakthroughs in neuroscience that have allowed us to see the brain in action as it learns and remembers and that are beginning to illuminate the basis of the seven sins. These studies have allowed us to see in a new light what's going on inside our heads during the frustrating incidents of memory failure or error that can have a significant impact on our everyday lives. I also discuss how our emerging knowledge of the seven sins can help us to counter them. For the new edition, I have included at the end of each chapter a section called "The Update," which highlights some notable developments since 2001 that add in an important way either to our understanding of the nature of one of the seven sins or to how they impact our day-to-day lives. Doing so forced me to focus on what we now know about the seven sins that we didn't know back in 2001. As an active participant in the field, I've tracked these new developments in real time as they have made their way into the literature. But pulling them together for this edition has highlighted to me that we've expanded our knowledge of each of the seven sins in intriguing and sometimes unexpected directions. Comprehensive coverage of developments in memory research during the past two decades is well beyond the scope of this updated edition, but I hope that my discussion of selected new findings and ideas will convey some of the progress we've made in understanding how and why memory can go astray.

This updating exercise also required me to reassess the current validity of the evidence that I included in the 2001 edition. After all, as science grows and develops, old findings are often superseded by new ones, and problems that were not initially apparent with an experimental procedure or result may come to light with further research. Moreover, during the past decade, psychology has been working through a painful "replication crisis" stimulated by the reporting of notable failures to replicate experimental results. Different psychologists have different views on the extent and severity of this crisis, but in light of these emerging concerns, I was curious to gauge the extent to which the findings I included in the 2001 edition have held up over time.

I've reviewed the studies reported in each chapter. As far as I can determine, only a few findings that I discussed in 2001 have failed to stand the test of time in a way that required me to change what I wrote previously in order to avoid perpetuating an unreliable experimental result or invalid conclusion. In those few instances, I have adjusted the main text as necessary, and in the notes section at the end of the book, I have briefly summarized the reasons for these changes. So please consult the notes if you are interested in checking for new developments that have led me to change statements or claims from the 2001 edition. I have also made a few other minor tweaks to the original text in the main part of each chapter, such as removing no longer current affiliations of researchers and deleting references to "recent" studies that are no longer recent, as well as adding brief mentions of a few new findings, ideas, or everyday examples that are closely related to the original text. But the vast majority of the 2001 text outside The Update sections is the same now as it was then.

A critical point that I made in the 2001 edition is that to understand the seven sins more deeply, we also need to ask why our memory systems have come to exhibit these bothersome and sometimes dangerous properties: Do the seven sins represent mistakes made by Mother Nature during the course of evolution? Is memory flawed in a way that has placed our species at unnecessary risk? I don't think so. To the contrary, I contend that each of the seven sins is a by-product of otherwise desirable and adaptive features of the human mind.

Consider by analogy the ancient seven deadly sins. Pride, anger, envy, greed, gluttony, lust, and sloth have great potential to get us into trouble. Yet each of the deadly sins can be seen as an exaggeration of traits that are useful and sometimes necessary for survival. Gluttony may make us sick, but our health depends on consuming sufficient amounts of food. Lust can cost a straying husband his wife's affections, but a sex drive is crucial for perpetuating genes. Anger might result in dangerous elevations of blood pressure, but it also ensures that we defend ourselves vigorously when threatened. And so forth.

I argue for a similar approach to the memory sins. Rather than portraying them as inherent weaknesses or flaws in system design,

I suggest that they provide a window on the adaptive strengths of memory. The seven sins allow us to appreciate why memory works as well as it does most of the time, and why it evolved the design that it has. Though I focus on problems that the seven sins cause in everyday life, my purpose is not to ridicule or denigrate memory. Instead, I try to show why memory is a mainly reliable guide to our pasts and futures, though it sometimes lets us down in annoying but revealing ways.

I begin by exploring the nature and consequences of the sin of transience in Chapter 1. Toward the close of the nineteenth century, pioneering psychologists first measured loss of retention over time and produced a famous curve of forgetting. Newer studies have taught us about what kinds of information are more or less susceptible to forgetting over time. This research has implications for such diverse topics as President Bill Clinton's grand jury testimony about what he recalled from meetings with Monica Lewinsky and Vernon Jordan, what you are likely to remember from a day at the office, and how forgetting changes with increasing age. I also consider exciting advances from neuroimaging technologies that provide snapshots of the brain in action as it learns and remembers. My research group has used neuroimaging to seek the roots of transience in brain activities that occur during the moments when a new memory is born. Insights into the basis of transience also suggest methods to counter it. I consider a range of approaches to reducing transience, including psychological techniques that promote enhanced encoding of new information, the effects of such popular products as ginkgo biloba, and advances in neurobiology that are illuminating the genes that are responsible for remembering and forgetting. In The Update, I delve into the discovery of an intriguing condition now known as "highly superior autobiographical memory," first described in 2006, which I think represents a naturally occurring form of "anti-transience" for personal memories. I consider this condition in relation to research that has emerged since the 2001 edition showing how to put the brakes on transience in all of us. I also address a question that has taken on increasing importance since 2001: Are we harming our memories by relying increasingly on Google, Instagram, and GPS instead of our own memory systems to retrieve information, archive our experiences, and navigate our environments?

Chapter 2 focuses on the most irritating of the seven sins: absent-mindedness. We've all had more encounters with lost keys and forgotten errands than we might care to admit. Absent-minded errors have the potential to disrupt our lives significantly, as the great cellist Yo-Yo Ma found out in October 1999 when he left his $2.5 million instrument in the trunk of a taxi. Fortunately for Ma, police recovered the instrument right away. To understand why absent-minded errors occur, we need to probe the interface between attention and memory, explore the role of cues and reminders in helping us to carry out everyday tasks, and understand the important role of automatic behavior in daily activities. We spend a great deal of our lives on autopilot, which helps us to perform routine tasks efficiently, but also renders us vulnerable to absent-minded errors. Research on what psychologists call "prospective memory" has illuminated how and why different types of absent-minded forgetting occur. In The Update, I consider the most tragic manifestation of any of the memory sins, something I first became aware of only a few months after the publication of *The Seven Sins of Memory* in the spring of 2001: absent-minded forgetting of a child in a hot car by otherwise high-functioning and caring parents, often resulting in the child's death. I also discuss the intriguing phenomenon of mind wandering — when our minds drift away from the main task at hand — which psychologists have only begun to study intensively during the past two decades. Mind wandering can produce absent-minded memory errors that are especially frequent and costly in the classroom.

There are few more jarring experiences than knowing that you know something cold — the name of an acquaintance or the answer to a trivia question — while failing to produce the information when you need it. Chapter 3 explains why we are occasionally susceptible to such episodes of blocking. Proper names of people and places are especially vulnerable to blocking, and the reasons why this is so help to explain the basis of the sin of blocking. In a fascinating neurological disorder known as "proper-name anomia," patients with damage to specific regions within the brain's left hemisphere cannot retrieve proper names of people (and sometimes places), even though they can easily summon up the names of common objects. These patients often know a great deal about the people or places whose names they block, such as a person's occupation or where a city is located on a map. The plight of these patients resembles the familiar tip-of-the-tongue state, where we can't come up with a proper name or a common name, yet often can provide a great deal of information about it, including the initial letter and number of syllables. In this chapter, I compare alternative theories of the tip-of-the tongue state and suggest ways to counter this and related forms of blocking.

Blocking also occurs when people try to remember personal experiences. I consider exotic cases in which patients temporarily lose access to large sectors of their personal pasts and neuroimaging studies that provide glimpses into what goes on in the brain during this sort of blocking. Laboratory studies of more mundane forms of blocking, in which retrieving some words from a recently read list impairs access to others, have intriguing implications for such real-world situations as interviewing eyewitnesses to a crime. The Update begins with perhaps the most famous case of blocking in modern times — then Texas governor Rick Perry's catastrophic "oops" retrieval failure in a 2011 presidential debate — and examines recent research on tip-of-the-tongue states and related kinds of blocking that can help us to understand it. I also delve into an exciting line of research on memory suppression that first appeared just after the publication of the 2001 edition and has since illuminated both cognitive and neural mechanisms that contribute to blocking.

Chapter 4 considers the first of the sins of commission: misattribution. Sometimes we remember doing things we only imagined, or recall seeing someone at a particular time or place that differs from when or where we actually encountered them: we recall aspects of the event correctly but misattribute them to the wrong source. I show how misattribution errors figure prominently in such seemingly disparate phenomena as déjà vu, unintentional plagiarism, and cases of mistaken eyewitness identification. Remember the infamous John Doe 2 from the Oklahoma City bombing back in 1995? I explain why he was almost surely the product of a classic misattribution error.

Psychologists have devised clever methods for inducing powerful misattribution errors in the laboratory. People incorrectly claim — sometimes with great confidence — having experienced events that have not happened. In addition to explaining why such false memories occur, I explore a question with important practical and theoretical ramifications: Is there any way to tell the differences between true and false memories? Our research team has used neuroimaging techniques to scan subjects while they experience true and false memories, and the results provide some insights into why false memories can be so subjectively compelling. In this chapter, we'll also encounter brain-damaged patients who were especially prone to misattributions and false memories. One patient believed that he was "seeing film stars everywhere" — mistaking unfamiliar faces for familiar ones. Understanding what has gone wrong in such individuals can help to illuminate the basis of misattributions in healthy people. The Update focuses on innovative experimental methods for inducing and exploring déjà vu that have uncovered key characteristics of the phenomenon. I also discuss the latest developments in research using neuroimaging to distinguish true from false memories, and I grapple with the important question of whether we are ready to apply our newfound knowledge in the courtroom.

Chapter 5 addresses one of the most dangerous of the seven sins: suggestibility. Our memories are sometimes permeable to outside influences: leading questions or feedback from other people can result in suggested false memories of events that never happened. Suggestibility is a special concern in legal contexts. I examine cases where suggestive questioning by law enforcement officials has led to serious errors in eyewitness identification, and where suggestive procedures used by psychotherapists have elicited memories of traumatic events that never occurred. Young children are especially vulnerable to the influences of suggestive questioning, as illustrated in a tragic Massachusetts daycare case in which an entire family went to prison because of children's recollections that I believe were tainted by suggestive questions. Suggestibility can also lead people to confess to crimes they did not commit. I discuss such cases and consider experimental evidence showing that it is surprisingly easy to elicit false confessions in noncriminal settings. In The Update, I examine recent experimental research that makes this point in a more shocking way than previous studies did, relate the evidence to recent high-profile cases of false confessions, and discuss how the views of both psychotherapists and experimental psychologists regarding suggestibility have evolved during the past couple of decades.

As I showed in my book *Searching for Memory*, we tend to think of memories as snapshots from family albums that, if stored properly, can be retrieved in precisely the same condition in which they were put away. But we now know that we do not record our experiences the way a camera records them. Our memories work differently. We extract key elements from our experiences and store them. We then re-create or reconstruct our experiences rather than retrieve copies of them. Sometimes, in the process of reconstructing, we add on feelings, beliefs, or even knowledge we obtained after the experience. In other words, we bias our memories of the past by attributing to them emotions or knowledge we acquired after the event.

Chapter 6 explores several different types of biases that sometimes skew our memories. For instance, "consistency biases" lead us to rewrite our past feelings and beliefs so that they resemble what we feel and believe now. We'll see how consistency biases shape memories in diverse situations, ranging from how supporters of Ross Perot remembered feeling when he quit the 1992 presidential race to how much married and dating couples recall liking or loving each other at different points in the past. "Egocentric biases," in contrast, reveal that we often remember the past in a self-enhancing manner. I show that egocentric biases can influence recall in diverse situations, ranging from how divorced couples recall their marital breakups to students' recall of their anxiety levels prior to an exam. "Stereotypical biases" influence memories and perceptions in the social world. Experience with different groups of people leads to the development of stereotypes that capture their general properties, but can spawn inaccurate and unwarranted judgments about individuals. I consider studies that explore how stereotypical bias fuels racial prejudice and can even lead people to "remember" the names of nonexistent criminals. Although little is known about the brain systems that give rise to bias, I discuss some intriguing clues from "split-brain" patients whose cerebral hemispheres have been disconnected from each other.

In The Update, I discuss evidence that links consistency bias with a development that most of us have become all too familiar with since the 2016 presidential campaign: fake news reports intended to sway political and social opinions. A study of voters in a 2018 Irish referendum on abortion rights provides some of the most compelling evidence that consistency bias can drive false memories for fake news items. I discuss this and related evidence that repeated exposure to fake news and false statements can heighten a bias to judge such statements as true. These effects have important implications for what has become a pressing problem in our society, as exemplified by the disruptive effects of Donald Trump's repeated false claims of widespread voter fraud in the 2020 presidential election despite the absence of evidence to support those claims. Another kind of bias that has captured widespread societal attention is "implicit bias," which is expressed outside of conscious awareness. I examined some early evidence on implicit stereotypical biases in the 2001 edition, but since then there has been an explosion of research — and controversy — about the role of implicit bias in racial prejudice. The wave of protests against the horrific death of George Floyd at the hands of

Minneapolis police in May 2020 brought the issue of systemic implicit racial bias to center stage once again. In The Update, I touch on some of the main ideas and findings of this research, including large-scale studies that have examined the effectiveness of implicit bias training.

Chapter 7 focuses on the most debilitating of the seven sins: persistence. Try to think of the single biggest disappointment in your life — a failure at work or school, or a romantic relationship gone sour. Chances are that you recollected this experience repeatedly in the days and weeks after it happened, even though you wished you could forget it. Persistence thrives in an emotional climate of depression and rumination and can have profound consequences for psychological health, as we'll see in the case of a baseball player who was literally haunted to death by the persisting memory of a single disastrous pitch. To understand the basis of persistence, I consider evidence that emotions are closely linked with the perception and registration of incoming information, which in turn influence the formation of new memories.

The force of persistence is greatest after traumatic experiences: wars, natural disasters, serious accidents, childhood abuse. Nearly everyone persistently remembers a traumatic event in its immediate aftermath, but only some people become "stuck in the past" for years or decades; I explore why this is so. Traumatic memories can be so overwhelming that it is only natural to try to avoid reexperiencing them. Paradoxically, however, attempting to avoid remembering a trauma may only increase the long-term likelihood of persistently remembering it. Studies of brain structure and physiology are providing important information about the neural underpinnings of traumatic persistence and also suggest potentially novel methods for reducing persistence. The Update considers some important recent developments in the battle to reduce the harmful effects of persistence, which are based on a phenomenon called "memory reconsolidation." When we retrieve a memory, we need to store or consolidate it all over again, which renders the memory temporarily vulnerable to disruption — a feature that may be useful in countering the effects of persisting memories. I also examine how some of the new research on memory suppression discussed in The Update in Chapter 3 is related to intrusive memories of traumatic experiences.

After reading the first seven chapters, you might easily conclude that evolution burdened humankind with an extremely inefficient memory system — so prone to error that it often jeopardizes our well-being. In Chapter 8, I take issue with this conclusion and argue instead that the seven sins are by-products of otherwise adaptive properties of memory. For instance, I show that transience makes memory adapt to important properties of the environment in which the memory system operates. I also consider unusual cases of extraordinary recall that illustrate why some apparent limitations of memory that produce absent-mindedness are in fact desirable system properties. I explain how misattribution arises, in part, because our memory systems encode information selectively and efficiently, rather than indiscriminately storing details, and I examine how bias can facilitate psychological well-being. I also argue that persistence is a price we pay for a memory system that — much to our benefit — gives high priority to remembering events that could threaten our survival. I draw on developments in evolutionary biology and psychology to place these suggestions in a broad conceptual context that allows us to appreciate better the possible origins of the seven sins.

In The Update, I first consider novel evidence that has emerged during the past two decades that illuminates adaptive aspects of memory errors, and then I discuss how the role of memory in imagining future experiences is related to an adaptive perspective on memory errors. According to a theoretical framework that my colleagues and I have developed over the past decade and more, using memory to think about the future requires a flexible memory system that allows us to recombine bits and pieces of relevant past experiences to prepare for novel possible future experiences. We possess such a memory system, but the very flexibility that makes it adaptive for future thinking and related processes can contribute to certain kinds of memory errors. Given its relatively recent development, this perspective on memory was entirely absent from the 2001 edition. However, taking this approach has significantly broadened my own thinking about the nature and functions of memory, and I explain how and why it has done so.

In Kawabata's "Yumiura," the woman who remembered a love affair that apparently never happened reflected on the gift of memory. "Memories are something we should be grateful for, don't you think?" she asked the bemused novelist. "No matter what circumstances people end up in, they're still able to remember things from the past—I think it must be a blessing bestowed on us by the gods." She offered this high praise even though the memory system she celebrated led her unknowingly down a path of delusion. The path through this book is in some ways analogous: we need to immerse ourselves in the dark sides of memory before we can fully appreciate this blessing bestowed by the gods.

1

The Sin of
Transience

ON OCTOBER 3, 1995, the most sensational criminal trial of the time reached a stunning conclusion: a jury acquitted O. J. Simpson of murder. Word of the not-guilty verdict spread quickly, nearly everyone reacted with either outrage or jubilation, and many people could talk about little else for days and weeks afterward. The Simpson verdict seemed like just the sort of momentous event that most of us would always remember vividly: how we reacted to it and where we were when we heard the news.

Can you recall how you found out that Simpson had been acquitted? Chances are that you don't remember, or that what you remember is wrong. Several days after the verdict, a group of California undergraduates provided researchers with detailed accounts of how they learned about the jury's decision. When the researchers probed students' memories again fifteen months later, only half recalled accurately how they found out about the decision. When asked again nearly three years after the verdict, less than 30 percent of students' recollections were accurate; nearly half were dotted with major errors.

The culprit in this incident is the sin of transience: forgetting that occurs with the passage of time. We are all familiar — sometimes painfully so — with the everyday consequences of transience. Imagine, for example, that you are attending an annual meeting of a professional or social group. A smiling face looms at the other end of the hallway, approaching with an extended hand, calling out your name, and saying how wonderful it is to see you again. You smile politely and try to buy some time, but inside you feel a mounting sense of panic: Who is this person? Why don't I remember having met him before? He senses your discomfort and reminds you of the pleasant cup of coffee you enjoyed together at the same meeting last year, where you discussed, among other things, mutual frustrations with the bad weather that disrupted your travel plans. If you had seen this person an hour or a day after you met, you surely would have recognized him. But a year later, you feel like the befuddled novelist in "Yumiura," who could not remember the woman who claimed he proposed marriage, as you struggle and still can't recall the incident. Muttering weakly something to the effect that "I sort of remember . . . ," you actually feel as though you are meeting this person for the first time.

Transience can sometimes leave us feeling rather embarrassed. A female acquaintance of mine attended the wedding of a friend, whose husband she had not met before. Several months later, at a fiftieth birthday party for her friend, she spotted an unfamiliar man in the corner. She discreetly asked her friend about the stranger — who was the woman's new husband. My acquaintance says she still cringes when thinking about that moment.

Perhaps the most pervasive of memory's sins, transience operates silently but continually: the past inexorably recedes with the occurrence of new experiences. Psychologists and neuroscientists have uncovered reasons for transience and are developing ways to counter it. The path to the modern era was set when a young German philosopher, traveling through Europe in the late 1870s, found inspiration that changed his future, and that of psychology, while browsing in a secondhand Parisian bookstore.

WHEN MEMORY FADES

The philosopher's name was Hermann Ebbinghaus, and the book that he encountered, authored by the great German philosopher-scientist Gustav Fechner, contained experimental methods for studying sensory perception. When Ebbinghaus began his first academic post in Berlin in 1878, he pursued the flash of insight that had come to him in the Parisian bookstore: memory, like sensory perception, could be studied using the methods of science. It would take him seven years to publish his findings, but Ebbinghaus's 1885 monograph shaped the field for decades to come. Probing his own memory for thousands of meaningless letter strings (psychologists call them "nonsense syllables") that he had dutifully tried to learn and relearn, Ebbinghaus produced the first experimental evidence of transience. He tested himself at six different times after studying a list of nonsense syllables, ranging from one hour to one month. Ebbinghaus noted a rapid drop-off in retention during the first few tests: nine hours after he studied a list of nonsense syllables, he had forgotten approximately 60 percent of the list. The rate of forgetting then slowed down considerably. After a month's delay, Ebbinghaus had forgotten just over 75 percent of what he had learned initially — not that much worse than the amount of forgetting at the nine-hour delay.

Ebbinghaus conducted his experiments in the sterile confines of the laboratory, far removed from the complexities of everyday life; he studied meaningless strings of letters, not rich and varied personal experiences, and tested only himself. Despite the evident limitations, these century-old findings concerning how one man learned and forgot nonsense syllables have something to say about whether we will recall last week's breakfast meeting six months from now or remember what we read in yesterday's newspaper for more than a few hours or days. His conclusion that most forgetting occurs during early delays, and then slows down after later ones, has been replicated in countless laboratory experiments. Modern memory researchers have also extended Ebbinghaus's curve of forgetting outside the confines of the laboratory, demonstrating that it defines a core feature of transience.

In the early 1990s, the psychologist Charles Thompson and his colleagues at Kansas State University probed the memories of college students who kept diaries over the course of a semester in which they recorded one unique event each day. Forgetting was not quite so rapid as in Ebbinghaus's study, but the shape of the forgetting curve for these everyday events was generally similar to what others had observed in the laboratory. Thompson's students recorded and tried to remember experiences that varied in significance. A minority were personally meaningful ("My boyfriend Jake and I broke up"), but most were rather humdrum ("Watched movies at Jim's house on the VCR from 8:00 p.m. to 3:45 a.m."; "Mark and I started to make caramel corn but we soon found out that we were out of baking soda"). Other evidence concerning an annual happening that most people value greatly — Thanksgiving dinner — shows clearly that even personally significant events are not immune from the kind of transience that characterizes the Ebbinghaus forgetting curve.

How well can you recollect the most recent Thanksgiving dinner that you attended? A study of more than five hundred college students suggests that what you remember very much depends on exactly when you are reading these words. At regular intervals for six months after Thanksgiving, students were asked about the overall vividness of their memories of the dinner and also about specific details. Vividness declined rapidly over the first three months, followed by a more gradual decline for the remaining three months. The basic form of the Ebbinghaus curve was again observed, but this time for an event of considerable personal significance.

The drop-off was not, however, quite so steep as in Thompson's diary studies. This difference may be because some aspects of our most recent Thanksgiving dinner can be "remembered" on the basis of general knowledge of previous ones. We know that we probably had turkey, even if we have forgotten the particulars of this year's bird; we also know that we probably gathered together with family. This type of general knowledge about what usually happens at Thanksgiving does not fade across just a few months. Consistent with this suggestion, students' memories for food and for who attended the dinner dropped off at a relatively slow rate. But memories of details that were specific to the most recent Thanksgiving — such as what clothes they and others wore and the contents of conversations — were lost much more quickly.

Similar processes operate when people recall a day at work. Try to answer in detail the following three questions: What do you do during a typical day at work? What did you do yesterday? And what did you do on that day one week ago? When twelve employees in the engineering division of a large office-products manufacturer answered these questions, there was a dramatic difference in what they recalled from the day before and a week earlier. The employees recalled fewer activities from a week earlier than from the day before, and the ones they did recall from a week earlier tended to be part of a "typical" day. Atypical activities — departures from the daily script — were remembered much more frequently after a day than after a week. Memory after a day was close to a verbatim record of specific events; memory after a week was closer to a generic description of what usually happens. Likewise, Thompson's diary studies showed that specific details, such as the location of an event, the people who were there, and the specific date, fade more rapidly than the general sense of what happened. These observations are backed up by other laboratory studies indicating that recollections of when and where an event occurred, or who said what, tend to be especially transient.

At relatively early time points on the forgetting curve — minutes, hours, and days, sometimes longer — memory preserves a relatively detailed record, allowing us to reproduce the past with reasonable if not perfect accuracy. But with the passing of time, the particulars fade and opportunities multiply for interference — generated by later, similar experiences — to blur our recollections. We thus rely ever more on our memories for the gist of what happened, or what usually happens, and attempt to reconstruct the details by inference and even sheer guesswork. Transience involves a gradual switch from reproductive and specific recollections to reconstructive and more general descriptions.

When attempting to reconstruct past events based on general knowledge of what usually happens, we become especially vulnerable to the sin of bias: when present knowledge and beliefs seep into our memories of past events (see Chapter 6). The combination of transience and bias can get us into trouble. A management consultant told me about a meeting at which a partner in a large company made a presentation to an important client in the presence of his company's CEO and several overseas investors. The partner related a story relevant to the client's situation about how a particular fast-food chain adopted a strategy of raising prices. The story was based on an incident the partner remembered from a year or two earlier. But rather than calling on a detailed reproductive memory, the partner had unknowingly reconstructed the specifics from his present knowledge — the chain had not actually raised prices. Worse yet, a manager who had previously worked at the fast-food chain fidgeted uncomfortably. "She started making faces while he was speaking," recalls the consultant. "As the partner was finishing his story, the manager spoke to the associate next to her in what she thought was a whisper. In a voice that regrettably carried halfway across the room, she said, 'He doesn't know what he's talking about. They never raised prices.'" The embarrassed partner had lost specific memory but was unaware of it.

Transience played the role of troublemaker in another, rather more public incident, where questions concerning the nature of forgetting assumed national prominence: the 1998 grand jury investigation of William Jefferson Clinton.

FORGETTING MONICA

The afternoon of August 17, 1998, was a watershed in the investigation and eventual impeachment of President Clinton. Testifying before a grand jury convened by the independent counsel Kenneth Starr, Clinton answered questions concerning the details of his relationship with Monica Lewinsky and about his related testimony in January 1998 in the Paula Jones lawsuit. Clinton's August 17 remarks will no doubt be remembered by many — and in the history books — for his verbal jousts with prosecutors regarding the exact definition of the term "sexual relations."

But from the perspective of a memory researcher, Clinton's terminological hairsplitting is not nearly so interesting as a second battle he fought that afternoon: a battle over the characteristics and limits of transience. Clinton's memory lapses in his grand jury testimony and earlier deposition in the Jones case were widely viewed as self-serving conveniences designed to avoid embarrassing admissions. Prosecutors' attempts to establish this point rested on their intuitions about what is — and is not — reasonable to forget about an experience at different times after it has occurred.

This debate over transience is vividly illustrated by an exchange between Clinton and the government counsel Sol Wisenberg concerning a meeting between the president and Vernon Jordan on the evening of December 19, 1997. Earlier that day, Jordan had met with an extremely upset Monica Lewinsky, who had just learned that she had been issued a subpoena by the independent counsel's office. Jordan had later told Clinton about this development. On August 17, 1998, nearly eight months later, Wisenberg focused on what Clinton had said back in January about this meeting with Jordan. When asked whether anybody other than his attorneys ever told him that Lewinsky had been served with a subpoena by the independent counsel's office, Clinton told the Jones attorneys, "I don't think so." But this claim seemed implausible to Wisenberg: "Mr. President, 3.5 weeks before, Mr. Jordan had made a special trip to the White House to tell you Ms. Lewinsky had been subpoenaed; she was distraught; she had a fixation over you. And you couldn't remember that 3.5 weeks later?"

Clinton says that his memory is not what it used to be, and offers up possible explanations of his recent forgetfulness:

> If I could say one thing about my memory — I have been blessed and advantaged in my life with a good memory. I have been shocked and so have members of my family and friends of mine at how many things I have forgotten in the last six years — I think because of the pressure and the pace and the volume of events in a president's life, compounded by the pressure of your four-year inquiry, and all the other things that have happened. I'm amazed — there are lots of times when I literally can't remember last week.

Wisenberg immediately picks up on Clinton's self-confessed memory problems. "Are you saying, sir," he queries, "that you forgot when you were asked this question that Vernon Jordan had come on December 19, just 3 weeks before, and said that he's met that day, the day that Monica got the subpoena?" While not explicitly agreeing, Clinton acknowledges that he might have forgotten certain aspects of Vernon Jordan's visit. "It's quite possible that I had gotten mixed up," he proffers. Clinton then asserts somewhat more emphatically, "All I can tell you is I didn't remember all the details of all this."

Given the obsessive pursuit of Clinton by the independent counsel's office, Wisenberg's questions might be viewed as indiscriminate badgering by an aggressive attorney. But other parts of the deposition indicate that Wisenberg did not cast doubt on Clinton's claims about forgetting when they seemed more plausible. Compare the contentious exchange about forgetting across a three-week interval with an incident that occurs later in the grand jury deposition. Clinton is asked about a meeting with his aide John Podesta that occurred seven months earlier. On January 23, two days after the Lewinsky affair became public, Clinton allegedly told Podesta that he had not engaged in any type of sex whatsoever with Lewinsky. When asked about this exchange, Clinton acknowledges making careful denials to a variety of people who might have included Podesta, but again appeals to faulty memory for particulars:

CLINTON: I do not remember the specific meeting about which you asked or the specific comments to which you referred.
WISENBERG: You don't remember . . .
CLINTON: Seven months ago, I'd have no way to remember, no.

In contrast to his pointed probing of Clinton's apparent forgetting of a three-week-old meeting, Wisenberg allows this assertion to pass unchallenged. He is willing to concede poor memory for a relatively routine exchange seven months earlier, but is dubious about any claims of forgetting across a mere three weeks. The crux of the problem goes all the way back to Ebbinghaus: How much forgetting is plausible at different times after an experience has occurred?

Whatever Clinton's motivations when he testified, his self-professed confusion about the details of what happened is exactly the type of forgetting expected based on both naturalistic and laboratory studies. Nonetheless, Wisenberg's skepticism that Clinton could have forgotten the entire meeting with Jordan after a mere three weeks is fully warranted. Clinton, on the other hand, showed acute awareness of the difference between specific and general memories. Thus, when describing his first encounters with Lewinsky in early 1996, he acknowledges that he probably met with her approximately five times, but has specific memory for only two meetings. Clinton draws a sharp distinction between his specific recollections and more general ones:

> I remember specifically—I have a specific recollection of two times. I don't remember when they were. But I remember twice when, on a Sunday afternoon, she brought papers down to me, stayed and we were alone.
>
> And I am frankly quite sure—although I have no specific memory, I am quite sure—that there were a couple of more times, probably two more, three times more. That's what I would say. That's what I can remember. But I do not remember when they were or at what time of day they were or what the facts were. But I have a general memory that I would say I certainly saw her more than twice during that period between January and April 1996 when she worked there.

Was Clinton twisting his testimony to avoid an embarrassing admission? Maybe so, but from the perspective of both naturalistic and laboratory memory research, one could hardly find a more apt illustration of how memory fades over time.

THE BOOMERS' LAMENT

Whatever the source of the memory complaints made by the fifty-something Clinton, he was certainly not alone among his contemporaries: aging boomers were grumbling in record numbers about their increasing propensity for forgetting. Laboratory studies show that some of these concerns may be warranted. Numerous experiments have documented that older adults (mainly in their sixties or seventies, sometimes fifties) have greater difficulty than college students remembering information that an experimenter asked them to learn. Further, even when older adults can remember lists of words or other experimental materials just as well as their younger counterparts across a delay of a few minutes, their memories deteriorate more rapidly across days or weeks. These memory deficits are particularly evident when older adults are required to recollect the particulars of an experience, such as exactly when and where an event occurred. Older adults lose specific details and tend to rely even more than younger adults on a general sense of knowing that something happened.

How early does aging begin to affect transience? This question is important to millions of people entering their forties and fifties (and is also relevant to the claims of Clinton, who was fifty-two years old in August 1998). Because most investigations of aging memory have compared college students with retirees, relatively less is known about people who occupy the in-between ages. In one study, people who had reached their thirties, forties, fifties, sixties, or seventies took various memory tests in 1978 and again in 1994. People who were fifty or older at the beginning of the experiment (in 1978) performed more poorly when learning and recalling word lists and stories in 1994 than they had back in 1978. Those who were in their thirties in 1978 performed more poorly in 1994 only on the stories. Among people who were in their thirties in 1978 and those who were in their fifties that year, the older group performed worse on both word recall and story recall. So problems with story recall begin, at the latest, in the early to mid-forties, whereas problems with word recall are not evident until people reach their fifties. The good news is that none of the declines were large, with the older groups generally recalling about 10 to 15 percent less than the younger groups.

By the time people reach their sixties and seventies, transience is more marked and consistent. But even in these older groups, poor recall is not an inevitable consequence of aging: transience varies considerably among older individuals. For example, in one study a significant minority of people in their seventies (roughly 20 percent) recalled about as many words from a recently presented list as college students did.

Why do some older adults continue to show more marked susceptibility to transience than their younger counterparts, whereas others show little evidence of decline? Several reports have raised the possibility that educational level plays a role. For example, in a Dutch study elderly adults aged sixty-five to sixty-nine, seventy to seventy-four, seventy-five to seventy-nine, and eighty to eighty-five were given a list of words to learn, then tried to recall them immediately and after a thirty-minute delay. Loss of information across the delay was faster and observed at an earlier age in less educated people than in more educated people. Whereas sixty-five- to sixty-nine-year-olds in both groups retained about 65 percent of what they learned across a delay, eighty- to eighty-five-year-olds with high education retained about 60 percent of learning across the delay, but those with low education retained less than 50 percent.

The researchers also noted that their results could reflect a higher prevalence of Alzheimer's disease or other forms of dementia among those with lower educational levels, possibly because they have less "mental reserve" to call on than more highly educated people. Scientists have long distinguished between normal declines in memory that accompany aging (sometimes referred to as "benign senescent forgetfulness") and more pronounced declines that accompany conditions involving actual brain pathology, such as Alzheimer's disease. The brains of Alzheimer's patients are disfigured by "senile plaques," deposits of a protein known as "amyloid," and by twisted nerve cell fibers called "neurofibrillary tangles," which interfere with the normal operations of nerve cells. Experiments have shown that compared with healthy older adults, Alzheimer's patients retain little of their recent experiences.

An important series of studies by the neurologist Herman Buschke and his colleagues shows that levels of forgetting in a word memory test can distinguish between healthy older individuals and those with

FIGURE 1.1

FIGURE 1.2

FIGURES 1.1 AND 1.2 *Although there is no simple one-to-one relationship between an individual brain region and a specific sin of memory, some brain regions are particularly relevant to specific memory sins. You can start to understand the regions' locations by recognizing that each hemisphere in the brain is divided into four major lobes: frontal, tempo-*

Alzheimer's disease. In the simplest version of the test, people see a sheet containing four words belonging to different categories. When the examiner says the appropriate category name (for example, *vegetable*), the individual points to the appropriate word (for example, *potato*). This procedure ensures that people pay attention to the words and understand them. After a few minutes, individuals try to remember the words on their own and are then given the category names again as prompts for any forgotten items. Failure to come up with a studied word when given a category cue probably reflects loss of memory across the brief delay. Poor performance on this test (defined by specific cutoff scores) is almost uniquely associated with the presence of Alzheimer's disease or some other form of dementia. The test works because Alzheimer's disease greatly magnifies transience above and beyond any changes associated with normal aging.

Psychologists and neuroscientists who study memory agree that transience is pervasive and increases as people age. But they have spent decades struggling with a seemingly straightforward yet maddeningly difficult question: Why does it happen?

ral, parietal, and occipital. FIGURE 1.1 *shows each of these lobes from the perspective of the surface of the brain's left hemisphere.* FIGURE 1.2 *allows us to peer through the surface and view a number of structures that occupy the inner parts of the brain.*

The hippocampus and nearby structures in the inner parts of the temporal lobe (Figure 1.2) are especially pertinent to the sin of transience. Parts of the frontal lobe (Figure 1.1) also play a role in transience, are even more centrally involved in the sins of absent-mindedness and misattribution, and may be related to the sin of suggestibility. The area near the front of the temporal lobe (Figure 1.1, lower left) appears to play a role in the sin of blocking. The amygdala (Figure 1.2) is closely related to the sin of persistence. Not much is known about the brain regions involved in the sin of bias, but regions within the left hemisphere may play a significant role. I elaborate on the relationship between brain function and each of the memory sins in Chapters 1–7.

Witnessing the Birth of a Memory

The human brain is perhaps the most complex object in the entire universe, consisting of some 86 billion nerve cells or neurons and an even larger number of connections or synapses between them. Neuroscientists, who typically study memory in rats, rabbits, monkeys, birds, and even sea slugs, can record electrical or chemical signals directly from individual neurons or carefully remove small portions of the brain. This kind of unfettered access to the brain has always elicited some jealousy on the part of psychologists such as myself. We haven't had the techniques to probe the inner workings of human brains with anywhere near the precision available to neuroscientists, and ethical grounds preclude the possibility of making experimental lesions in a person's brain. It is as if the scientific gods have decided to allow neuroscientists into an inner sanctum of the brain but restricted psychologists to a remote observation deck.

Straining to catch a glimpse into the inner sanctum, psychologists have relied, for the most part, on experiments of nature: cases in which people suffer memory loss as a result of damage to particular parts of the brain. In the most famous case ever reported, a young man known by the initials HM was operated on for relief of intractable epilepsy in 1953. The neurosurgeon, William Beecher Scoville, removed the inner parts of the temporal lobe on both sides of HM's brain (see Figures 1.1 and 1.2). After the operation, HM seemed normal in most respects; he could perceive the world around him, carry on a normal conversation, and perform on IQ tests as well as he had before the operation. But there was something terribly wrong: HM seemed to forget his daily experiences as fast as they occurred. He couldn't remember conversations from minutes earlier. He failed to recognize doctors who worked with him every day. He forgot that he had eaten lunch almost as soon as his plate was cleared from the table. HM was plagued by this extraordinary form of transience for over fifty years until his death in 2008: his memory never showed even a hint of improvement.

HM revealed a stunning link between transience and the inner parts of the temporal lobe. Because his amnesia was so profound, the structures that were removed — including the horseshoe-shaped hippocampus and part of a region behind it called the parahippocampal gyrus — have fascinated memory researchers ever since HM's case was first reported. These structures are among the earliest affected and hardest hit by the senile plaques and neurofibrillary tangles of Alzheimer's disease, which probably explains why affected patients have such great difficulty remembering recent experiences.

The scientific gods have grown kinder to psychologists. Recent decades have seen the development of powerful new neuroimaging tools that allow us to peer into the brain while it learns and remembers. The technique that researchers have used most frequently is called functional magnetic resonance imaging, or fMRI. This technology works by detecting changes in the brain's blood supply. When a region of the brain becomes more active, it requires more blood than it does in a less active condition. But when blood flow rises, something odd happens: there is a temporary oversupply of oxygenated hemoglobin relative to deoxygenated hemoglobin, which magnifies the fMRI signal. Using this technique, researchers can determine which parts of the brain "light up" during cognitive activities.

Using fMRI allows us to localize these changes in blood flow quite precisely, within a few millimeters. Just as the telescope allowed astronomers to see the heavens and the microscope allowed biologists to peer into cells of living organisms, fMRI (and a related neuroimaging technique known as "positron emission tomography," or PET scanning) has opened up the human brain for psychologists and neuroscientists.

When memory researchers first began to use fMRI and PET scans, there was great excitement about finally witnessing firsthand what goes on in the parts of the temporal lobe that were removed from HM, such as the hippocampus — regions that are clearly central to understanding transience. But promising early reports were followed by a string of failures.

In late 1997, my research team seized on a new way to examine the issue with fMRI. Consider the following questions: If I measure activity in your brain while you are learning a list of words, can I tell from this activity which words you will later remember having studied and which words you will later forget? Do measurements of brain activity at the moment when a perception is being transformed into a memory allow scientists to predict future remembering and forgetting of that particular event? If so, exactly which regions allow us to do the predicting? Because of technical limitations, early fMRI (and PET) studies could not address these questions. But by 1997, fMRI had advanced to the point at which it was possible, at least in principle, to pose these questions and obtain answers.

In a collaborative effort led by two young stars of fMRI research, Anthony Wagner and Randy Buckner, our group at the imaging center of Massachusetts General Hospital came up with an experiment that was undoubtedly taxing for the participants. The MRI scanner is not a luxury suite: a technician gently pushes you, while you lie flat on your back, headfirst into a narrow tube. You then lie extremely still for an hour or two (motion disrupts recording of the fMRI signal) while carrying out a task the experimenter has devised. All the while, the scanner emits loud beeps as a strong magnetic field is used to detect brain activity.

While holding still in this cacophonous tunnel, participants in our experiment saw several hundred words, one every few seconds, flashed at them from a computer by specially arranged mirrors. To check that they paid attention to every word, we asked our volunteers to indicate whether each word referred to something abstract, such as "thought," or concrete, such as "garden." Twenty minutes after the scan, we showed subjects the words they had seen in the scanner, intermixed with an equal number of words they hadn't seen, and asked them to indicate which ones they did and did not remember. We knew, based on preliminary work, that people would remember some words and forget others. Could we tell from the strength of the fMRI signal which words participants would later remember and which ones they would later forget?

We could. Two regions of the brain showed greater activity when people made abstract/concrete judgments about words they later remembered compared to those they later forgot. Critically, one area was in the inner part of the temporal lobe: the parahippocampal gyrus in the left cerebral hemisphere — one of the regions that HM's surgeon had removed.

The other region whose activity predicted subsequent memory was located farther forward, in the lower left part of the vast territory known as the frontal lobes. This finding was not entirely unexpected, because previous neuroimaging studies indicated that the lower left part of the frontal lobe works especially hard when people elaborate on incoming information by associating it with what they already know. Cognitive psychologists had known for years that transience is influenced by what happens as people register or encode incoming information: more elaboration during encoding generally produces less transient memories. For instance, suppose I show you a list of words to remember, including *lion, CAR, table,* and *TREE.* For half of the words, I ask you to judge whether they refer to living or nonliving things; for the other half, I ask you to judge whether they are in uppercase or lowercase letters. All other factors being equal, you will later remember many more of the words for which you had made living/nonliving judgments compared to words for which you had made uppercase/lowercase judgments. Thinking about whether the word refers to a living or nonliving thing allows you to elaborate on the word in terms of what you already know about it; making the uppercase/lowercase judgment does little to link the word with what you already know. Other experiments have shown that subsequent memory improves when people generate sentences or stories that tie together to-be-learned information with familiar facts and associations.

We thought that something similar might be going on in our fMRI experiment. When the left frontal lobe was strongly activated, people may have been more successful in elaborating on a study list word in terms of what they already knew about it — dredging up associations or images — than when the left frontal lobe was more weakly activated. The left parahippocampal region, we hypothesized, would then help to "save" this elaboration in memory. Working together, these two parts of the brain helped to transform perception of a word into an enduring memory of its presentation.

At about the same time that we carried out our fMRI study, a group at Stanford University completed a related project. During scanning, people studied pictures of everyday scenes (instead of words) and then tried to remember the pictures a few minutes later. Their results were virtually identical to ours, except that the right cerebral hemisphere was prominently involved. Levels of activity in the lower part of the right frontal lobe, and in both the right and left parahippocampal gyrus, predicted subsequent remembering and forgetting of pictures that volunteers had studied in the scanner. These findings made good sense, because earlier studies suggested that the right hemisphere is primarily responsible for coding pictures, whereas the left hemisphere is responsible for processing words.

The results from these two studies were exciting in part because there is something fascinating, almost like science fiction, about peering into a person's brain in the present and telling what they will likely remember and forget in the future. And beyond an exercise in scientific fortune-telling, these studies managed to trace some of the roots of transience to the split-second encoding operations that take place during the birth of a memory. What happens in frontal and parahippocampal regions during those critical moments determines, at least in part, whether an experience will be remembered for a lifetime or follow the curve described by Ebbinghaus en route to the oblivion of the forgotten.

FIRST SECONDS AFTER PERCEPTION

In the late 1950s, two articles appeared in psychological journals that astounded the few scientists who then specialized in memory research. Trained in the tradition of Ebbinghaus, they were accustomed to observing the trajectory of forgetting across hours, days, and weeks. The new studies showed that when people were given the seemingly simple task of remembering three nonsense syllables, they forgot them almost completely in less than twenty seconds. Nothing like it had ever been reported.

The key to understanding the apparent anomaly lies in a crucial transition that takes place in the moments when a memory is born: from temporary or short-term memory to more permanent long-term memory. Retaining information across days, weeks, and years depends on two major forms of long-term memory. Episodic memory supports remembering of personal experiences that occurred in a particular time and place: recollections of the surprise birthday party you attended last week, or of the Broadway play you saw on your first visit to New York as a child. Semantic memory allows the acquisition and retrieval of general knowledge and facts: knowing that John Adams and Thomas Jefferson were principal architects of the Declaration of Independence, or that Yankee Stadium is the House That Ruth Built.

But a third type of memory intervenes between the moment of perception and the eventual establishment of long-lasting episodic or semantic memories. Referred to as "working memory," it holds on to small amounts of information for short periods of time — usually a few seconds — while people engage in such ongoing cognitive activities as reading, listening, problem solving, reasoning, or thinking. You need working memory to understand each and every one of the sentences I have written thus far. If you did not have a way to hold on to the beginning of the sentence as the rest of it unfolds, you would not know what I meant by the time you reached the sentence's end. Consider, for example, the following two sentences:

> The long and demanding course was so difficult that he never shot below 90.
> The long and demanding course was so difficult that he never passed an exam.

You cannot tell whether the word *course* refers to golf or school unless you hold on to this word until the end of the sentence. Working memory allows you to do so, but the system must constantly discard what is no longer needed at the moment and devote its resources to the temporary storage of incoming information. Unless a special effort is made — such as repeating a sentence over and over again — information is lost from the system almost immediately after it enters.

The stunning demonstrations of rapid forgetting in the late 1950s exploited this property of working memory. Immediately after presentation of a nonsense syllable for study, people were required to count backward from one hundred by threes. Unable to rehearse the nonsense syllable and thus keep it in mind, the participants were victimized by rapid loss of information from working memory.

We've all experienced this kind of transience. After calling directory assistance to obtain a phone number, you are faced with the choice of paying an extra few cents for automatic dialing or doing it yourself. If you take the time to decide which option to pursue, the number will vanish because you aren't mentally repeating it. Perhaps the phone company understands the consequences of rapid transience: having forgotten the number while considering the options, people may be more likely to pay the extra cost for automatic dialing rather than looking up the number again. And we've all been frustrated by rapid transience in the course of casual conversations. While listening to a friend, you are reminded of something important to tell them. But when they unexpectedly change the topic and start spilling the latest gossip about a mutual acquaintance, you suddenly realize that you've forgotten that critical tidbit you wanted to pass on. It can take considerable effort to recapture your train of thought and regenerate what you wanted to tell your friend.

The main culprit in rapid transience is a part of the working memory system called the "phonological loop." First postulated by the British psychologist Alan Baddeley, the phonological loop allows us to temporarily hold on to a small amount of linguistic information. Baddeley conceived the loop as a "slave" subsystem that assists the "central executive" system of working memory. This system orchestrates the flow of information into and out of long-term memory, but because of the continual bombardment of inputs, the executive frequently needs assistance. The phonological loop helps out by providing extra temporary storage of words, digits, and other bits of speech.

This slave subsystem's existence was initially revealed by studies of brain-damaged patients whose memory problems are virtually a mirror reversal of those seen in the amnesic patient HM. Even though his long-term memory for daily experiences was nonexistent, HM had no difficulty when presented with a string of digits and asked to repeat them immediately. He could easily reproduce sequences of six or seven digits — the same number that can be recalled by healthy people. In the early 1970s, the neuropsychologists Tim Shallice and Elizabeth Warrington described an intriguing patient, known by the initials KF, who had no difficulty remembering daily experiences from long-term memory but was unable to remember immediately more than a single digit! KF (and other patients like him) had suffered a stroke that destroyed the back part of his parietal lobe on the surface of the left cerebral hemisphere but did not affect the inner parts of the temporal lobes that were removed from HM's brain.

The mirror-image strengths and weaknesses in HM and KF showed that the phonological loop can function independently of long-term memory. But the results from studies of KF also raised questions about the function of the phonological loop. If people with a dysfunctional loop have no difficulty establishing new long-term memories, then why do they need it in the first place? Surely this system did not evolve solely to help us remember telephone numbers for a few seconds. By the 1980s, the function of the phonological loop seemed so obscure that one cynic derided it as "a pimple on the face of cognition."

We now know that the kind of rapid transience associated with a damaged phonological loop has significant, even grave, consequences. The early clues came from studies of another brain-injured patient with a damaged phonological loop. The patient could learn word pairs in her native language, Italian, as quickly as healthy controls. But in contrast to healthy native Italian speakers, the patient could not learn Italian words paired with unfamiliar Russian words. Subsequent studies showed similar results: patients with damage to the phonological loop were almost totally unable to learn foreign vocabulary.

The phonological loop turns out to be a gateway to acquiring new vocabulary. The loop helps us put together the sounds of novel words. When it is not functioning properly, we cannot hold on to those sounds long enough to have a chance of converting our perceptions into enduring long-term memories. Rapid transience of this kind has consequences that extend beyond adults with brain damage. Studies of young children show that the ability to repeat nonsense words provides a sensitive measure of the phonological loop's functioning. Children who perform at a high level on this test have an easier time acquiring new vocabulary than do children who perform at a low level; the number of nonsense words a child can repeat immediately is an excellent predictor of vocabulary acquisition. Baddeley and the psychologist Susan Gathercole have found that children with language deficits perform especially poorly on tests of the phonological loop. In contrast, other studies have revealed that gifted language learners — polyglots who have mastered several languages — do especially well on the same kinds of tests. Far from being a mere "pimple on the face of cognition," the phonological loop is a key player in one of the most fundamental human abilities: learning a new language.

Neuroimaging studies using fMRI and PET scans have begun to illuminate some of the neural subsystems that are relevant to short-term transience. For instance, neuroimaging studies have isolated the storage compartment of the phonological loop to the back part of the parietal lobe — an important finding because, as we have already seen, this part of the system is damaged in brain-injured patients who are plagued by short-term transience. Another part of the phonological loop, critical for actively repeating information held in short-term storage, depends on lower portions of the left prefrontal cortex — in the general vicinity of the region discussed earlier that contributes to elaborative encoding. This same region plays an important role in language output. When a healthy person suffers the kinds of short-term transience considered so far — such as forgetting what he or she is about to say, or forgetting a phone number looked up seconds ago — it's probably because the person fails to activate this part of the left frontal cortex. The information is then lost from working memory and unavailable for further elaborative encoding into long-term memory. Healthy people can circumvent short-term transience by making a concerted effort to rehearse information, which stimulates the lower left frontal cortex. But brain-damaged individuals, like the patient KF, are perpetually doomed to endless bouts of rapid transience because they lack the necessary brain structures.

After the First Few Seconds

Working memory and encoding processes are keys to understanding transience, but they are not the entire story. Whether an experience is quickly forgotten or remembered for years also depends on what happens after those first few seconds when a memory is born. Human beings are storytellers, and we tend to tell stories about ourselves. Thinking and talking about experiences not only helps to make sense of the past but also changes the likelihood of subsequent remembering. Those episodes and incidents we discuss and rehearse are protected, at least partially, from transience; those that we don't ponder or mention tend to fade more quickly. Of course, the experiences that cause us to ponder and discuss them repeatedly might simply be more memorable in the first place. After the Loma Prieta earthquake struck the Bay Area in 1989, those who experienced it firsthand were so eager to relate their memories of this distinctive and disturbing event that others quickly became saturated by endless tales of "where I was when the earthquake hit." Soon a popular T-shirt appeared admonishing people to refrain from sharing their earthquake stories.

In the diary study conducted by Charles Thompson and associates, experiences that students reported talking and thinking about most often were remembered in the richest detail. Numerous laboratory studies have demonstrated clearly that even when possible differences in initial memorability are controlled, thinking or talking about a past event enhances memory for that event compared to experiences that are not rehearsed. These findings have direct implications for countering transience in everyday life: thinking and talking about everyday experiences is one of the best ways to retain them later.

Transience can also be exacerbated by what happens after an experience is initially encoded. Consider the study discussed earlier that probed what people remember from a typical day at work. The next day, their memories were rich and detailed; a week later, they were little more than generic descriptions of what usually happens. Imagine, however, that after leaving work on Monday, some people left for a week's vacation instead of working for the remainder of the week. Chances are excellent that upon returning, they would possess a richer and more detailed recollection of what happened at work on the previous Monday than those who worked for the entire week. Experiences that are similar to those we wish to remember create interference that impairs memory. People who don't leave for vacation carry out many activities on Tuesday, Wednesday, Thursday, and Friday that are highly similar to those they carried out on Monday, and thus create substantial interference. People who take off on vacation engage in entirely different activities that create little or no interference.

But long-term transience is probably not entirely attributable to interference from similar experiences: loss of information over time occurs even when there is little opportunity for interference to play a role. For example, the psychologist Harry Bahrick tested retention of Spanish vocabulary in those who had studied Spanish during high school or college. He conducted tests at various time points after people stopped taking Spanish, ranging from immediately to fifty years later. Bahrick reported a rapid drop-off in memory for Spanish vocabulary during the first three years after classes had stopped, followed by tiny losses in later years. The drop-off during the initial years is probably attributable to spontaneous decay or loss of information.

What happens to those experiences that we can remember after a day but not after a year? Do they disappear entirely? Or are they lurking in the background, requiring only the right trigger—a distinctive voice or a pungent smell—to call them to mind? Memory researchers have debated these questions for decades. The answer —or at least my answer—involves a partial "yes" to both scenarios. Neurobiological studies of nonhuman animals provide mounting evidence that forgetting sometimes involves literal loss of information. Memories, according to most neurobiologists, are encoded by modifications in the strengths of connections among neurons. When we experience an event or acquire a new fact, complex chemical changes occur at the junctions—synapses—that connect neurons with one another. Experiments indicate that with the passage of time, these modifications can dissipate. The neural connections that encode memories thus may weaken as time passes, perhaps mirroring the shape of the decay curve first reported by Ebbinghaus. Unless strengthened by subsequent retrieval and recounting, the connections become so weak that recall is eventually precluded.

At the same time, however, countless studies have also shown that seemingly lost information can be recovered by cues or hints that remind us of how we initially encoded an experience. As time passes and interference mounts, information may be gradually lost to the point that only a powerful reminder can breach the seemingly inexorable effects of transience by dredging up the remaining fragments of an experience from ever-weakening neural connections.

This latter point is nicely illustrated by the psychologist Willem Wagenaar's diary study of his personal memories. Every day for four years, Wagenaar recorded various aspects of a distinctive event: who was involved, what happened, when and where the event occurred, and a further distinguishing detail of the event. He did not review the memory diary at any point during the four years when he was re-cording entries. Wagenaar commenced testing himself the day after the recording phase concluded, probing his memory with different combinations of cues (for example, who, what, where, when).

Wagenaar found that the more cues he provided, the more likely he was to remember key details of the event. There were, however, many events in which no amount of cueing elicited any form of rec-ollection. Intrigued by the question of whether these experiences had disappeared from his memory altogether, Wagenaar interviewed people who were involved in ten of the events he had scored as "com-pletely forgotten." In all cases, they were able to provide additional details that allowed Wagenaar to remember the event.

Wagenaar's study reveals a common result of transience over months and years: incomplete rather than total forgetting that leaves in its wake scattered shards of experience. Vague impressions of fa-miliarity, general knowledge of what happened, or fragmentary de-tails of experiences are the most common legacies of transience.

REDUCING TRANSIENCE

We'd all like to remember more than what remains in the wake of transience. Any attempt to reduce transience should include trying to seize control of what happens in the early moments of memory formation, when encoding processes powerfully influence the fate of a new memory. All popularly available memory improvement pack-ages recognize and build on this fundamental insight by trying to teach people how to elaborate on incoming information; a number of books and articles provide helpful reviews of specific techniques. The most frequently prescribed technique involves some form of visual imagery mnemonics: people are encouraged to elaborate on information they wish to remember by converting it into vivid and even bizarre visual imagery. So, for instance, if you want to remem-ber that my name is Daniel Schacter, you might imagine me sur-rounded by a group of lions (Daniel in the lions' den), eyeing a shack into which I hope to flee for protection.

Visual imagery mnemonics were first discovered by the Greeks more than two thousand years ago and are used by most professional mnemonists to perform the spectacular feats of their trade — memorizing a telephone book or the names of hundreds of people based on just a few seconds of exposure. Controlled studies in the laboratory also clearly show that ordinary people can use imagery mnemonics to boost memory for lists of words, names, and other materials. There is a problem, however. Many of the imagery techniques are complex, require considerable cognitive resources to implement, and are therefore difficult to use spontaneously. The first few times you generate bizarre mental pictures and stories to encode new information, the process may be challenging and fun. But the task of repeatedly generating memorable images can eventually become burdensome enough so that people stop engaging in it. In one study, for example, older adults were able to use mnemonics when instructed to do so in the lab, but barely one-third of them reported using the techniques in their everyday lives.

Widely advertised memory improvement programs, such as Mega Memory, rely heavily on the use of visual imagery and related techniques. Promotional materials for Mega Memory hold out the enticing prospect that training can result in a "photographic memory" that will enable you to remember names and faces, recall lists or appointments without writing anything down, and even impress your friends and family with demonstrations of mental gymnastics. Glowing testimonials suggest spectacular gains by individuals who have tried the program.

There is little reason to doubt that these programs will be helpful to those who make the effort to use the techniques on an ongoing basis. But I suspect that some people do not realize that to be successful, they must use the techniques each and every time they want to remember a particular event or fact. When I took questions during a radio interview, one caller asked me whether completing the Mega Memory course would "train my brain" to "take pictures" that ensure subsequent memory. She expected — or at least hoped for — a method that would boost her memory in much the same way that glasses help you to see better: just put them on, and without any effort you notice an immediate improvement in your vision. Unfortunately, I explained, mnemonic techniques are not the memory equivalents of eyeglasses: improvements are possible, but they require effortful use of the technique to encode each individual face, name, event, or fact.

Although there have been few controlled investigations of commercially available memory programs, one study examined the effects of training using Mega Memory and similar memory power audiotapes with groups of older adults. After completing a variety of memory tasks, participants attempted to complete one of the two training programs or were assigned to a waiting list. Most of the participants managed to complete the programs, reported generally high levels of satisfaction with them, and had the subjective sense that their memories had improved as a result of training. Disappointingly, there was no evidence of memory improvement in those adults who successfully completed either the Mega Memory or memory power program as compared with the other participants. The researchers concluded that the benefits of these programs for older adults had been "grossly exaggerated."

To profit from mnemonics or any technique purported to improve elaborative encoding, the method must be simple enough to use regularly. One approach that meets this criterion has been documented in numerous laboratory studies: generating elaborations that relate information you wish to remember to what you already know. A simple way to achieve this goal is to ask questions about what you wish to remember that force you to elaborate: What are the distinctive features in the face of the woman I just met? What acquaintance does she remind me of, and what are their similarities and differences?

Promising results have been reported using a variant of this approach derived from encoding studies in an unlikely population: professional actors. During the early 1990s, the psychologists Helga and Tony Noice made an intriguing discovery while studying how professional actors learn and remember their lines. Rather than using a verbatim memorization strategy, actors learn a script by asking questions about how the specific words that a character uses provide insights into the nature of the character and his goals. The precise grammar, punctuation, and other linguistic elements serve as clues to the character's plans, motivations, and intentions. For instance, when one actor encountered a brief response by his character — "Yes, I did" — he noted when analyzing the script, "I don't say anything more than I need to say. Short answers." Another actor, considering the line "Er . . . thanks. Thanks," thought that it suggested "trying to be cool and man-of-the-worldish, but I stutter a little."

Noice and Noice also examined whether college students and older adults can benefit from instruction in the kinds of "active experiencing" used by actors. Results have been encouraging. Several studies have shown that brief training in this strategy enhanced verbatim recall of a script in psychology students and senior citizens compared to participants who simply tried to memorize the script. As with imagery mnemonics, active experiencing demands considerable effort, so it remains to be seen whether people will use the technique on a regular basis. But the promising early results remind us that a major principle for countering transience — enhance elaborative encoding — along with some tools for realizing it, have been established experimentally. The main stumbling block involves effective implementation of encoding techniques in everyday life.

Because elaborative encoding, imagery mnemonics, and related approaches all require cognitive effort, there is undeniable appeal to the prospect of finding an easy and permanent antidote to transience — the mnemonic equivalent of corrective lenses. To judge by the amount of advertising it has received, you might guess that the magical mnemonic lenses have been found in the extracts of leaves from one of the oldest deciduous trees, the ginkgo biloba. We've all seen the ads claiming that ingestion of ginkgo will produce heightened mental sharpness and enhanced memory function. And, indeed, many studies have shown that ginkgo does have a salutary effect on cerebral circulation. In the few well-controlled studies of memory that compare ginkgo to placebo controls, modest improvements have been reported in people who reported serious memory problems prior to taking ginkgo, but little or no improvement has been observed in people who reported slight or no memory problems beforehand. Other studies have revealed that patients with Alzheimer's disease show small improvements in a variety of symptoms after taking ginkgo, probably because of general improvements in alertness. But there is no evidence that ginkgo exerts specific effects that reduce transience. Given a choice between taking ginkgo and investing some time and effort in developing elaborative encoding strategies, healthy people would be well-advised to focus on the latter approach.

Various other herbs and vitamins have also been touted as memory aids, but for the most part the evidence supporting their efficacy is slim or nonexistent. Some suggestive positive results have been reported in several studies of a nutritional supplement called phosphatidylserine, or PS. Like ginkgo, PS appears to exert generally beneficial effects on a wide variety of tasks, including some memory tests. Some have gone so far as to tout it as a "memory cure" for all manner of memory problems associated with advancing age. However, the apparent ubiquity of PS effects — modest gains in attention, concentration, speed of responding, and so forth — suggests that it may operate mainly to augment arousal and alertness, much like a stiff cup of coffee. Indeed, the authors of a six-step memory-cure program that advocates regular doses of PS also endorse the kinds of elaborative encoding techniques discussed earlier. It is a safe bet that this part of the program is responsible for some of the clinical successes they describe.

Other approaches have focused on hormones that seem related to transience. For instance, researchers have been examining the possible benefits of estrogen hormone replacement in postmenopausal women. After menopause, women often complain about memory problems, and laboratory evidence from studies of older women suggests that low levels of estrogen are associated with poor retention of verbal information, such as lists of words or word pairs, across a time delay. Experimental results indicate that estrogen replacement can improve delayed retention of verbal and pictorial information.

Treatments that effectively combat transience are likely to operate directly on the physiological processes responsible for preserving memories. A group of neurobiologists led by Joseph Tsien took a dramatic step forward in this direction by identifying a gene that significantly improves retention in experimental mice. The gene makes a protein for a neural gateway that plays a key role in memory: the NMDA (N-methyl-D-aspartate) receptor. The NMDA receptor helps to orchestrate the flow of information from one neuron to another across the gap known as the synapse. Several decades ago, the Canadian psychologist Donald Hebb proposed that memories form when the strength of synaptic connections rises among neurons that are active at the same time—a state of affairs summed up by the slogan "Neurons that fire together wire together."

The NMDA receptor opens when it receives two different signals at roughly the same time, triggering facilitated neural processing called "long-term potentiation," which is believed to help increase synaptic connections and thus promote memory formation. At a relatively young age, the receptor stays open for longer than at an older age, boosting long-term potentiation and making it easier for youthful organisms to form new connections. Tsien's group overexpressed the critical gene in experimental mice, leading to more activity in NMDA receptors. Mice with extra copies of the gene performed several different kinds of tasks—learning a spatial layout, recognizing familiar objects, and recalling a fear-inducing shock. The mutant mice showed enhanced long-term potentiation during learning, and also showed better performance on each of the three memory tasks than did normal mice. The benefits persisted into adulthood, in effect allowing older mice to learn like younger ones.

The Tsien group concluded their article with the tantalizing suggestion that the beneficial gene expression effect in mice "reveals a promising strategy for the creation of other genetically modified mammals with enhanced intelligence and memory." As exciting as their results may be, however, nobody yet knows when this kind of approach will lead to the development of treatments that counter- act transience in patients with memory disorders or even in people with normal memories. The possibilities are both enticing and trou- bling. Tim Tully, a neurobiologist who has carried out pioneering research on the genetic basis of memory, wonders whether memory- enhancing drugs might eventually find applications that he would deem personally distasteful. "Think about the pressure on a general who has thirty minutes to communicate a data-rich conversation of specifics of bombing missions to a group of pilots before going off to drop bombs," suggests Tully. "Do you think he'd cram, then take a memory enhancer? They'd be chomping at the bit for drugs that could modulate memory in that fashion." Tully is a pacifist who views this type of application as a perversion of the intent of his and others' research. "I would hate to see this understanding perfected for the art of war, for all the covert and overt atrocities that humans push over on each other."

The potential educational implications of memory-enhancing drugs are also both auspicious and troubling. "What would it be like if a child popped a memory enhancement pill every day before school?" wonders Tully. "What would that child's head be like after twelve years of education? What would the child accomplish with that store of information?" The possibility of producing a genera- tion of superlearners, free from the limitations of transience, seems highly desirable. But could the brain handle such an onslaught of information? What happens to those children who don't have access to the latest memory enhancer? Are they left behind in school and in later life? "We don't know," concedes Tully. Some of the same ques- tions apply to adults in the workplace. Imagine that your likelihood of obtaining a promotion grows if you learn and retain more job-re- lated information, and you can do so by taking a memory enhancer.

Failing to take the drug could put you at a competitive disadvantage. Would you take it, even if the drug produced worrisome side effects, or if the side effects were unknown? These are the kinds of questions that we will have to face eventually, given the pace of progress in research on the neurobiology of memory.

Public excitement over the prospects of genes and drugs that would reduce or eliminate forgetting perhaps reflects an underlying fear of the catastrophic consequences of Alzheimer's disease, or even of the milder effects of normal age-related memory decline. This fear cuts to the heart of why transience is perhaps the most terrifying of the seven sins: it undermines memory's role in connecting us to past thoughts and deeds that define who we are. The great British poet William Wordsworth recognized this connection. In his "Ode: Intimations of Immortality from Recollections of Early Childhood," Wordsworth meditated on the qualities of faded childhood memories, acknowledging with some regret, "The things which I have seen I can now see no more." He celebrated the importance of the faint echoes that remained from his ever-receding past:

> But for those first affections,
> Those shadowy recollections,
> Which, be they what they may,
> Are yet the fountain-light of all of our day,
> Are yet a master-light of all of our seeing.

The Update
ANTI-TRANSIENCE: FROM HIGHLY SUPERIOR AUTOBIOGRAPHICAL MEMORY TO RETRIEVAL PRACTICE AND REWARD EFFECTS

In 2006, I was fascinated to read a just-published case study that described an adult woman, referred to by the initials AJ, who possessed a prodigious memory for her past experiences unlike any other individual previously reported in the scientific literature. AJ lived in Southern California, and several years earlier she had written a letter to the eminent memory researcher James McGaugh at the University of California, Irvine, describing her extraordinary ability. "I am thirty-four years old and since I was eleven I have had this unbelievable ability to recall my past," she explained, going on to say, "Whenever I see a date flash on the television (or anywhere else for that matter) I automatically go back to that day and remember where I was, what I was doing, what day it fell on and on and on and on and on. It is non-stop, uncontrollable and totally exhausting."

Intrigued by this description, McGaugh and his colleagues studied AJ for several years during the early 2000s and provided formal evidence that supported her claims. When they gave AJ a specific date from 1974 or later, she could recall which day of the week the date fell on and something specific about what she had been doing on that day. AJ kept diaries throughout that time, allowing the researchers to check the accuracy of her recollections in those diaries. Especially compelling were the results of the "Easter Test," where the researchers asked AJ, with no warning beforehand, what she had been doing on every Easter from 1980 through 2003. AJ produced the correct date for Easter in each of those years and also provided some details about what had happened on those days, ranging from "just returned from AZ, sick as a dog" for April 7, 1985, to "hang all day, spaghetti dinner with R" for April 11, 1993. All of AJ's memories were confirmed by her diary entries.

Can you recall what you were doing on each Easter for the past two decades? Or on randomly chosen specific dates during that time? (Try May 13, 2012, or October 22, 2005, to get a feel for it.) Undoubtedly, the answer is no. What made AJ's ability to accomplish these feats even more remarkable was that she did not use visual imagery mnemonics or other similar techniques that, as discussed earlier in this chapter, are routinely used by professional mnemonists to store and recall vast amounts of information. Indeed, AJ's performance on standard laboratory tests of memory that involved encoding and retrieval of word lists or similar materials was overall unremarkable and on some tests below average. Her extraordinary memory abilities were restricted to recalling everyday personal experiences.

In 2008, AJ published a book about her jaw-dropping memory, *The Woman Who Can't Forget,* in which she revealed that her real name was Jill Price. Jill appeared in multiple television interviews, including a *60 Minutes* piece that also featured Dr. McGaugh, which generated widespread interest and numerous inquiries to McGaugh from other individuals who claimed that they, too, possessed exceptional memory abilities similar to Jill's. McGaugh and his colleagues screened the inquiries and found that most of the people did not possess these abilities, though a few of them did. In a 2012 paper, the McGaugh group described eleven cases similar to Jill's and labeled the condition "highly superior autobiographical memory," now commonly known as HSAM. In addition to carrying out behavioral testing that confirmed that these HSAM individuals, like Jill, did not do exceptionally well on standard laboratory tests of memory, the researchers performed structural MRIs that revealed differences in the volume of nine brain regions between the HSAM and control groups. Several of these regions, such as the parahippocampal gyrus in the medial temporal lobe, have been implicated in autobiographical memory, leading the researchers to suggest that "structural changes found in the HSAM population may contribute to the more efficient use of the same hardware." In a 2018 fMRI study, individuals with HSAM and a matched control group were instructed to recall past personal experiences during scanning. The HSAM individuals showed increased activity in twice as many brain regions as the controls when they remembered these experiences. They also showed stronger coupling between the hippocampus and the prefrontal cortex, regions that are important for autobiographical memory.

These findings highlight some important features of HSAM, but they leave open the question of how Jill and other people with HSAM achieve their remarkable feats of memory. Given that Jill kept diaries of her everyday experiences, perhaps she simply studied her diary entries in preparation for her testing sessions and thus literally memorized her past. McGaugh and his colleagues convincingly shot down that theory in their original 2006 paper, pointing out that Jill indicated that she rarely reviewed her diaries, and also that she did not know in advance which of the thousands of diary entries she would be asked about. Further, not all HSAM individuals report keeping diaries. Perhaps Jill and others possess some kind of "photographic" memory, making literal recordings of experiences in a way that the rest of us cannot. That, too, flies in the face of the evidence: when given standard laboratory tests that reveal memory distortions and errors in ordinary people (tasks that I will discuss in the chapters on misattribution and suggestibility), HSAM individuals made the same kinds of mistakes that other people did.

Importantly, however, there is evidence that people with HSAM are not as susceptible to transience when recalling personal experiences as the rest of us are. A 2016 study by the McGaugh group of thirty HSAM individuals revealed that they didn't recall any more details than the non-HSAM controls about personal events that had occurred a day or a week earlier, but they did recall significantly more details about events that had occurred a month, a year, and ten years earlier. This study also documented that HSAM individuals are characterized by high levels of obsessive behaviors that resemble those observed in patients diagnosed with obsessive-compulsive disorder, such as a compulsive need to organize their environments and a tendency to ruminate about their past experiences. This description is consistent with Jill Price's characterization of her own recollections as "non-stop, uncontrollable and totally exhausting." Indeed, the original 2006 case report on Jill noted that she "always needed order in her life" and "has trouble inhibiting her constant remembering of her personal past."

Based on these observations, HSAM individuals may be protected from the normal effects of transience because they frequently retrieve their past experiences. That idea fits well with experimental findings that have emerged during the past two decades concerning a phenomenon referred to in the memory literature as "retrieval practice": asking people to retrieve information from memory can be more beneficial to later remembering than simply having them restudy that information. The general idea that retrieving information from memory can strengthen that information and benefit subsequent retention has a long history in psychology (I discussed some of this evidence earlier in the chapter), but it received renewed attention during the early 2000s based on striking demonstrations from the psychologists Henry Roediger and Jeff Karpicke concerning the dramatic benefits of retrieval practice. These benefits have important implications for student learning that have had an increasing impact on educational practices in recent years. Most relevant to our discussion are the results of a 2006 study in which Roediger and Karpicke (1) presented participants with stories to remember, (2) either allowed the participants to restudy the stories or gave them a test on the contents of the stories that required them to retrieve the information, and (3) gave them a final test either five minutes, two days, or one week later. Retrieval practice, compared with restudying, didn't benefit final recall after the five-minute delay — in fact, there was a small advantage of restudying the stories — but retrieval practice dramatically improved final story recall compared to restudying after the two-day and one-week delays. In other words, retrieval practice slowed down the rate of forgetting over time, similar to what the McGaugh group found in their 2016 study of HSAM individuals. Putting those two findings together supports the idea that HSAM is characterized by "anti-transience" for personal experiences, which results from a kind of "autobiographical retrieval practice": repeatedly recalling and perhaps obsessing over past experiences.

The parallel findings in both HSAM and retrieval practice that the rate of forgetting over time slows down are especially noteworthy because it is difficult to find conditions or experimental manipulations that specifically impact the rate of forgetting (as opposed to impacting the encoding or retrieval processes). Recently, though, evidence has mounted showing that a reward can also impact transience selectively. For example, in one experiment, people encoded pictures from one category that were linked to a monetary reward and pictures from another category that were not. A monetary reward did not benefit memory on an immediate test, but it had a large beneficial effect after a three-week delay. Another study showed the boosting effect of a monetary reward on memory for trivia items: the reward increased retention after a one-week delay but not after a ten-minute delay. A similar effect has been observed with drug manipulations that affect the brain's reward system: administering L-dopa improved retention after a six-hour delay but not after a two-hour delay.

The finding that a reward can reduce forgetting over time is potentially important because any manipulation that slows down transience could have practical implications. It's unclear whether reward plays a role in the exceptional memories of HSAM individuals, but future studies that explore the issue would be informative. More generally, findings from the past two decades that HSAM, retrieval practice, and reward all serve to reduce transience puts us in a stronger position today to develop effective interventions to help preserve our memories over time.

GOOGLE, SMARTPHONES, AND SOCIAL MEDIA: FRIENDS OR ENEMIES OF TRANSIENCE?

When I wrote *The Seven Sins of Memory* back in 2001, the Internet was already a force in everyday life, but Google was just coming on the scene, and smartphones (as we know them today) and social media were still several years away. Now many of us routinely rely on Google as a kind of external memory for facts and general knowledge. We use our ever-present smartphones both to navigate our environments with GPS and to record experiences that we wish to preserve and then share through social media. Facebook and Instagram are overrun with photos of everyday happenings. In 2019, Senator Elizabeth Warren boasted about having taken more than 100,000 selfies with people who had attended her presidential campaign events. Recent research has shown that people are biased toward relying on external reminders rather than internal cognitive resources to retrieve memories — a process known as "cognitive offloading" — even when this is not an optimal strategy. Is the increasing reliance on external devices to archive our experiences, navigate our environments, and retrieve information helping or hurting our ability to remember over time?

I've long been interested in the effects of photographs on memory. Back in the late 1990s, my lab conducted a series of studies in which we examined how viewing a photograph of a recent videotaped event affected subsequent memory. Viewing a photo strengthened memory for the event but impaired memory for related events that were not reviewed. (For more on this finding, see Chapter 3. For a discussion of how photos can serve as misinformation that creates false memories, see Chapter 5.) Based on this research, it seems likely that reviewing personal photos on Facebook or Instagram has multiple effects on later memory, both heightening recall of the events depicted in the photos and impairing recall of related events that aren't reviewed.

More recently, researchers have studied how taking a photo of an event impacts subsequent memory for that event. In 2014, the cognitive psychologist Linda Henkel published a study in which people took a museum tour and were instructed to take photos of some objects but just look at others. When given a memory test for the objects on the tour, participants remembered fewer objects and the locations of those objects when they had taken photos of them than when they hadn't. In a later study, people toured a church on the Stanford University campus. Some participants were given an iPod Touch to use as a camera and were told to take as many photos as they liked (minimum of five), either for themselves or to post on Facebook; other participants did not have a camera. Participants who took photos for themselves as well as those who took photos to post on Facebook recalled fewer details of the tour a week later compared with participants who didn't take any photos at all.

Does this photo-induced memory impairment occur because people engaged in cognitive offloading rely on the photo as a memory aid rather than on their own recall? Probably not. Researchers who evaluated this hypothesis using a virtual museum tour found a photo impairment effect even when participants deleted the photo shortly after taking it. These findings suggest that focusing on the act of taking a photo (i.e., focusing on optimal lighting, angle, and so forth) might affect encoding of the experience in a way that impairs subsequent memory. However, it's an oversimplification to suggest that taking a photo of an object or event will inevitably lead to impaired memory. Henkel's work showed that the memory-impairing effect of taking a photo disappeared when people took a photo by zooming in on a specific part of the object. Moreover, other research indicates that when people tour a museum and decide for themselves when to take a photo, taking the photo can enhance subsequent memory for visual aspects of the experience while at the same time impairing memory for auditory aspects. Thus, the impact of taking a photo on what we later remember likely depends on our goal when taking the photo and how memory is later probed.

Using a computer rather than our own memories to store information might have memory-impairing effects. Indeed, a 2011 study indicated that participants exhibited worse memory for trivia items that they typed into a computer (e.g., "An ostrich's eye is bigger than its brain") when they were informed that the computer would save this information than when they were informed that the computer would delete the information. However, subsequent research hasn't revealed similar costs. And one study showed that when people saved a pdf that contained a word list to the computer instead of trying to memorize the words on their own, they were better able to remember a different list of words from a second pdf presented a few seconds later. So, while relying on a computer to store and retrieve information is potentially harmful to memory, it can also be helpful.

People (like me) who frequently rely on a GPS platform such as Google Maps or Waze to navigate when driving or just walking around a new area may not learn much about their environments. Could such reliance produce a persisting impairment in our spatial memory processes? A 2017 study from the laboratory of the London neuroscientist Hugo Spiers provides some intriguing evidence. In this study, participants were taken on a live tour of the Soho neighborhood in London, where they acquired extensive spatial knowledge of the area. The next day, during fMRI they either actively navigated through a filmed simulation of Soho, relying on the memories acquired the previous day to plan their navigation, or simply followed navigation directions provided to them, as when relying on GPS. The study revealed extensive navigation-related activity in the hippocampus, a structure long implicated in memory and spatial navigation, as well as in a region of the prefrontal cortex previously linked to spatial planning — but only in the condition that required memory-based navigation. These hippocampal and prefrontal responses were absent when participants relied on GPS-like directions to navigate. Although this finding does not speak directly to the question of whether relying on GPS impairs spatial memory, several earlier studies show that various measures of hippocampal volume are positively associated with the use of spatial navigation strategies and reliance on spatial memory. Taken together, these lines of research at least raise the possibility that overreliance on GPS to the exclusion of memory-based navigation strategies could contribute to hippocampal atrophy and associated memory decline, although there isn't any direct evidence yet to support this possibility.

Researchers have only just begun to examine how Google, smartphones, social media, and GPS are impacting our memories, and while it's already clear that there is an effect, it's also clear that my initial framing of the question — "Is the increasing reliance on external devices to archive our experiences, navigate our environments, and retrieve information helping or hurting our ability to remember over time?" — is too simplistic. Relying on these external devices doesn't always impair memory and can even produce some benefits. And as we will see in The Update in the next chapter on the sin of absent-mindedness, reliance on external devices to aid memory can sometimes be a life-or-death matter.

2

The Sin of
Absent-Mindedness

ON A BRUTALLY COLD DAY in February 1999, seventeen people gathered on the nineteenth floor of a Manhattan skyscraper to compete for a title known to few others outside that room: National Memory Champion. The winner of the US competition would go on to the world memory championship several months later in London.

The participants were asked to memorize thousands of numbers and words, pages of faces and names, lengthy poems, and rearranged decks of cards. The victor in this battle of mnemonic virtuosos, a twenty-seven-year-old administrative assistant named Tatiana Cooley, relied on classic elaborative encoding techniques: generating visual images, stories, and associations that linked incoming information to what she already knew. Given her proven ability to commit to memory vast amounts of information, one might expect that Cooley's life would have been free from the kinds of memory problems that plague others. Yet the champ considered herself dangerously forgetful. "I'm incredibly absent-minded," Cooley told a reporter. Fearful that she would forget to carry out everyday tasks, Cooley depended on to-do lists and notes scribbled on sticky pads. "I live by Post-its," she admitted ruefully.

The image of the National Memory Champion being dependent on Post-its has a paradoxical, even surreal, quality: Why does someone with a capacity for prodigious recall need to write down anything at all? Couldn't Tatiana Cooley call on the same abilities and strategies she used to memorize hundreds of words or thousands of numbers to help her remember that she needed to pick up a jug of milk at the store? Apparently not: the gulf that separated Cooley's championship memory from her forgetful everyday life illustrates the distinction between transience and absent-mindedness.

The mnemonic techniques that Cooley mastered helped her to counter the effects of the sin of transience. Give ordinary people a long string of numbers to memorize, and by the time they have gone much past the seventh or eighth digit, the first few on the list have faded. Not so for a skilled mnemonist like Cooley, who encoded the numbers in a manner that made them readily accessible even when time passed and more numbers were encoded. But the kinds of everyday memory failures that Cooley sought to remedy with Post-it Notes — errands to run, appointments to keep, and the like — have little to do with transience. These kinds of memory failures instead reflect the sin of absent-mindedness: lapses of attention that result in failing to remember information that was either never encoded properly (if at all) or is available in memory but is overlooked at the time we need to retrieve it.

To appreciate the distinction between transience and absent-mindedness, consider the following three examples:

A man tees up a golf ball and hits it straight down the fairway. After waiting a few moments for his partner to hit, the man tees up his ball again, having forgotten that he hit the first drive.

A man puts his glasses down on the edge of a couch. Several minutes later, he realizes he can't find the glasses and spends a half hour searching his home before locating them.

A man attempts to rob a bank but is easily caught because he forgot to put on his mask during the robbery.

Superficially, all three examples appear to reflect a similar type of rapid forgetting. To the contrary, it is likely that each occurred for very different reasons.

The first incident took place back in the early 1980s, when I played golf with a patient who had been taking part in memory research conducted in my laboratory. The patient was in the early stages of Alzheimer's disease, and he had severe difficulty remembering recent events. Immediately after hitting his tee shot, the patient was excited because he had knocked it straight down the middle; he realized he would now have an easy approach shot to the green. In other words, he had encoded this event in a relatively elaborate manner that would ordinarily yield excellent memory. But when he started teeing up again and I asked him about his first shot, he expressed no recollection of it whatsoever. This patient was victimized by transience: he was incapable of retaining the information he had encoded elaboratively, and no amount of cueing or prodding could bring it forth.

In the second incident, involving misplaced glasses, entirely different processes are at work. Sad to say, this example comes from my own experience — and happens more often than I would care to admit. Without attending to what I was doing, I placed my glasses in a spot where I usually do not put them. Because I hadn't fully encoded this action to begin with — my mind was preoccupied with a scientific article I had been reading — I was at a loss when I realized that my glasses were missing. When I finally found them on the couch, I had no particular recollection of having put them there. But unlike the problem facing the golfing Alzheimer's patient, transience was not the culprit: I had never adequately encoded the information about where I put my glasses and so had no chance to retrieve it later.

The third example, featuring the bungled bank robbery, took place in Auckland, New Zealand, in 2009 and culminated with the capture of the robber and an accomplice because the robber's unmasked face was easily visible to the bank tellers. The robber had also initially forgotten to bring his gun to the teller's counter and then had to retrieve it from his accomplice before demanding and receiving the money.

There is, of course, no way to know exactly what the robber was thinking about when he initially approached the teller without a gun or a mask on his face, but it seems safe to assume that he knew perfectly well that his plan called for bringing a gun to the counter and wearing a mask. Thus, forgetting in this case was probably not a result of transience, or failure to encode the information initially, but was instead likely attributable to an absent-minded retrieval failure at the moment when the robber approached the teller's counter.

Absent-minded memory failures are both amusing and frightening. To understand the basis for them, we need to probe the role of attention in encoding processes, and also to explore how retrieval cues and reminders help us to remember what we intend to do.

ATTENDING AND REMEMBERING:
HOW MUCH DO WE NOTICE?

We have already seen that the degree and type of elaborative encoding that people carry out can strongly affect transience. When such encoding fails altogether, however, conditions are ripe for the annoying kinds of absent-minded memory failures that sometimes seem a regular part of daily existence: misplaced glasses, lost keys, forgotten appointments, and so forth. One way to prevent elaborative encoding is to disrupt or divide attention when people are acquiring new information. In studies of divided attention, experimental participants are given a set of target materials to remember, such as a list of words, a story, or a series of pictures. At the same time, they are required to perform an additional task that draws their attention away from the to-be-remembered material. For example, people might be asked to monitor an ongoing series of tones and to respond when they hear a high-pitched or low-pitched tone, while at the same time they try to study a list of words for a later test. Or, while studying the words, they might be asked to listen to a series of numbers and respond whenever a series of three consecutive odd numbers appears. Compared to a condition in which they are allowed to pay full attention to the study list, people exhibit extremely poor memory for the words studied under divided-attention conditions.

Some studies suggest that divided attention during encoding does not necessarily prevent people from registering some information about an experience. Memory researchers have found it useful to distinguish between two ways in which we remember past experiences:

recollection and familiarity. Recollection involves calling to mind specific details of past experiences, such as exactly where you sat in the restaurant you dined at last week, the tone of voice used by the waiter who served you, or the kind of spices used in the Cajun-style entrée that you ordered. Familiarity entails a more primitive sense of knowing that something has happened previously without dredging up particular details. In the restaurant, for example, you might have noticed at a nearby table someone you are certain you have met previously despite failing to recall such specifics as the person's name or how you know them. Laboratory studies indicate that divided attention during encoding has a drastic effect on subsequent recollection, and has little or no effect on familiarity. This phenomenon probably happens because divided attention prevents us from elaborating on the particulars that are necessary for subsequent recollection, but it allows us to record some rudimentary information that later gives rise to a sense of familiarity. When our attention is divided, we may still record enough information about a face so that it seems familiar when we encounter it again, even though we do not engage in sufficient elaboration to recollect the person's name, occupation, or other details later.

Many absent-minded errors are probably attributable to a kind of divided attention that pervades our daily lives. Mentally consumed with planning for a critical presentation the next day, you place your car keys in an unusual spot as you are reading over your notes. Or, thinking about how much money is left in your checking account after writing the latest check, you leave the checkbook on the dining room table. Even if some residual familiarity remains from these encounters, it is not sufficient to prevent forgetting later on: you need to be able to recollect the details of where you put the keys or the checkbook. Lew Lieberman, a retired psychology professor, relates a particularly irritating incident of this kind:

A day does not go by when I do not spend time looking for something. Today I needed a new booklet of checks for my checkbook.

When I went to get it, I found the very next booklet was missing. Apparently, at some earlier time, I could not find my checkbook and had to use a check from the next booklet to write a check, but then I could not find the missing booklet and have NO recollection of having done this. But then, where is the booklet?

Insufficient attention at the time of encoding may be an especially important contributor to absent-minded errors in older adults. Experiments carried out in the laboratories of the psychologists Fergus Craik and Larry Jacoby indicate that aging can produce a state that resembles a kind of chronic divided attention. Their studies found similar patterns of memory performance in older adults (aged sixties to seventies) who were allowed to pay full attention to incoming information during encoding and college students whose attention was divided during encoding. For instance, in Jacoby's experiments both groups showed less recollection of past experiences than did college students who paid full attention at the time of encoding, even though all three groups showed similar levels of familiarity. Divided attention reduces the overall amount of cognitive resources — the "energy supply" that fuels encoding — that can be devoted to incoming information. Likewise, Craik and others argue that aging is associated with a decline in cognitive resources, thereby resulting in patterns of performance that resemble those produced by divided attention.

Attentional lapses that yield absent-minded forgetting are particularly likely for routine activities that do not require elaborative encoding. During the early stages of performing complex activities, such as driving a car or typing, we need to pay careful attention to every component of the activity. But as our skill improves with practice, less and less attention is required to perform the same tasks that initially demanded painstaking effort. Numerous experiments have shown that practice on various kinds of tasks and skills results in a shift from attention-demanding, effortful task execution to automatic execution involving little or no deployment of attention. "Operating on automatic" provides us with the cognitive freedom to focus on unrelated matters as we perform what once was an attention-consuming task, such as driving a car. But automaticity has a cost: the virtual absence of recollection for activities that were performed "on automatic." Most seasoned drivers, for example, are familiar with the unsettling experience of cruising along at sixty-five miles per hour on a six-lane interstate and suddenly realizing that they have no recollection of the road for the past five miles. Absorbed with concerns that have nothing to do with driving, and relying on the well-learned skills that allow them to drive safely even when on automatic, the experienced driver does not elaborate on what is going on around them and hence remembers nothing of it. Over a century ago, the British novelist Samuel Butler, who developed a grand theory of mental evolution that assigned great importance to the development of automatic behavior, insightfully characterized memory for automatic actions in a concert pianist who has just played a five-minute piece:

> For of the thousands of acts . . . which he has done during the five minutes, he will remember hardly one when it is over. If he calls to mind anything beyond the main fact that he has played such and such a piece, it will probably be some passage which he has found more difficult than the others, and with the like of which he has not been so long familiar. All the rest he will forget as completely as the breath which he has drawn while playing.

This kind of amnesia for the automatic can lead to some jarring incidents of forgetting. It is probably responsible for the kind of forgetting I experienced when, on automatic, I put my eyeglasses down in an unlikely location. Even worse, people report frantically searching for glasses that, only moments ago, they casually pushed up on top of their heads, or running around the house looking for keys they are still holding. My own most frustrating "amnesia for the automatic" story occurred after finishing a round of golf. I carried my clubs back to my car and prepared for the drive home. I usually put my car keys in my golf bag during the round but could not find the keys there. Panicking, I emptied the contents of the bag to no avail. I couldn't find the keys in my pockets and, assuming they had fallen out of the bag when I was playing, began silently cursing under my breath as I contemplated what to do next. Out of the corner of my eye, I then noticed the raised trunk of the car with the keys dangling from the back. Operating on automatic, I had already used the keys to open my trunk but had no memory of it.

Neuroimaging techniques provide insights into what happens in the brain during conditions of divided attention and automatic behavior. Tim Shallice and his collaborators studied the effects of divided attention by performing PET scans while volunteers tried to learn a list of word pairs. Some scans were conducted while people performed an easy, distracting task that diverted little attention away from encoding the word pairs: volunteers moved a bar in the same predictable direction on all trials. Other scans were carried out while the volunteers performed a difficult, distracting task that drew most of their attention away from encoding the word pairs: they moved the bar in novel, unpredictable directions on each trial. There was less activity in the lower left part of the frontal lobe during the difficult distraction scans than during the easy distraction scans. As we saw in the previous chapter, activation in the lower left frontal region during encoding is closely related to subsequent remembering and forgetting. Shallice's experiment suggests that divided attention prevents the lower left frontal lobe from playing its normal role in elaborative encoding. When this region is not involved in encoding new information, or only minimally involved, subsequent recollection will suffer greatly, and absent-minded types of forgetting are likely to occur.

Related neuroimaging studies also link the left inferior frontal lobe with automatic behavior. The neuroscientist Marcus Raichle and his group performed PET scans while they showed volunteers a series of common nouns and asked them to generate related verbs.

So, for example, when shown the noun *dog,* participants might come up with *bark* or *walk.* When subjects first performed this task, generating verbs was associated with extensive activity in the lower left frontal lobe (and many other parts of the brain). This activity probably reflects a kind of elaborative encoding related to thinking about properties of dogs and the kinds of actions they perform. But as the volunteers practiced the task repeatedly with the same nouns and generated the verbs more quickly and automatically, activity in the lower left frontal lobe gradually declined. This result raises the possibility that automatic behaviors in everyday life — a key source of absent-minded errors — may be associated with low levels of left prefrontal activity.

In a related fMRI study conducted by Anthony Wagner in my laboratory, we saw further evidence of how automatic behavior, reflected by reduced activity in the left inferior prefrontal cortex, works against forming vivid recollections. Memory researchers have known since the pioneering studies of Hermann Ebbinghaus over a century ago that repeating information improves memory for what is repeated. Further, distributing the repetitions over time often results in better memory than massing them all together. So, for instance, if you want to study for a test you will be taking in a week's time and are able to go through the material ten times, it is better to space out the ten repetitions during the week than to squeeze them all together. (Students often engage in massive cramming just before taking an exam, which can produce short-term gains in retention, but spacing out repetitions generally produces better long-term results.)

We showed people words to encode for a later test, either a day before we showed them the same words again in the scanner (spaced repetition) or just a few minutes before they saw the same words again (massed repetition). Predictably, people showed better memory on the test for the spaced words than for the massed words. Most important, there was less activity in the left inferior prefrontal region when people studied the massed words they had just seen a few minutes earlier than when they studied the spaced words they had seen a day earlier. Repeating the words close together in time apparently led to more automatic encoding on the second repetition, which was associated with reduced left prefrontal activity and poorer subsequent memory. These results fit nicely with those from Raichle's verb-generation experiment and might help us to understand why automatic kinds of encoding can lead to absent-minded memory errors.

Automatic or superficial levels of encoding can result in other kinds of absent-minded errors, too. One of the most intriguing is known as "change blindness." In studies of change blindness, people observe objects or scenes that unfold over time. Experimenters make subtle or large changes to the objects or scenes in order to determine whether people notice the changes. Change blindness occurs when people fail to detect the changes that the experimenter has made. The psychologists Daniel Levin and Daniel Simons have performed some of the most inventive research on change blindness. In one study, for instance, they showed participants a movie in which a young blond man sits at a desk. He then gets up, walks away from the desk, and exits the room. The scene shifts outside the room, where a young man makes a phone call. Unknown to the observers, the man sitting at the desk is not the same person as the man who makes the phone call. Although both are young and blond and wear glasses, they are clearly different people when examined at all carefully. Only one-third of the observers noticed the change.

In another film, two women are shown sitting across a table from each other, sipping colas and munching on food as they chat. As the camera cuts back and forth between the two, it all seems pretty normal and mundane. When asked if they noticed whether anything changed during the brief duration of the film, most people say they did not detect any changes, or perhaps noticed one. Yet in every frame, there were numerous changes in the women's clothes, props on the table, and so forth.

Not satisfied with merely demonstrating change blindness in film segments, Levin and Simons asked whether such effects could also be demonstrated in live interactions. To test this idea, one experimenter asked someone on a college campus for directions. While they were talking, two men walked between them carrying a door that hid a second experimenter. Behind the door, the two experimenters traded places, so that when the men carrying the door moved on, a different person from the one who had been there just a second or two earlier was now asking for directions. Remarkably, only seven of fifteen participants reported noticing this change!

In successive experiments, Simons has demonstrated even more dramatic effects by further restricting attention to an object. Consider this: If you were watching a circle of people passing a basketball and someone dressed in a gorilla costume walked through the circle, stopped to beat his chest, and exited, of course you would notice him immediately — wouldn't you? Simons and the psychologist Chris Chabris filmed such a scene and showed it to people who were asked to track the movement of the ball by counting the number of passes made by one of the team. Approximately half of the participants failed to notice the gorilla.

Focused on tracking the ball's movement, people are blind to what happens to unattended objects and thus do not encode the sudden change. Brain imaging evidence from a related experimental procedure supports this idea. When people are instructed to pay attention to letter strings superimposed on line drawings of objects, parts of the left frontal, temporal, and parietal lobes respond more strongly to meaningful words than to random letters. But when they are instructed to pay attention to the line drawings, these regions no longer respond differently to words and random letters — even though participants look directly at the letter strings.

In the earlier examples, where people were free to attend to whatever they wished, change blindness probably occurred because people encode features of a scene at an extremely shallow level, recording the general gist of the scene but few of the specific details. To paraphrase Simons and his collaborators, successful change detection tends to occur when people encode elaboratively the exact features that distinguish the original object or person from the changed one. In the door study, the people who most often failed to notice that a different person emerged from behind the door were middle-aged and older adults; college students tended to notice the change. Older individuals might have encoded the initial (young) experimenter generically as a "college student," whereas the college students (for whom the person asking directions was a peer) might have encoded the experimenter in a more specific way. To find out whether college students would be more susceptible to change blindness when induced to encode at a generic level, Simons and Levin repeated the door study attired as construction workers. They thought the college students might now tend to encode them more generically and, hence, show higher levels of change blindness. And they did: only four of twelve students noticed when a different construction worker emerged from behind the door to ask directions. Thus, shallow encoding that does not proceed beyond a general level results in poor recollection of the details of a scene and consequent vulnerability to change blindness. Change blindness is attributable, at least in part, to the same kinds of automatic encoding activities that sometimes leave us searching for glasses perched atop our heads or keys clenched in our fists.

Remembering What You Want to Do

In Marcel Proust's monumental exploration of his own memory, *Remembrance of Things Past,* the author's yearning to recapture lost moments from childhood seems to epitomize what memory is for: providing a connection between the present and the past. Yet in our daily lives, memory is just as much about the future as it is about the past. We are all familiar with the seemingly endless to-do lists that remind us of what we need to remember in the future: pick up milk and cereal on the way home; call to make that airline reservation; drop off a manuscript at an associate's office; confirm tomorrow's lunch date; mail in the mortgage payment on time; transfer money from savings to checking — the list could go on indefinitely.

Psychologists nowadays use the term "prospective memory" to describe remembering to do things in the future. Until recent decades, however, researchers had focused almost exclusively on the remembrance of things past, which constituted the object of Proust's yearnings and writings, even though people express more concern about remembering to carry out future actions than about other, retrospectively oriented aspects of memory. This distinction may be because when retrospective remembering fails — forgetting a name or a fact, or confusing when and where two events occurred — memory is seen as unreliable. But when prospective remembering fails — forgetting a lunch appointment or failing to drop off a package as promised — the person is seen as unreliable. Have you ever forgotten to send in your monthly mortgage or credit card payment? If so, you know that faulty memory is not a sufficient excuse to escape the late-payment fee. Absent-minded errors of prospective memory are annoying not only because of their pragmatic consequences, but also because others tend to see them as reflecting on credibility and even character in a way that poor retrospective memory does not.

Why does prospective memory fail? To begin to answer this question, I find it useful to adopt a distinction first proposed by the psychologists Gilles Einstein and Mark McDaniel. They distinguish between "event-based" and "time-based" prospective memory. Event-based prospective memory involves remembering to carry out a task when a specific event occurs. If your friend Frank says, "When you see Harry at the office today, tell him to call me," Frank is asking you to remember to perform a particular action (tell Harry to call me) when a specific event occurs (you see Harry at the office). Time-based prospective memory, in contrast, involves remembering to carry out an action at a specific time in the future. Remembering to take the cookies out of the oven in twenty minutes and remembering to take your medicine at 11:00 p.m. are examples of time-based prospective memory tasks.

Forgetting can occur for different reasons when we are faced with event-based and time-based prospective memory tasks. In event-based tasks, problems occur if the event that is designated to trigger recall of the intended action fails to do so: if, for instance, we see Harry in the office and are not reminded to tell him to call Frank.

In time-based tasks, by contrast, problems usually arise because we fail to encounter or generate a cue that can remind us to carry out the target action. When faced with the task of remembering to take medicine at 11:00 p.m., either I must spontaneously remember to do so at 11:00 p.m. or think ahead and arrange cues that will likely trigger recall at the right time. Knowing that I am likely to be brushing my teeth before bed at 11:00 p.m., for example, I might place the medicine in a spot by the sink where I can't miss it. From this perspective, event-based prospective memory requires understanding of why cues or hints do or do not spontaneously trigger recall of an intended action; time-based prospective memory requires understanding of how we generate cues that will help us to remember at a later time.

Consider first event-based prospective memory. Frank has asked you to tell Harry to call him, but you have forgotten to do so. You indeed saw Harry in the office, but instead of remembering Frank's message, you were reminded of the bet you and Harry had made concerning last night's college basketball championship, gloating for several minutes over your victory before settling down to work. When Frank later asks you what happened with Harry, you apologize profusely and wonder out loud whether something has gone terribly wrong with your memory. In all likelihood, nothing is wrong. Prospective memory failed because Harry is a potential reminder of many things other than the message to call Frank. The best prospective memory triggers tend to be highly distinctive cues that have few other associations in long-term memory, and hence are not likely to remind us of irrelevant information.

Experiments by Gilles Einstein and Mark McDaniel using a simple laboratory analogue of event-based prospective memory demonstrate the importance of cue distinctiveness. Participants were given lists of words to learn for a later test. For the prospective memory task, some people were instructed to push a button whenever a particular familiar word appeared, such as *movie,* and others were instructed to push the button whenever a particular unfamiliar item appeared, such as the nonsense word *yolif*. Einstein and McDaniel reasoned that people have many associations to *movie* and, hence, might sometimes think of them instead of remembering to press the button. They have no associations to *yolif* and, hence, would not be distracted by irrelevant information and forget to push the button. Results indeed showed that people were much more likely to remember to press the button when cued with *yolif* than with *movie*.

A reminder also has to be sufficiently informative, as well as distinctive, to aid prospective recall. How many times have you jotted down a phone number that you need to call, thinking that it will remind you later to do so, only to discover that you do not recollect whose phone number it is? When I visited a college campus to lecture on memory, my host's secretary showed me a "reminder" she had scrawled on a sticky pad earlier that day which said only "Nat." She now had no idea who or what she meant by "Nat." When we write a note to ourselves, all the surrounding information is available in working memory, so the reminder seems perfectly adequate. But we may fail to take into account the main lesson in the previous chapter: memories are frequently transient. The reminder that seemed self-evident when related information was available in working memory becomes a cryptic — and frustrating — puzzle when that information has faded with time. To aid future recall, we need to transfer as many details as possible from working memory to written reminders.

Event-based prospective memory can also fail because we are preoccupied with other concerns and devote so little attention to the target event that we are not spontaneously reminded of anything. If you saw Harry in the office only minutes before you had to give a major presentation to your CEO, you may have been devoting so much mental effort to preparing for the talk that the sight of Harry failed to trigger any recollections at all. Experiments using a variant of the Einstein-McDaniel procedure support this possibility. People were shown a series of words and were instructed to remember to press a button whenever a particular word appeared. Some participants also performed an additional attention-demanding task. For example, in one experiment some participants tried to generate a sequence of digits rapidly in a random order while they were also studying the word list and remembering to perform the prospective memory task. Compared to participants who were allowed to generate digit sequences at a more leisurely pace, the group that generated digits rapidly showed many more lapses of prospective memory—that is, they forgot to press the button when the target word appeared. They were preoccupied with trying to generate random digit sequences quickly, so the word cues frequently failed to remind them of what they were supposed to do, much as someone preoccupied with preparing a talk might fail to pass on a message to a coworker she encounters while in the midst of preparations. In other experiments in which participants were given relatively mindless additional tasks to perform, such as continually repeating the word *the* while studying words and trying to remember to press a button when the target appeared, prospective memory did not suffer.

A study that used PET scans to examine brain activity during an event-based prospective memory task further illuminates these findings. While in the scanner, participants were instructed to repeat a series of spoken words. In a condition that also required prospective memory, they tried to remember to tap whenever a designated target word was spoken. Compared to when participants repeated words but did not have to remember to carry out a future action, prospective remembering was associated with greater activity in several parts of the frontal lobe. Some of these same frontal regions have been implicated previously in working memory—holding information online for brief time periods. Although we do not yet know how these laboratory findings relate to everyday absent-minded errors, it is tempting to speculate that some of the frontal regions that showed heightened activity during prospective remembering are "captured" by distracting activities that preoccupy us and contribute to failed prospective memory. Consider, for example, what might happen when we are told to pass on a message to an associate but are preoccupied with competing task demands — thinking about what we said, or didn't say, at this morning's meeting when we encounter that associate. Some of the frontal regions that contribute to successful prospective remembering may be tied up by our internal monologue, and thus do not play their usual role in enabling prospective recall. This could result in a failure to be reminded by a cue to carry out an intended action.

Stressed-out aging adults who worry that each new absent-minded memory slip signals the onset of age-related cognitive decline, or perhaps even Alzheimer's disease, should take comfort in the finding that prospective cues frequently fail to trigger recall of appropriate actions when people are preoccupied with attention-consuming matters. The source of their worries may well lie in the multitude of competing professional and personal concerns that absorb mental energy and can reduce the effectiveness of reminders to carry out mundane but necessary everyday tasks. Indeed, several laboratory studies have shown that older adults who have reached their sixties and seventies perform almost as well as younger adults on event-based prospective memory tasks. When given cues that remind them to carry out a target task, older adults have little problem remembering what to do.

Aging does have more noticeable effects on time-based prospective memory tasks. When we need to carry out an action at a particular time in the future, such as remembering to take medication before bed, we must generate cues or reminders on our own. For example, in laboratory studies by Einstein and McDaniel, older and younger adults were instructed to remember to press a key after ten and twenty minutes had passed; a clock was positioned behind the subjects to help them keep track of time. In this time-based task, older adults forgot to press the key more often than did younger adults. With no cue available to trigger recall of the target action, older adults were less likely than younger adults to summon up the action on their own. This finding fits well with other data indicating that self-initiated recall is a difficult task for older adults, probably because it requires extensive cognitive resources that decline with age.

Older adults can, however, perform well on time-based prospective memory tasks by taking steps to convert them into event-based tasks — that is, by generating cues that will be available at the appropriate time to trigger recall of what must be done. When asked by an experimenter to make a phone call at a specified time, some older adults changed the time-based task to an event-based task by linking it with an incident in their daily lives that occurred when the call had to be made. For example, one participant placed a reminder note to make the call next to where she washed dishes, and another tied in the phone call with a morning coffee.

These findings have implications for such important everyday prospective memory tasks as taking medication. Many older adults need multiple medications, and taking them at the right time is crucial for their health. Surveys suggest that between one-third and one-half of elderly adults do not adhere to their medication schedules. Direct observations indicate that such problems are mainly characteristic of people in their seventies and eighties; "young" older adults (in their sixties) generally adhere well to medication schedules. As noted earlier, remembering to take a medication at 11:00 p.m. is a time-based task, but it can be converted to an event-based task by, say, placing the needed medication next to one's toothbrush and regularly brushing one's teeth before retiring at 11:00 p.m. Many factors contribute to poor medication adherence, but improvements can be realized by arranging cues that convert this time-based task to an event-based task.

Perhaps even more than event-based prospective memory, time-based prospective memory often fails because people are preoccupied with other concerns that prevent them from even attempting to generate appropriate retrieval cues. In the study that required participants to make a phone call at a particular time, the most common reasons they gave for failing to do so were that they were "absorbed" or "distracted." Unfortunately, we often merely admonish ourselves to remember to carry out a task at a future time rather than generating concrete cues or reminders that will help us to do so. Sitting at a desk in your home office, you tell yourself earnestly, "Okay, don't forget to mail that credit card payment tomorrow morning." But unless you convert this time-based task to an event-based task by generating a reminder, such as putting the bill in a place where you will see it when you leave for work the next morning, the bill will likely remain unsent on top of your desk. The psychologist Susan Whitbourne related to me a particularly vexing incident of this sort:

> In leaving for an overnight trip to Baltimore, I "told" myself to be sure to pack my contact lens case in the morning, after I was through with it at home. However, I forgot to do so, as I found when I looked for it in my bag that night. Spotting two empty water glasses with handy paper covers, I thought I would put one lens in each glass and cover them up and that would do it. At the time, I was quite weary after a long day of travel and an evening of socializing. In the morning, I went to the sink and, to my horror, saw that the right glass had been removed and was empty! The glass of water I helped myself to in the middle of the night had an extra little treat in it that would never make it to my eye. Fortunately, I was able to give my talk that day wearing only one contact lens, but it was a pretty miserable experience, not to mention an expensive memory slip.

Despite the health risk of swallowing a contact lens, Whitbourne's absent-minded error led to a relatively benign, if irritating, outcome. But in other contexts, more serious consequences can follow from failed time-based prospective recall. Air traffic control provides a compelling example. Controllers are frequently faced with situations in which they must postpone an action and remember to carry it out at a later time. For example, if a pilot requests a higher altitude that cannot be granted until nearby aircraft pass, the controller must remember to give the clearance later. To help remember, controllers use rectangular strips of paper, called "flight progress strips," which provide information about the altitude, route, destination, and other features of each flight for which the controller is responsible. A controller who defers a request for higher altitude, for example, might try to use the strip for that flight as a reminder by marking it or offsetting it from other strips.

Flight progress strips are being replaced by automated electronic strips that do not allow controllers to manipulate them physically. To help determine how controllers could use such automated reminders most effectively, researchers at the University of Oklahoma collaborated with the Federal Aviation Administration in a simulated study of air traffic control. Consider a controller who has just deferred a request from Delta flight 692 for higher altitude until passing traffic clears, and enters a prospective command to remind himself to grant higher altitude to Delta 692 in one minute. One scenario would be to make the electronic reminder visible during the minute waiting period, to help the controller "rehearse" the command, but not at the moment the command is to be executed. A second scenario would be to make the electronic reminder visible only at the moment when the command needs to be retrieved and executed. Yet a third scenario would be to keep the reminder visible both during rehearsal and at the moment of intended retrieval. Compared to a control condition in which no electronic reminder was provided, prospective recall improved only when the cue was available at the time needed for retrieval (the second and third scenarios). Providing the reminder during rehearsal alone produced no benefit, and providing the reminder during both rehearsal and at the moment of retrieval was no more effective than providing it at retrieval alone.

The importance of having a cue available at the time an intended action is carried out, rather than beforehand, was painfully illustrated when I received a call at home one morning from my wife. She reminded me to leave cash for our housecleaners, who would make their weekly visit later that day. She also reminded me not to set the security alarm, because the cleaners do not know the code.

I immediately removed the cash needed to pay them and placed it on the kitchen table. I then resumed what I had been doing (writing this very chapter) and left for the office later that morning. Two hours later, I received a message from a friend who had been notified by our security company that the alarm in our house had gone off. Police arrived quickly, and the cleaners faced the awkward task of explaining that they intended to clean — not to clean out — our house. My wife's reminder to leave the money worked because I was able to act on it immediately. Her reminder to refrain from setting the alarm induced me to "rehearse" — admonishing myself not to forget, just as Susan Whitbourne told herself to pack the case for her contact lenses — but it ultimately failed because it was not present when I needed to avoid setting the alarm at the time I left the house a couple of hours later.

Because prospective memory so heavily depends on the availability of cues that trigger intended actions, the most effective way to counter absent-minded prospective memory failures is to develop and use effective external memory aids. The most effective such cues pass two key criteria considered earlier: they are sufficiently informative, and they are available at the time an action needs performing. The quintessential external memory aid — a string tied around one's finger — passes the latter of these two criteria but not the former. Tying a string around a finger is potentially helpful because it's always visible. But it renders us vulnerable to the same problem that frustrated the secretary who puzzled over what she meant by the reminder saying only "Nat": it is easy to forget what a string around the finger means. Even if we do write down sufficiently detailed notes to remind us of what we intend to do, we still must find a way to ensure that they are available around the time the action is to be performed. Sticky-pad notes hidden in our pockets or a notebook that we never look at may contain all the necessary details but will not help us remember unless they are consulted.

A number of elementary and secondary schools have instituted effective programs that use external memory aids to combat a common absent-minded error among students: forgetting to do home-work. For example, in one Atlanta-area elementary school, students record assignments to be carried out in a central planning notebook that parents are asked to sign each night. The school's principal spot-checks the planners, awarding ice cream and candy kisses to those students whose parents sign off every day of the week. To encourage its use, one high school requires students to carry the planner as a hall pass, and another requires them to take it with them to the water fountain or restroom. Informal reports suggest a reduction of forgot-ten homework assignments.

Many effective everyday memory aids that we take for granted meet the two key criteria of informativeness and availability at the time of retrieval. A whistling teakettle, for instance, reminds you of exactly what you need to do at the time you need to do it. Like-wise, some electronic irons come with a built-in prospective mem-ory cue, sounding an alarm when left facedown for too long. Even more sophisticated electronic devices are now available to help us record and plan our future actions. A survey conducted in the early 1990s identified thirty different kinds of external memory aids that were then available commercially, and the list has grown since then. Interestingly, there were variations in the perceived usefulness of dif-ferent types of external aids as a function of age and lifestyle. Back then, teens and adults in their twenties tended to be most interested in high-tech reminders such as electronic memo pads that could be used at school or on the job. Middle-aged adults with families viewed products that reduced forgetting of tasks around the house, such as the "memory iron," as particularly helpful. And older, mainly retired adults were most interested in products that helped them to execute routine daily tasks at home and elsewhere, such as an elec-tronic "plant reminder" that is inserted into soil and sounds when the plant needs to be watered.

When Joseph Tsien and his group published their groundbreak-ing study of genetically engineered memory improvements in mice, the media were awash in speculations about high-tech memory drugs that might put an end to forgetting altogether. But just as National Memory Champion Tatiana Cooley forgot to do things and struggled to overcome her absent-minded memory failures, there is likewise no guarantee that any future drugs that combat transience will also reduce absent-mindedness. As Cooley discovered, however, combating absent-mindedness does not require genetic interventions: the Post-its that she relied on, or other more sophisticated external memory aids, are adequate remedies when used effectively. Absent-mindedness is most troublesome for busy individuals who are perpetually trying to balance multiple tasks and must therefore constantly organize future actions. The psychologist Ellen Langer has pointed out that when we misplace our car keys or eyeglasses, it is usually because we are devoting our mental resources to more important things: wrestling with a personal dilemma or thinking about how to handle an upcoming meeting at work. Are there also absent-minded mice, preoccupied with pressing concerns that lead to automatic behaviors and associated forgetting? Might there be a specific gene responsible that could help us to overcome such memory failures? If one exists, would we want to make use of it? These are intriguing questions without clear answers. But I suspect that for the foreseeable future, cognitive engineers, not genetic engineers, will lead the way forward in efforts to combat absent-mindedness.

The Update
FORGOTTEN CHILDREN

Several months after the first edition of *The Seven Sins of Memory* was published in the spring of 2001, I received a phone call from an attorney concerning a startling and tragic case of forgetting that he had taken on in Dallas County, Iowa. Kari Engholm, then a thirty-five-year-old hospital executive, drove to work on a hot late-June morning focused on a busy day ahead filled with meetings. But that morning was different from most mornings because Kari, who normally drove her three-year-old son, Eric, to a daycare center before going to work, was also responsible for driving her seven-month-old daughter, Clare, to a babysitter. Kari's husband, Dennis, usually drove Clare to the babysitter, but he couldn't do so that morning. So Kari dropped off Eric and then drove directly to work—as she always did—without stopping to leave Clare with the babysitter. The babysitter left messages on the Engholms' home phone asking why Clare had not been dropped off, but they never reached Kari and Dennis. At the end of a steamy, ninety-degree day, Kari picked up Eric at daycare and, when she opened the door to let Eric into the car, finally became aware of the horror that had transpired: Clare had died in the back seat of the oven-hot car.

I was taken aback by the attorney's phone call because I had never heard of a case in which forgetting produced such a catastrophic result. I had read about parents who made an ill-considered decision to leave a child in a hot car while running an errand, but this was different—Kari Engholm never made a conscious choice to leave Clare in the car and wasn't even aware that Clare was in the car after dropping off Eric. Instead, what happened to Kari was an extreme example of absent-minded forgetting that closely followed the principles of prospective remembering and forgetting established in psychological studies. Earlier in this chapter, I discussed the critical importance of having a reminder cue available at the moment an action needs to be executed. Kari did not notice Clare sleeping in her car seat when she dropped off Eric and thus had no reminder to drive to the babysitter at the moment she needed one. I also discussed evidence that people forget to carry out intended actions because they are preoccupied with other matters and don't attempt to generate retrieval cues. Kari was focused on upcoming meetings, and it surely wouldn't have occurred to her that she could possibly forget that her baby was in the car, so why would she even try to generate a reminder? Other evidence shows that automatic behavior can contribute to absent-minded forgetting. Kari's normal routine changed on that awful June day: As she left Eric's daycare, habits took over, and she automatically drove directly to work. In effect, Kari encountered a "perfect storm" of conditions that conspired to produce a nearly unimaginable kind of absent-minded forgetting.

News coverage of the tragedy contained incredulous and even

contemptuous assertions. A July 5, 2001, column in the *Orlando Sentinel* discussing Kari's case and two similar ones raised a question that no doubt crossed the minds of many: "How do you forget your child is in the car? How do you become so preoccupied with work that you forget to drop your child at the babysitter's, as two of these women claim to have done?" Kari was indeed charged with felony neglect of a dependent child and involuntary manslaughter, and she stood trial for those offenses. But in December 2001, Judge Paul Huscher rendered a verdict of not guilty, reasoning that Kari had not acted with reckless disregard for Clare's safety.

Sadly, cases similar to Kari's have appeared with numbing regularity during the past two decades. But as pointed out by Gene Weingarten in his Pulitzer Prize–winning *Washington Post* article "Fatal Distraction," these tragic deaths started occurring with regularity only after a well-intentioned policy change produced unintended consequences:

> Two decades ago, this was relatively rare. But in the early 1990s, car-safety experts declared that passenger-side front airbags could kill children, and they recommended that child seats be moved to the back of the car; then, for even more safety for the very young, that the baby seats be pivoted to face the rear. If few foresaw the tragic consequence of the lessened visibility of the child . . . well, who can blame them? What kind of person forgets a baby?

Unfortunately, events since have shown that pretty much anyone can forget a baby in the back seat. People who have forgotten young children in hot cars leading to death include numerous caring, responsible, and highly accomplished parents. According to a 2018 report from the National Safety Council, about forty children died in hot cars each year since 1998, and 54 percent of those deaths were attributable to forgetting (by contrast, only 19 percent resulted from a parent knowingly leaving a child in a hot car, and 26 percent resulted from a child gaining access to the car). The perfect storm of circumstances that led Kari Engholm astray — absence of retrieval cues at the moment they are needed most, change in routine, absorption with pressing concerns unrelated to the child, and reliance on automatic behavior — show up again and again in these heartbreaking stories.

Who is to blame? Online comments concerning cases like Kari's tend to be split sharply. Some provide a harsh response to Gene Weingarten's question "What kind of person forgets a baby?": anyone who could do so is not fit to be a parent and has committed a crime. Others view the bereaved parents as victims of an extreme kind of forgetting that does not deserve to be punished as a crime, especially given that the parents are already suffering from severe and unrelenting self-inflicted guilt. Not surprisingly, my own view fits the latter perspective for the reasons just discussed. Yet the legal system has had difficulty settling on a consistent approach to child hot car deaths, with charges ranging from no criminal charges in some cases all the way up to felony involuntary manslaughter in others. In a 2019 *New York Times* article on whether the legal system should treat these tragedies as accidents or crimes, Amber Rollins of Kidsandcars.org — an organization that is devoted to keeping children and pets safe in and around motor vehicles and has analyzed more than eight hundred child hot car cases — stated flatly: "All in all, there is no rhyme or reason to how these cases are treated."

Although there has been little systematic research on factors that influence the assignment of blame when parents forget a child in a hot car, a 2015 study provided some initial evidence in this regard. Male and female participants read a brief scenario that described an event similar to what happened with Kari Engholm: While driving to work on a hot summer day, a parent (either male or female) forgets to drop off their child at daycare. In the severe outcome condition, the child remains in the car for several hours and dies before being found. In the mild outcome condition, the child is found soon after being left in the car, is treated at a hospital for mild dehydration, and is released the same day. Participants then completed questionnaires that included assessments of blame and responsibility. Male participants assigned greater responsibility and blame to the parent than did females, regardless of whether the parent in the story was male or female. Participants of both genders assigned greater responsibility and blame when the outcome was severe than when it was mild. In light of these preliminary findings, we should expect that assignment of blame and responsibility in hot car deaths attributable to forgetting will vary depending on who is assigning the blame and the circumstances that impacted the outcome.

Wherever one comes down on the question of whether or to what extent parents are to be blamed in such cases, the good news is that approaching the problem as a reversible failure of prospective memory can lead to two potential solutions: create awareness that this type of catastrophic forgetting is possible, and find a way to provide external retrieval cues that mitigate its occurrence. Awareness is crucial because what makes this form of absent-minded forgetting truly perverse is that the very idea that one could possibly forget one's own child in the back seat of a car is to most people preposterous, even though studies have shown that it is not. Websites that bring attention to the problem, such as Kidsandcars.org and the National Safety Council (www.nsc.org), do an excellent job of promoting awareness, as do media reports, which typically peak during the summer in response to new cases of hot car deaths. Many reports emphasize the value of parents putting a visual reminder in the front seat (such as a toy or doll) alerting them that a child is in the back seat. New products also provide useful reminders, such as the Elepho eClip, which attaches to a car seat and sends visual and auditory alerts to a smartphone to remind the driver that there is a baby in the car. Car manufacturers have begun to develop optional features as well, such as rear seat reminder systems. Even the traffic app Waze has a feature that can remind drivers to check the back seat upon reaching their destination. Eschewing a high-tech approach, in 2019 a nine-year-old girl invented a device that uses a stretchy cord and Velcro loops to attach car keys to a car seat, thus reminding the driver that a baby is on board.

Although not all reminder systems may be entirely foolproof, I am unaware of any cases of forgetting that have led to the death of a child in a hot car equipped with a reminder device, which raises an important question: Why isn't potentially lifesaving reminder technology mandatory in every new vehicle? The reason cited by the Alliance of Automobile Manufacturers (AAM) in a May 2019 statement is that only 13 percent of new car buyers have children aged six or younger. That argument may not survive mounting pressure: the Hot Cars Act of 2019, introduced by Ohio congressman Tim Ryan, would make reminder technology mandatory in new vehicles, and the US Senate has drafted a similar companion bill. Because previous bills have faced stiff resistance from the AAM, it is perhaps not surprising that Ryan's bill did not receive a vote in the 116th Congress, which ended on January 3, 2021; only time will tell whether these new proposals ever become law. But let's hope we are on the road to reducing and perhaps eliminating absent-minded forgetting as a source of the devastating infant and child deaths that haunt the lives of Kari Engholm and too many other parents.

WHEN THE MIND WANDERS

If you've been reading this chapter for more than a few minutes, it's likely that there was a moment (maybe even a few) when you suddenly realized that you were no longer attending to the words on the page and had drifted away from the book — "zoning out" into an inner world of fantasies, plans, or memories. That's no insult to me as a writer: laboratory studies have shown that when participants read various kinds of texts for more than a few minutes — even a literary masterpiece such as Tolstoy's *War and Peace* — zoning out is a frequent occurrence. Nowadays, psychologists refer to such events as "mind wandering."

When I wrote the first edition of *The Seven Sins of Memory*, mind wandering was barely a blip on psychologists' radar screens. But that changed within a few years, largely due to the research and writing of the psychologists Jonathan Schooler and Jonathan Smallwood, who recognized that mind wandering occurs frequently, developed experimental paradigms to study it, and proposed theoretical models to explain it. As a result, mind wandering became, and still is, a hot topic in psychological research.

Mind wandering is related to the sin of absent-mindedness because it is often implicated in everyday cases of divided attention during the encoding stage of memory, such as those I discussed earlier in this chapter, which produce forgetting. If you are engaged in mind wandering while reading a book, you are not likely to remember much of what you've read, and once you catch yourself, you may decide that you need to go back and reread the pages for which you were "absent."

One of the most important lines of recent research linking mind wandering with absent-minded forgetting has focused on educational settings, especially classroom and video lectures. College professors such as myself aren't shocked to learn that students occasionally engage in mind wandering during our lectures, but I was surprised to learn how often it can happen. In a 2011 study of undergraduates, researchers probed students' thoughts as they sat through three 50-minute psychology lectures: they sounded an alert five times during each lecture and asked students to record what they were thinking about at the moment when the alert sounded. On about one-third of these occasions, students recorded thoughts that were unrelated to the lecture. Perhaps most important, more frequent mind wandering was associated with poorer retention of lecture material as measured on an exam given several weeks later.

For any lecturer, it is disturbing to think that a substantial proportion of their audience is engaged in mind wandering rather than focusing on what they are saying. Perhaps the lecturer in this particular class was especially boring? Probably not. Similar results were obtained in a study of mind wandering while students watched video-recorded lectures by three different Yale professors in psychology, economics, and classics. There was an overall 43 percent incidence of mind wandering in response to visual probes during these lectures, and a substantial increase in mind wandering from the beginning of the lecture to the end. Moreover, greater increases in mind wandering across each lecture were linked with poorer retention of lecture material as measured on a test given shortly after the lecture. More recent research indicates that mind wandering during live lectures is relatively stable across time compared with video-recorded lectures, and that during live lectures, distraction from media multitasking, such as engaging with social media on smartphones and laptops, is even more damaging to retention than mind wandering. In fact, one study showed that people who reported frequently engaging in media multitasking in their daily lives were especially prone to attentional lapses during a laboratory memory task that resulted in retrieval failures.

Is there anything that can be done to reduce attentional lapses such as mind wandering during lectures and thus increase attention to and memory for lecture content? Several years ago, the Toronto psychologist Karl Szpunar, then a postdoctoral researcher in my laboratory, led a study in which we hypothesized that embedding brief quizzes in a video-recorded lecture would improve attention to the lecture, reduce mind wandering, and increase retention of lecture material. And that is exactly what we found. When watching a twenty-minute statistics lecture, students who received quizzes after each five-minute lecture segment engaged in mind wandering about half as often as students who either restudied the same material or did arithmetic problems after each lecture segment instead of receiving a quiz. The quizzed group, compared with the other two groups, also showed a significant increase in retention of lecture content on a test given to all students at the end of the lecture. A subsequent study from my lab showed that periodic quizzing also enhanced students' ability to integrate information from different parts of a video-recorded lecture.

In 2001, I concluded this chapter by suggesting that "cognitive engineers" will lead efforts to combat absent-mindedness. I think the developments during the past twenty years are largely consistent with that suggestion. We've made progress in the urgent battle to reduce the extreme form of absent-minded forgetting that causes children to die in hot cars by generating retrieval cues that can remind parents of something they could never imagine forgetting. And the use of intermittent quizzing during lectures has been shown to be helpful in reducing the absent-minded forgetting that can result from mind wandering. Absent-mindedness remains a common and sometimes dangerous sin of memory, but thankfully there are simple ways to mitigate its influence.

3
The Sin of Blocking

"What's the name of that stuff I wanted to tell your mother to use?"

"Wait a second. I know."

"It's on the tip of my tongue," she said.

"Wait a second. I know."

"You know the stuff I mean."

"The sleep stuff or the indigestion?"

"It's on the tip of my tongue."

"Wait a second. Wait a second. I know."

IN THIS EXCHANGE from Don DeLillo's novel *Underworld*, Nick Shay and his wife, Marian, exemplify the sense of urgency associated with a familiar but frustrating experience: blocking on a bit of information that we know we know. Sometimes an episode of blocking is little more than a mildly irritating curiosity, as with Nick and Marian. But in other contexts, it can cause great anxiety. At an office party, for instance, you are conversing over a drink with your colleague Martin. A young woman you've worked with on numerous occasions, but haven't seen for several months, approaches to join the conversation. You will be expected to introduce her to Martin, and ordinarily you would be delighted to do so. But even though you know exactly what position she holds, how long she has worked at the firm, and even what kind of food she likes, you shudder as you block on her name. You think it begins with a *C* or a *K* and contains several syllables; the name feels as if it is on the tip of your tongue. But no matter how hard you try, the entire name simply will not come to mind. Seeking to avoid embarrassment for all, you nimbly attempt to steer the interaction so that your two colleagues introduce themselves to each other rather than relying on you. "You two know each other, don't you?" you ask innocently. You feel at once relieved and angry with yourself when Katrina extends her hand to Martin and introduces herself.

The sin of blocking involves a kind of forgetting that differs from absent-mindedness and transience. Unlike absent-minded memory failures, the recalcitrant name or word has been encoded and stored, and sometimes a retrieval cue is available that would ordinarily trigger recall. And unlike memory failures resulting from transience, the information has not faded from memory: it is lurking somewhere, seemingly poised to spring to mind with more prodding, but remains just out of reach when needed. Blocking is peculiarly vexing because at one and the same time, it seems perfectly clear that you should be able to produce the sought-after information in the face of irrefutable evidence that you cannot.

Name Blocking

Blocking can occur in diverse situations. Engaged in casual conversation, you block on a word in the middle of a sentence. Stage actors fear those relatively rare but embarrassing moments in a scene when they block on their lines. And students dread the awful realization that they have blocked on an exam answer they studied diligently and might even recall spontaneously after finishing the test. But blocking occurs most often with people's names. In surveys that probe different types of memory failures in everyday life, blocking on the names of familiar people invariably emerges at or near the top of the list. Name blocking is especially troublesome for older adults: the single biggest complaint of cognitive difficulties by adults past age fifty — by far — involves problems retrieving the names of familiar people.

These sentiments are backed up by objective data. Twenty-year-olds, forty-year-olds, and seventy-year-olds kept diaries for a month in which they recorded spontaneously occurring retrieval blocks that were accompanied by the tip-of-the-tongue sensation. Blocking occurred occasionally for the names of objects (for example, *algae*) and abstract words (for example, *idiomatic*). In all three groups, however, blocking occurred most frequently for proper names, with more blocks for people than for other proper names such as countries or cities. Proper-name blocking occurred more often in the forty- and seventy-year-old groups than in the twenty-year-old group; blocking on the names of personal acquaintances occurred more frequently in the seventy-year-olds than in either of the other two groups.

Why do we block on the names of people? To begin to answer this question, consider what psychologists call the Baker/baker paradox. Two groups of experimental participants are shown, one at a time, pictures of unfamiliar male faces. The first group is given a name to associate with the face, whereas the second group is given an occupation. The trick is that the names and occupations are designated by the same words. For instance, the name group is told that the first person is called Baker and the second Potter, whereas the occupation group is told that the first person is a baker and the second is a potter. When later shown the face and asked to try to come up with the accompanying word, recall of occupations was higher than recall of names. This outcome defines the Baker/baker paradox: Why should recall of the same word differ as a function of whether it is treated as a proper name or an occupation?

Contemporary approaches to resolving the Baker/baker paradox begin with a variant of the observation made by John Stuart Mill over 175 years ago: "Proper names are not connotative: they denote individuals who are called by them: but they do not indicate or imply any attributes as belonging to those individuals." In other words, when I tell you that my friend's name is John Baker, I tell you little or nothing about him, beyond the fact that he has a relatively common Anglo-Saxon name. When I tell you that my friend is a baker, however, I tell you quite a bit about him: a general sense of how and where he spends his days, what kinds of materials he uses at work, and what kinds of products he creates. The occupation name *baker* calls up a wealth of associations and knowledge based on prior experience with bakers; the proper name *Baker* pretty much stands on its own. In the Baker/baker experiment, people can use preexisting associations and knowledge to more easily encode and remember the occupation name *baker* than the proper name *Baker*.

The idea that proper names tell us little about the characteristics of their bearers helps to explain why *new* names of people are difficult to learn and remember. This idea has also led to the proposal that blocking of familiar names occurs because proper names, relative to common names, are not as well integrated with related concepts, knowledge, and associations. Consider a neat experiment reported by the cognitive psychologists Serge Brédart and Tim Valentine. They showed people pictures of cartoon and comic-strip characters, some with descriptive names that highlight salient features of the character (Grumpy, Snow White, Scrooge) and others with arbitrary names (Aladdin, Mary Poppins, Pinocchio). Even though the two types of names were equally familiar to participants in the experiment, they blocked less often on the descriptive names than on the arbitrary names.

Although the names of people in modern Western cultures do not usually incorporate attributes of their bearers, names in other cultures do. For instance, members of the Yuman Indian tribes of Arizona are given names that uniquely capture some aspect of the time and place of their birth. In certain Greek villages, wealthy farmers bear surnames that signify important religious practices, members of the middle class have surnames generated from masculine first names, and poor shepherds bear surnames formed from absurd nicknames. In these and other cultures in which names reflect specific properties of individuals, blocking might be less problematic than in modern Western societies.

Theoretical models of memory for common and proper names can help us to appreciate more fully how blocking of proper names can result from tenuous links with conceptual knowledge. Most models distinguish between several kinds of knowledge that are required to produce a common name or a proper name. To begin, let's consider three fundamental elements. One is a visual representation of what an object or a person looks like — the rectangular shape of a book, the sharp edge of a knife, or the bulging nose and thinning black hair of your colleague Martin. The visual representation for *baker* would consist of an amalgam of shapes, features, and textures from different bakers you've encountered. The visual representation for *John Baker* might include the angular shape of his face plus idiosyncratic features such as his horn-rimmed glasses, knotty gray beard, and so on.

The second element is a conceptual representation that specifies what functions an object performs, what tasks a person carries out, or other biographical facts about an individual. The conceptual representation for *baker* would include such information as "works in kitchen," "bakes bread," "gets up early," and so forth. The conceptual representation for *John Baker* might include "attorney," "neighborhood president," and "good golfer."

Third, a phonological representation specifies the constituent sounds, such as syllables, that comprise the name: *ba* and *ker*. Phonological representations are the same for *Baker* and *baker*.

If you saw John Baker and your brain activated only a visual representation of him, his face would seem familiar, but you would not know his name or anything about him. If your brain activated only the visual and conceptual representations, John Baker would seem familiar, and you would know he is the attorney from your neighborhood who enjoys golf, but you would block on his name.

Most models of name retrieval hold that activation of phonological representations occurs only *after* activation of conceptual and visual representations. This idea explains why people can often retrieve conceptual information about an object or person whom they cannot name, whereas the reverse does not occur. For example, diary studies indicate that people frequently recall a person's occupation without remembering his name, but no instances have been documented in which a name is recalled without any conceptual knowledge about the person. In experiments in which people named pictures of famous individuals, participants who failed to retrieve the name "Charlton Heston" could often recall that he was an actor. But nobody who correctly named "Charlton Heston" failed to recall that he was an actor. Thus, when you block on the name *John Baker,* you might very well recall that he is an attorney who enjoys golf, but it is highly unlikely that you would recall Baker's name and fail to recall any of his personal attributes.

If name retrieval occurs as the final stage in a multistep sequence, then it makes sense that we can block on the name of a familiar person about whom we know many things. But by itself, this framework does not help us to understand why people block more frequently on proper names than on common names. To understand this frustrating feature of memory, it is necessary to complicate the picture a little by adding another level of representation.

Language-processing models typically include a level of representation that intervenes between the conceptual and phonological levels, and that I refer to as the "lexical" level. Lexical representations specify how a word or name can be used in a larger linguistic utterance, such as a sentence. Critically, the links between the conceptual and lexical levels may differ in an important way for common and proper names.

Consider a model developed by the psychologists Deborah Burke and Donald MacKay, which consists of a network of interconnected representations that can excite or activate one another. As shown in Figure 3.1, for a common name such as *baker,* the visual representation is connected to each of the conceptual representations, such as "works in kitchen," "bakes bread," and "gets up early." Each of these representations has a direct link with the lexical representation *baker,* which is in turn connected to the phonological representations (syllables). In Burke and MacKay's scheme, this breakdown means that when we see a baker, the visual representation of *baker* becomes active, which in turn passes along excitation to the conceptual representations. Each of these conceptual representations becomes active, and the resulting excitation converges on the lexical representation for *baker.* And when that level becomes strongly activated, it excites the phonological representations. In turn, the word *baker* pops out.

FIGURE 3.1 *Deborah Burke and Donald MacKay have proposed a theory to explain why people block more often on proper names such as John Baker than common names such as baker. The figure presents a schematic version of the theory. The circles are nodes in a network that represent specific types of information. A visual representation of a person or an object is linked to conceptual representations that specify what a person or object does. For a common name, these conceptual representations converge directly on a lexical representation that allows access to the phonological representations (sounds) needed to retrieve the name. For a proper name, however, the conceptual representations converge on a "person identity node," which is in turn connected to the lexical representations by a single link. According to Burke and MacKay, this single, fragile link between the person identity node and the lexical representation makes proper names more susceptible to disruption and blocking than common names.*

For proper names, however, each of the individual conceptual representations converges on a single, special representation of a person's identity—a "person identity node," according to the psychologist Andrew Young. Thus, the conceptual representation "attorney" connects via a link to a person identity node for *John Baker.* Likewise, the conceptual representations "neighborhood president" and "good golfer" connect to that person identity node. In this way, all of the different things we know about *John Baker* converge to identify him.

The biggest difference between proper and common names occurs at the next level in the network: the person identity node for *John Baker* connects by a single link to the lexical level representations for *John* and *Baker*. This single link contrasts sharply with the arrangement for common names, where the conceptual representations all converge directly on the lexical representation, passing forward summed excitation that reliably activates it. Instead, the lexical representation that comprises the proper name receives weaker and more fragile excitation through a single link. This lack makes proper names much more vulnerable to retrieval blocks, even when visual and conceptual representations are strongly activated and we feel we know everything about the person except their name.

This model may also help to explain why blocking on the names of personal acquaintances seems to occur more frequently as people age. Because the link between conceptual and lexical representations is especially tenuous for proper names, it is more easily disrupted by factors such as general slowing of cognitive processing. Numerous studies have shown that cognitive processes slow down in older adults, perhaps because of reduced speed of neural transmission. According to Burke and MacKay's model, the names most susceptible to retrieval blocking are familiar ones that have not been encountered recently. Encountering a person activates both the conceptual and lexical representations for that person and thus strengthens their interconnections. Conversely, when we do not see someone for a long period of time, the already fragile link between lexical and conceptual representations is weakened. Additionally, because older adults have lived longer than younger adults, they are more likely to know people whom they have not encountered for lengthy time intervals. And, indeed, a diary study conducted by Burke and MacKay revealed that participants most often experienced name blocking when they encountered familiar individuals whom they had not been in contact with for at least several months; this interval was considerably longer for older adults.

The Burke and MacKay model formalizes the idea that proper names are linked less directly to preexisting knowledge and associations than are common names. But there are probably other reasons why proper names are especially susceptible to retrieval blocks. With proper names, a single phonological representation — a person's exact name — must be called up. But with common names, multiple phonological representations are often available. For example, synonyms can be used to refer to the same object: if you cannot come up with the word *davenport* when you are about to sit down on one, *couch* or *sofa* will do. Objects can also be described at multiple levels: you can refer to the moving object in front of you as an *Accord,* a *Honda,* or a *sedan,* not to mention *car, automobile,* or *vehicle.* These multiple labels give us flexibility in generating names, thus reducing the likelihood of blocking.

To examine whether the requirement to retrieve a specific label contributes to proper-name blocking, Serge Brédart asked people to name pictures of actors. Some were known both by their stage names and by the names of characters depicted in the photos, such as Harrison Ford/Indiana Jones and Sean Connery/James Bond. Others were known by their stage names but not by the names of the characters in the photos, such as Richard Gere/Zack Mayo and Julia Roberts/ Vivian Ward. Participants could respond with either the actor's stage name or the character's name. Even though the actors in the two sets of photos were equally familiar to participants, there were fewer retrieval blocks for those actors who were also known by the names of their characters.

Such findings might have interesting cross-cultural implications. As noted earlier, in some societies personal names reflect specific features of their bearers. In others, individuals may be known by several different names. In some African tribes, the same person has a whistled name that is distinct from their drummed and spoken names, or may be called different names by different members of the family. It is not uncommon in some Indian tribes for an individual's name to change at different stages of life. Brédart's experiment suggests that name blocking could be less frequent in such societies than in our own.

Though blocking on names of familiar acquaintances is annoying and sometimes embarrassing, most people manage to retrieve the great majority of proper names they try to remember. Even those who are especially vulnerable to name blocking — older adults in their seventies, for example — report on average no more than two or three blocks per month for the names of personal acquaintances. But there is a small group of individuals for whom no cognitive task is more difficult than retrieving the name of a familiar person. For them, name blocking is as much a part of everyday life as a morning cup of coffee or an evening stroll.

THE MAN WHO COULDN'T NAME ANYONE

In July 1988, a forty-one-year-old Italian man who worked in a hardware store injured his head during a riding accident. The man, known in the medical literature only by the initials LS, had sustained damage to parts of the frontal and temporal lobes in the left cerebral hemisphere. Fortunately, however, LS's cognitive abilities were largely unaffected by the brain damage. He had no difficulty understanding language, could speak fluently and clearly, and scored perfectly on standard tests of language skills. Perception, memory, and general intelligence also were largely intact.

The accident had, however, caused a quite specific but debilitating problem: LS was virtually unable to produce proper names, even though he had no difficulty producing common names. When he encountered familiar people, LS recognized them easily but could not retrieve their names. Laboratory testing revealed that the deficit was remarkably clear-cut. When shown fifty common objects, he came up with the names for all of them. But when shown photos of twenty-five famous people whom others could name effortlessly, he could produce the names of only two. The names had not disappeared from his memory, however. When LS was shown a picture of a famous person and was asked to select the correct name from several choices, he had no difficulty doing so. And he was perfectly able to pronounce the names that he could not retrieve: when an examiner said a name aloud, LS could repeat it back immediately. But try as he might, LS could rarely generate names when he was shown faces or was given detailed descriptions of people.

These retrieval difficulties were also evident with other types of proper names. For instance, LS could not retrieve the names of cities or countries when the examiner pointed to a spot on a blank atlas or read a description of a particular place. However, LS was able to retrieve a good deal of conceptual knowledge related to the people and places he could not name. He stated correctly, for example, that a face he failed to name was that of the prime minister, and on a blank atlas he could point correctly to the cities and countries whose names he could not produce. It was as if he was living in a perpetual tip-of-the-tongue state, at least as far as familiar people and places were concerned.

LS was one of the first brain-damaged patients ever described with problems restricted to retrieving proper names — a condition now referred to as "proper-name anomia." Since his case was published in 1989, additional reports of patients characterized by similar difficulties have accumulated steadily. Some of these patients, like LS, have problems retrieving both person and place-names. Other patients have problems exclusively with retrieving the names of people. Looking at all the cases together, the psychologists Richard Hanley and Janice Kay concluded that impairments in retrieving the names of places are seen only in those patients with the most serious problems retrieving the names of people. Patients with milder difficulties retrieving person names tend not to have difficulties retrieving the names of places, thus suggesting that retrieving the names of places is not as hard as retrieving the names of people. This idea fits well with evidence from healthy individuals indicating that more retrieval blocks occur for the names of people than places.

Patients with proper-name anomia are especially striking because of how much they may know about the people and places they cannot name. One patient could retrieve the names of only two of forty famous people (compared to twenty-five of forty for healthy controls), yet she could still recall correctly occupations for thirty-two of those people — the same number as healthy people. When shown pictures of celebrities with famous spouses, the patient could hardly name any of the celebrities or their spouses. But she could describe the occupations and other characteristics of the famous spouses in just as much detail as the control subjects.

In cases of proper-name anomia, then, the connection between conceptual information about a person and the phonological code needed to pronounce a proper name — which depends on a single fragile link even in an uninjured brain — is severed. This disruption still leaves the patient able to recognize faces as familiar, identify people on the basis of conceptual knowledge, match names and faces easily, repeat names without error, and produce the names of common objects that have more robust connections to conceptual information. Yet such patients are almost totally hapless when they must produce a name themselves.

These observations suggest that understanding the neural location of damage in proper-name anomia should illuminate what parts of the brain allow retrieval of proper names from conceptual information. In all reported cases of proper-name anomia, the left cerebral hemisphere was damaged. Although the exact location within the left hemisphere varies from patient to patient, proper-name anomia is sometimes associated with damage to a region in the front of the left temporal lobe known as the temporal pole. The neuroscientists Hanna and Antonio Damasio reported that in a group of over one hundred neurological patients who had each suffered a single lesion, injury to the left temporal pole tended to result in proper-name retrieval deficits. Their observations are supported by a case study in which surgeons removed the left temporal pole (but no other parts of the brain) from a forty-seven-year-old carpenter to provide relief from epilepsy. The man developed a severe case of proper-name anomia but was otherwise largely free of cognitive problems. However, damage to the left temporal pole doesn't always lead to name-retrieval problems, and some cases of proper-name anomia are linked with damage to other regions in the left temporal lobe or elsewhere in the left hemisphere.

Neuroimaging studies of healthy volunteers provide further evidence: in experiments using PET scans, activation of several regions within the left temporal lobe, including the temporal pole, was observed when people retrieved proper names. Retrieval of common names, though activating some of the same left temporal areas, tended to produce elevated activity farther back in the temporal lobe. Other parts of the brain outside the temporal pole are, no doubt, also involved in retrieving proper names. But the left temporal pole appears to play a role in allowing people — most of the time — to make the fragile link between a person's characteristics and the arbitrary label by which they are known to others.

On the Tip of the Tongue

The town of Greenwich, England, a neighbor of London located on the prime meridian, is best known for serving as the world's official timekeeper. But in the late 1990s, the area near Greenwich also became known as the construction site for the vast and expensive Millennium Dome, which would become one of the largest sports and entertainment complexes in Europe. Deputy Prime Minister John Prescott could not have been too surprised, then, when at a January 1998 London youth conference he was asked to justify the massive and ever-increasing cost of the Dome before several thousand teenage attendees. "The money came from the . . . you know . . . what do they call it," stammered the flustered Prescott. He had blocked on the name of the national lottery, finally blurting out in desperation, "The raffles." In response to laughter and jeers from the audience, Prescott tried to show that he knew something about the word he could not produce: "I don't do it myself," Prescott offered weakly. The conference chair leaned over and whispered discreetly, "The lottery," but by then it was too late to cover up the retrieval failure or to avoid the indignity of an article describing Prescott's gaffe in the next day's *Times*.

As the deputy prime minister learned in an unusually public manner, proper names are not the only items that sometimes get stuck on the tips of our tongues. The description offered in 1966 by the Harvard psychologists Roger Brown and David McNeill, who reported the first investigation of the tip-of-the-tongue (TOT) state and vividly depicted its emergence in an experimental participant, would no doubt have resonated with Prescott. "The signs of it were unmistakable," observed Brown and McNeill. "He would appear to be in mild torment, something like on the brink of a sneeze, and if he found the word his relief was considerable." Evidence from diaries of TOT experiences suggests that college students experience roughly one or two TOTs each week, compared to about two to four TOTs per week in elderly adults, with middle-aged adults somewhere in between. Though TOTs happen most often for names of people, they also occur for other proper names, including places, titles of books and movies, and names of familiar tunes, as well as for common words.

The feeling that a blocked word or name is on the tip of the tongue appears to be a near-universal experience. The cognitive psychologist Bennett Schwartz surveyed speakers of fifty-one different languages and found that forty-five of them contain expressions using "the tongue" to describe situations in which a blocked item feels as though it is on the verge of recovery. The most frequently used expressions across languages are the near-literal equivalent of "on the tip of the tongue," such as *"sulla punta della lingua"* in Italian and *"op die punt van my tong"* in Afrikaans. Other close variants include the Estonian *"keele otsa peal,"* or "at the head of the tongue," and the Cheyenne *"navonotootse'a,"* or "I have lost it on my tongue." The most poetic is the Korean *"Hyeu kkedu-te mam-dol-da,"* which translates as "sparkling at the end of my tongue." The only six languages in Schwartz's survey that do not use a "tongue" or similar expression are Icelandic, Amharic, two sub-Saharan African languages, Indonesian, and American Sign Language.

Why is the tip-of-the-tongue expression (or other close variants) used so widely? Probably because of the sense of imminence captured by Brown and McNeill — the unmistakable sensation of being "on the brink of a sneeze" — and the simultaneous sense that one knows a good deal about the blocked word. As we saw earlier with name blocking, people often know the occupation and other characteristics of people whose names remain perched on the tips of their tongues, and the same holds for other kinds of blocked words. For example, Brown and McNeill and many others since have induced TOT experiences by giving people word definitions. Below are ten such definitions from an experimental study; try to produce the target word for each definition. (The answers are listed in the preceding note.) When you cannot generate the word, note whether or not it feels as if it is on the tip of your tongue.

1. metal or metal-tipped spear used in contests of distance throwing
2. yarn-dyed cotton fabric woven in stripes, checks, plaids, or solid colors
3. mild or hot, red condiment often used on deviled eggs
4. inscription on a tomb
5. incombustible, chemical-resistant material used for fireproofing
6. navigational instrument used for measuring the angular elevation of the sun or a star above the horizon
7. tough, elastic tissue forming part of the skeleton
8. heavy, broad-bladed knife or hatchet used especially by butchers
9. essential living matter of all plant and animal cells
10. crystalline sugar occurring naturally in fruits, honey, etc.

Now ask yourself the following questions about each of the words that you failed to generate: What is the first letter of the word? What other letters do you think you know? How many syllables does the word have? Do any words related to the blocked target come to mind, even though you are pretty sure that these are not the target words?

Beginning with Brown and McNeill, researchers have found that people in a TOT state often know the first letter of the blocked word, less frequently know the final letter, and even less often know the middle letters. Information about the number of syllables in the word is usually available, too. People are generally more accurate in providing letters from a blocked word, and the number of syllables in it, when they are in a TOT state than when they are not. Chances are that if you experienced a TOT for any of the preceding ten items, you knew at least the first letter or the number of syllables in the word.

This kind of partial retrieval is exploited as a gag in the screwball comedy play *The Mystery of Irma Vep*, in which an ancient Egyptian princess is brought back to life by an eccentric archaeologist. The awakened princess excitedly calls out, "Cairo! Cairo!" But rather than referring to the capital city, she is desperately trying to resolve a TOT state brought on by her sudden need for treatment of back pain resulting from 3,500 years of mummification. The audience understands when she triumphantly finds the final two syllables: "Practor!"

When experiencing a TOT, people not only retrieve a blocked word's sound and meaning; they also know some of its grammatical properties. This phenomenon has been shown most clearly in studies of Italian speakers in TOT states. All Italian nouns are marked as either masculine or feminine. A noun's gender has important grammatical (syntactic) implications: it determines what articles are used and also the form of adjectives. But the gender of a noun has no relation to its meaning: *sasso* and *pietra* both mean stone, but the former is masculine and the latter is feminine. There are also nouns in which gender is unrelated to sound. Nonetheless, several studies have shown that when experiencing a TOT, Italian speakers can indicate with greater than chance accuracy whether the blocked word is masculine or feminine — they can retrieve abstract lexical information that is stored independently of sound and meaning. Just as studies of proper-name TOTs show that people can produce virtually everything they know about a person except their name, studies of common-name TOTs show that people can produce nearly everything they know about an item except its label.

During TOT states, people frequently come up with words that are related in sound or meaning to the sought-after item. If you blocked on any of the ten test items, you might have thought of a word that was similar to the one you were seeking, even though you were sure it was not the blocked target. Deputy Prime Minister Prescott came up with "raffles" when he wanted "lottery," and he knew that the blocked word referred to an activity in which he did not engage. Something similar happened when experimenters induced TOT states by playing subjects theme songs from 1950s and 1960s television shows and asking for the names of the shows. People who were blocked on *The Munsters* sometimes came up with *The Addams Family*," and some of those who were blocked on *Leave It to Beaver* thought of *Dennis the Menace*.

Some researchers have gone as far as to suggest that the related but incorrect words that come to mind during a TOT state cause blocking of the sought-after target. In a diary study in which more than forty people recorded TOTs in their everyday lives for four weeks, well over half of the TOTs involved the recurrent retrieval of a word that was related in sound or meaning to the blocked target. Eventually, the blocked words were retrieved. The diarists judged that they had encountered the recurrent interlopers more frequently or recently than the blocked targets. These observations led the authors to suggest that the related words served to suppress or inhibit retrieval of the target. Recent or frequent exposure to these unwanted items had rendered them so easy to retrieve that they dominated conscious awareness and crowded out target words that would ordinarily have come to mind.

Invoking the story of Cinderella and her hideous stepsisters who tried unjustly to insinuate themselves into the prince's good graces as rightful owners of a lost slipper, the British psychologist James Reason called the unwanted but intrusive words that block a sought-after target "ugly sisters." Through their close relation to the target, ugly sisters may attract undue attention and interfere with retrieval of the sought-after item. Experimental studies published in the late 1980s appeared to provide strong evidence that ugly sisters are indeed the main culprits in instigating TOT states. When experimenters explicitly provided words that were similar in sound to the target, people experienced more TOTs than when they presented words that did not sound like the target. Thus, TOTs occurred more frequently when the target word *alchemy* was cued with the definition "medieval forerunner of chemistry" plus the ugly sister *axial*, than when the target word *incubate* was cued with the definition "to keep eggs warm until hatching" plus the unrelated word *simulation*.

However, the ugly sisters hypothesis has since fallen on hard times. Studies using additional control conditions that were omitted from the prior experiments have undermined the idea that ugly sisters cause TOT blocks. In these more tightly controlled studies, providing similar-sounding ugly sisters had no effect on the incidence of TOTs. Another study compared the frequency of TOTs for words that sound like many other words and those that sound like few other words. For example, words such as *pawn* and *cold* sound like many other words: they have lots of "phonological neighbors." In contrast, *public* and *syntax* sound like few other words: they have few phonological neighbors. If ugly sisters that sound like blocked words cause TOTs, then there should be more TOTs for words with many phonological neighbors than for words with only a few. But the experiments showed the exact opposite. They also revealed that irrespective of phonological similarity, there were more TOTs for infrequently used words (*pawn, syntax*) than for frequently used words (*cold, public*).

Although these results are bad news for the ugly sisters hypothesis, they support the Burke and MacKay model I described earlier in relation to name blocking. In that model, blocking and TOTs occur when phonological representations activate only partially because of a weakened connection to lexical representations. It follows, then, that factors that contribute to weak activation of phonological representations should raise the incidence of TOTs. This idea fits nicely with the finding that TOTs tend to occur for infrequently used words: failure to use such words on a regular basis may weaken the connections between phonological and lexical representations. The idea is also consistent with results showing that name blocking occurs most often for names of people who have not been encountered recently. It also suggests that the incidence of TOTs should be reduced by exposing people to target words on which they are likely to block just before asking them to produce the items in response to definitions. Burke and her colleagues have reported experiments that yielded precisely this result.

Recall also that names are highly susceptible to blocking and TOTs because they are isolated from conceptual knowledge. Data showing that TOTs are especially likely to occur for words with few phonological neighbors provide additional evidence that isolated knowledge is especially vulnerable to blocking.

If ugly sisters aren't the main cause of TOTs, do they play any role at all? Yes. Burke and MacKay suggest that ugly sisters may help to prolong TOT states. Although the initial block may be caused by weak activation of an infrequently used phonological node, when similar-sounding words do come to mind, they may get us off track and thereby delay resolution of the TOT state. Unfortunately, we often tend to embrace the ugly sisters because they provide a comforting feeling of being "close" to the target and thus reassure us that we are about to resolve the TOT. So we may continually repeat the ugly sisters to ourselves in order to bring forth the blocked target, even though such a strategy may, paradoxically, prolong the TOT.

The idea that ugly sisters are a consequence — not the initial cause — of TOT states also helps us to make sense of results concerning aging and TOTs. We've already seen that older adults are more prone to TOTs for both proper and common names than are younger adults. But several studies have also shown that older adults produce fewer ugly sisters than do younger adults. If ugly sisters were the cause of TOTs, the opposite should have been observed. Further, the same studies have shown that when experiencing a TOT, older adults are able to call up less partial information about a word—first letter, number of syllables, and so on—than young people. Older adults tend to describe their TOTs as "drawing a blank," whereas young people often generate a flurry of partial information and ugly sisters.

Partial information about a word can help to resolve TOTs by providing cues that eventually trigger recall of the entire word. And even though ugly sisters may prolong TOTs by sidetracking the search, some words that sound like the target can help to resolve TOTs in the same manner as partial information—by providing cues that elicit the correct target. Burke and MacKay describe a person who blocked on the name of the California city Ojai (pronounced "oh-hi") and muttered in frustration, "Oh hell." This similar-sounding expression immediately triggered recall of the word. It did not play the role of an ugly sister and sidetrack resolution of the TOT because "Oh hell" was not part of the search domain (California cities) on which the individual was focused. So, though young people may be more likely than older adults to get caught up in some lengthy TOTs because of distracting ugly sisters, they are also more likely to resolve quickly other TOTs because they generate potential cues—partial information and similar sounds—rather than merely "drawing a blank."

Perhaps because ugly sisters can lengthen TOTs when they shift our attention away from the correct target, people sometimes advise one another to turn to something else, hoping that the blocked target will spontaneously spring to mind once attention has been removed from the ugly sister. An acquaintance's mother, for instance, advised her daughter to think of chocolate cake when she became blocked on a word. And, indeed, diary studies indicate that approximately one-third to one-half of TOTs are resolved when target words suddenly "pop up," seemingly out of nowhere. Other TOTs are resolved either by conscious use of cueing strategies—searching through the alphabet or generating similar-sounding words—or by consulting external sources such as a dictionary or an encyclopedia.

Resolution of TOTs by unexpected "pop-ups" of the target may occur because the influence of ugly sisters has dissipated over time.

Pop-ups might also reflect the outcome of "incubation" processes that operate outside of awareness: perhaps the mind continues to work on "solving" the retrieval block even when conscious attention is shifted elsewhere. However, there's little evidence for this idea, and I suspect that many seemingly spontaneous pop-ups result from the operation of cues that we fail to notice, yet that nonetheless remind us of the target. A person who had blocked on the name of Al Capp's heroine went for a bike ride several days later. He thought to himself how wonderful it was to ride during "days in May" and then suddenly recalled the blocked name: Daisy Mae. In the excitement of resolving a TOT, it would be easy to overlook or forget the cue that triggered recovery, thus producing inflated estimates of how often "spontaneous" pop-ups occur. Indeed, in laboratory studies in which people are asked to think aloud while they try to resolve retrieval blocks, almost all resolutions occur through deliberate self-cueing strategies; hardly any spontaneous pop-ups are observed. This result may be because in the laboratory setting, where people are fully focused on their own cognitive processes, they are highly likely to notice subtle cues that trigger recall.

Findings and ideas concerning the resolution of TOTs have implications for attempts to combat blocking when it occurs in everyday life. Many TOTs resolve within a minute or so of onset. In some situations, then, simply waiting out the block, perhaps with an appeal (in appropriately aged individuals) to the tribulations of a "senior moment," may be the most painless solution. Even if the TOT does not resolve immediately, it is probably best not to give up too quickly: studies have shown that the more time people spend trying to retrieve a blocked name, the more likely they are to come up with it.

But what about those social situations like the one I sketched at the beginning of this chapter, in which you have blocked on the name of a very familiar person, are embarrassed to show it, and desperately wish to come up with the name quickly? If you don't spontaneously recall partial phonological information—the first letter or the number of syllables—it may be helpful to run through the alphabet. Studies have shown that when people view a famous face and block on the person's name, providing the name's initial letters is a more effective aid than giving semantic information about the person's occupation. If you are already able to retrieve the initial letters of the name, try using that information to recall previous situations in which you have encountered that person and uttered their name. Avoiding the false lure of ugly sisters may aid resolution, too. Ugly sisters probably contain some sounds that are similar to the target and thus can be used as a cue to trigger recall, but endlessly repeating a word or name that you know is incorrect because it makes you feel close to the target will likely prolong the agony.

For the names of people, it is also possible to adopt a proactive stance. Guided by the idea that proper names are difficult to retrieve because they are isolated from conceptual knowledge, you might find it worthwhile to review systematically the names of personal acquaintances — especially people you see infrequently or sporadically — in a way that makes them more meaningful. For example, knowing that your tax accountant's name is Bill Collins doesn't tell you anything meaningful about him, and because you tend to see him only once or twice a year — usually in the early spring — he is a good candidate for blocking. However, you can elaborate on the name in a way that makes it meaningful: imagine a dollar bill being snatched from your accountant's pocket by a playful collie. This kind of encoding technique has been used effectively in teaching people entirely novel names. It should also be helpful in "reencoding" familiar names because it helps to strengthen the otherwise fragile link between conceptual and phonological information that renders proper names so susceptible to blocking. Making proactive encoding efforts for names that have proven troublesome in the past or that are likely candidates for a TOT experience (individuals not encountered recently or frequently) should reduce the chances of blocking on those names again.

REPRESSION REVISITED

In March 1998, a twenty-year-old woman named Cynthia Anthony pleaded not guilty in a Toronto court to the murder of her twenty-three-day-old baby. A March 19 *Toronto Sun* headline trumpeted the basis for her defense: "Mom: I Blocked Memory of Fall." Anthony claimed that she had tripped over a cable TV cord and dropped the baby on hard ceramic tile. But she had made no mention of this accident when questioned by police shortly after the baby's death. At the trial, Anthony explained that she had been "in shock" as a result of the horrific incident and had "blocked it" from her memory. She explained to the jury that she had recovered the memory only months later when she was looking at photographs of the baby. The next day, a psychiatrist testified in support of her story. "Memory Block Possible — Doctor," declared the *Sun*. "The enormity of the tragedy she suffered may render her more vulnerable to amnesia," affirmed Dr. Graham Glancy.

It is one thing to block on the name of a person not encountered recently or on an infrequently used word, but quite another to block on an emotionally traumatic event that happened just minutes or hours earlier. Does blocking occur for episodic memories of personal experiences — even traumatic ones?

Several lines of evidence suggest that blocking for personal experiences can occur under specific conditions and within certain limits. The kind of amnesia claimed by Cynthia Anthony — selectively and completely forgetting a trauma only minutes, hours, or days later — is not infrequently reported but rarely happens without physical insult to the brain. Quite to the contrary, as I elaborate in Chapter 7, recent traumas are usually remembered vividly and persistently. Head injury, alcohol, drugs, or loss of consciousness is usually involved whenever people fail to recall a trauma that has just occurred. And in these instances, blocking is probably not responsible for amnesia: it is more likely that the memory was never encoded or stored properly to begin with. Nonetheless, Anthony's blocking defense convinced the Toronto jury: they acquitted her of second-degree murder.

Stronger evidence for blocking of episodic memories comes from rather more mundane laboratory studies that involve nontraumatic, emotionally neutral experiences. Consider the following experiment. I show you a list of words drawn from categories such as fruits or birds: *apple, canary, robin, pear, crow, banana,* and so forth. On a subsequent memory test, I provide some words from the list, such as *pear* and *canary,* and ask for recall of the other words. Do you think that providing *pear* and *canary* will increase recall of the other words, compared to a test in which I do not provide any words from the study list? Intuitively, the answer to this question would seem to be a clear "yes" — giving some words from the study list should serve as reminders for the others. Surprisingly, however, experiments have shown the exact opposite. The words that are provided as test cues seem to behave like the "ugly sisters" that pop up during TOT states, serving to sidetrack memory search and thus to block or inhibit access to other studied words.

Experiments have also revealed that the act of retrieving information from memory can inhibit subsequent recall of related information. Imagine that after studying word pairs such as *red/blood* and *food/radish,* you are given *red* as a cue and recall that *blood* went with it. This act of recall strengthens your memory of the two words appearing together, so that next time you are given *red,* it will be easier for you to recall *blood.* Remarkably, however, recalling that *blood* went with *red* will also make it more difficult later to recall *radish* when given *food!* When practicing *red/blood,* it is necessary to suppress retrieval of recently encountered "red things" other than blood, so that your mind is not cluttered with irrelevancies that could interfere with recall of the word you seek. But there is a cost to suppressing retrieval of unwanted items such as *radish:* they are less accessible for future recall, even to a cue (*food*) that would seem to have nothing to do with "redness."

Is this kind of retrieval-induced inhibition an isolated curiosity, observed only in studies of word-list recall, or does it happen regularly? When you review photographs from a European vacation and a snapshot of Westminster Abbey reminds you of its stained-glass windows, will this recollection make it more difficult to recall the windows of Notre-Dame? Evidence from experiments conducted by the psychologist Wilma Koutstaal in my laboratory suggests that it might. Participants carried out simple activities, such as pounding a nail into a block of wood or pointing to Australia on a globe. Then they saw photographs of some of these actions, which increased recall of the reviewed activities on a later test. More interestingly, reviewing these same photos lowered later recall of activities that were not shown in photographs (compared to a condition in which no photographs were reviewed).

Something similar can happen in a context with important legal ramifications: eyewitness recall. Eyewitnesses are typically questioned selectively about specific aspects of an event. Could repeated retrieval of these incidents in response to questions make it more difficult to recall aspects of the experience about which no questions are asked? This outcome would be a highly undesirable side effect of questioning, because investigators might later need to revisit parts of an event that they did not probe initially.

In a laboratory analogue of an eyewitness situation, people saw color slides of a crime scene — a student's room where a theft had occurred. The experimenters then questioned them selectively about certain categories of objects in the scene. For example, they asked about some of the college sweatshirts that were visible in the room, but not about other sweatshirts. No questions were asked about other categories of objects in the room, such as textbooks. Compared to memory for the textbooks, subsequent recall improved for the sweatshirts that the experimenters asked about, but declined for the sweatshirts that they did not ask about. Access to nonretrieved items from reviewed categories seemed to be blocked by successful recall of items from the same category.

The psychologist Michael Anderson has theorized that whenever we selectively retrieve some memories in response to a particular cue but not others, inhibition of the nonretrieved information occurs. If you spend an enjoyable evening reminiscing about college days with an old roommate, other experiences that you shared together but did not discuss may become inhibited as a result of being suppressed during retrieval of the experiences that you did discuss.

Anderson further suggests that this idea might shed some light on the controversial phenomena of forgetting and recovery of childhood sexual abuse. The 1990s were marred by a heated and often ugly debate concerning the accuracy of traumatic memories that had seemingly been forgotten for years or decades, only to be recovered in psychotherapy or in response to some triggering incident. Early discussions were divided sharply, with one side arguing that virtually all such memories are accurate and the other that virtually all are false. Although the bitter division has persisted, some discussions have contended that both accurate and false recovered memories of childhood traumas exist, and have attempted to characterize the mechanisms responsible for each. I consider false memories of childhood when I discuss suggestibility in Chapter 5.

Studies of people who say that they were sexually abused as children suggest, somewhat surprisingly, that reports of temporary forgetting of the abuse are more common when the abuser is a family member than a nonfamily member. Why? Anderson suggests one possible interpretation. When a parent or other trusted caregiver perpetrates abuse, a child is still emotionally and physically dependent on that person, and thus still needs to maintain a functional relationship with the abuser. Memories of the abuse may undermine this objective by creating anxiety and distrust, whereas recalling more positive experiences with the caregiver could facilitate an adaptive relationship. Thus, Anderson suggests, the child needs selectively to retrieve nontraumatic, rather than traumatic, experiences associated with the caregiver. This type of situation may promote retrieval-induced inhibition — when we need to retrieve some selective memories in response to a particular cue (in this case, the family member) but not others. It remains to be determined whether this type of blocking plays a role in genuine instances of forgetting and recovery of trauma perpetrated by a family member, but the hypothesis is plausible and worth examining empirically.

Not all instances of forgetting childhood abuse involve family members, however. For example, the University of Pittsburgh psychologist Jonathan Schooler carefully documented a case in which a thirty-year-old man referred to by the initials JR became agitated while watching a movie in which the main character struggled with recollections of sexual molestation. Later that evening, JR was over-whelmed by a sudden and vivid recollection that a parish priest had sexually abused him on a camping trip when he was twelve years old. As far as Schooler could determine, JR had not thought about this incident for many years. "If you had done a survey of people walking into the movie theater when I saw the movie," JR reflected, "asking people about child and sexual abuse, 'Have you ever been, or do you know anybody who has ever been,' I would have absolutely, flatly, unhesitatingly, said no!" This incident occurred in 1986, well before the eruption of the recovered memories controversy in the early 1990s: "I was stunned, I was somewhat confused, you know. The memory was very vivid and yet . . . I didn't know one word about repressed memory."

Why had JR forgotten about the abuse for so long? Transience no doubt played some role — the memory may have weakened over time — but the reported vividness of JR's recollection suggests that transience is not the entire story. The incident may have become blocked or inhibited through a process known as "directed forget-ting." Experiments have shown that when people are instructed to forget about a list of words they have just studied, they later recall fewer of those words on a surprise memory test compared with words they had been instructed to remember. The UCLA psychol-ogist Robert Bjork and his colleagues have argued persuasively that such directed-forgetting effects are sometimes attributable to the form of blocking known as retrieval inhibition. Such inhibition can be "released" when we encounter sufficiently powerful cues that lead us to reexperience an event in the way that we did initially. Perhaps JR consciously attempted to avoid retrieving memories of his en-counter with the priest, and thus, over a long period of time, success-fully inhibited access to them. The potent triggers contained in the movie may have elicited emotions like those JR felt during the initial experience, allowing him to overcome the inhibition.

Concepts such as "retrieval inhibition" inevitably call to mind the

Freudian notion of repression. Is retrieval inhibition simply code for Freud's old idea, which has been maligned because it lacks experimental support? Not really. Freud's concept of repression entails a psychological defense mechanism that is inextricably bound up with attempts to exclude emotionally threatening material from conscious awareness. But in modern discussions by such theorists as Bjork and Anderson, retrieval inhibition is a far more ubiquitous construct that applies to both emotional and nonemotional experiences.

Nonetheless, there are some interesting intersections between the modern notion of retrieval inhibition and the Freudian concept of repression that have implications for blocking. For example, the clinical psychologists Lynn Myers and Chris Brewin examined the operation of retrieval inhibition in a group of people known as "repressors." Repressors tend to report low levels of anxiety and stress even when physiological measures indicate strong emotional reactions to a person or situation — a beet-red face, for instance, accompanied by denial of any embarrassment. Repressors are the kinds of people whom others would likely label "defensive." Several studies have shown that repressors tend to recall fewer negative events from their lives than do nonrepressors.

Myers and Brewin used a directed-forgetting procedure in which participants studied pleasant or unpleasant words and were then given directed-forgetting instructions. Repressors were more adept than nonrepressors at using retrieval inhibition to block recall of recently studied unpleasant words, even though there were no differences between the two groups in blocking recall of pleasant words.

How far can repressors go in using retrieval inhibition to block memories of unpleasant events? Could they forget a recent trauma, as in the Toronto murder case of Cynthia Anthony, or even block out larger chunks of their lives? We do not yet know the answers to these questions. We do know, however, that retrieval inhibition on a large scale can occur in cases of "psychogenic" amnesia, where patients block out large parts of their personal pasts after various kinds of psychological stresses. Such patients usually retain the ability to form and retrieve new memories but can remember little about their autobiographies — including their personal identities — prior to the onset of amnesia. For the most part, such patients have been relegated to the realm of psychiatric disturbances. Studies using neuroimaging techniques provide a glimpse into the neural mechanisms that are involved in blocking episodic memories. In one German case, a patient referred to by the initials NN unexpectedly disappeared from home, turning up days later in a city hundreds of miles away, unaware of his personal identity and unable to recall almost anything about his past experiences. He eventually landed in a hospital, and his family was tracked down. NN had been suffering from various stresses in his daily life prior to his disappearance, but there was no sign of overt brain damage. The patient underwent PET scans while he listened to descriptions of events from various points in his past. When healthy people carried out a similar task involving recollection of emotionally salient past experiences, the scans revealed increased activity in parts of the right cerebral hemisphere, especially toward the back part of the frontal lobe and front parts of the temporal lobe. But NN showed no activation in these regions, and instead activated a much smaller part of frontal and temporal regions within his *left* hemisphere.

These observations are particularly intriguing because other studies have revealed that neurological patients who cannot recollect large parts of their personal pasts, even though they can form new memories, have frequently sustained damage to the back of the right frontal lobe and to the front of the right temporal lobe.

A PET scan study of a striking neurological patient provides further clues. Patient PN suffered a cerebral hemorrhage while in his forties that damaged his left frontal lobe. He had also recently suffered several personal setbacks, including divorce, job difficulties, and personal bankruptcy. Perhaps as a result of both the neurological damage and psychiatric complications from his recent troubles, PN developed amnesia for the nineteen years prior to his hemorrhage. He underwent PET scans while looking at family photographs that had been taken during the nineteen years that he could not remember, or while looking at family photographs taken before or after that time (which he had no difficulty remembering). When looking at photographs taken during the nineteen-year amnesic gap, PN showed less activity in a part of the right frontal lobe than when he was looking at photographs taken before or after that period. The right frontal region that showed reduced activity was quite close to a similar region that failed to show activation in patient NN but that is active under similar conditions in healthy people.

An additional finding is especially intriguing. When looking at photographs from the nineteen years he could not remember, PN showed increased activity in a region near the back center of the brain — the precuneus — that frequently activates when healthy people recall past experiences. The researchers suggested that this activity might signal the earliest stages of the retrieval process beginning to go forward. To continue to develop the search, and ultimately recollect the event shown in the photo, the frontal lobe system that directs and controls the retrieval process must kick in. But at this point during PN's attempt to retrieve experiences from the nineteen-year gap, the frontal control system seemed to shut down, thus leaving him unable to recollect anything.

Why would the frontal system shut down only for those experiences in the nineteen-year gap? The system itself was not dysfunctional, because it activated when PN tried to remember experiences before or after the amnesic period. But the gap contained the key adverse events in PN's life, raising the possibility that the negative emotion brought on as PN began to retrieve those negative autobiographical events (the early-stage retrieval indicated by the precuneus activation) led to or allowed the shutdown of the frontal system.

Could this interplay between the precuneus and the frontal system represent the neural signature of a type of blocking that resembles Freud's dynamically inspired concept of repression? Might those individuals characterized as repressors show a similar pattern of greater activity in the precuneus and reduced activity in the frontal control system when they are asked about negative events from their past?

Neuroimaging research holds out the tantalizing possibility of allowing us to reconceptualize, and perhaps explain, these rare but fascinating cases. Neuroimaging studies might even help physicians treat patients who present with extensive amnesia in the absence of detectable brain damage. Clinicians often suspect that such patients are faking amnesia in order to avoid legal or other personal difficulties. But there are no tests that reliably distinguish between genuine and feigned amnesia. If neuroimaging studies turn up reliable brain signatures of memory blocking that are different from those that accompany attempts to fake memory loss, this could provide an important clue to clinicians who need to formulate a plan for managing amnesia patients. Though we are still a long way from understanding the vicissitudes of blocking, imaging studies provide a real chance for illuminating even this most vexing of memory's sins.

The Update
Oops!

On November 9, 2011, eight candidates for the Republican presidential nomination gathered to debate at Oakland University in Rochester, Michigan. Pundits expressed differing views about who won the debate, but there was no doubt about the biggest loser: Texas governor Rick Perry. Blustering that "it's three agencies of government when I get there that are gone," Perry quickly named the Departments of Commerce and Education before stumbling badly when he tried to recall the third, searching unsuccessfully for the next forty-five seconds before reluctantly concluding that "the third one I can't . . . sorry . . . oops!" Several minutes later, Perry did recall that the third agency was the Department of Energy, but it was too late to save him from the humiliation of the moment and the brutal press coverage that depicted this gaffe as the likely end of his candidacy. University of Virginia political scientist Larry Sabato went so far as to tweet, "To my memory, Perry's forgetfulness is the most devastating moment of any primary debate." That moment still lingered for Perry a little over five years later when Perry was chosen to lead the Department of Energy. It was revived in headlines such as this one from Vox:

> Rick Perry is Trump's pick to run Energy. He once forgot the agency's name.

I watched the 2011 debate and received e-mails the next day from the *Washington Post,* the *Boston Globe,* ABC News, NPR, and other media outlets interested in my take on what had happened. For a memory researcher, this was a textbook example of name blocking. We already saw earlier in the chapter that name blocking occurs increasingly often as we age. Perry, though not quite a senior citizen in 2011, was eight months past his sixty-first birthday at the time of the debate — old enough that age could plausibly have heightened his risk of blocking. We also saw that names that haven't been retrieved frequently or recently show heightened susceptibility to blocking. Although Perry knew "Department of Energy" well enough to retrieve the name later in the debate, perhaps stronger preparation would have avoided the problem altogether. Perry also had some partial knowledge of the name he couldn't produce, which is typical with blocking. Recall the example of blocking by Britain's deputy prime minister John Prescott discussed earlier in this chapter. Prescott also had some partial knowledge of the word he blocked on: he blurted out "raffles" when searching for "lottery." Similarly, when fellow debater Ron Paul suggested that the third agency might be the Environmental Protection Agency and CNBC's debate moderator, John Harwood, asked Perry directly whether it was, Perry knew enough about the blocked name to reject the suggestion.

The stress of a prime-time, nationally televised debate could also have played a role. Intuitively, it seems plausible that high stress could increase the chances of blocking. Surprisingly, however, the topic received little research attention until the past few years, when experiments from the laboratory of the cognitive psychologist Lori James examined the effects of stress on one of the most salient forms of retrieval blocking — the tip-of-the-tongue (TOT) state that I discussed at length earlier. To induce stress, the researchers used a well-validated method known as the Trier Social Stress Test (TSST), which requires participants to prepare and give a speech as they would for a job interview, explaining why they should be hired and describing their skills, strengths, and qualifications to observers who will evaluate their performance. After giving the speech, participants performed a mental arithmetic task (as in the standard TSST), followed by a word definition task that James and her colleagues designed to elicit TOTs by asking about difficult-to-retrieve words (e.g., "What do you call a word puzzle in which letters are rearranged to form new words or phrases?" Answer: anagram). Compared with a control condition in which participants had to prepare a speech, do mental arithmetic, and complete the word definition task *without* any observers evaluating their performance, evaluation-related stress resulted in a significant increase in TOTs. These findings were based on a sample of college students, but in subsequent research, James and her colleagues demonstrated the same stress-related increases in TOTs with adults ranging in age from eighteen to eighty. We can't know for certain whether these findings apply to Rick Perry, but they are consistent with a role for stress in his epic retrieval block.

It's also interesting to consider whether Ron Paul's suggestion that the EPA might be Perry's third targeted agency contributed to prolonging Perry's retrieval block. Recall that "ugly sisters" — words that are related to a blocked item — are probably not the cause of TOT states and related retrieval failures. Recall also, however, that Deborah Burke and Donald MacKay suggested that ugly sisters might play a role in prolonging a TOT state. If so, then we would expect that when someone is experiencing a TOT state, drawing their attention away from the "ugly sisters" should help to resolve it. Evidence supporting this idea emerged from a 2005 study showing that there is a higher likelihood of resolving a TOT state after a delay during which people aren't thinking about the item they can't retrieve, because they are responding to other, unrelated questions. A subsequent study revealed that this finding applies both when an ugly sister accompanies a TOT and when it doesn't, but both studies suggest that focusing attention away from the TOT item increases the chances of eventually recalling it.

That doesn't necessarily mean that Ron Paul's mention of the EPA prolonged Perry's retrieval failure, but his delayed recovery of "Department of Energy" later in the debate likely benefited from a focus on other matters during that time. Regardless, given the frequency of retrieval blocking in older adults, we can be pretty sure that Perry won't be the last aging politician to suffer from an "oops" moment in a political debate. Indeed, a possible case of blocking came up during the Democratic presidential debate in Las Vegas, Nevada, on February 19, 2020, when Telemundo reporter Guadalupe Venegas asked Amy Klobuchar about her inability to name Mexican president Andrés Manuel López Obrador (aka AMLO) in a Telemundo interview just before the debate. Klobuchar, fifty-nine at the time, attempted to write off the incident as an innocent example of "momentary forgetfulness," but as Venegas and others pointed out, she could not provide any information about AMLO or his policies in the interview, raising legitimate questions about whether blocking was the culprit there.

Despite some progress during the past two decades in understanding factors that impact retrieval blocks such as TOT, we are still largely in the dark when it comes to understanding what goes awry in the brain to produce such short circuits. Shortly after *The Seven Sins of Memory* appeared in 2001, my research group published an fMRI study led by the Israeli psychologist Anat Maril in which we induced TOTs in the scanner by giving people two cues (e.g., *"Chinatown"* and "director") for a difficult-to-retrieve target ("Roman Polanski"). This procedure yielded enough TOT states to analyze associated brain activity. The most striking finding was that brain regions that had previously been associated with cognitive control and detecting cognitive conflicts, including parts of the prefrontal cortex and the nearby anterior cingulate, became highly active during a TOT state, compared to when retrieval was either successful or when it failed but did not elicit a TOT state. Our study focused on young adults, but a more recent fMRI study replicated our findings with elderly adults and further suggested that age-related changes in TOT experiences involve specific cognitive and neural mechanisms that are distinct from those that produce other kinds of age-related memory declines.

TO THINK OR NOT TO THINK

Although we still can't pinpoint the neural causes of TOT states, we have made some progress in understanding the brain basis of other memory processes that are implicated in blocking. Earlier in the chapter, I discussed experiments by Michael Anderson and his colleagues that provided evidence for retrieval inhibition. In 2001, Anderson introduced a novel experimental paradigm for studying retrieval inhibition called the "think–no think" procedure. Participants encoded a series of unrelated word pairs such as *moss/north*. Then, when they were presented with the first word of the pair, they were instructed to try either to recall the associated word (the "think" condition) or to suppress the associated word from conscious awareness (the "no think" condition). Later, on a final memory test, when participants tried to recall each associated word in response to the first word of the pair, they remembered fewer "no think" words than "think" words. This finding alone might simply indicate that memory for "think" words improved because of practice rather than revealing impaired recall of "no think" words. Critically, however, final recall of "no think" words was worse than final recall of words that were studied initially but that were not included in the think–no think phase of the experiment. This result shows that final recall was impaired by participants' prior attempts to suppress a word during the "no think" phase. The results were the same even when Anderson paid participants to try to recall the "no think" words on the final test. Suppressing them earlier during the "no think" phase blocked subsequent retrieval to such an extent that participants couldn't come up with these items even when money was at stake.

These findings were initially controversial because researchers using similar think–no think procedures reported a failure to observe any effects of suppression in a 2006 paper. With replication failure in psychology emerging as a hot-button issue around the same time, skeptics wondered whether retrieval inhibition in the think–no think paradigm was real. But by 2012, a review of think–no think data from thirty-two published articles, some from Anderson's lab and some from other researchers, revealed consistent evidence for a modest impairment of recall of suppressed items in the think–no think paradigm. A 2020 meta-analysis of twenty-five studies that used the think–no think procedure to compare suppression effects in healthy individuals and depressed or anxious individuals confirmed a modest but significant suppression effect in the healthy individuals and a reduced suppression effect in individuals who were anxious or depressed. These and other recent studies confirm that the suppression effect in people who are not depressed or anxious is, though not large, real.

In fact, this suppression effect has been considered robust enough to investigate with fMRI and related imaging procedures. In 2004, Anderson's group found that when people are trying to suppress a target item during the "no think" phase, parts of the prefrontal cortex associated with cognitive control show *increased* activity, whereas the hippocampus — a brain region frequently associated with successful recollection — shows *decreased* activity. Crucially, these brain changes predict the extent to which a specific item suffers from impaired recall that is attributable to retrieval blocking. Building on these findings, a 2017 study from Anderson's group focused on the possible role of GABA — an inhibitory neurotransmitter that can be measured in the human brain with a technique known as "magnetic resonance spectroscopy" — in modulating retrieval inhibition in the think–no think paradigm. Results revealed that a higher resting concentration of GABA in the hippocampus is associated with a greater ability to suppress "no think" items and with stronger coupling between the hippocampus and the prefrontal cortex during attempted suppression. Collectively, these findings not only provide new insights into the brain mechanisms that produce retrieval blocking, but as we will see in The Update in Chapter 7, they also have implications for addressing the unwanted and psychologically debilitating intrusive memories associated with persistence, memory's seventh sin.

4
The Sin of
Misattribution

I have been here before,
But when or how I cannot tell:
I know the grass beyond the door,
The sweet keen smell,
The sighing sound, the lights around the shore . . .
— "Sudden Light," Dante Gabriel Rossetti, 1854

ON FEBRUARY 24, 1896, members of the Société Médico-Psychologique in Paris learned about a bizarre case of memory disturbance. Accounts of patients suffering from amnesia were not uncommon in the 1890s, but the thirty-four-year-old man described that day had a different problem: he remembered events that never occurred. After suffering from malaria several years earlier, Louis was regularly overwhelmed by feelings of familiarity when he encountered situations that were, in reality, entirely novel. In the midst of his brother's marriage ceremony, he felt certain he had attended the same event a year earlier. Admitted to a new hospital because of emotional problems, Louis was sure he had been there before. When he first met Dr. François-Léon Arnaud, the French psychiatrist who reported his case to the Société Médico-Psychologique, he insisted, "You know me, doctor! You also welcomed me last year, at the same time of the day, and in this same room. You asked me the same questions, and I gave you the same answers."

Louis was of great interest to the psychologists and psychiatrists who had assembled in Paris to hear Arnaud's presentation. The late nineteenth century has been called a golden age for the study of memory, and French psychology played a large part in it. Although

Ebbinghaus's groundbreaking 1885 experiments are best known to-day, four years earlier the French psychologist Théodule Ribot had written a classic book, *Diseases of Memory,* which described how brain damage or psychological disturbance could produce amnesia for the recent or remote past. Ribot also described cases where memory is present but wrong. Called "paramnesias" or "false memories," these distortions had sparked a spirited and sometimes heated debate: How widespread are such false memories in the general population? Do they signal the presence of clinical pathology? Is there just one type of paramnesia, or are there many? Proponents of opposing views debated in a special 1893 issue of the *Révue Philosophique.*

When Arnaud presented Louis to the Paris meeting of the society in 1896, he placed his problems squarely in the context of the ongoing debate by rejecting the terms most commonly used to describe the aberrant remembering that Louis displayed. "I believe that it would be better to abandon the words false memory and paramnesia," he boldly asserted, going on to argue — seemingly paradoxically — that "the phenomenon in question may not be associated with memory at all." Arnaud suggested a new expression to describe the inappropriate familiarity that plagued patients like Louis: the illusion of déjà vu. He insisted that déjà vu is a special experience, distinct from other kinds of memory distortions because of its intensity, the conviction that a present experience is identical to a past one, and the feeling that one knows precisely what is going to happen next.

Arnaud helped to propel the term *déjà vu* into common usage, but he was not the first to describe the experience. Dante Gabriel Rossetti captured the feeling of déjà vu in his 1854 poem "Sudden Light," and as early as 1849, Charles Dickens wrote of a similar experience in *David Copperfield.* "He seemed to swell and grow before my eyes," David relates upon encountering Uriah Heap. "The room seemed full of the echoes of his voice; and the strange feeling (to which no one is quite a stranger) that all this had occurred before, at some indefinite time, and that I knew what he was going to say next, took possession of me."

But what did Arnaud mean when he claimed that Louis's déjà vu experiences "may not be associated with memory at all"? Many prior interpretations of déjà vu tended toward the mystical, conjecturing that it reflects memory for a past life and thus provides evidence for reincarnation, or perhaps involves telepathic eavesdropping into someone else's memory. Other, less exotic explanations held that people have feelings of déjà vu when a present experience stirs up a similar — though not identical — past experience. For Arnaud, however, déjà vu had nothing to do with either the paranormal or partial memories of a similar past episode. Instead, he characterized it as a kind of bad judgment: a misattribution of current sensations and experiences onto the past.

To understand better what Arnaud had in mind in 1896, fast-forward a century and consider a 1993 experiment by the Canadian cognitive psychologist Bruce Whittlesea. Participants first studied a list of common words. On a later memory test, some words from the study list and some new words appeared in capital letters at the end of a sentence; participants judged whether the capitalized words had appeared earlier. In some of the sentences, the word at the end of the sentence was highly predictable from the preceding words: "The stormy seas tossed the BOAT." In other sentences, the final word was less predictable: "She saved her money and bought a LAMP."

When the capitalized word had not appeared previously on the study list and participants should have responded "new," they sometimes incorrectly responded "old." Most important, people were more likely to claim incorrectly that they had previously seen the highly predictable new words than that they had seen the less predictable new words. Participants also named highly predictable words faster than they named less predictable words. Whittlesea suggested that participants misattributed their fast responses for the highly predictable words to an earlier encounter that, in fact, had never occurred: speedy, fluent responding — a consequence of the word's predictability — was misinterpreted as familiarity.

In this experiment, then, people claimed that they had a prior experience — seeing a word on a study list — for reasons having nothing to do with memory, just as Arnaud had asserted about déjà vu a century earlier. Déjà vu, he thought, might occur because features of a present situation trigger responses, perhaps analogous to the fluent processing of predictable words in Whittlesea's experiment, that are mistakenly attributed to a past experience.

Déjà vu occurs relatively infrequently, and as we will see in The Update in this chapter, only recently have scientists developed innovative experimental procedures to explore which features of a present experience can produce the kinds of mistaken judgments that Arnaud theorized about to his Parisian audience. Yet misattributions in remembering are surprisingly common. Sometimes we remember events that never happened, misattributing speedy processing of incoming information or vivid images that spring to mind, to memories of past events that did not occur. Sometimes we recall correctly what happened, but misattribute it to the wrong time or place. And sometimes misattribution operates in a different direction: we mistakenly credit a spontaneous image or thought to our own imagination, when in reality we are recalling it — without awareness — from something we read or heard. We know more about déjà vu today than we did back in the days of Arnaud, and we have learned a great deal more about other forms of misattribution. This is hard-won knowledge with potentially vital consequences for society: misattribution can alter our lives in strange and unexpected ways.

EYEWITNESS MISATTRIBUTIONS AND SOURCE MEMORY

Anybody who remembers the Oklahoma City bombing in 1995 probably also recalls the failed search for John Doe 2. John Doe 1 — soon identified as Timothy McVeigh — was apprehended shortly after the bombing in April of that year. At the same time, the FBI mounted a nationwide manhunt for a second suspect they believed had accompanied McVeigh when he rented a van from Elliott's Body Shop in Junction City, Kansas, two days before the bombing. An artist's sketch of John Doe 2, depicting a young, square-faced man with dark hair and a stocky build wearing a blue and white cap, appeared continually on television and was featured in newspapers around the country. Despite massive efforts that resulted in the successful prosecution of McVeigh and his friend Terry Nichols, and polls indicating that seven in ten Americans believed that another accomplice had eluded the law, John Doe 2 was never found. What happened?

After tracing McVeigh's rental van, the FBI interviewed employees at Elliott's Body Shop. A secretary and the shop owner recalled that only one man, matching McVeigh's description, had rented a van on April 17, 1995, two days before the bombing; he had made his reservation under the alias "Robert Kling." The mechanic, Tom Kessinger, who watched the transaction, recalled seeing two men. One fit McVeigh's description: tall and fair with short blond hair. The other was shorter and stockier, had dark hair, wore a blue and white cap, and had a tattoo beneath his left sleeve. Based on Kessinger's recollection, the search for John Doe 2 began.

The source of Kessinger's memory, however, appears to lie in an unrelated visit to Elliott's Body Shop a day later, when Army Sergeant Michael Hertig and his friend Private Todd Bunting also rented a van in Kessinger's presence. Hertig, like McVeigh, was tall and fair. Bunting was shorter and stockier, had dark hair, wore a blue and white cap, and had a tattoo beneath his left sleeve — a match to the description of John Doe 2.

After initiating the unsuccessful manhunt for the elusive second suspect, FBI agents reviewed records of Hertig and Bunting's visit to Elliott's Body Shop. They reluctantly concluded that John Doe 2 was Private Todd Bunting, an innocent man with no connection to the bombing. Kessinger had correctly recalled Bunting's features, depicted in the infamous picture of John Doe 2 that circulated nationwide, but had misattributed them to the wrong episode a day earlier.

This kind of mistaken identification is not unprecedented. In a famous case from the mid-1950s, a British ticket agent robbed at gunpoint later identified an innocent sailor as the gunman. The sailor had previously purchased tickets from the same agent, who had misattributed the familiarity of the sailor's face to the robbery. In a later incident, the psychologist Donald Thomson was accused of rape based on a victim's detailed memory of his face. Thomson was cleared because he had an impeccable alibi: he was in the midst of a live television interview (ironically, on the fallibility of memory) at the moment the rape occurred. The victim had been watching the show and misattributed her memory of Thomson's face to the rapist.

Both Thomson and the British sailor were fortunate to escape wrongful imprisonment. But how many other times have similar misattributions produced inaccurate eyewitness testimony leading to the conviction of an innocent person? According to data reported by the Innocence Project in 2021, mistaken eyewitness identifications have been involved in 69 percent of approximately 375 wrongful convictions overturned by DNA evidence. There are no doubt other such mistakes that have not yet been rectified.

These chilling numbers create a sense of urgency regarding the need to understand better the nature of eyewitness misattributions and to take steps to minimize them. The specific type of misattribution in the John Doe 2 incident is sometimes referred to as "unconscious transference." The idea is that a witness such as Kessinger incorrectly attributes a face's familiarity to the wrong source because he unconsciously transfers memory of the individual from one context to another. Laboratory studies indicate that when individuals make an eyewitness misidentification, they are not necessarily unaware of having previously encountered a person in multiple contexts. For example, participants who watched a film of a robbery that included an innocent bystander in a separate scene sometimes later mistakenly identified the bystander as the robber. But the process that led to the misidentification was not entirely unconscious: many participants believed — incorrectly — that the bystander and the robber were the same person.

Whether unconscious or not, the kinds of eyewitness misidentifications observed in cases such as John Doe 2 and others fit well with research showing that people often have sketchy recollections of the precise details of previous experiences — when and where they encountered a person or object. This vagueness creates fertile soil for the occurrence of "source misattributions," in which people recall correctly a fact they learned earlier or recognize accurately a person or object they have seen before, but misattribute the source of their knowledge. Experiments have shown, for instance, that people may remember perfectly well that they saw a previously presented face but misremember the time or place that they saw it, much as happened to Tom Kessinger in Elliott's Body Shop. Sometimes eyewitnesses have sketchy, uncertain memories of the face itself. In a paper published in 2018, the cognitive psychologist John Wixted points out that in all the cases he examined where DNA evidence exonerated a wrongfully convicted individual and where information about the certainty of the initial identification was available, the eyewitness was at first uncertain about their identification of the accused person. Problems arise when further questioning produces a higher confidence about an incorrect identification that contributes to a wrongful conviction (see Chapter 5 on suggestibility for a related discussion).

Consider what's involved in remembering the details of what a person looks like and where you saw them. You attend a business meeting at a palatial downtown office on Tuesday morning and meet two executives with whom you will be negotiating: Thomas Wilson, a silver-haired vice president wearing horn-rimmed glasses and a conservative blue suit, and Frank Albert, a thirtysomething financial analyst wearing a bow tie and colorful suspenders. Later that afternoon, you head out to the suburbs to meet with two prospective clients who have just started a new company in rather cramped quarters. The computer programmer, Eric Merton, is a recent college graduate wearing jeans and a silver earring; the company president, Elaine Green, is a slightly older woman dressed in a more traditional business suit.

If I ask you a week later about your meetings last Tuesday, to provide an accurate report you will need to remember the individual features of the people and places you visited. But it is not sufficient to recall a vice president, financial analyst, computer programmer, and president; horn-rimmed glasses, colorful suspenders, a bow tie, silver earring, jeans, and traditional business suits; Mr. Wilson, Mr.

Albert, Mr. Merton, and Ms. Green; a large downtown office and a smaller one in the suburbs. You also need to remember which person was wearing what and which face goes with which name, who works out in the suburbs and who works downtown, and what position each person holds. In addition to recording and retrieving the individual features, you need to link them together in memory so that you can recall the correct conjunctions of people, attire, positions, and places.

Psychologists refer to this linking process as "memory binding": gluing together the various components of an experience into a unitary whole. When individual parts of an experience are retained but memory binding fails, the stage is set for the kinds of source misattributions seen in the John Doe 2 incident and in other episodes of mistaken eyewitness recollection.

Source confusions are sometimes attributable to a binding failure: at the time an event occurs, an action or object is not properly bound to a particular time and place. Binding failures may also contribute to memory confusions between events we actually experience and those we only think about or imagine. About to leave your house, you think about closing the basement door. An hour later in the car, you are suddenly gripped by a sense of panic: "Did I actually close the door, or did I only imagine doing it?"

After he retired, the psychology professor Lew Lieberman became increasingly vexed by such confusions. "It is as if before you do something," he reflected, "you kind of picture yourself doing it and then later, you do not remember whether it was just the picture or the reality." He wondered whether others experience something similar. In fact, numerous experiments have shown that when people imagine seeing an object, or carrying out an action, they sometimes later claim that they actually perceived the object or performed the action.

In one particularly neat experiment, younger and older adults saw an object such as a magnifying glass and researchers later asked them to imagine a lollipop (similar object), or they saw a hanger and later were asked to imagine a screwdriver (unrelated object). Older adults were more likely than younger adults to insist that they had actually seen the imagined lollipop, but were no more likely than younger adults to claim they had seen the imagined screwdriver. Older participants seemed to have special difficulty binding the appearance of perceived objects (for example, a "round shape") to the context of presentation. So, after seeing one "round shape" — the magnifying glass — and imagining another similar shape — the lollipop — elderly participants could not recall details associated with the actual perception of the magnifying glass, and were thus prone to source misattribution.

If associated details are bound together with an object or action, it becomes easier to recall whether an incident actually occurred. Fretting in the car about whether you've left your basement door wide open, you carry out a frantic mental search, trying to recall some specific object or action that proclaims that you indeed carried out what you had thought about doing. Your mind eases as you remember seeing a cat running away when you closed the door. But if you hadn't bound together the perception of the frightened animal with the act of closing the door, you might still be trying to sort out imagination from reality.

Binding failures can also result in a striking illusion known as a "memory conjunction error." Having met Mr. Wilson and Mr. Albert during your business meeting, you reply confidently the next day when an associate asks you the name of the company vice president: "Mr. Wilbert." You remembered correctly pieces of the two surnames but mistakenly combined them into a new one. Cognitive psychologists have developed experimental procedures in which people exhibit precisely these kinds of erroneous conjunctions between features of different words, pictures, sentences, or even faces. Thus, having studied *spaniel* and *varnish,* people sometimes claim to remember *Spanish.* Or having seen drawings of the first two faces shown in Figure 4.1, people often claim to remember having seen a different face (the third face in the figure) when later given a recognition test. The third face combines features of the two they saw earlier. If individual features of the words or faces are retained, but are not bound together adequately when people initially study them, memory conjunction errors can result.

FIGURE 4.1 *After seeing the faces on the left and in the center of the figure, people later claim erroneously to remember seeing the face on the right, which contains conjunctions of elements from the other faces. This type of misattribution is known as a "memory conjunction error."*

Studies of brain-injured patients suggest that the hippocampus plays an important role in binding processes that, when disrupted, contribute to memory conjunction errors. Patients with damage restricted to the hippocampus are even more likely than healthy controls to make memory conjunction errors for recently studied words and faces. The patients perceive faces and words as wholes, but when tested only a few seconds or minutes later, they are likely to miscombine features of separate faces or syllables of different words. The damaged hippocampus no longer provides the mnemonic glue needed to hold together parts of a face or word in memory. This idea receives further support from brain imaging studies using PET scans. The hippocampus became especially active when people learned pairs of unrelated words (for example, *level/need*), which places heavy demands on binding processes.

Source misattributions and memory conjunction errors can also occur because of faulty memory retrieval processes. When a face seems familiar, people need to reflect on, or "monitor," the outputs of memory to determine why. Patients whose frontal lobes have been damaged by stroke or partially removed during surgery have difficulty engaging in such retrieval-monitoring processes. They tend to make snap judgments about the source of a feeling of familiarity, and hence make more source misattribution errors than do healthy controls.

Healthy elderly adults who perform poorly on tests that are sensitive to frontal lobe abnormalities also tend to be especially prone to source misattributions. Recall that older adults often claimed that they had previously seen a lollipop they had only imagined, when in reality they had actually seen a similarly shaped magnifying glass. When participants took this test two days after seeing and imagining objects, older adults who scored most poorly on other tests that are sensitive to frontal lobe damage also made the most confusions between perceived and imagined objects. But when memory testing was carried out only fifteen minutes after seeing and imagining objects, there was no relationship between these source misattributions and scores on frontal lobe tests. Monitoring processes that depend on the frontal lobes are probably most heavily taxed after a two-day delay, when trying to recall whether you perceived or imagined an object is very difficult and requires considerable reflection. If only fifteen minutes have passed, then the memory task is easier and does not draw on the frontal lobes as much.

Related retrieval failures also contribute to memory conjunction errors. Susan Rubin and her collaborators found that in a sample of older adults, those who performed most poorly on tests of frontal lobe function also tended to make many memory conjunction errors, such as claiming to remember *barley* from an earlier list when they actually saw *barter* and *valley*. These elderly adults failed to scrutinize their memories sufficiently, relying instead on the strong sense of familiarity engendered by seeing a conjunction word like *barley*.

In studies of eyewitness identifications reported during the 1980s and 1990s, Gary Wells at Iowa State University argued that common lineup identification practices may often promote memory errors because people are encouraged to rely on familiarity. In standard lineup procedures, witnesses are shown a number of possible suspects *simultaneously;* after seeing all of them, they attempt to identify the culprit. Wells claimed that under such conditions, witnesses tend to rely on relative judgments: they choose the person who, relative to the others in the lineup, looks most like the suspect. The problem is that even when the real suspect is not in the lineup, witnesses still tend to choose the person who looks most like them. Witnesses rely on general similarities between a face in the lineup and the actual culprit, even when they lack specific recollections. The early research by Wells and his colleagues suggested a way to minimize reliance on such relative judgments: use a *sequential* lineup and instruct the witness to make a "thumbs-up or thumbs-down" decision about each possible suspect right after seeing the face instead of waiting until all the potential suspects' faces have been displayed. Wells produced experimental evidence suggesting that this sequential procedure encourages people to scrutinize their memories carefully and examine whether the pictured person matches the details of their recollections.

In the late 1990s, this evidence led a working group formed by former US attorney general Janet Reno to determine that sequential lineups produce more reliable identifications than simultaneous lineups, although they stopped short of specifically recommending that police switch to using the sequential procedure. Beginning in the early 2000s, however, researchers employing more sophisticated analysis approaches than those used in Wells's studies failed to find convincing evidence that sequential lineups selectively reduce false identifications compared with simultaneous lineups. Instead, sequential lineups have both benefits and costs: they often reduce the likelihood of an eyewitness incorrectly identifying an innocent individual, but they also reduce the likelihood of a witness correctly identifying a guilty individual. This new line of research led one prominent group of memory researchers to conclude that "if there is any difference in diagnostic accuracy between the two lineup formats, it likely favors the simultaneous procedure."

Studies on eyewitness misattributions are important because the stakes are so high for both accused individuals and victims of crimes. To me, they also lead to a fundamental question with far-reaching implications: Is it possible to tell true memories from false ones?

LOOKING FOR A TRUTH MACHINE

In the summer of 1996, I helped to run a cognitive neuroscience institute at Dartmouth College. My family and I stayed at a lovely country inn located in the nearby Vermont countryside. Returning there after a day of lectures by distinguished speakers, I was stunned by an unexpected, even surreal, sight: the door to our room was virtually covered with slips of paper, each containing a phone message from a newspaper, television news show, or radio program. Media from all over the world wanted to talk to me — right away.

That morning, an article in the Tuesday science section of the *New York Times* described new PET scan studies I had conducted with several colleagues examining brain activity while people experienced true and false memories. Though other studies had used PET scans and fMRI to peer inside the brain as participants recalled true memories of previous experiences, none had looked at brain activity when they called up false memories of incidents that had never occurred. The possibility that brain imaging might function as a kind of high-tech lie detector, flawlessly sorting out true from false memories, is undeniably intriguing.

It is easy to have people recall true memories during a scan: ask them about words or pictures that you showed them before scanning, or inquire about past experiences outside the laboratory. But how does one induce false memories in a PET scanner? A year before our PET scan study, the psychologists Henry L. Roediger and Kathleen McDermott rediscovered a procedure developed by James Deese in the 1950s that reliably leads people to insist that they experienced an event — the appearance of a word in a list — that never actually happened. This procedure is now referred to as Deese/Roediger-McDermott, or DRM. The experimenter first reads out lists of associated words. One list, for instance, might contain *thread, pin, eye, sewing, sharp, point, prick, thimble, haystack, thorn, hurt, injection, syringe, cloth, knitting.* Another list might contain *bed, rest, awake, tired, dream, wake, snooze, blanket, doze, slumber, snore, nap, peace, yawn, drowsy.* On a later memory test, subjects decide whether each of several words was read aloud earlier: *sewing, door, needle, sleep, candy, awake.* Most of the time, people correctly remember that they heard *sewing* and *awake,* and correctly state that they did not hear *door* and *candy.* More interestingly, people frequently claim — confidently but incorrectly — that they heard *needle* and *sleep.* You might even have made this error yourself as you looked over the test words.

This false memory effect occurs because all the words in the first set are associated with *needle* and all the words in the second set are associated with *sleep.* Hearing each word in the study list excites or activates related words. Because *needle* and *sleep* are related to all the associates, they become more activated than other words — so highly activated that only minutes later, people swear that the experimenter said the word. Could PET scans distinguish between these true and false memories, even though the experimental participants themselves do not?

A few minutes before they entered the scanner, participants in our experiment heard a series of associate lists. Then, during one scan they made recognition judgments about previously presented words, such as *sewing* or *awake,* and during another scan, they made judgments about associated words that had not been presented, like *needle* and *sleep.* As expected, people claimed to remember the nonpresented words almost as often as they claimed to remember the presented ones. Brain activity was, overall, remarkably similar during true and false recognition: a network of regions showed heightened activity regardless of whether people were claiming to remember words they had heard previously or associates they only thought they had heard. The frontal lobes responded very strongly, and there were also signs of activity in the inner parts of the temporal lobe, near the hippocampus, during both true and false recognition.

Because the hippocampus and surrounding areas play such an important role in true memories, we thought that activation in this area during retrieval of a false memory might mislead people into feeling confident of hearing a word that was never actually presented.

But despite the striking similarities between the regions activated during true and false recognition, there were also tantalizing hints of differences. A part of the frontal lobe thought to be involved in scrutinizing or monitoring memories showed greater activity during false than true recognition. It was as if people sensed something odd about words like *sleep* and *needle* and were scrutinizing them especially carefully before capitulating to the powerful memory illusion. There was also more activity during true than false recognition in a part of the temporal lobe on the surface of the left hemisphere — a region that stores the sounds of words. Was the PET scan picking up a faint echo of hearing a word that had actually been presented?

The possibility of using brain imaging to separate truth from fiction — perhaps in a therapist's office or court of law — has a surreal, futuristic appeal. In James Halperin's imaginative novel *The Truth Machine,* brain-scan technology has advanced to the point at which it unfailingly separates truth from deceit. Politicians must now make promises under the watchful eye of the scanner, which will immediately reveal devious intentions (a prospect that was amusing enough in the 1990s but took on then-unimaginable relevance after the 2016 US presidential election; see The Update in Chapter 6). Though telling truth from intentional deceit is different from distinguishing between true and false memories — the liar intends to be deceptive, whereas the faulty rememberer tries to be truthful — the prospect of a "memory truth machine" captured the imagination of the reporters whose phone numbers were plastered across my door. Could we now use PET scans to settle disputes over recovered memories of childhood abuse, where one person vividly remembers horrific abuse and another denies it just as firmly? Could they help to decide whether the memory of an eyewitness is accurate?

These kinds of questions are fascinating, and their potential implications for society are enormous. But our results forced me to throw cold water on speculations about these far-reaching consequences. The similarities between true and false recognition were striking and widespread, the differences small and no more than suggestive. We had used an experimental task whose relation to everyday life is unknown and had looked at only one type of testing condition. We didn't know whether we'd get the same results if we changed any aspect of our procedure. Based on our experiment, brain imaging would not be used soon to decide between true and false memories in the courtroom or anywhere else.

We followed up on our initial findings, and the results justified my caution. Differences in brain activity during true and false recognition turned out to depend on the details of the testing procedure. Because of limits on PET technology, we had to test all previously studied words during one scan, all nonpresented associates of studied words in a second, and unrelated new words in a third. This feature of testing encouraged subjects to scrutinize their memories carefully before responding "old" or "new," because all the words within a particular scan would tend to seem equally familiar (or unfamiliar) to them. We reasoned that such careful scrutiny contributed to the different patterns of brain activity during true and false recognition.

To test this idea, we recorded electrical activity in the brain from various scalp locations using "event-related potentials," which reflect the brain's electrical response to specific sensory stimuli. Event-related potentials offer the ability to track brain activity over just a few thousandths of a second. Unlike PET scanning — which provides a picture of brain activity averaged across a minute or so — the event-related potential technique allows us to mix together studied words, nonpresented associates, and unrelated new words during a single memory test. Under these conditions, previously studied words or associate lures tend to jump out as familiar in comparison to unrelated new words, so people are more likely to make snap judgments about them. With this type of test, we saw no reliable differences in electrical activity during true and false recognition.

These results contain an important positive lesson: test conditions that encourage people to carefully examine their memories broaden differences between true and false memories. Further studies using various procedures for inducing false recognition support this conclusion.

Other researchers have used electrical recordings to examine brain activity during memory conjunction errors (for example, remembering *Spanish* after seeing *spaniel* and *varnish*). Memory conjunction errors occur because people misattribute the strong familiarity elicited by two previously exposed syllables to having seen them together as a single integrated unit. Results suggest that it is possible to tell memory conjunction errors apart from true recollections. Electrical responses differed when college students correctly remembered words that were shown earlier, compared to when they incorrectly claimed to remember totally new words, or "syllable lures" (new words that shared a syllable with a previously studied word, such as *Spanish* after seeing only *varnish*). When students made memory conjunction errors, electrical responses were clearly distinguishable from those associated with accurate remembering, but were indistinguishable from electrical responses that accompanied false alarms to new words or syllable lures.

False alarms were produced by a general sense of familiarity that was strongest for conjunction words and weakest for entirely new words. Conjunction words were, to some extent, just as familiar as the words that were actually presented: in each case, participants had seen both of the word's syllables. But correct "old" responses involved specific recollections of having seen the two syllables together. These detailed memories were associated with very different patterns of electrical activity than were the general feelings of familiarity that misled people to say they had seen the new conjunction words.

Several related studies using electrical recordings or fMRI have also shown that brain activity differs when people call up specific recollections of past experiences compared with when they respond on the basis of general familiarity. Further, people who are highly susceptible to the Deese/Roediger-McDermott memory illusion — they remember falsely as often as they remember accurately — show identical brain electrical activity during true and false memories. But people who are less susceptible to the illusion — they remember accurately more often than they remember falsely — show different patterns of brain activity during accurate and inaccurate remembering.

These results suggest that misattribution can be mitigated by encouraging people to base their memory decisions on specific recollections rather than relying on overall familiarity. In the Deese/Roediger-McDermott procedure, for example, having heard numerous associated words, people may be lulled into basing their memory decisions on whether a test word is strongly associated with previous studied words and thus seems highly familiar, rather than demanding specific recollections.

Lana Israel and I tested this idea by showing people pictures at the same time they heard lists of semantic associates. So, for example, when they heard a list including *butter, flour, milk,* and *dough,* each word was accompanied by a picture — a stick of butter, pile of flour, carton of milk, and ball of dough. Later, we asked participants whether they remembered studied words, like *butter,* and associates that had not been studied, such as *bread.* We thought that the pictures would be so distinctive and memorable that people would later claim to remember having heard a word only when they could also recollect having seen a picture. That is exactly what we found.

Based on several experiments, we hypothesized that studying pictures along with words helped experimental participants to invoke a "distinctiveness heuristic": a rule of thumb that leads people to demand recollections of distinctive details of an experience before they are willing to say that they remember it. Consider the following question: Do you recall that one page earlier in this book I confessed that I suffer from a multiple personality disorder and that I actually have nineteen separate personalities, each with a different name? You can confidently assert that I never said any such thing because you invoke a distinctiveness heuristic: if I had made such a confession one page earlier, you would have been startled; surely you would possess a detailed recollection of what I wrote and how you reacted to it. We can invoke a distinctiveness heuristic whenever we expect that our memories will contain rich and detailed information about an experience. In experiments that use the Deese/Roediger-McDermott word associates procedure, however, people typically do not expect to retrieve distinctive recollections of specific words, and so are misled into falsely recognizing associates that they had never studied. But after studying pictures along with the words, participants expect more from their memories. They easily reject items that do not contain the distinctive pictorial information they are seeking — much as you easily rejected my assertion about multiple personalities.

The distinctiveness heuristic can help older adults to avoid false recognition. Elderly adults are sometimes especially prone to false recognition. They have a harder time than younger adults calling up specific recollections and tend to rely more on general familiarity — a potent combination for producing misattribution. Yet when provided with highly memorable information to study, older adults can invoke a distinctiveness heuristic as effectively as younger adults to reduce false memories.

However, older adults often do not expect to recollect specific details of past experiences; in fact, they may expect to recall little or nothing. Unfortunately, expecting little from their memories can create serious problems for the elderly. As the cognitive psychologist Larry Jacoby has pointed out, con artists know precisely how to exploit this feature of aging memory. Back in the late 1990s, the Cleveland Better Business Bureau warned of a familiar scam called "Where's the Check?" Con artists collect personal information from older adults during a telephone conversation. When they call back the next day, the crooks determine whether the senior has forgotten the conversation, and hence would be likely to forget other events. If so, the con artist makes a false claim about an incident that never occurred, such as, "We received your check for $1,200, but it should only have been for $950. Send us another check for $950, and we'll simply return the first check to you." In another variant, the scam artist asserts, "Our records indicate that you paid $2,400, leaving a balance of only $600. Let's make out a check today to clear the balance." Not remembering the conversation—and not expecting to —many embarrassed seniors send along the check to avoid further problems.

This sad, expensive outcome results from a failure to invoke a distinctiveness heuristic: "If I sent a check for $1,200 or $2,400, I surely would remember it." Because many seniors ordinarily tend to recall relatively little distinctive information about past experiences, some don't expect to remember writing the check and are therefore not surprised when it seems that they've forgotten. Our studies using the Deese/Roediger-McDermott procedure and related tasks show that when armed with specific recollections, older adults can use the distinctiveness heuristic effectively. With the aging of the baby boom generation, growing numbers of people will no doubt become targets of similar frauds that prey on fuzzy memories and low expectations for specific recall. To reduce the vulnerability of an aging population to such scams, it would be worthwhile to try to alter older adults' expectations of their own memories, perhaps by incorporating training into memory courses for senior citizens that explains the distinctiveness heuristic and how to use it effectively.

The good news from our research is that with a little guidance, older adults can guard against false memories by learning to scrutinize their memories carefully in order to avoid distortions and errors.

SEEING FILM STARS EVERYWHERE

When defenses against misattribution are seriously damaged, however, people make bewildering, even bizarre, claims about the past that sever the connection between memory and reality. In 1991, a British photographer in his mid-forties, known in the medical literature by the initials MR, started to have problems with vision and then memory. He had difficulty recalling events from the recent and remote past. More disturbingly, MR experienced intense feelings of familiarity about people he did not know. He began asking his wife regularly whether a passing stranger was "somebody"—a screen actor, television newsperson, or local celebrity. MR became so convinced that his feelings were real that he often could not resist approaching befuddled strangers and asking whether they were indeed famous celebrities. Vexed by the sensation that he was "seeing film stars everywhere," MR sought help from a psychiatrist, who concluded that the false familiarity did not originate from psychological problems.

When given formal tests, MR recognized the faces of actual celebrities as accurately as healthy volunteers. But MR also "recognized" more than three-quarters of unfamiliar faces, whereas healthy controls hardly ever did. Neurological exams revealed that MR had been afflicted by multiple sclerosis. The disease, which attacks the myelin sheath that protects nerve cells, had caused damage in the vicinity of the frontal lobes.

The fact that MR's frontal lobes were compromised by multiple sclerosis provides an important clue to the origin of his unusual disorder (most multiple sclerosis patients are not afflicted with this type of recognition disorder). A similar clue comes from work by the University of Arizona neurologist Steven Rapcsak, who has described patients who falsely recognize new faces after damage to the lower and inner parts of the right frontal lobe.

The damaged frontal regions normally play an important role in assessing or monitoring signals provided by other neural systems. In cases of false facial recognition, brain damage may have resulted in faulty connections between frontal systems and those elsewhere, which seem to be involved in face recognition. The British neuropsychologist Andrew Young has proposed that encountering a familiar face excites a "face recognition unit," containing a description of what the person's face looks like. When activated, this unit sends out signals that we take as a sign that the face is familiar to us. These signals, however, do not provide any details concerning the person's identity. Recall of such information requires activation of a separate "person identity node" (see Chapter 3), which contains details of a person's occupation, interests, background, and related information.

Rapcsak suggests that patients with frontal lobe damage do not sufficiently monitor or scrutinize signals generated by weakly activated face recognition units located elsewhere. Several lines of research indicate that regions near the back of the brain, in the lower parts of the temporal lobe and nearby areas in the occipital lobe, record and retrieve visual descriptions of faces. Single-cell recordings from monkeys, for instance, have revealed "face cells" that respond more strongly to faces than to other objects. And fMRI studies in people have shown something similar. The fusiform gyrus, a key part of the visual regions in the rear of the brain, shows exceptionally strong activity when people look at faces compared to many other kinds of visual objects. Damage to the fusiform gyrus typically results in loss of the ability to recognize well-known faces as familiar.

According to Rapcsak and others, when we encounter a face, the fusiform region becomes highly activated, which excites face recognition units. But because these units contain only visual information, the source of familiarity is left unspecified — we don't know whether the face seems familiar because we have encountered it before or because it resembles other faces we know. For a familiar face, a face recognition unit should excite a related person identity node, allowing us to recall details about the person. Problems arise when a novel face excites a face recognition unit — producing a weak feeling of familiarity — but does not call forth detailed information about the person from a person identity node. Frontal monitoring systems must now intercede and demand recall of person-specific information. The patients with frontal lobe damage studied by Rapcsak and his coworkers failed to engage spontaneously in such monitoring operations, instead blithely accepting signals from an activated face recognition unit as indicators of familiarity. Importantly, Rapcsak was able to reduce false recognition of faces in his patients by requiring them to respond "familiar" only when they could also produce specific information about a person. Because the patients could not produce specific information about unfamiliar faces, they managed to resist the impulse to call the face familiar.

In addition to "seeing film stars everywhere," MR also frequently claimed to recognize made-up names that were constructed to sound like pop stars (Sharon Sugar) or historical figures (Horatio Felles). When asked about the identity of the nonfamous people who seemed so familiar to him, MR could do no better than generic labels: singer, politician, sports star. In striking contrast, however, MR did not falsely recognize made-up place-names: he knew that Jakarta is an actual city and that Wabera is not. Likewise, MR did not falsely recognize such made-up words as *legify* or *florrical*. MR's problems were restricted to recognizing people, suggesting that frontal systems can fail miserably in a specific domain while performing normal monitoring operations in other areas.

We don't precisely understand this phenomenon. However, the finding could illuminate one of the weirdest of all misattributions: the Fregoli delusion. In 1927, the French psychiatrists P. Courbon and G. Fail described a schizophrenic woman who believed she was a "victim of enemies." The patient felt certain that two French actresses were attempting to persecute her. Courbon and Fail named the delusion after the Italian actor Leopoldo Fregoli, who delighted Parisian audiences of the time with his ability to mimic other people. The hallmark of the Fregoli delusion is an unshakable belief that a stranger is "inhabited" by a friend, relative, or famous person. Whereas patients such as MR experience general feelings of false familiarity, Fregoli patients are victimized by specific false memories.

The Fregoli delusion usually occurs in psychiatric patients, but neurologists and neuropsychologists have reported cases in which the delusion occurs after brain injury even when patients do not have a prior psychiatric history. In one case, a twenty-seven-year-old woman from Madeira who was studying English in London suffered a severe head injury when she fell to the road from a bus that unexpectedly moved forward as she was about to exit. Patient IR suffered severe damage to the lower and inner parts of the right frontal lobe —

regions implicated previously in abnormal false recognition — as well as injury to other parts of the frontal cortex. As she was recovering in the hospital, IR became convinced that a female patient in a nearby bed was her mother. The subjective conviction was so powerful that IR attempted to get into bed with the bewildered patient several times and followed her to other parts of the hospital after she was moved. The Fregoli delusion finally subsided after a month, when IR's father confirmed that her mother was in a hospital back home in Madeira. IR had twisted one bit of accurate knowledge — that her mother was in a hospital — into a compelling delusion.

Formal testing showed that IR was plagued by memory problems, from time to time came up with stories or confabulations about events that had never occurred, and even developed a delusion that a young nephew was being cared for elsewhere in the hospital. The researchers who studied IR concluded that part of her problem involved a breakdown in frontal lobe monitoring systems that normally scrutinize memories for plausibility and coherence. IR's difficulties seemed to involve misinterpretation of signals from *particular* person identity nodes. IR did not "see film stars everywhere" but instead became confused about the identity of a specific individual. We still don't know exactly why different patients develop different forms of misattribution, but I suspect that brain imaging techniques will soon help to unravel that.

What a Great Idea I Had: The Perils of Cryptomnesia

William Wallace is a legendary figure in Scottish history. Popularized by Mel Gibson's portrayal in the 1995 film *Braveheart*, Wallace was also the subject of an acclaimed biography authored in the same year by the Scotsman James Mackay. But Mackay's world soon fell apart amid allegations that he had plagiarized large sections of his book from a 1938 biography of Wallace written by the Scottish historian Sir James Fergusson.

"I'm just totally unaware of it, this is purely unconscious, I do assure you," pleaded Mackay. "I have tried always to find new material on the people I've written about." Is it possible to reproduce significant parts of another person's work without being aware of the material's origin? Mackay's plea of unconscious influences should be viewed with some skepticism: he was accused of blatant plagiarism in other books, and the Scottish historian Geoffrey Barrow called his biography of Wallace "the worst case of plagiarism I've seen for quite a while, and maybe even the worst ever." But there is other evidence that people can, in good faith, produce from memory another individual's writings or ideas while unknowingly misattributing these creations to themselves — a type of misattribution known as "cryptomnesia." Cryptomnesia constitutes a mirror image of some of the misattributions considered earlier in the chapter. In false recognition, for example, people misattribute a feeling of familiarity to a novel event, whereas in cryptomnesia, people misattribute novelty to something that should be familiar.

During the early 1900s, the psychoanalyst Carl Jung discovered that Friedrich Nietzsche had taken parts of *Also sprach Zarathustra* from a story he had read in his youth. Nietzsche wrote:

Now about the time that Zarathustra sojourned on the Happy Isles, it happened that a ship anchored at the isle on which the smoking mountain stands, and the crew went ashore to shoot rabbits. About the noontide hour, however, when the captain and his men were together again, they suddenly saw a man coming towards them through the air, and a voice said distinctly: "It is time! It is high time." But when the figure drew close to them, flying past quickly like a shadow in the direction of the volcano, they recognized with the greatest dismay that it was Zarathustra.

Jung noted the resemblance to an old ghost story written by the German physician and poet Justinus Kerner:

The four captains and a merchant, Mr. Bell, went ashore on the island of Mount Stromboli to shoot rabbits. At three o'clock they mustered the crew to go aboard, when, to their inexpressible astonishment, they saw two men flying rapidly towards them through the air . . . They came past them very closely, in the greatest haste, and to their utmost dismay descended amid the burning flames into the crater of the terrible volcano, Mount Stromboli. They recognized the pair as acquaintances from London.

The similarities between the two passages are unmistakable, but Jung concluded that Nietzsche had not intentionally copied Kerner's work; he had simply forgotten the source of his ideas. A remarkable example of unintentional plagiarism came to the fore after George H. Daniels's 1971 book, *Science in American Society,* received a warm review in the journal *Science.* In a letter to *Science,* Daniels wrote that soon after the review appeared, he became aware that parts of the book incorporated quotations from other sources that he had only acknowledged in a general way. "To first cite as a major source the author of a still current book," explained Daniels, "who, in many cases, would be a likely reviewer of my book, and then to deliberately steal from him, would require a degree of naivete much greater than mine." What had happened? Reconstructing his efforts, Daniels wrote, he realized he had memorized and unconsciously reproduced the content of several books; when he thought he was describing them generally he was in fact quoting from them. "I have certainly been aware that I had an extraordinary ability to remember material when I wanted to," Daniels reflected ruefully, "but I have never before realized that I did it unconsciously."

We are all potentially susceptible to cryptomnesia, and in some instances we can catch ourselves in the act. The psychologist Graham Reed describes a time when he woke up in the middle of the night with a catchy tune running through his mind. He excitedly developed the tune the next morning and worked feverishly on it throughout the day. When he thought about a title for his wonderful new creation, Reed realized it already had one — "The Blue Danube," a waltz written by Johann Strauss II! People can even unintentionally "plagiarize" their own ideas. The psychologist B. F. Skinner wrote that "one of the most disheartening experiences of old age is discovering that a point you have just made — so significant, so beautifully expressed — was made by you in something you published a long time ago."

On the face of it, cryptomnesia is difficult to study under controlled conditions: how does an experimenter induce people to unintentionally plagiarize the ideas of others? In 1989, cognitive psychologists Alan Brown and Dana Murphy came up with a procedure for doing so. They asked groups of four people to produce examples from a specified category, one person after another. For example, if the experimenter said "fruit," the group members might say, in turn, "apple," "pear," "orange," and "peach." On a later test, people were required to generate new examples from the same categories that no one in the group had previously mentioned. Despite explicit instructions not to produce what others had said, participants sometimes "plagiarized" answers, such as "apple" or "pear," even though others had previously given them.

Cryptomnesia in this experiment is probably attributable to an unconscious influence of memory known as "priming." When people hear other group members generate such words as *apple* or *pear*, the words become activated, or primed, in memory. The priming persists over time, so that when participants attempt to generate new category members later, the activated words spring to mind easily. Failing to recollect that they previously heard a primed word, people believe that they are producing it for the first time themselves.

Research indicates that cryptomnesia can be reduced by requiring people to pay careful attention to the source of their ideas. The psychologist Richard Marsh asked groups of college students to generate novel solutions to each of two problems: (1) "What are some ways in which the University might be improved?" and (2) "How can the number of traffic accidents be reduced?" Similar to the research described in the previous paragraphs, one group of participants returned a week later and were asked to generate novel solutions that no one in the group had mentioned the week before. Sometimes these students produced ideas that others had suggested the previous week. But when a second group of students returned a week later and tried to generate novel solutions, the researchers explicitly encouraged them to consider carefully whether the idea was new or related in some way to ideas that other group members had proposed the previous week. These students plagiarized less frequently than those in the first group. People sometimes do not spontaneously scrutinize the origins of their ideas, leaving themselves open to the undue influence of priming. Instructions to consider possible origins of an idea can, at least to some extent, override the influence of priming and allow people to take advantage of the information they possess about the source of an idea.

Misattributions in cryptomnesia are produced by two of the same factors that create false recognition: an absence of specific recollections about the source of recalled information, and a failure to carefully consider source information that is potentially available. The resulting misattributions can wreak havoc in everyday life: witness the misguided search for John Doe 2, con artists who exploit the elderly, and the bizarre manifestations of the Fregoli delusion.

Larry Jacoby has noted the similarity between attributions in remembering and those invoked in social situations. In famous experiments conducted by the social psychologist Stanley Schachter, people were injected with adrenaline in a pleasant or a frustrating situation. Subjects in the former group felt happy; those in the latter group became angry. The adrenaline created an ambiguous sense of arousal that people attributed to positive or negative features of the situation. The adrenaline-induced arousal resembles the fluent or speedy mental activity that people sometimes attribute — rightly or wrongly — to a feeling of familiarity rooted in a past experience. Perhaps this sensation is what the French psychiatrist Arnaud had in mind when he tried to explain the peculiar illusion of déjà vu that so often gripped his patient. It was as if Louis received jolts of adrenaline that he struggled to interpret, ultimately attributing them to past experiences that had never occurred.

The odd experiences of a patient like Louis, and the annoying misattributions that happen frequently in everyday life, teach an important lesson about the nature of memory. We often need to sort out ambiguous signals, such as feelings of familiarity or fleeting images, that may originate in specific past experiences or arise from subtle influences in the present. Relying on judgment and reasoning to come up with plausible attributions, we sometimes go astray.

The Update
DÉJÀ VU: FROM PAST TO FUTURE

Most people have experienced déjà vu at least once, but few of us experience it regularly. What would that be like? I began this chapter with Dr. Arnaud's 1896 case report of Louis, which gives a glimpse into a world of perpetual déjà vu. More than a century later, Pat Long, a journalist at the *Times* of London, entered that world after he developed epilepsy as a result of a brain tumor that was eventually removed in 2012. He started to experience déjà vu on a regular basis, as frequently as ten times in a day. Writing about his experience in 2017, Long gave his article a disturbing title: "My Déjà Vu Is So Extreme I Can't Tell What's Real Anymore." Trying to understand the basis of these bewildering experiences is no easy task. As I mentioned at the outset of the chapter, possible explanations of déjà vu abound, including exotic ideas rooted in the paranormal. Yet because of the infrequent occurrence and ephemeral nature of déjà vu, historically it has been difficult for scientists to evoke and study it systematically. Happily, that has begun to change over the past decade.

Some of the most innovative research has been conducted by the cognitive psychologist Anne Cleary and her colleagues. Cleary has attempted to test a long-standing idea about déjà vu: the compelling sense of familiarity that characterizes the experience reflects memory for a similar or related experience. If I go to a newly opened restaurant for the first time and am suddenly gripped by the sensation that I've been there before, maybe I have been to a restaurant with a similar arrangement of tables, but I've never been to *this* restaurant. To test the idea, Cleary first presented participants with pictures of everyday scenes, such as a bathroom. She later showed them novel scenes that had a similar or dissimilar configuration of elements and asked whether they could recall a related scene that they had seen earlier. When participants failed to recall the original scene, they were more likely to report an experience of déjà vu to a configurally similar novel scene than to a configurally dissimilar novel scene. Cleary and her collaborators then developed a more lifelike virtual reality video version of this procedure in which people explored a virtual environment, such as a hedge garden, comprising a sequence of turns. In the test phase, they saw novel scenes that were configurally similar or dissimilar to the scenes they had encountered during their virtual exploration. Once again, when they did not recall the original scene, they were more likely to report déjà vu to a configurally similar than to a configurally dissimilar scene.

In their most recent version of this procedure, Cleary and her colleague Alexander Claxton looked into one of the most fascinating subjective aspects of déjà vu: the feeling that we know what is going to happen next. Pat Long called this a feeling of "precognition" and experienced it so intensely that he had difficulty telling the difference between real events and illusory ones. In an extension of the virtual reality video paradigm, Cleary told participants as they viewed novel scenes: "Without knowing why, you may also feel a sense of which way to turn next. Indicate which way to turn. Press L for Left and R for Right." Strikingly, she found that participants claimed to have a feeling of which way to turn more frequently when they reported an experience of déjà vu to a novel, configurally similar scene than when they did not report an experience of déjà vu to this kind of scene. But did they actually know which way to turn? Absolutely not: participants could not predict with above-chance accuracy what the next turn would be, despite their conviction that they knew it. So déjà vu isn't just a misattribution about what happened in the past, it's also an illusion about what's going to happen in the future. As I discuss in The Update in Chapter 8 concerning whether the seven sins are vices or virtues, the link between past and future has become increasingly prominent in memory research during the past decade and may provide key insights into adaptive aspects of memory errors.

HAVE WE FOUND THE TRUTH MACHINE YET?

When we published our first study using brain scanning to distinguish true from false memories back in 1996, my colleagues and I were excited that we could see neural differences between the two. As discussed earlier in this chapter, we soon learned that our success depended on the design details of our experimental procedure: different procedures yielded different results. Now, more than two decades on from that first study, have we come any closer to finding a "memory truth machine"? Yes and no.

Dozens of studies, most of them using ever more sophisticated fMRI procedures and analysis techniques, have attempted to distinguish between actual memories and illusory ones. And we've made some progress toward that goal. For example, in 2004 the cognitive neuroscientist Scott Slotnick and I published the results of fMRI experiments in which participants viewed drawings of novel shapes composed of lines and colors that were variations on visually similar prototype shapes the participants had never seen. When given a recognition memory test in the scanner after studying many similar novel shapes, people correctly recognized most of the shapes they had seen earlier—but almost as often, they incorrectly claimed that they had seen a nonpresented prototype. (In contrast, people had little difficulty correctly responding that they had never seen nonpresented shapes that were visually dissimilar to the studied ones.) Even though many of the same brain regions showed similar levels of activity during true and false recognition, there was greater activity in several areas of the visual cortex when people correctly recognized shapes they had actually seen compared with when they falsely recognized prototypes they hadn't seen. These findings suggest that sensory reactivation could be responsible for this difference: that is, areas in the visual cortex that initially encoded specific features of studied shapes were reactivated by those features on the recognition test, but sensory reactivation occurred to a much lesser extent for nonstudied prototype shapes.

After the publication of our paper, subsequent experiments from my lab and others provided more evidence that this kind of neural sensory reactivation can distinguish true from false memories in other experimental paradigms. And sensory reactivation isn't the only way that fMRI can tell the difference between true and false memories. For example, a review of the combined results of numerous fMRI studies revealed that areas within the frontal lobe are consistently more strongly engaged during the retrieval of false memories than true memories. These results are exciting, and they reflect hard-earned progress in the quest for what at one time seemed a fanciful notion of an fMRI truth machine. But does this mean that we are ready to bring fMRI into the courtroom to help determine, for example, whether an eyewitness identification is accurate or an alleged victim is recalling a crime correctly? Not so fast.

One problem is that fMRI evidence for distinguishing true from false memories is the product of averaging across both *items* (e.g., many novel shapes) and *participants* (most fMRI studies now use groups of twenty to forty participants). Researchers use averaging in an attempt to boost the strength of the fMRI signal. In the courtroom, however, we need to determine the objective memory status of a *single event* in a *single person,* and we don't yet have evidence that any fMRI truth machine is up to that task.

But we are making some progress toward that goal. A promising technique that has become increasingly popular in fMRI research involves training a "pattern classifier" to "decode" a person's mental state. For example, in a study of face recognition, the cognitive neuroscientists Jesse Rissman and Anthony Wagner fed a pattern classifier large amounts of data regarding both brain activity associated with successful recognition of a recently seen face and brain activity associated with a failure to recognize a recently seen face.

The next question was whether, armed with this information, the classifier could determine whether a *single participant* subjectively recognized a *single face* on which the classifier had not been explicitly trained. The answer was yes: the pattern classifier could reliably decode whether or not a person *believed* that they were remembering a previously encountered face.

That's very impressive, but could the classifier also tell whether a person had *actually* seen a specific face, regardless of what the person believed? There was little evidence that it could. However, to distinguish a true from a false memory for a single event, a classifier would have to be able to determine the objective status of the memory. We don't have evidence yet that this feat can be achieved convincingly for a single event in a single person. Still, research using pattern classifiers is progressing rapidly, and there is a growing emphasis in the field on using data from individuals rather than group averages. These trends provide reasons for optimism that an eventual fMRI truth machine is not just a flight of fancy.

Nonetheless, problems remain. For example, lab studies of true and false memories typically require people to remember shapes and word lists, but we don't know whether results obtained with these kinds of materials apply to the rich, multimodal experiences that occur in everyday life outside the lab. Neuroimaging research, including work from my own lab, has increasingly focused on examining brain activity associated with everyday experiences outside the lab, but more of this kind of work will be needed before we can apply fMRI to true and false memories in the courtroom.

Even if these limitations can be overcome, couldn't people use strategic countermeasures in an attempt to "beat the test"? Consider a 2015 study that employed a version of the face recognition paradigm developed by Rissman and his colleagues. The researchers instructed participants to respond truthfully to some faces and to use countermeasures when responding to others. They used two kinds of countermeasures. First, when participants believed they had seen a face earlier, they were instructed to call the face "new" (a lie) and to focus on features of the face, such as exposure and lighting, that they had not attended to previously. The idea here was to enhance the brain's novelty response and thus hide the participants' experience of remembering. Second, when participants believed they had not seen a face earlier, they were instructed to call the face "old" (another lie) and to dredge up personal memories related to someone they knew who looked like the target face. The idea was that this memory would mislead the pattern classifier into determining that the participant had actually seen the novel face. Both countermeasures worked: when people used them, the classifier failed to decode memories that it could successfully decode when people responded truthfully.

What does this all mean? We've made advances in understanding the neural basis of misattribution during the past two decades, but we need to make a lot more progress before we can apply this understanding to decoding specific memories in the courtroom. Evidence on wrongful convictions, extreme déjà vu, cryptomnesia, and other examples considered in this chapter highlight the fact that misattribution can create significant problems in everyday life. In addition, when misattribution combines with another of memory's sins — suggestibility — people can develop detailed and strongly held recollections of complex events that never occurred. Beginning in the 1990s, such recollections were linked with deeply troubling events concerning eyewitnesses in court cases, false memories of childhood sexual abuse, and abuse allegations against daycare centers and preschools. The resulting shock waves fractured families and shattered lives.

5
The Sin of Suggestibility

SHORTLY AFTER AN El Al cargo plane took off from Schiphol Airport in Amsterdam on October 4, 1992, two engines failed and the pilots attempted to return to the airport. They never made it back: the plane crashed into an eleven-story apartment building in a southern suburb, killing thirty-nine residents and all four members of the airline crew. Reporters and television cameras descended on the chaotic scene, and the tragedy dominated news in the Netherlands for days. People throughout the country saw, read, heard, and talked about the catastrophe.

Ten months later, a group of Dutch psychologists probed what members of their university communities remembered about the crash. The researchers asked a simple question: "Did you see the television film of the moment the plane hit the apartment building?" Fifty-five percent of respondents said "yes." In a follow-up study, two-thirds of the participants responded affirmatively. They also recalled details concerning the speed and angle of the plane as it hit the building, whether it was on fire prior to impact, and what happened to the body of the plane right after the collision. These findings are remarkable because there was no television film of the moment when the plane actually crashed.

The psychologists had asked a blatantly suggestive question: they implied that television film of the crash had been shown. Respondents may have viewed television footage of the postcrash scene, and they probably read, imagined, or talked about what might have happened at the moment of impact. Spurred on by the suggestive question, participants misattributed information from these or other sources to a film that they never watched.

In 1997, a PBS television audience watching a *Scientific American Frontiers* documentary on memory hosted by Alan Alda learned that something similar can result from a seemingly innocent everyday activity: looking at photographs. In collaboration with the show's producers, I devised a memory experiment based on my laboratory's research; Alda was the naive but willing subject. We met at a park in Brookline, Massachusetts, on a sunny fall morning; the camera rolled as we sat on a bench in front of a young man and woman about to begin a staged picnic. Alda knew they were actors and suspected that his memory would be tested. He paid close attention as the pair enjoyed a drink, put on sunscreen, combed their hair, ate a sandwich, took a picture, and did various other things that people would be more or less likely to do while enjoying a picnic on a beautiful day.

Two days later, we met in my Harvard office. I showed photographs of the bucolic scene to Alda, asking him only to judge the aesthetic quality of each one. He quickly sensed that I was up to something. When he saw a photo of the actors eating potato chips — and failed to remember any potato chips at the picnic — he identified the experiment's key feature. Some photos showed events that had actually occurred at the picnic, whereas others were visual suggestions: they showed actions that might have happened but did not. He wondered aloud whether we had set out to play tricks on his memory.

After finishing up with the photos, I told Alda that I was going to read out loud a series of objects and actions and instructed him to say "yes" when he remembered an item from the picnic. He had to be careful, I warned, because — just as he suspected — some of the items had appeared only in the photos he had just seen and were not part of the actual picnic. Despite his skepticism and generally accurate memory, Alda soon stumbled: he claimed to remember seeing the young woman file her nails at the picnic, but she had done so only in a photo he had seen minutes earlier. He stumbled again moments later when he recalled a bottle of water at the picnic that had appeared only in a photo. Alda accepted his erroneous recollection with characteristic good humor, and I assured him that his experience was common.

Suggestibility in memory refers to an individual's tendency to incorporate misleading information from external sources — other people, written materials or pictures, even the media — into personal recollections. Suggestibility is closely related to misattribution in the sense that the conversion of suggestions into inaccurate memories must involve misattribution. However, misattribution often occurs in the absence of overt suggestion, making suggestibility a distinct sin of memory.

Suggested memories can seem as real as genuine ones. On May 31, 2000, a front-page story in the *New York Times* described the baffling case of Edward Daly, a Korean War veteran who made up elaborate — but imaginary — stories about his battle exploits, including his involvement in a terrible massacre in which he had not actually participated. While weaving his delusional tale, Daly talked to veterans who had participated in the massacre and "reminded" them of his heroic deeds. His suggestions infiltrated their memories. "I know that Daly was there," pleaded one veteran. "I know that. I know that."

Suggestibility is worrying for multiple reasons: leading questions can contribute to eyewitness misidentifications; suggestive psychotherapeutic procedures may foster the creation of false memories; and aggressive interviewing of preschool children can result in distorted memories of alleged abuses by teachers and others. The stakes are high in these cases, so understanding and countering suggestibility is just as important for addressing social and legal concerns as it is for furthering psychological theory.

Influencing Eyewitnesses

In the Dutch study of El Al crash memories, researchers provided factually incorrect information regarding the existence of film that captured the plane colliding with an apartment building. In so doing, they followed a procedure pioneered by the University of Washington psychologist Elizabeth Loftus that has since been used in numerous laboratory studies. People first witness an everyday event on slides or videotape, then answer a question containing misleading suggestions about the event, and finally take a memory test that probes their recollections of the original incident. For example, in a study by the psychologist Philip Higham, participants viewed videotape of a staged robbery at a convenience store. They were then given misleading suggestions about an item of clothing worn by the store attendant and later tried to remember the attendant's clothing and other details of the scene.

Describing the procedure to a psychology class from his own memory, a research student who had helped to carry out the project explained that in the video the attendant wears a white apron. He confidently elaborated on the details of his recollection to convey to the students exactly what happened. Much to his shock, the student soon discovered that he had unwittingly demonstrated the power of the effect he was investigating. The attendant did not wear a white apron in the video; it had been suggested later by the experimenter.

Previous experiments had shown that suggestive questions produce memory distortion by creating source memory problems like those in the previous chapter: participants misattribute information presented only in suggestive questions about the original video. Higham's results provide an additional twist. He found that when people took a memory test just minutes after receiving the misleading question, and thus still correctly recalled that the "white apron" was suggested by the experimenter, they sometimes insisted nevertheless that the attendant wore a white apron in the video itself. In fact, they made this mistake just as often as people who took the memory test two days after receiving misleading suggestions, and who had more time to forget that the white apron was merely suggested. The findings testify to the power of misleading suggestions: they can create false memories of an event even when people recall that the misinformation was suggested.

The results have potentially important implications for police interrogations of eyewitnesses because they imply that when suggestive questioning is used, memories for an original event may be altered even when people realize that the interrogator mentioned a critical bit of information. Although few data are available regarding the extent of suggestive questioning of eyewitnesses, a British study using actual interviews indicates that approximately one of every six questions that police posed to eyewitnesses was in some way suggestive.

In the numerous misinformation studies based on the work of Elizabeth Loftus, memory distortion results from suggestions that provide blatantly inaccurate information, such as a nonexistent white apron. But even more subtle suggestions that do not contain specific inaccuracies can also influence eyewitness testimony. Consider this excerpt from a Missouri case:

EYEWITNESS TO A CRIME ON VIEWING A LINEUP: Oh, my God . . . I don't know . . . It's one of those two . . . but I don't know . . . Oh, man . . . the guy a little bit taller than number two . . . It's one of those two, but I don't know.

EYEWITNESS THIRTY MINUTES LATER, still viewing the lineup and having difficulty making a decision: I don't know . . . number two?

OFFICER ADMINISTERING LINEUP: Okay.

DEFENSE ATTORNEY, MONTHS LATER . . . AT TRIAL: You were positive it was number two? It wasn't a maybe?

EYEWITNESS: There was no maybe about it . . . I was absolutely positive.

The eyewitness spent about thirty minutes viewing a lineup of four people while trying to identify her attacker from among them. She expressed considerable doubt while making her choice, but later at trial disavowed that she had experienced even a hint of uncertainty. The psychologist Gary Wells wondered whether confirming feedback from the administering officer — simply saying "okay" — served as a suggestive procedure, increasing the witness's confidence in her memory. If so, the implications for courtroom testimony would be significant: an eyewitness's level of confidence is the single most important determinant of whether a jury believes that the witness has identified a suspect correctly. When confronted with a highly confident eyewitness, juries tend to focus more on that person's believability than on the original witnessing conditions that may have made it difficult for the witness to perceive or identify the perpetrator. Even though juries believe confident witnesses more than uncertain ones, and a growing body of research indicates that confidence can be a highly reliable indicator of the accuracy of a memory, there are also conditions in which eyewitness confidence bears a tenuous link to eyewitness accuracy. To make matters worse, eyewitness confidence can be inflated when a witness is told that another witness identified the same suspect, or when witnesses rehearse their testimony repeatedly during trial preparations. Clearly, eyewitness confidence is not set in stone at the time an event occurs. But is it so malleable that seemingly innocuous confirming feedback—a mere "okay"—can inflate it significantly?

To find out, Wells and Amy Bradfield showed people a security video in which a man enters a Target store, and told them that in the moments following the scene they witnessed, the man murdered a security guard. The subjects then tried to identify the gunman from a set of photos—even though the actual gunman did not appear in any of the photos. Some participants received confirming feedback: "Good, you identified the actual suspect." Others received no feedback, and still others received disconfirming feedback that the suspect was in one of the photos they had not selected. Finally, all subjects assessed how well they had been able to view the suspect and evaluated the certainty, clarity, and other features of their memories.

Compared with those who received disconfirming or no feedback, people who received confirming feedback claimed higher confidence and trust in their memories, a better view and clearer recollection of the gunman, and heightened recall of facial details. There was, of course, no basis for these claims: subjects in all three conditions had the same opportunity to perceive and remember the gunman. Despite the fact that the witnesses were dead wrong, their confident assertions of a good initial view of the suspect and a clear, detailed recollection would have been extremely convincing to a jury.

These findings are especially important in light of the legal criteria for evaluating the validity of eyewitness reports. Faced with evidence that suggestive questioning could influence eyewitness testimony, in 1972 the Supreme Court ruled in *Neil v. Biggers* that such procedures do not necessarily disqualify an eyewitness account if there are grounds to believe that the report is fundamentally accurate. The Biggers criteria hold that the probable accuracy of an eyewitness account depends on the witness's certainty, ability to describe the suspect, and initial opportunity to view and pay attention to a crime (as well as on the amount of time between the incident and attempted identification). As Wells and Bradfield point out, however, their results show that confirming feedback, for instance, can influence several of the very criteria used to evaluate the credibility of evidence obtained with suggestive procedures, creating a type of Catch-22:

> An argument that the use of feedback is suggestive would not result in a successful motion to suppress the evidence because the eyewitness is certain, claims to have had a good view, and so on. Of course, the eyewitness is certain, claims to have had a good view, and so on because of the suggestive procedure, but the Biggers criteria do not allow for such an analysis . . . Arguing that a suggestive procedure is not a problem because of the eyewitness's high standing on the Biggers criteria is a bit like arguing that a forensic DNA procedure that contaminated the suspect's blood with the sample at the crime scene is not a problem because the lab results show that the match is virtually perfect.

In light of Wells and Bradford's results and the court's reliance on the Biggers criteria, it is difficult to overemphasize the importance of limiting suggestive procedures during police interviews.

But suggestibility is not the only concern that police confront when interviewing an eyewitness: they want to elicit as much accurate information as possible. To improve eyewitness recall, some police professionals advocate the use of hypnosis. The hypnotist uses an induction technique that directs the subject to relax and concentrate on a specific object or activity: staring at a picture on the wall while experiencing the sensation that one's eyelids are becoming heavy, or imagining oneself lying on a warm beach. Once a sufficiently deep hypnotic state has been established, the hypnotist attempts to prod recall by asking the subject to go back in time and reexperience the original event, or perhaps imagine a giant television screen that depicts the incident they witnessed.

Hypnotic procedures sometimes produce spectacular outcomes in actual crimes. One of the most impressive occurred in the 1976 kidnapping of twenty-six children and their bus driver in Chowchilla, California. Three masked men hijacked the bus at gunpoint, took the children and the driver to a quarry, and buried them six feet underground. After the children and driver miraculously escaped, FBI agents tried unsuccessfully to obtain information from them about the kidnappers. The bus driver then submitted to a hypnotic interview and recalled correctly five of six numbers from the license plate of the kidnappers' van. This crucial information ultimately led to the arrest and conviction of all three criminals.

Despite this and other impressive successes, the status of testimony obtained through the use of hypnosis remains controversial. Hypnotic procedures frequently elicit inaccurate reports and sometimes amplify the suggestive effects of misleading information. Reviews of the scientific literature have turned up little or no evidence that hypnosis reliably enhances the accuracy of eyewitness memory. But hypnosis can bolster witness confidence. In view of its potentially powerful impact on juries, the specter of confident — but inaccurate — testimony from a witness who had been hypnotized continues to be a source of grave concern.

Advocates of hypnotically aided testimony, such as the forensic psychologist Martin Reiser, highlight dramatic successes and point

out that hypnosis does not invariably lead to heightened suggestibility. And, indeed, if an investigation is stalled and other procedures
have failed, hypnosis might be useful for obtaining leads that can
be subsequently checked by independent evidence. Hypnosis can
also serve as a kind of "face-saving" device. Sometimes witnesses
are initially reluctant to provide information for fear of reprisals or
personal embarrassment. If they later change their minds but want
to avoid admitting having lied earlier, they can "recover" a memory
through hypnosis. Indeed, such face-saving incidents could account
for some of the apparent successes of hypnotic interviews.

Because of problems with hypnotically aided testimony, researchers have sought to develop other procedures for increasing
the retrieval of accurate information from eyewitnesses without
also increasing suggestibility. One effective approach is known as
the "Cognitive Interview." Developed initially in the 1980s by the
cognitive psychologists Ronald Fisher and Edward Geiselman, the
Cognitive Interview is based on findings and ideas established in
controlled studies of memory and specifically avoids the use of suggestive or leading questions. The original Cognitive Interview included four components. The first involves asking a witness to try
to report everything about the relevant incident, important because
police often ask highly specific questions that do not maximize witness recall, such as "What color was his shirt?" instead of "Describe
your attacker." To stimulate recall of details that may not be retrieved
initially, a second component of the Cognitive Interview requires the
witness to try to reinstate mentally the context or setting in which
the incident occurred. Numerous laboratory studies have shown that
such mental reinstatement of context can enhance memory retrieval.
Third, witnesses are asked to try to recall events in different temporal
orders: starting at the beginning and proceeding to the end, and vice
versa. This procedure, too, has yielded improved recall in controlled
studies. Finally, witnesses are asked to try to take different perspectives on an event, such as mentally viewing the event from the perspective of the perpetrator or the victim, to help them notice fea-

tures of the incident that they otherwise might have overlooked. In the early 1990s, these four cognitive procedures were supplemented with procedures that foster social interaction and communication between the interviewer and the witness.

Many experiments have compared the Cognitive Interview to standard police interviewing techniques. Virtually all of them find that the Cognitive Interview yields significant — and sometimes extremely large — gains in witness recall. These effects have been observed with various types of interviewers, ranging from novice college students to experienced police officers, and with different types of witnesses, including a range of adults, elderly individuals, and children.

As with hypnosis, however, the Cognitive Interview can yield greater reporting of inaccurate information. But the amount of inaccurate information is typically small — many studies find no sign of it at all — and there is no evidence that the Cognitive Interview reduces eyewitness accuracy. Because the results so far indicate that the Cognitive Interview raises recall without a corresponding increase in suggestibility, many police — including all police forces in England and Wales — receive training in the Cognitive Interview and use it routinely when interrogating witnesses. Further, several features of the Cognitive Interview are included in the guidelines for collecting eyewitness evidence developed by former attorney general Janet Reno's working group in the 1990s (see Chapter 4).

Suggestibility is also a concern in relation to a highly disturbing outcome of some police interrogations: false confessions. Some false confessions occur because suspects wish to terminate mental or physical abuse even though they know they did not commit a crime; others happen spontaneously, without coercion, and may reflect attention seeking or related pathology. But in a subset of false confessions — nobody knows exactly how many — people develop the false belief that they committed a crime. The Harvard professor Hugo Munsterberg was the first psychologist to call attention to this latter type of false confession. In his classic 1908 book, *On the Witness*

Stand, Munsterberg observed that emotional stress, combined with social pressure and suggestion, could distort memory to the point that people falsely believe they have committed a crime.

False confessions by political prisoners were widespread in the Soviet Union during the heyday of totalitarian rule. "The Communists are skilled in the extraction of information from prisoners and in making prisoners do their bidding," observed the authors of a 1956 article on Communist interrogation techniques. "It has appeared that they can force men to confess to crimes which they have not committed, and then, apparently, to believe in the truth of their confessions and express sympathy and gratitude toward those who have imprisoned them."

Even in modern Western societies, people continue to make false confessions in which they mistakenly believe in their own guilt. In a bizarre case reported in the 1970s, Peter Reilly came home to discover the body of his murdered mother. He immediately notified the police, who identified him as a suspect and administered a polygraph test, which Reilly failed. Though initially he denied the murder, Reilly eventually became convinced that he must have committed the crime and signed a written confession. Two years later, he was exonerated by new evidence showing that he could not have murdered his mother.

Reilly's experience illustrates what the clinical psychologist Gisli Gudjonsson calls a "memory distrust syndrome." Although Reilly did not develop detailed recollections of having committed murder, in the face of coercive questioning by police he began to distrust his own memory and eventually disregarded it entirely. To abandon trust in his memory for such a grisly event — more precisely, in his failure to recollect the murder — Reilly would have had to abandon the memory monitoring strategy called the "distinctiveness heuristic": expecting to remember distinct details of an experience (see Chapter 4). Normally, someone who participated in a horrific event such as murdering his own mother would surely expect to remember the incident. The memory distrust syndrome can develop when it is plausible that one might forget even a violent crime — perhaps when a person is intoxicated or believes he could have repressed a horrendous event. When somebody no longer expects to remember an event clearly, it is easier to distrust memory.

In some instances of false confessions, suspects initially believe in their own innocence, but in the course of suggestive police questioning, they may eventually develop specific recollections of a crime they did not commit. In a highly publicized case from the mid-1990s, the Washington State sheriff's deputy Paul Ingram confessed to the sexual abuse of his two daughters and participation in a bizarre cult that included satanic rituals, animal sacrifices, and the murder of babies. In response to coercion and bullying from local police officers, Ingram had reported full-blown "memories" of these ghastly activities — memories that he came to believe he had previously repressed. Even though no hard evidence for any of the confessed activities was ever produced and Ingram eventually retracted his confession, he was sent to prison and served time until his release in 2003.

Coercive questioning by police is frequently involved in false confessions. Gisli Gudjonsson and associates in London described the bizarre conclusion of a case involving a seventeen-year-old man who had been routinely interviewed by police in connection with the investigation of a brutal murder. He became preoccupied with "visions" of the victim's face and began to wonder whether he had committed the crime. The young man turned himself in to police voluntarily, initially stating that "it might have been me," but that "I don't know if I killed her or not. I keep seeing her." During the course of the next twenty-four hours, he developed the belief that "I must have done it because I can see a picture of her," and then finally asserted with conviction that "I am sure I killed her . . . I know I did it." Although there was no other evidence to support this claim, the man was imprisoned on the basis of his written confession. He served twenty-five years of his sentence before new evidence led to a reversal of his conviction.

This latter case raises the possibility that some individuals may be especially prone to false confessions because they are easily suggestible. Gudjonsson has developed a scale for measuring individual differences in what he calls "interrogative suggestibility": the tendency to change claims about the past in response to misleading information and suggestive questions. Gudjonsson found that people who had made a criminal confession that they later retracted were more influenced by suggestive questions than "deniers" who steadfastly refused to acknowledge any involvement in a crime despite forensic evidence against them. The memory performance of the two groups on standard clinical tests did not differ.

It is still hard to fathom how anyone could admit to carrying out an act — much less a violent crime — that he or she did not commit. The memory sins considered earlier in the book — transience, absent-mindedness, blocking, and some types of misattribution — are so familiar from our daily experience that we can relate to them all too easily. But the kind of suggestibility involved in false confessions is alien to the realities of everyday remembering and forgetting. Not surprisingly, mock juries are highly skeptical of the possibility that people would ever confess to crimes they did not commit.

Experiments by Saul Kassin and his colleagues showed that false confessions may not be as aberrant as they first seem. College students seated at a computer were instructed to type in a series of spoken letters — one group typed at a hurried pace, another at a more leisurely rate. All of the students had been instructed not to press the Alt key because it would cause the program to crash. None of the students actually hit the Alt key, but the experimenter falsely accused them of doing so. After denying the charge, half the students in each group heard a confederate "witness" say that she saw the error; there was no witness for the other students. Nearly 70 percent of the students eventually signed a false confession that they had hit the Alt key. The effect was particularly striking in the group that had typed quickly and also heard a witness back up the experimenter: all of them signed the confession, and 35 percent produced a detailed false recollection of how they had made the error.

Kassin's results are troubling, because they suggest that under the right conditions many of us can be induced to confess to an act that we never performed. Of course, people may not expect to remember hitting the Alt key on a computer, whereas they would ordinarily expect to remember committing a violent crime. It may be relatively easier to make people confess to hitting the Alt key than to committing a crime because they are less likely in the experimental situation to invoke the distinctiveness heuristic: "If I committed this act, I surely would remember it." This interpretation is supported by the finding that false confession was especially common in people who typed rapidly during the initial task. These individuals probably expected less from their memories than those who typed more slowly, perhaps reasoning that because they typed so quickly, they were likely to make a mistake and unlikely initially to remember doing so.

The consequences of suggestibility in eyewitness testimony and police interrogation can be shattering, but its harmful effects are not confined to these public arenas. Suggestibility can even shape recollections of the mostly intensely personal and private aspects of our pasts.

THE RISE AND FALL OF FALSE MEMORY SYNDROME

In 1992, a group of alarmed middle-aged adults formed the first organization ever dedicated to the topic of memory distortion: the False Memory Syndrome Foundation. Comprised mainly of parents in the midst of disturbing conflicts with their adult daughters, the early members of the foundation told stories that seemed shocking at the time but became numbingly familiar as the 1990s progressed. Educated and intelligent middle-class women entered psychotherapy for depression or related problems, only to emerge with recovered memories of previously forgotten childhood sexual abuse, typically perpetrated by fathers and sometimes by mothers. The parents who formed the foundation, and many others like them, angrily disputed the validity of the memories their children embraced. Accusers and their supporters castigated the parents for denying a reality they could not accept.

As I mentioned in Chapter 3, some recovered memories of childhood abuse that people had not thought about for years have been corroborated and appear to be accurate. But when the crisis first boiled over in 1992, many professionals and accused parents were quick to blame an alleged epidemic of false memories on suggestive techniques used by some psychotherapists — hypnosis, guided imagery exercises where people imagine possible abuse scenarios, and the like — to call up supposedly forgotten traumas. As the 1990s unfolded, several kinds of evidence indicated that many recovered memories are inaccurate: implausible recollections of bizarre practices in satanic cults whose existence was never documented; the lack of scientific support for commonly used memory recovery techniques; and a steadily increasing number of women who retracted their memories. Early on, however, memory researchers were roped into the fray as potential arbiters of the reality of recovered memories. Many pressing questions required solid scientific answers: Is it possible to create false memories of traumatic autobiographical events? What kinds of techniques are most likely to promote illusory recollections? Are certain kinds of people especially susceptible to implantation of memories for events that never happened?

In the early 1990s, memory researchers did not have good answers to these questions. Psychologists knew in general terms that memory is suggestible, but for the most part they had to rely on evidence from such experimental techniques as those pioneered by Elizabeth Loftus, in which suggested details of an event seep into the recollections of eyewitnesses. Critics objected — and rightly so — that these kinds of suggested memories involve little more than the minutiae of an experience; they do not demonstrate or imply that people can develop full-blown false recollections of a trauma such as sexual abuse. Memory researchers, the critics contended, would have to do far better before their findings could inform the ongoing debate. And they did. In an ironic contrast to its devastating effects on families, and the bitter divisions it produced within psychology and psychiatry, the recovered memories debate had a salutary effect on memory research by stimulating a new wave of studies on suggestibility.

Appropriately enough, Elizabeth Loftus — a pivotal figure in earlier suggestibility studies and a lightning rod in the recovered memories debate — reported one of the first attempts to implant experimentally a mildly traumatic autobiographical incident. In what came to be known as the "lost in the mall" study, a teenager named Chris was asked by his older brother Jim to try to remember the time Chris had been lost in a shopping mall at age five. He initially recalled nothing, but after several days Chris produced a detailed recollection of the event. The study achieved instant notoriety because, according to Jim and other family members, Chris never was lost in a shopping mall. Following up with a larger group of twenty-four participants, Loftus documented that after several probing interviews, approximately one-quarter of the participants falsely remembered being lost as a child in a shopping mall or a similar public place.

The psychologist Ira Hyman and his group at Western Washington University successfully implanted false memories of other childhood experiences in a significant minority of participants in their experiments. Hyman asked college students about various childhood experiences that, according to their parents, had actually happened. He also asked them about a false event that, their parents confirmed, had never happened. For instance, students were asked: "When you were five you were at the wedding reception of some friends of the family and you were running around with some other kids, when you bumped into the table and spilled the punch bowl on the parents of the bride." Participants accurately remembered almost all of the true events but initially reported no memory for the false events. However, approximately 20 to 40 percent of participants in different experimental conditions eventually came to describe some memory of the false events in later interviews. In one experiment, more than half of the participants who produced false memories described them as "clear" recollections that included specific details of the central event, such as remembering exactly where or how they spilled the punch. Just under half reported "partial" false memories, which included some details but no specific memory of the central event.

Hyman's results implicate visual imagery as a culprit in suggested memories. People in his studies who produced false memories of childhood experiences scored higher on scales that measure vividness of visual imagery than did individuals whose recollections were more accurate. Further, when Hyman and associates specifically instructed people to try to imagine an event if they could not recall it initially, they found more false memories compared with when participants were allowed to sit quietly and think about whether the event had occurred. These results make sense in light of other evidence that true recollections of actual events are often characterized by rich and detailed visual imagery. If imagery is a kind of mental signature of true recollections, then embellishing a false memory with vivid mental images should make it look and feel like a true memory.

In collaborative work with Elizabeth Loftus, the Italian psychologist Giuliana Mazzoni asked whether another type of suggestive procedure can produce false memories: dream interpretation. Some therapists use their patients' dreams to make inferences about what happened to them in the past. Could dream interpretation help to create, rather than reveal, past experiences? To find out, Mazzoni and Loftus asked people to rate their confidence that various kinds of experiences had or had not happened to them. One group then participated in an ostensibly unrelated task two weeks later in which a clinical psychologist interpreted their dreams. The psychologist suggested to them that their dreams included repressed memories of events that had happened to them before the age of three — upsetting experiences such as being abandoned by parents, getting lost in a public place, or being lonely and lost in unfamiliar surroundings. The participants previously indicated that such events had never happened to them. Nonetheless, when they were again asked about early experiences two weeks after having their dreams interpreted, the majority now claimed to remember one or more of the three suggested experiences for which they had previously denied any memory. Nothing of the sort was found in a control group that did not receive any suggestions regarding their dreams.

The kinds of events falsely recollected in the studies by Loftus, Mazzoni, and Hyman are sometimes mildly upsetting but do not involve serious trauma. Additional experiments obtained similar results with more disturbing events. Using procedures like those reported by Hyman, the Canadian psychologist Stephen Porter and his coworkers successfully implanted false childhood memories of a serious animal attack, serious outdoor accident, and serious harm perpetrated by another child in approximately one-third of the college students in their experiments. Of course, there may be limits to the kinds of memories that can be successfully suggested. In one study, for example, 15 percent of participants generated false recollections of being lost in a shopping mall, but none generated false memories of a childhood enema.

Still, it's hard not to be impressed by just how many different kinds of memories can be suggested. Consider, for instance, your very earliest recollection: What is the first thing you can recall from childhood? The psychoanalyst Alfred Adler believed that earliest memories have great psychological significance, providing important insights into the very core of an individual's personality. For most of us, earliest memories date from three to five years of age; there is no evidence that people can remember incidents that occurred before they were two years old, most likely because the brain regions necessary for episodic memory are not yet fully mature until that age.

In one study, people generally reported earliest memories from when they were three or four years old, as in most previous research. The experimenters then introduced a suggestive procedure in which they asked subjects to visualize themselves as toddlers and try to "get in touch" with even earlier memories. They offered assurances that just about anyone can remember very early events, such as a second birthday, by "letting go" and working hard to visualize the event. Following the suggestive procedure, people reported earliest memories that dated, on average, to approximately eighteen months — well before the accepted offset of childhood amnesia. Indeed, one-third of those exposed to the suggestive procedure reported an earliest recollection from prior to twelve months, whereas nobody did so without suggestion. Because there is no other evidence that people can recall events from this early in their lives, these newly discovered "memories" almost certainly do not reflect accurate recall of events. Consistent with this idea, those individuals who came up with earliest memories from prior to twenty-four months were more suggestible on Gudjonsson's interrogative suggestibility scale than those who did not.

Visualization is not the only suggestive procedure that can influence what people claim to remember about early childhood. In a separate study, hypnotic suggestions yielded earlier autobiographical memory reports than hypnotists' instructions to relax or to count numbers visually; nearly four of every ten participants who received hypnotic suggestions claimed to remember events that occurred at or before their first birthday.

If doubts linger about whether memories dating prior to the age of two years are products of suggestion rather than accurate recovered memories, results from the laboratory of the Canadian hypnosis researcher Nicholas Spanos should end the debate. Consider the following question: Can you recall whether at the hospital where you were born a colored mobile hung above your crib? Of course you cannot. Spanos and his collaborators told people they wanted to find out whether there were colored mobiles above their birth cribs. They informed one group that hypnosis allows people to remember events from the first days of life by regressing them to an earlier time so that they can relive those experiences. These individuals then received a hypnotic regression treatment and mentally "returned" to the day after their birth. A second group listened to the same speech that hypnosis can unlock early memories and then heard that they would receive an equally effective nonhypnotic treatment called "guided mnemonic restructuring." They were encouraged to "reexperience" the day after their birth but were not administered a hypnotic regression treatment. A control group was told nothing about hypnosis or memory enhancement and simply tried to recall what dangled over their cribs the day after they were born.

No one in the control group came up with memories of a mobile over their crib, but about half of the individuals in the other two groups did. Regardless of whether they actually received hypnotic regression treatment, some people who had been led to expect that they would be able to recall experiences from the first day after their birth expressed a strong belief that they had done so.

Though not unprecedented — other evidence shows that people sometimes "remember" past lives and alien abductions, usually under the influence of hypnosis — these results are important because they underscore the key role of expectancies in producing false memories. The mere suggestion that participants should expect to recall something from the first day of life was sufficient to lead half of an otherwise ordinary sample of introductory psychology students to believe that they had recovered a patently preposterous memory.

Based on what I said in Chapter 4 about the distinctiveness heuristic and what we expect from our memories, it is perhaps not surprising that people readily come up with false memories from early childhood and infancy. Ordinarily we would not expect to recall the incidents of early life with vividness or clarity in the same way that we would expect to do so for a recent event. It is extremely difficult to implant false memories of salient personal experiences that allegedly occurred yesterday, such as becoming lost in a shopping mall, because we expect to remember yesterday's events with some clarity and detail. For recent events, we can invoke a distinctiveness heuristic: if the suggested event occurred, we would remember it vividly. But we expect little of recollections from early childhood and thus are more likely to interpret fuzzy images or vague feelings of familiarity as signs of an emerging memory, particularly if we are instructed to expect that such recollections are possible.

Suggestibility's pernicious effects highlight the idea that remembering the past is not merely a matter of activating or awakening a dormant trace or picture in the mind, but instead involves a far more complex interaction between the current environment, what one expects to remember, and what is retained from the past. Suggestive techniques tilt the balance between these contributors so that present influences play a much larger role in determining what is remembered than does what actually happened in the past.

At the same time, results like those reported by Spanos and others provide a sobering perspective on the recovered memories controversy. Recollections of early experiences are extremely malleable, more so than many would have believed before these studies were reported. When suggestive techniques such as hypnosis and guided imagery are used to hunt for memories from vulnerable periods of childhood, they comprise a potentially dangerous recipe for producing false memories. Surveys of psychotherapists conducted in the early and mid-1990s indicate that many believe that hypnosis and guided imagery can unlock buried childhood memories, and therefore use these techniques to stimulate clients' recollections. In view of the data we've considered, it should not be at all surprising if a subset of those clients recalled events that never occurred.

People with especially vivid imagery and those who score high on interrogative suggestibility scales appear to be at risk for creating some types of false memories. Ira Hyman also found that individuals who obtain high scores on a scale that measures self-reported tendencies toward lapses in attention and memory are more likely to create false childhood memories than people who obtain lower scores on that scale. Experiments with college students reveal that higher scores on that scale are also associated with greater false recognition of semantic associates — words such as *sweet* after the study of related words such as *candy, sour, sugar, bitter,* and so forth (see Chapter 4). A study in my laboratory led by Susan Clancy documented a similar relationship in adult women. In that study, we found that women who reported recovered memories of childhood sexual abuse showed elevated false recognition of semantic associates on the *sweet* test compared with women who were abused as children and always remembered it and with nonabused control subjects.

It is conceivable that the women reporting recovered memories were abused as children, forgot about it, and later recalled the abuse; the early trauma might have been responsible for heightened susceptibility to false recognition. However, this hypothesis does not explain why women who reported recovered memories showed more false recognition than women who always remembered their abuse. An alternative possibility is that the recovered memories were inaccurate, reflecting a vulnerability to memory distortion, which also results in more false recognition of semantic associates. We cannot be certain about the causal sequence: early trauma produces heightened false memories, or greater susceptibility to false memories produces inaccurate reports of early trauma. However, Clancy led another study that found that people who "remembered" being abducted and abused by aliens also showed increased false recognition of semantic associates. Because such abduction memories are surely false, these results indicate that heightened false recognition of semantic associates in the laboratory may indeed reflect elevated risk for experiencing false memories outside the lab. At the very least, our results add to the evidence that some people are more vulnerable to false recognition than others.

As the 1990s concluded, there were clear signs that the recovered memory crisis had started to ease. Perhaps because of new knowledge about suggestibility and memory that encouraged therapists to adopt a more conservative approach to memory recovery, and perhaps because of successful lawsuits brought against them by retractors, the incidence of new cases involving disputed recovered memories plummeted. In the False Memory Syndrome Foundation's Winter 1999 issue of its newsletter, the director, Pamela Freyd, reported that the foundation "now receives dramatically fewer calls and letters from people asking for assistance." She concluded, "The drop is of such magnitude that we can finally phase out that part of the FMSF organization that responded to those calls." The rise and fall of the recovered memories controversy paralleled a related crisis that hinged on the suggestibility of the most vulnerable memories of all.

SUGGESTIBILITY IN PRESCHOOL

On April 19, 1999, the Boston attorney James Sultan sent me a copy of an amicus brief filed days earlier in the case of *Commonwealth of Massachusetts v. Cheryl Amirault LeFave*. Amirault LeFave, along with her brother Gerald Amirault and mother, Violet Amirault, had been convicted over a decade earlier of molesting children at their family-run Fells Acres daycare center in Malden, a small suburb just north of Boston. The Amiraults' story resembles other highly publicized daycare cases that seemed to spread like wildfire in the 1980s and early 1990s, such as those concerning the McMartin preschool in Los Angeles and the Little Rascals daycare center in Edenton, North Carolina. In the latter cases, preschool-age children reported that they had been subject to revolting, even horrific, acts. The children's accusations involved not only sexual abuse but also bizarre claims of bloody torture, murder, being forced to eat dead babies, and even taking trips on alien spaceships. Yet there was a lack of medical evidence that the children had suffered abuse, and no adult visitors ever noticed anything amiss in the daycare centers where wrongdoing allegedly occurred. None of the schools had a prior history of problems: Fells Acres, for example, had been operating for eighteen years without any accusations of impropriety prior to the initial charges against Gerald Amirault in 1984. The children who made the accusations had almost invariably endured suggestive questioning by police or childcare professionals.

There was, however, a critical difference between the Fells Acres case and the other two cases, reflected in the amicus brief I received. Prosecutors failed to obtain a conviction in the McMartin case and finally gave up trying. The convicted teachers from the Little Rascals daycare center eventually were released after new evidence became available. In contrast, despite concerted efforts on the part of her defense attorneys and the urging of leading researchers in the area of child memory, the Commonwealth of Massachusetts maintained that Cheryl Amirault LeFave belonged in prison.

Amirault LeFave and her mother, Violet, had been offered parole during 1992 in exchange for an admission of guilt, but they refused to admit to crimes that they claimed they had not committed. (No such offer was made to Gerald.) They were granted new trials in 1995 and released from prison. But prosecutors successfully appealed, and in 1997 the Supreme Judicial Court of Massachusetts overturned the decision to award the Amirault women new trials, ordering them to return to prison. Culminating a subsequent frenzy of legal maneuvers, in May 1997 Judge Isaac Borenstein overturned the convictions of Cheryl and Violet on the technical grounds that they had not been allowed (literally) to face their accusers — the Fells Acres children — directly in court. Violet Amirault died of cancer in September 1997. The prosecution was preparing an appeal of the decision that had freed Cheryl when her attorney, James Sultan, told the court that he had novel evidence warranting a new trial.

Sultan had enlisted the aid of Dr. Maggie Bruck, a respected expert on the suggestibility of children's recollections. Dr. Bruck contended that the Commonwealth of Massachusetts owed Cheryl another trial because new research on child suggestibility spoke directly to the possibility that the interviewing techniques used with the Fells Acres children had led them to provide inaccurate reports. The amicus brief that James Sultan sent me in April 1999 backed up Dr. Bruck's interpretation of the new research and its potential relevance to the guilt or innocence of Cheryl Amirault LeFave. Twenty-nine researchers with established credentials in the study of memory, including me, had signed the brief.

The bulk of the evidence described in the amicus brief came from striking demonstrations regarding the nature and extent of suggestibility in children's recollections of personal experiences. Beginning in the early 1900s, researchers had shown that suggestive questions can distort children's reports about the past — sometimes to a greater extent than seen in adults. But prior to 1990, almost all of this research had examined children who were older than the preschoolers whose memories were disputed in the Fells Acres case and other similar instances. At the time of the Amiraults' convictions, there were only a handful of studies available concerning the suggestibility of preschoolers like those who testified against them. Further, the early studies had focused on whether small details of an incident could be suggested to children through misleading questions. If asked about the hair color of a bald man who had visited them, children who "remembered" that the man had black hair were considered suggestible. But this type of research fell far short of determining whether suggestive questions could lead children to provide an inaccurate recollection of an entire event that, in reality, never occurred.

Sultan and Bruck's concerns about the Amirault case centered on interviews with the Fells Acres children conducted by the pediatric nurse Susan Kelley. None of the Fells Acres children had spontaneously reported abuse to their parents, and they denied being abused when asked about it initially. Reports of abuse emerged only after questioning by parents, police, Kelley, and others (based on concerns stemming from an incident in which one child engaged in sex play with a cousin). This observation is key because research has shown that children's spontaneous recollections tend to be accurate, whereas their responses to specific questions are more likely to include distortions. For instance, in a 1996 study two- to five-year-old children were interviewed about treatment that they had just received in an emergency room. The researchers found that when children were asked open-ended questions such as "What happened?" they provided accurate details of their experiences. But when they were asked more specific questions such as "Where did you hurt yourself?" the incidence of inaccurate details grew dramatically, from 9 percent in response to open-ended questions to 49 percent in response to specific questions.

Bruck noted that in Susan Kelley's interviews of the Fells Acres children, she never began by asking an open-ended question such as "What happened?" Instead, she proceeded directly to specific questions: queries about teachers, whether they were nice, and so forth. Kelley also frequently repeated specific questions, seeming to refuse to take no for an answer. For instance, investigators developed the hypothesis that a clown whom the children had mentioned in connection with the daycare center was in some way related to the alleged abuse. In the following exchange, Kelley repeatedly asks the child about the clown's action:

KELLEY: Did the clown touch you?

CHILD: No . . .

KELLEY: You said the clown took your clothes off.

CHILD: Yeah.

KELLEY: And then what happened?

CHILD: Well, nothing really.

KELLEY: Did the clown touch any . . . Will you show me if the clown touched any part of you?

CHILD: No, he didn't touch me any —

KELLEY: Now, pretend this was you. Did the clown touch you? Where did the clown touch you?

CHILD: Right there [indicates foot].

KELLEY: Did he take your underpants off?

CHILD: [No response]

KELLEY: Then what did he do?

CHILD: Nothing else.

KELLEY: No? Did he touch you?

CHILD: I want to wear that now.

KELLEY: Oh, but I want you to tell if the clown touched you.

CHILD: Yeah.

With other Fells Acres children, repeated interviews were conducted on separate occasions when an initial interview failed to yield satisfactory answers, with results much like those depicted in the quoted transcript: negative responses were eventually replaced by positive ones. Such repeated questioning is alarming because studies conducted by Bruck and others have found that when children are interviewed twice and produce details in a second interview that were not mentioned in the first, the new details are highly likely to be inaccurate. In related studies, Bruck and the Cornell psychologist Stephen Ceci repeatedly asked children questions about events that their parents indicated had never occurred, such as getting a finger caught in a mousetrap and going to the hospital. The children were encouraged to think about and imagine the events. After repeated questioning, 58 percent of preschoolers reported detailed recollections of at least one event that they initially said had never occurred; 25 percent generated false memories for a majority of such events.

Some of the deleterious effects of suggestive questioning are attributable to basic vulnerabilities of young children's memory systems. A number of laboratory studies indicate that young children have special difficulties remembering source information — exactly when and where a particular incident or action occurred. When children are repeatedly asked about particular events, the incidents may begin to feel familiar simply because the examiner has mentioned them numerous times. Lacking detailed memory for the source of the feeling of familiarity, preschoolers may begin to mix together bits and pieces of different past episodes, or even intrude elements of fantasy and imagination. Source memory problems may also explain why parents can sometimes inadvertently suggest experiences to children that actually never occurred. In one study, preschoolers visited "Mr. Science" at a university laboratory and watched him conduct some experiments. Four months later, the children's parents received written descriptions of the experiments, others that the child had not witnessed, and a further incident that had not actually occurred: "Mr. Science wiped [child's name] hands and face with a wet-wipe. The cloth got close to [child's name] mouth and tasted really yucky." Parents read the stories to their children three times. When asked later about what they had seen in the laboratory, children frequently remembered experiments that had been mentioned only by their parents. When asked whether Mr. Science put something yucky in their mouths, more than half the preschoolers said "yes." Poor source memory is the likely culprit.

Some of the reports generated by children in daycare cases such as Fells Acres may also be attributable to social pressures that often surround the interview situation. For example, Maggie Bruck documented a number of instances in which Susan Kelley held out promises and even bribes in exchange for testimony.

At the time of Cheryl Amirault LeFave's trial, little was known about the effect of social influence on the accuracy of a child's recollection. Researchers had typically examined the effects of suggestive questioning in isolation from the social pressures that were often present during interviews in the 1980s daycare cases. And, indeed, some studies found that when preschoolers received only a single suggestive question, they rarely produced false reports about the central features of an event, such as whether strangers had taken off their clothes.

Additional studies filled in the gap. In 1998, the psychologists Sena Garven, James Wood, and their coworkers from the University of Texas at El Paso took advantage of a new resource that had not been available during the Fells Acres trial: transcripts of interviews from the McMartin case. As with the Susan Kelley interviews, investigators in the McMartin affair applied various kinds of social pressures in an attempt to elicit information from recalcitrant preschoolers. In addition to asking suggestive questions, interviewers offered praise and rewards for sought-after information, expressed disappointment or disapproval when children failed to come up with a desired answer, repeated questions that initially yielded no responses, and invited children to speculate about what might have happened by pretending or imagining.

Garven and associates compared the McMartin techniques to a control condition involving suggestive questioning only. Preschoolers watched and listened as a graduate student introduced as Manny Morales told them the story of *The Hunchback of Notre Dame*. After the story, he gave out cupcakes and napkins, said goodbye, and departed. A week later, children in the control group were asked about a few things that Manny had done, such as taking off his hat and asking the children to sit quietly and listen. They were also asked suggestive questions about things that Manny had not done: tearing a book, putting a sticker on a child's knee, saying a bad word, throwing a crayon at a child who was talking, and so forth. Children in the social incentive group were asked the same questions, except that the interviewers also used the influence techniques identified in the McMartin transcripts.

The results were disturbing. In the social incentive condition, five-and six-year-olds said "yes" to just over half of the misleading questions, whereas five- and six-year-olds in the control group said "yes" to fewer than 10 percent of the misleading questions. Results were similar for four-year-olds and even worse for three-year-olds: they said "yes" to 81 percent of the misleading questions in the social incentive condition compared to 31 percent in the control condition. These findings leave little room for doubt that social incentive techniques like those used by investigators in McMartin and Fells Acres have a devastating effect on the accuracy of what preschoolers report about past experiences.

In another highly publicized case, nineteen adults in the small town of Wenatchee, Washington, were convicted of running a child sex ring in the mid-1990s. The convictions were questioned because a thirteen-year-old girl who served as a key witness recanted her testimony, claiming that the chief police investigator forced her to generate allegations of sexual abuse. "I had to make it all up," she reflected. "First I said it didn't happen . . . and then he forced me to make up a lie." Experiments by the psychologists Jennifer Ackil and Maria Zaragoza have shown that forcing elementary school children to answer a suggestive question about what happened in a video they saw earlier creates a serious source memory problem: the children confused their own answers with what had happened in the video.

Despite the persuasiveness of the new research on child suggestibility to the twenty-nine scientists who signed Dr. Bruck's amicus brief, prosecutors continued to insist to the court that grounds were insufficient to warrant a new trial for Cheryl Amirault LeFave. In the winter of 1998, Maggie Bruck described the new research to Judge

Isaac Borenstein, highlighting important differences from the earlier work that was available at the time of the initial Amirault trial. Despite rebuttals from the prosecution, Judge Borenstein found Bruck's arguments convincing. He enumerated stinging criticisms of the prosecution's evidence and ruled in favor of a new trial. Borenstein did not, however, have the final word. In August 1999, the Supreme Judicial Court of Massachusetts, siding with the prosecution's claim that evidence concerning child suggestibility was available at the time of trial and that Bruck had not added anything fundamentally new, overturned Judge Borenstein's decision and reinstated Amirault LeFave's conviction. The decision seemed to ensure that she would return to prison. But days before she was scheduled to do so, in late October 1999, prosecutors and defense attorneys agreed to a deal: Amirault LeFave was set free on time served, but remains a convicted felon. Gerald Amirault remained in prison until 2004, when he was released on parole.

Though tragic for the Amiraults, the Fells Acres parents and children, and those entangled in related preschool cases, the interviewing errors of the 1980s were also responsible for the novel research in the 1990s, which has provided benefits for children and the rest of society. Knowing more about what factors raise suggestibility in young children — leading questions, social incentives, forced responding, and the like — also means knowing more about how to lower it. Interviewers who rely on simple open-ended questions and avoid the risky techniques used in the past stand an excellent chance of obtaining accurate information from even very young witnesses.

Suggestibility remains a worrisome vulnerability of memory, especially in young children. Yet despite its potential to wreak more havoc than any of the other seven sins, suggestibility is probably the easiest to neutralize. Whereas countering such problems as transience and absent-mindedness, for instance, requires putting forth the effort to perform elaborative encoding techniques or to construct external memory aids, avoiding suggestibility's harmful consequences mainly involves knowing what *not* to do. There is no longer any reason for police and mental health professionals who interview children or adults in legal or therapeutic contexts to repeat the kinds of errors that were made before psychologists declared a kind of research war on suggestibility during the 1990s. By revealing just how permeable to suggestions our recollections can be, the studies cited in this chapter provide weapons that can allow society to better protect the integrity of memory from external influences that, if left unchecked, are likely to corrupt it.

The Update
FALSE MEMORIES AND FALSE BELIEFS:
IMPLICATIONS FOR FALSE CONFESSIONS

One of the important accomplishments of the 1990s was the development of experimental paradigms for reliably inducing what Elizabeth Loftus has since called "rich false memories" — illusory recollections of complex real-world experiences. By the end of the 1990s, various studies using procedures such as the "lost in the mall" paradigm had established that suggestive procedures could induce approximately 20 to 30 percent of participants to produce false memories of events ranging from spilling punch at a wedding to more traumatic experiences such as an animal attack.

In 2015, a study by the psychologists Julia Shaw and Stephen Porter upped the ante on the type and frequency of rich false memories that psychologists could induce in the lab. Shaw and Porter used suggestive procedures they claimed induced *70 percent* of their college student sample to develop a false memory of committing a crime as an adolescent! That is a headline-grabbing number, and indeed their finding received widespread media coverage. Even for grizzled memory researchers such as myself, this was a shocking result for two reasons. First, no prior study had come close to inducing rich false memories in 70 percent of any sample. Second, recall that in earlier studies, young adults falsely remembered events that allegedly had occurred in childhood. As I pointed out in this chapter, we typically don't expect to recall early life experiences vividly, which makes it plausible to interpret vague ideas or images that pop up in response to suggestion as evidence of an emerging memory. But we do expect to remember recent events with greater clarity and detail, allowing us to invoke a "distinctiveness heuristic" and avoid developing false memories. Could 70 percent of college students really develop false memories for committing crimes alleged to have occurred only a few years earlier? Are our memories that easily corrupted by suggestion?

To address these questions, let's look more closely at what Shaw and Porter actually did. They enlisted the aid of parents or other caregivers, who confirmed that the students in the study had never had police contact or participated in any criminal event. Caregivers also provided the researchers with a description of an emotional noncriminal event that each student had actually experienced. Students completed three interviews spaced about a week apart. In each interview, they were first asked about the true event, which all of them recalled easily. For the false event, half of the students were told that they had committed a crime resulting in police contact (an assault, an assault with a weapon, or a theft). The other half were told that they had experienced an emotional but noncriminal event (an injury, a dog attack, or losing a large sum of money).

At first, none of the participants recalled any of the false events, which is typical in studies of rich false memories. But then the experimenters started applying social pressure: they told students that their parents had said the events had happened and that most people can recall these kinds of disturbing events if they just try hard enough. They also put the students' imaginations to work, encouraging them to repeatedly visualize the event during the week between the experimental sessions. The deadly combination of social pressure and repeated visualization produced the headline number that grabbed so much attention: in a final interview, 70 percent of students who were asked about crimes they had not committed met the experimenters' criteria for having false memories. That number was no fluke: just over 76 percent of participants who were asked about emotional but noncriminal events that had never occurred met these criteria.

Although these findings set the memory world abuzz, not all researchers were buying what Shaw and Porter were selling. Kimberley Wade and her colleagues published a critique claiming that there was a problem with the criteria that Shaw and Porter used to classify a student's report as a "false memory." The researchers classified a student's event description as a false memory if the student believed the event had occurred and also provided details about what had happened, including some of the false information the experimenter had suggested. But does that really indicate that students were having an experience of "remembering" an event that never occurred? Wade and her colleagues pointed to earlier research that distinguished between false *beliefs*, where people accept a suggestion as true and speculate about specifics of what might have happened, and false *memories*, where people report a subjective experience of remembering the event and recall details of what happened. They rescored Shaw and Porter's results using criteria from previous studies that made that distinction, and they found that only about 25 to 30 percent of Shaw and Porter's participants falsely *remembered* committing a crime — pretty much the same proportion as in earlier studies of rich false memories and far from the 70 percent that had made headlines. The other reports of committing crimes were classified as false beliefs.

That's a dramatic difference from the original claim, but it's still unsettling that 25 to 30 percent of students could be induced to falsely remember committing a crime, and perhaps even more unsettling that 70 percent falsely *believed* they had committed a crime, even if that belief fell short of a full-blown false memory. Relevant here are studies of false confessions I discussed in this chapter. Saul Kassin's work in the 1990s showed that about 70 percent of participants signed a confession that they had hit the Alt key on a computer even though they hadn't, and 35 percent falsely recalled doing so. Shaw and Porter's results fit nicely with those findings, but they involved a much more high-stakes event than accidentally hitting a computer key.

False confessions have seized public attention in recent years, in part because of the saga of the Central Park Five. These five men were convicted of committing the brutal 1989 assault and rape of a jogger in Central Park named Trisha Meili after falsely confessing to the crime as a result of police coercion. The men were eventually exonerated in 2002 when another man confessed to the attack. The 2012 PBS documentary *The Central Park Five* and the 2019 Netflix miniseries *When They See Us* brought the story to a wide audience and sparked discussion of the dangers of false confessions. So did a disputed case of a possible false confession depicted in the Netflix documentary series *Making a Murderer*. In 2005, sixteen-year-old Brendan Dassey confessed to assisting his uncle Steven Avery in the sexual assault and murder of photographer Teresa Halbach. Brendan later recanted what he claimed was a coerced confession, but he was nonetheless convicted and sentenced to life in prison. A judge subsequently ruled that Brendan's confession was coerced and that he should be released. But the judge's decision was overturned on appeal, a clemency petition for Dassey's release was denied in December 2019, and as I write these words he remains in prison.

John Grisham's 2006 book, *The Innocent Man,* and a 2018 Netflix documentary with the same title described two other cases involving apparent false confessions to murders that took place in Ada, Oklahoma. In the first case, Ron Williamson and Dennis Fritz were convicted of the 1982 murder of cocktail waitress Debra Sue Carter in part because Williamson admitted to having a dream in which he committed the murder, which was treated as a confession. In 1999, Williamson and Fritz were released from prison after DNA evidence exonerated them. In the second case, Karl Fontenot and Tommy Ward were convicted of a 1984 murder of store clerk Denice Haraway based mainly on highly dubious forced confessions. The two men's cases were appealed separately. On December 19, 2019, Fontenot was released from prison. As of this writing, Ward's case remains under appeal.

Inevitably, discussions of alleged false confessions touch on a deeply troubling question: Why would anyone confess to a crime that they did not commit? As discussed earlier in the chapter, there are multiple reasons why this happens, and it's only in a subset of false confessions, which Saul Kassin and his colleagues refer to as "internalized false confessions," that people mistakenly come to believe that they actually committed a crime. But Shaw and Porter's results remind us that a potent cocktail combining coercion and imagination can lead a surprisingly high proportion of people to develop a false belief that they have committed a crime when in fact they have not. The qualification that a much smaller proportion develop full-blown false memories in response to coercive questioning is significant theoretically. However, it may be of less practical importance for false confessions in legal settings, because developing a false belief that one has committed a crime, even without developing a false memory, must surely increase the chances of someone providing a false confession. Psychologists have tended to focus on trying to understand how suggestion can lead to false memories, but it is now clear that we need to focus at least as much attention on understanding how suggestion can lead to false beliefs.

Have the Memory Wars Ended?

The outcries over false memories in adults and children during the 1990s and the new research we just considered amply illustrate the dangers of suggestibility. Still, as I was completing this chapter two decades ago, there were reasons to be optimistic that the kinds of false memories that tore families and communities apart were beginning to vanish. I pointed out earlier that in 1999 Pamela Freyd proclaimed that the False Memory Syndrome Foundation was receiving so few new case reports that they phased out the part of the organization that had been responding to these cries for help. Research into children's memories by Maggie Bruck, Stephen Ceci, and others had by then made it clear how vulnerable preschoolers' memories are to the corrupting influence of suggestion, and many convictions of falsely accused daycare workers had been overturned. Twenty years on, have we held on to these gains in the battle against suggestibility's damaging consequences? To a large extent, yes, but dangers still lurk.

On December 31, 2019, the False Memory Syndrome Foundation was dissolved because, according to its website, "the need for the FMS Foundation has diminished dramatically over the years." Moreover, in recent years we have not seen the emergence of new daycare center cases that feature horrific claims of abuse created by the use of suggestive techniques. The studies of researchers such as Bruck and Ceci during the 1990s are no doubt partly responsible for this change. So are the efforts of individuals who have made the general public aware of the injustices that occurred in McMartin, Fells Acres, and other similar cases, notably Dorothy Rabinowitz in both a series of *Wall Street Journal* articles and her 2003 book, *No Crueler Tyrannies*. As pointed out by Richard Beck in his 2015 analysis of the egregious daycare cases of the 1980s and 1990s, *We Believe the Children*, protocols for interviewing children have changed for the better as a consequence of the mistakes that led to past debacles. This is likely a major reason why, although real child abuse continues to be a serious problem, suggestion-related illusory recollections of daycare abuses are not.

Another important question is whether awareness that suggestion can lead to potentially damaging false memories has led to reduced use of suggestive therapeutic procedures to recover memories. In 2012, the memory researcher Lawrence Patihis and his colleagues administered a survey to fifty-three board-certified psychotherapists asking whether they agreed with various statements, including the following: "It is possible to suggest false memories to someone who then incorporates them as true memories." Ninety-six percent of the therapists agreed with this statement, which is significantly higher than the 86 percent who agreed with the same statement in a survey administered to a similar group of therapists back in 1992. Even more dramatic, in the 1992 survey 48 percent of psychotherapists agreed with the statement "Hypnosis can be used to recover memories of actual events from as far back as birth," but only 9 percent agreed with that statement in 2012.

These are encouraging signs that psychotherapists are increasingly aware of the dangers of suggestive memory procedures. Still, Patihis and his colleagues found that memory researchers are even more skeptical about the possibility of recovering accurate memories in therapy than psychotherapists are. And a 2019 large-scale survey by Patihis and the writer Mark Pendergrast regarding the experiences of people who have been in therapy suggests that a minority of contemporary therapists continue to probe for repressed memories of sexual abuse during therapy. The incidence of such probing appears to be less frequent now than during the 1990s, but it has not disappeared completely. While that doesn't necessarily mean that a new firestorm of false memories is about to erupt, given the well-established dangers of suggestive probing, we would do well to remain on guard going forward.

6

The Sin of Bias

IN GEORGE ORWELL'S chilling novel of life in a totalitarian political system, *1984*, the ruling party achieves psychological mastery over its subjects by willfully altering the past. "Who controls the past," runs the party slogan, "controls the future: who controls the present controls the past." The government's Ministry of Truth tries to alter the written historical record and even to manipulate the actual experience of remembering:

> Past events, it is argued, have no objective existence, but survive only in written records and in human memories. The past is whatever the records and the memories agree upon . . . Control of the past depends above all on the training of memory. To make sure that all written records agree with the orthodoxy of the moment is merely a mechanical act. But it is also necessary to *remember* that events happened in the desired manner. And if it is necessary to rearrange one's memories or to tamper with written records, then it is necessary to *forget* that one has done so. The trick of doing this can be learned like any other mental technique.

Totalitarian societies like the one envisioned by Orwell have declined since the collapse of the Eastern European communist regimes. But forces that in some sense resemble the Ministry of Truth continue to operate in individual minds: our memories of the past are often rescripted to fit with our present views and needs. The sin of bias refers to distorting influences of our present knowledge, beliefs, and feelings on new experiences or our later memories of them.

In the stifling psychological climate of 1984, the Ministry of Truth uses memory as a pawn in the service of party rule. Much in the same manner, biases in remembering past experiences reveal how memory can serve as a pawn for the ruling masters of our cognitive systems.

Five major types of biases illustrate the ways in which memory serves its masters. *Consistency and change biases* show how our theories about ourselves can lead us to reconstruct the past as overly similar to, or different from, the present. *Hindsight biases* reveal that recollections of past events are filtered by current knowledge. *Egocentric biases* illustrate the powerful role of the self in orchestrating perceptions and memories of reality. And *stereotypical biases* demonstrate how generic memories shape interpretation of the world, even when we are unaware of their existence or influence.

THE WAY WE WERE DEPENDS ON THE WAY WE ARE

When Ross Perot unexpectedly announced his withdrawal from the presidential race on July 16, 1992, he dealt a cruel blow to his fervent supporters. Perot was widely reviled in the press — *Newsweek* ran a cover story on him titled "The Quitter" — and his allies experienced a complex mixture of sadness, anger, and hope that he might reconsider the decision. When he reentered the campaign in early October, those who had supported him reacted in different ways. "Loyalists" never wavered from Perot and renewed their efforts on his behalf. "Returning supporters" had initially switched to another candidate but quickly came back. "Deserters" abandoned Perot as soon as he left the race and never returned.

A few days after Perot quit in July, the University of California, Irvine, psychologist Linda Levine asked his supporters how they felt; she probed their memories again after the election in November. Loyalists, returning supporters, and deserters all accurately recalled, at least to some degree, the sadness, anger, and hope they had felt when Perot made his stunning July announcement. But they also rewrote their memories to be consistent with how they felt in November. After the election, loyalists underestimated how sad they felt when Perot quit. Returning supporters recalled feeling less angry in July than they actually said they were at the time. And deserters recalled being less hopeful than they actually were.

This consistency bias has turned up in several different contexts. Recalling past experiences of pain, for instance, is powerfully influenced by current pain level. When patients afflicted by chronic pain are experiencing high levels of pain in the present, they are biased to recall similarly high levels of pain in the past; when present pain isn't so bad, past pain experiences seem more benign, too. Attitudes toward political and social issues also reflect consistency bias. People whose views on political issues have changed over time often recall incorrectly past attitudes as highly similar to present ones. In fact, memories of past political views are sometimes more closely related to present views than to what people actually believed in the past. In one study, high school students stated their opinions on school busing and then heard arguments for or against busing. Despite changing their views in line with the arguments they heard, the students mistakenly recalled that they had always held the views they expressed after hearing the pro or con arguments.

To appreciate why people are so prone to consistency biases, try to recall your views on capital punishment five years ago. Can you specifically recall what you believed in those days? The Canadian social psychologist Michael Ross has observed that people often do not have clear memories of exactly what they believed or felt in the past, and instead infer past beliefs, attitudes, and feelings from their current states. Unless there is good reason to believe that your views on capital punishment have changed, you are likely to assess your present opinion and assume you felt the same way five years ago. Invoking what Ross calls an "implicit theory of stability" will lead to accurate recall if your views haven't changed over time, but will produce a consistency bias if they have.

People don't always invoke a theory of stability, however; sometimes we believe that we have, or should have, changed over time. Self-help programs may exploit such feelings. Once people invest time and energy in a program that is supposed to help them change

—lose weight, prepare for college entrance exams, or exercise more —they may exaggerate the degree of change they've actually experienced. Students who completed a program purported to enhance their study skills remembered their initial level of skill as being lower than they said it was before beginning the program, whereas students who were on a waiting list for the program showed no change bias.

Change bias also influences how women recall their emotional states during menstruation. Surveys indicate that women generally believe that they are likely to become highly irritable and depressed during their periods. Studies of women during menstruation clearly show a higher incidence of such physical symptoms as backaches, headaches, and abdominal pains—but there's little evidence for greater depression or related mood changes. Physical discomfort may lead women to theorize that menstruation results in negative moods and related kinds of psychological distress. In a study from Michael Ross's group, women who were menstruating reported more physical symptoms compared to when they were not, but the results showed little change in self-reported mood or personality measures. Yet during menstruation, these women recalled intermenstrual emotional states as more positive than they actually were, supporting their theories that menstruation produces bad moods. Such theories can also inflate recall of negative menstrual symptoms: the more a woman believes that she experiences bad moods during menstruation, the more she shows exaggerated recall of such symptoms after her period has concluded.

The effects of consistency and change bias are perhaps nowhere more evident than in recollections of close personal relationships. Recall the 1970s Barbra Streisand tune "The Way We Were," which holds that we try to forget currently painful memories of a past relationship and focus instead on past moments of laughter. As implied by the song, as well as by the evidence and ideas considered so far, it is difficult to separate recall of "the way we were" from current appraisals of "the way we are." Consistency biases often color couples' retrospective assessments of how they once felt, with the present state of the relationship dictating memory for how things used to be. Consider, for instance, dating college students who were asked, in separate sessions conducted two months apart, to evaluate themselves and their dating partners on such traits as honesty, kindness, and intelligence and also on how much they liked and loved their partners. During the second session, the couples also recalled their earlier evaluations. The students whose evaluations of their partners became more negative over time recalled their initial impressions as more negative than they actually were. Students who reported liking or loving a partner more in the second session than in the first also recalled having felt more love or liking in the past. Memories of past impressions and feelings were filtered through, and made consistent with, their current impressions and feelings.

Consistency biases are prevalent in both married and dating couples. Consider the following questions in relation to your own partner: How attached do you feel? How happy are you in your relationship? How often does your partner get on your nerves? How much do you love him or her? Then try to answer the same questions again, this time focusing on how you felt a year ago. Married and dating couples who were asked similar questions twice, over a period of eight months or four years, often remembered correctly that they had given similar ratings on the two occasions. But those men and women whose feelings had changed over time tended to mistakenly remember that they had always felt the same way. Trying to remember what they felt four years earlier, four out of five people whose feelings remained stable showed accurate recall, but only one in five of those whose feelings had changed recalled accurately "the way they were." Results were even more dramatic when couples recalled how they had felt eight months earlier: 89 percent of women and 85 percent of men whose feelings remained stable accurately remembered their earlier feelings, but only 22 percent of women and 15 percent of men whose feelings had changed showed accurate recall. The couples seemed to be saying "What I feel now is what I've always felt" — regardless of whether that was true or not.

These kinds of biases can sometimes accentuate troubles that some married couples experience during their first few years together. Once the "honeymoon" is over, many couples experience a sharp drop-off in levels of satisfaction with their marriages. Difficulties in the present are hard enough to address during the early years of marriage, but consistency biases can make matters worse by coloring the past with the unpleasant tones of the present. Consider a study that followed nearly four hundred Michigan couples through the first years of marriage. In those couples who expressed growing unhappiness over the four years of the study, men mistakenly recalled the beginnings of their marriages as negative even though they said they were happy at the time. "Such biases can lead to a dangerous downward spiral," noted the researchers who conducted the study. "The worse your current view of your partner is, the worse your memories are, which only further confirms your negative attitudes."

Though consistency biases are potent forces in shaping relationship memories, change biases can also occur — and sometimes in a positive direction. Remember the popular late-1960s song with the line "I love you more today than yesterday"? People would no doubt like to believe that their romantic attachments grow stronger over time. When dating couples were asked annually over four years to assess the present quality of their relationships and to recall how they felt in past years, their recollections embodied the same sentiments as the line from the song. Couples who stayed together for the four years recalled that the strength of their love had grown since they last reported on it. Yet analysis of their actual ratings at the time failed to show any increases in reported love and attachment. Objectively, the couples did not love each other more today than yesterday. But through the subjective lenses of memory, they did.

This pattern differs from the consistency biases seen in other dating and married couples, instead revealing a kind of improvement bias. The couples mistakenly remembered the past as less positive than it actually was, making the present seem rosier by comparison. Consistency and change biases can each occur at different points in a relationship, with the predominant bias at a particular time depending on the nature and stage of the relationship. The social psychologists Benjamin Karney and Robert Coombs analyzed a twenty-year longitudinal investigation of wives' feelings about their marriages. The study was initiated in 1969, when the women were in their mid-twenties. The scientists separately considered the first ten years of the women's marriages, when couples were making the transition to parenthood, and the second ten years, as they entered a period of personal and economic stability. On each occasion, wives answered questions, some very general ("How happy are you with your marriage?") and others more specific ("How many interests do you and your husband share?").

When reflecting back on the first ten years of their marriages, wives showed a change bias: they remembered their initial assessments as worse than they actually were. The bias made their present feelings seem an improvement by comparison, even though they actually felt more negatively ten years into their marriage than they had at the beginning. When they had been married for twenty years and reflected back on their second ten years of marriage, the women now showed a consistency bias: they mistakenly recalled that feelings from ten years earlier were similar to their present ones. In reality, however, they felt more negatively after twenty years of marriage than after ten. Both types of bias helped women cope with their marriages. The more women's recollections were biased toward improvement at the ten-year mark, the happier they were with their marriages at the twenty-year mark. By the twenty-year mark, wives who were most satisfied with their marriages showed the least memory bias, whereas those who were least satisfied showed the most bias — perhaps reflecting ongoing attempts to cope with an unhappy present by distorting the past. Memories of "the way we were" are not only influenced by but also contribute to "the way we are."

Consistency and change biases may help to reduce what social psychologists call "cognitive dissonance" — the psychological discomfort that results from conflicting thoughts and feelings. People will go to great lengths to reduce cognitive dissonance. A heavy drinker who reads the latest health statistics highlighting the dangers of excessive alcohol intake might try to reduce dissonance by convincing himself that he is only a light social drinker or by disparaging the statistics. Likewise, an unhappily married woman who believes that her marriage should be successful may reduce cognitive dissonance by distorting the past with consistency or change biases that make the present seem more bearable.

Dissonance reduction can occur even when people don't recall the event that is responsible for the dissonance. Consider the following scenario. You visit an art gallery and fall in love with two prints by the same artist but have only enough money to purchase one. After almost deciding on one and then the other, you finally make your choice, but as you leave with your new purchase, you still feel conflicted about passing over the remaining print. By the next day, however, you realize that you like the print you purchased quite a bit more than the one you passed up, and the dissonance created by the difficult decision dissipates.

Studies have shown that just this sort of dissonance reduction occurs when people are forced to decide between two art prints that they previously indicated they liked equally: after making the choice, they claim to like the chosen print more and the bypassed print less than they did earlier. In a study led by the social psychologists Matthew Lieberman and Kevin Ochsner, we found that amnesic patients also reduced dissonance created by choosing between two art prints they liked equally by later inflating how much they liked the chosen relative to the shunned print. But the amnesic patients had no conscious memory for making the choice that produced dissonance in the first place! These findings suggest that a variety of dissonance-reducing operations, including consistency and change biases, occur even when people have limited awareness of the source of the conflicts they are trying to manage.

I KNEW IT ALL ALONG

When the Boston Red Sox beat the Cleveland Indians in the deciding game of their playoff series in October 1999, Boston sports fans relished the prospects of taking on the world champion New York Yankees in the American League Championship Series. Euphoric callers to sports radio talk shows enumerated reason after reason why the long-suffering Red Sox had an excellent chance to dethrone the mighty — and hated — Yankees. The Red Sox had built up tremendous momentum in their come-from-behind win against Cleveland; no team could hit their dominating pitcher, Pedro Martínez; and in a short baseball series, anything can happen.

After the Red Sox lost the series, the talk show callers (at least the ones I heard when tuning in to the radio) reasoned very differently. I never thought the Red Sox had a chance, caller after caller grimly stated. I was sure they didn't have enough hitting to compete, recollected some. I always felt their bullpen was too weak, remembered others. I knew that the Yankees were too good, even die-hard Red Sox fans conceded.

The memories of the talk show callers seemed to be powerfully influenced by the outcome of the championship series: with the benefit of hindsight, the fans felt that they had known all along that the Red Sox were doomed to lose. Although it's difficult to draw firm conclusions based on an unscientific sampling of opinions on radio talk shows (perhaps only optimistic callers phoned in before the championship series, and the pessimists held off until later), controlled studies of other sports fans back up this interpretation of what the Red Sox callers said. During the fall of 1995, followers of the Northwestern University football team were asked, either before or after their home games against Wisconsin, Penn State, and Iowa, what they thought the team's prospects of winning were. Northwestern, which enjoyed a highly successful season in 1995, won all three games. Fans who were asked after each game to recall their predictions before the game reported giving Northwestern a much greater chance of winning than fans who rated the team's chances before the game.

Sports fans aren't the only ones who say they "knew it all along." Consider another public event that people expressed strong opinions about: the jury decision in O. J. Simpson's criminal trial. Can you recall how likely you thought the jury was to convict O.J.? Students were asked to estimate the likelihood that the jury would convict O.J. two hours before the jurors returned a not-guilty verdict and again two days later, after the students knew the verdict. They rated the likelihood of conviction as lower after the jury made its decision than before.

Judgments about sports events and the O.J. trial illustrate a familiar occurrence in everyday life: once we learn the outcome of an event, we feel as though we always knew what would happen. Called "hindsight bias" by psychologists, this tendency to see an outcome as inevitable in retrospect is a close cousin of consistency bias: we reconstruct the past to make it consistent with what we know in the present.

Hindsight bias seems particularly common around the time of political elections, with various pundits rushing to explain why the outcome of a particular race could hardly have gone otherwise. But did they see things so clearly before the votes were counted? On the day before the 1980 presidential election, students were asked to predict the outcome. Others were asked the day after to indicate what they would have predicted before the Tuesday election. Those who were asked on Wednesday said they would have predicted a higher percentage of the vote for Reagan and lower percentages for Jimmy Carter and Independent candidate John Anderson than those who were asked to predict the outcome on Monday.

Hindsight bias is especially pronounced when people come up with after-the-fact explanations that specify a deterministic cause of the outcome. Consider, for instance, people who judged alternate outcomes of a nineteenth-century war between the British and the Gurkhas of Nepal. In the foresight condition, people read about the incident and judged the likelihood of various outcomes. In the hindsight condition, people were told the result (the British won), and the experimenter then instructed them to judge the likelihood of various outcomes as if they did not know what had actually happened.

Despite this instruction, when participants knew the outcome, they exhibited hindsight bias. The bias was especially strong when experimenters provided a deterministic cause of the British victory: the superior discipline of their troops. But hindsight bias was practically nonexistent when experimenters suggested a chance cause — a freak rainstorm. Likewise, hindsight bias was especially pronounced in a subset of Northwestern football fans who, when asked after a game to recall their earlier predictions, also generated causal explanations of the outcome, such as "Our defense shut them down" or "They missed a crucial field goal." People feel most strongly that they always knew the results when they can construct a satisfying causal scenario that makes the outcome seem inevitable in hindsight.

Hindsight bias is so powerful that it occurs even when people are explicitly instructed to disregard the actual outcome of an event. It is as if knowledge of the outcome becomes instantly integrated with other general knowledge in semantic memory, and people simply cannot treat this new bit of information any differently from other information relevant to the judgment they are trying to make. That hindsight bias persists even when people are explicitly attempting to ignore outcome knowledge has potentially important implications for everyday situations in which hindsight bias occurs. When you seek a second medical opinion regarding a debatable diagnosis, you want the new doctor to take a fresh look at your condition, unbiased by the opinion of the first physician. But given the potent influence of hindsight bias, knowing the first physician's opinion may inexorably influence the judgment of the second, even if the second doctor tries to ignore what the first one said. This inevitable result is just what happened when doctors who received a diagnostic label for a particular case, such as leukemia or Alzheimer's disease, together with instructions to ignore it, were asked to make an independent diagnosis. These physicians were more likely to make a diagnosis consistent with the label than were others who made their diagnoses without having the benefit of a label.

Something similar occurs among courtroom jurors. Suppose that the prosecution introduces evidence from a seemingly incriminating telephone conversation, the defense objects to it, and the judge rules that the evidence is inadmissible. He then sternly instructs the jurors to disregard the evidence in their deliberations. Numerous studies have shown that mock jurors placed in such a situation cannot disregard inadmissible evidence, even in the face of explicit instructions to ignore it: they are more likely to convict than are jurors who don't hear the evidence. The same holds true for incriminating pretrial publicity that jurors are instructed to ignore. Once the publicity enters the memories of jurors, they are biased to feel that they knew all along that the defendant was guilty.

Hindsight bias, then, is ubiquitous: people seem almost driven to reconstruct the past to fit what they know in the present. In light of the known outcome, people can more easily retrieve incidents and examples that confirm it. Experimental evidence links this selective recall to the combined influences of two forces: general knowledge that influences the perception and comprehension of events, and vulnerability to misattribution.

Consider the following scenario. Barbara, a twenty-four-year-old single woman living in New England, meets an outgoing and intelligent man named Jack in her graduate business class and begins working on a course project with him. They begin to socialize after class, talking about school, careers, and their mutual love of skiing. At one point, they go to a restaurant, and Jack argues with a waiter and yells at Barbara, who then walks home alone in tears. After the conclusion of the course, Jack and Barbara stay out all night drinking and celebrating, and Barbara accepts Jack's invitation to spend a weekend at his parents' ski lodge in Vermont. The first night, Barbara drinks wine at dinner and kisses Jack. After skiing the next day, Jack takes Barbara out for a special dinner; they drink wine, and Jack holds Barbara's hand. After dinner, they return to the lodge, where Jack tells Barbara she is sexy and that he loves her, and Barbara tells Jack that she cares for him.

The psychologist Linda Carli asked Wellesley College undergraduates to read a passage about Jack and Barbara, presented as a case history of a woman who had been interviewed in a study of important life experiences. Carli constructed two different endings to the story. After the part in which Barbara tells Jack that she cares for him, half of the students read that Jack proposes marriage, whereas the other half read that Jack rapes Barbara. Two weeks later, all of the students were asked to rate the likelihood of alternative endings to the story "as if they did not know the actual ending," and they also took a memory test involving specific incidents that did or did not occur in the story.

Carli found strong evidence for hindsight bias: Students who had read the version ending in a marriage proposal judged the proposal as a more likely outcome than students who had read the version ending in rape, and vice versa. Students who had read the proposal ending tended to recognize falsely incidents that did not actually occur in the story but are expected precursors of a marriage proposal, such as "Jack gave Barbara a ring," "Barbara and Jack dined by candlelight," or "Barbara wanted a family very much." But students who had read the rape ending tended to recognize, also falsely, possible precursors of a rape, such as "Jack was unpopular with women," "Barbara was a tease," and "Jack and Barbara often went out drinking after work." Further, students' tendencies to misremember the precursors predicted the magnitude of hindsight bias: more false memories resulted in more hindsight bias.

The results suggest that as students tried to reconstruct what happened in the original passage, they activated general knowledge related to the story ending that they had read — proposal or rape. Sometimes they misattributed this knowledge to the story, leading them to misremember what happened and also to believe that they knew all along that the story would end in a manner consistent with the one they had read.

Hindsight biases are worrisome insofar as they can reduce or even prevent learning from experience: if we feel that we knew all along what would happen, then we may be less inclined to profit from the lessons a particular event or incident can teach us. But at the same time, the comforting sense that we always knew the way things would turn out makes us feel good about ourselves, inflating estimates of our own wisdom and prescience. This feature of hindsight bias no doubt contributes to its potency, because self-enhancing biases are pervasive features of attempts to reconstruct the personal past.

I REMEMBER IT WELL

In the 1958 musical *Gigi,* former lovers, played by Maurice Chevalier and Hermione Gingold, reflect back over the years and recall their final date together. As illustrated in the song "I Remember It Well," even though each one remembers the occasion vividly, their recollections could hardly be more different — they recall meeting at different times, whether they dined alone or with friends, and even whether the fateful date was in April or June. One of the pair must be wrong on each point, but neither one ever backs off from his or her side of the story. Most couples can likely recall similar, if not so extreme, examples from their lives. At a party during the December holiday season, a graduate student working in my laboratory almost came to blows with her husband because of a memory conflict over who had made jelly doughnuts for the previous year's holiday get-together. She recalled in vivid detail making the treats and serving them; so did he.

We are likely to give more credence to our own recollections of events than to those of others when our memories readily spring to mind and are accompanied by vivid, compelling details. We have direct access to these qualities of our own recollections in a way that we never do for the memories of others, which can lead us to dig in and insist on the unique validity of our own view of the world. This kind of egocentric bias contributes to some of the disagreements that couples experience about their shared pasts. Studies of married and dating couples have shown, for instance, that each member of the couple tends to remember himself or herself as more responsible for various kinds of incidents than the other. When asked to recall how much they contributed to deciding how money should be spent, planning a vacation together, or similar activities, one spouse might claim 80 percent credit while the other claims 40 percent. Although both agree that one of the pair was more responsible, one or both of them are claiming too much credit for their own contributions. This egocentric bias occurs even for negative incidents, such as shouldering too much responsibility for causing arguments in the relationship. The bias likely occurs because each member of the pair can more easily recall his or her own actions and feelings than what the partner did or said. Laboratory studies have shown that we tend to recall our own actions and words more readily than those of others.

Egocentric biases in memory reflect the important role that "the self" plays in organizing and regulating mental life. Many psychologists conceive of the self as a richly interconnected knowledge structure — the sum total of stored information about personal attributes and experiences. Numerous experiments have shown that when we encode new information by relating it to the self, subsequent memory for that information improves compared to other types of encoding. If I ask you to think about whether such attributes as "honest" or "intelligent" describe you or not, you are more likely to remember those words than if I ask you to make the same judgments about somebody else, such as a friend or a celebrity. Self-encoding also produces higher levels of subsequent memory than my asking you to elaborate on the words by focusing on their meaning or other properties that are not directly related to the self.

But the self is hardly a neutral observer of the world. Individuals in our society are motivated to think highly of themselves and often hold unrealistically flattering opinions of their abilities and achievements. Studies summarized by the social psychologist Shelley Taylor and her associates indicate that people are commonly subject to "positive illusions" characterized by inflated estimates of self-worth. For instance, most people tend to view desirable personality traits as more descriptive of themselves than of the average person, but they view undesirable personality traits as less descriptive of themselves than the average person. Because most people cannot be better than average, for some of us this sunny self-assessment must be illusory. Likewise, people are more likely to attribute successes than failures to themselves, and to attribute failures to forces outside the self.

The self's preeminent role in encoding and retrieval, combined with a powerful tendency for people to view themselves positively, creates fertile ground for memory biases that allow people to remember past experiences in a self-enhancing light. Consider, for example, college students who were led to believe that introversion is a desirable personality trait that predicts academic success and then searched their memories for incidents in which they behaved in an introverted or extroverted manner. Compared with students who were led to believe that extroversion is a desirable trait, the introvert-success students more quickly generated memories in which they behaved like introverts than like extroverts. The memory search was biased by a desire to see the self positively, which led students to select past incidents containing the desired trait.

Similar processes operate in everyday situations in which people are highly motivated to recount their pasts in ways that enhance current self-assessments. Do you recall what grades you obtained in high school courses? Can you remember how many As and Ds appeared on your report cards? Chances are that you can recall more of the good grades than the bad ones. When college students tried to remember high school grades and their memories were checked against actual transcripts, they were highly accurate for grades of A (89 percent correct) and extremely inaccurate for grades of D (29 percent correct).

Divorce can also accentuate self-enhancing memory biases. Recently divorced couples' retrospective assessments of their failed marriages reveal that the members of each pair tend to portray the past from very different, consistently self-serving perspectives. Looking back on why their marriage ended, one man recalled that "all she wanted was money to put in the bank," whereas his ex-wife remembered that "my husband seemed to be obsessed with making money." Another man attributed his breakup to the fact that he met another woman who was "younger and better-looking," whereas his ex-wife characterized the new woman as "a real bimbo," recounting that "people were prone to using descriptions such as 'the elevator doesn't go quite to the top.'"

Self-enhancing biases can also result from exaggerating the difficulty of past experiences. Consider a situation in which you anxiously study for a tough exam, take the test, and later find out that you passed. Just how anxious were you prior to the exam? Graduate students who recorded their anxiety levels before taking an important set of comprehensive examinations were asked a month later to recall how anxious they were during the pre-exam period. Students tended to exaggerate their pre-exam anxiety levels; the memory bias was particularly pronounced in those who knew that they had passed the exam. Recalling greater levels of anxiety than they actually experienced enhanced the students' sense of accomplishment, increasing pride and confidence in their abilities to cope with adverse events. Blood donors show a similar memory bias, retrospectively inflating their levels of pre-donation anxiety in a way that heightens their sense of bravery in overcoming obstacles to accomplish a courageous deed.

People sometimes deprecate past selves to maintain and enhance a favorable view of the current self. "Of all the lives that I have lived, I would have to say that this one is my favorite," the actress Mary Tyler Moore reflected in a 1997 magazine interview. "I am proud that I have developed into a kinder person than I ever thought I would be. I am less critical than I ever was and, as a result, I'm less critical of myself." Perhaps Moore had indeed changed for the better over time. But by recalling her past self as less kind and more critical than she was in 1997, suggests the psychologist Michael Ross, she was enhancing the value of her present self. Ross has found that people generally speak more favorably of present selves than of past selves. As with Moore, this inclination could reflect either a genuine improvement over time or a tendency to deprecate past selves. Consistent with the latter possibility, a substantial majority of college students and middle-aged adults rate their present selves, but not past selves, as above average relative to their peers. As noted earlier, a large majority of people cannot be above average compared with their peer group. These results therefore suggest that people inflate estimates of current self-worth by deprecating the way they were in the past.

Egocentric memory biases, then, are reflected in several related maneuvers — selective recall, exaggerating past difficulties, and deprecating past selves — that surround the present self in a comforting glow of positive illusions.

WHISTLING VIVALDI

When the Black journalist Brent Staples arrived as a student at the University of Chicago, he enjoyed walking near the lakeshore at night. Staples became unnerved one evening when he noticed that a white businesswoman, suddenly aware of his presence on the street, walked away quickly and then began to run. "I'd been a fool," reflected Staples. "I'd been walking the streets grinning good evening at people who were frightened to death of me." Attempting to ease concern that he was stalking white pedestrians or was otherwise ill intentioned, Staples started whistling Vivaldi's *The Four Seasons* to signal that he was a benign stroller. "The tension drained from people's bodies when they heard me," Staples recalled. "A few even smiled as they passed me in the dark."

Staples whistled Vivaldi because his presence activated in white strangers' memories a powerful stereotype that biased their perceptions of him: when walking on a quiet street at night, a Black man poses danger. The resourceful Staples came up with an effective method to avoid being viewed in such stereotypical — and erroneous — terms.

Stereotypes are generic descriptions of past experiences that we use to categorize people and objects. Many social psychologists think of stereotypes as "energy-saving" devices that simplify the task of comprehending our social worlds. Because it may require considerable cognitive effort to size up every new person we meet as a unique individual, we often find it easier to fall back on stereotypical generalizations that accumulate from various sources, including discussions with other people, printed and electronic media, and firsthand experience. Though relying on such stereotypes may make our cognitive lives more manageable, it can also lead to undesirable outcomes: when a stereotype diverges from reality in a specific instance — as happened with Brent Staples — the resulting biases can produce inaccurate judgments and unwarranted behavior.

The great social psychologist Gordon Allport was one of the first psychologists to recognize how the dual nature of stereotypes contributes to racial biases. While acknowledging that stereotypes help us to categorize the world, Allport held that "we often make mistakes in fitting events to categories and thus get ourselves in trouble." In his classic 1954 book, *The Nature of Prejudice,* Allport foresaw quite clearly the situation that Brent Staples would confront decades later. "A person with dark brown skin will activate whatever concept of Negro is dominant in our mind," contended Allport. "If the dominant category is one composed of negative attitudes and beliefs we will automatically avoid him, or adopt whichever habit of rejection is most available to us."

Allport's assessment was especially prescient because research has underscored that stereotypical biases can occur automatically, outside of conscious awareness. Early evidence for this view came from experiments that activated stereotypes by presenting words too quickly to register in conscious perception (a procedure known as "subliminal priming"). After subliminal priming with words intended to activate a stereotype of "Blacks," such as *welfare, busing,* and *ghetto,* white American students were more likely to judge an imaginary male of an unspecified race as a hostile person than when they were primed with neutral words. Further, the biasing effect was just as powerful in those students who expressed little racial prejudice on a questionnaire as in those who overtly expressed considerable racial prejudice.

The latter finding is particularly troubling because it suggests that even people who consciously experience little prejudice automatically activate stereotypical biases. But results from a British study point toward differences between high- and low-prejudice individuals. Like American students, high- and low-prejudice white British students were both biased to see a race-unspecified person as hostile after subliminal priming with negative words that directly activate a racial stereotype, such as *drugs, rude,* and *crime.* But only high-prejudice individuals showed a biasing effect after subliminal priming with neutral words that activate the general category of "Black people," such as *colored, afro,* and *West Indians.*

Stereotypical biases can also result in disturbing tendencies for people to "remember" hearing about nonexistent Black criminals. Mahzarin Banaji and her coworkers showed college students male names, indicating that some might seem familiar because they were names of criminals who had appeared recently in the media. Although none were actually names of criminals, the students were almost twice as likely to identify stereotypically Black names (Tyrone Washington, Darnell Jones) as those of criminals compared to stereotypically white names (Adam McCarthy, Frank Smith). The bias occurred even when people were instructed that "people who are racist identify more black names than white names; please do not use the race of the name in making your judgment."

Bias effects are not restricted to racial stereotypes. In another series of studies, Banaji and her collaborators exposed people to names of famous and nonfamous people, and later asked them to judge whether these and other names were famous or not. Previous studies had shown that after seeing nonfamous names, people sometimes later mistakenly classify them as famous. The nonfamous names seem familiar because they were presented earlier in the experiment, but participants forgot where they encountered the name —a misattribution error similar to those we considered in Chapter 4. In Banaji's experiment, people were far more likely to make this "false fame" error for male names than for female names. A gender stereotype — men are more likely to be famous than women — biased participants to make erroneous claims about the supposed fame of made-up male names.

A case can be made that such stereotypical biases are defensible and even reasonable. After all, in our society men are more likely to be famous than women; likewise, a higher proportion of Black than white men are in prison. The latter consideration probably motivated the behavior of the night strollers who conspicuously avoided Brent Staples: the University of Chicago area where he lived borders on largely Black and crime-ridden neighborhoods. Considered in statistical terms that apply to groups of people — men and women, Blacks and whites — stereotypical biases are not necessarily erroneous. The problem arises because people are sometimes willing to act on these biases in cases in which they are entirely unwarranted, resulting in what Banaji calls "guilt by association" rather than "guilt by behavior": individuals are perceived negatively based on their membership in a group rather than because of their specific behaviors or attributes.

Activated stereotypes not only bias how we think and behave; they can also influence what we remember. If I tell you that Julian, an artist, is creative, temperamental, generous, and fearless, you are more likely to recall the first two attributes, which fit the stereotype of an artist, than the latter two attributes, which do not. If I tell you that he is a skinhead and list some of his characteristics, you're more likely to remember that he is rebellious and aggressive than that he is lucky and modest. This "congruity bias" is especially likely to occur when people hold strong stereotypes about a particular group. A person with strong racial prejudices, for example, would be more likely than a less prejudiced person to remember stereotypical features of a Black man's behavior and less likely to remember behaviors that don't fit the stereotype. This tendency can create a self-perpetuating cycle in which a stereotype biases recall of congruent incidents, which in turn strengthens the stereotypical bias.

Stereotype bias also tends to occur when we don't make an effort to consider an individual's particular characteristics because we are mentally preoccupied with other matters. In controlled experiments, for instance, stereotype bias is most pronounced when people are given difficult tasks to carry out at the same time that they form impressions of people. You are most likely to recall only that Julian the artist is creative and temperamental if, when you first meet him, you are devoting most of your attention to thinking about an important meeting or an exam you will soon be taking. When you can devote more cognitive effort to sizing up Julian as an individual, you may actually recall more information that is incongruent with the stereotype. If you notice that Julian seems unusually even-keeled, for instance, you may wonder why he is so different from your stereotypical expectation of a temperamental artist. As a result of carrying out elaborative encoding to resolve the apparent discrepancy, you later remember clearly Julian's even-keeled demeanor.

When events unfold in a way that contradicts our expectations based on stereotypes and related knowledge of the world, we may be biased to fabricate incidents that never happened in order to bring our memories in line with our expectations. Consider two versions of a story about a man, Bob, who dearly wanted to marry his girlfriend, Margie, but did not want children and was anxious about how Margie would react if he told her. In one version of the story, Margie was thrilled to hear that Bob wished to remain childless because this desire fit well with her career plans. In another version, Margie was horrified because she desperately wanted children. Now consider two possible endings: Bob and Margie married, or Bob and Margie ended their relationship.

If you had read that Margie was thrilled by Bob's disclosure, then, based on your general knowledge of relationships, you would expect them to marry and find it surprising if they split up. But if you had read that Margie was horrified by Bob's disclosure, you might expect a breakup and be surprised if they married. Experiments have shown that when trying to recall the story, people who received incongruous endings mistakenly remembered critical incidents in a way that made sense of the outcomes. For instance, participants who read that Margie was horrified, and then learned that Bob and Margie married, recalled incorrectly, "They separated but realized after discussing the matter that their love mattered more." But participants who read that Margie was thrilled, and later learned that the couple split, incorrectly recalled such incidents as "There was a hassle with one or the other's parents" or "They *disagreed* about having children."

Much as the Ministry of Truth in Orwell's *1984* revises the historical past to fit its current precepts, general knowledge biases story recall so that memory fits neatly with expectations. In *1984*, responsibility for revision and fabrication fall on the shoulders of workers within the Ministry of Truth, such as the novel's protagonist, Winston Smith. In the world of memory, revisionist biases have been linked with one of the most puzzling subsystems in the human brain.

THE BASIS OF BIAS

In the late 1960s, neuropsychologists described an arresting syndrome that immediately captured the imagination of scientists and the general public alike. Patients who had undergone surgical separation of the left and right cerebral hemispheres as a treatment for intractable epilepsy — "split-brain" patients — behaved as if they housed two minds in a single body. The left hemisphere handled language and symbols, the right specialized in nonverbal information such as images and spatial locations. Though these patients seemed normal in casual conversation and social interaction, careful psychological testing revealed that situations could be devised in which each hemisphere digested incoming information without awareness of what the other was experiencing.

Despite its ignorance of happenings in the right hemisphere, the left hemisphere is nonetheless quite adept at coming up with various explanations and rationalizations for the strange situations that result from its surgical disconnection. The Dartmouth neuroscientist Michael Gazzaniga, who pioneered much of the research on split-brain patients, used clever experimental procedures to create conflicts between the left and right hemispheres to reveal the left brain's propensity for explanation and rationalization. For instance, after flashing the command "walk" to a split-brain patient's right hemisphere, without the knowledge of the left hemisphere, the patient would get up as instructed. When asked why he was walking, the patient — now relying on the verbal left brain — rationalized that he was going to get a soda. In another classic demonstration, Gazzaniga exposed a picture of a snow-covered house to the right brain and a chicken claw to the left. The patient was instructed to pick (from several choices) a line drawing of an object that related to the picture he saw. The patient's right hand (controlled by the left hemisphere) chose a rooster to match the chicken claw, whereas his left hand (controlled by the right hemisphere) chose a snow shovel to match the winter scene. The patient, faced with the bizarre sight of his two hands pointing to different drawings, consulted his verbal left hemisphere (which had no knowledge of the winter scene presented to the right brain) and immediately offered an explanation. He chose the shovel with his left hand, the patient claimed, because it could be used to clean out the chicken coop! Innocent that the left hand actually chose the shovel because it fit the winter scene shown to the nonverbal right hemisphere, the left brain confidently — but erroneously — generated an after-the-fact rationalization that made sense of the otherwise bewildering choice.

Based on these and other similar observations, Gazzaniga postulates that the left brain contains an "interpreter" that is continually drawing on general knowledge and past experience to try to bring order to our psychological worlds. These activities can produce memory biases not unlike those considered earlier in this chapter. For instance, Gazzaniga and his colleague Elizabeth Phelps showed split-brain patients slide sequences of such everyday activities as a man getting up for a day's work. Later, they tested the memories of the left and right hemispheres for incidents shown earlier, such as the man looking at his alarm clock, and novel incidents that had nothing to do with the studied sequences, such as the same man fixing a television. Most important, each hemisphere was also asked about incidents that fit the stereotype (or "schema") of getting up for work but that did not actually appear in the initial slide sequence — sitting up in bed, brushing teeth, and the like.

The left hemisphere often falsely recognized novel incidents that were consistent with the stereotype, whereas the right hemisphere hardly ever did. The left-brain interpreter was at work again, showing a bias to respond on the basis of general knowledge about activities usually involved in getting up for work. Though the left hemisphere's responses made sense in general terms — people do typically sit up in bed or brush their teeth when they get up for work — they were wrong when applied to the particular slides shown on this specific occasion.

The resemblance to the stereotypical biases considered earlier is striking. The left-brain interpreter relies on inferences, rationalizations, and generalizations as it tries to relate past and present, and in so doing probably also contributes to consistency, change, hindsight, and egocentric biases. The interpreter may help to confer a sense of order in our lives, allowing us to reconcile our present attitudes with our past actions and feelings, generating a comforting sense that we always knew how things would turn out, or enhancing our opinions of ourselves. But it also has the potential to lead us down the path of delusion. If the facile explanations and rationalizations offered by the interpreter generate powerful biases that prevent us from seeing ourselves in a realistic light, we are clearly at risk for repeating past failures in the future.

Fortunately, the left-brain interpreter is balanced by systems in the right hemisphere that are more attuned to the constraints of the external world. In Phelps and Gazzaniga's memory study, for instance, the right brain claimed to remember only the exact incidents it witnessed and almost never falsely recognized similar events that hadn't happened. In fMRI studies led by Wilma Koutstaal in my laboratory, we discovered that part of the right visual cortex is sensitive to whether an identical object is presented on two occasions (the same picture of a table) compared with two different examples of the same object (pictures of different tables). But the left visual cortex responds similarly whether objects shown on two occasions are identical or merely alike.

The right hemisphere's proclivity for responding on a literal basis can help to keep in check its more expansive and error-prone cerebral neighbor. In Orwell's *1984*, the Ministry of Truth enjoys sovereign rule, unfettered by any countervailing forces; the result is a totalitarian disaster. The left-brain interpreter, left to its own devices, might well produce a similarly calamitous outcome in individual minds: unchecked bias and rationalization could lead us to a bottomless abyss of self-delusion. Happily for our species, however, the brain has engineered a system of checks and balances missing in Orwell's nightmare vision. Still, the various forms of bias are so deeply embedded in human cognition that few good remedies exist for overcoming or avoiding them altogether. Perhaps the best we can do is to appreciate that current knowledge, beliefs, and feelings can influence our recollections of the past and shape our impressions of people and objects in the present. By exercising due vigilance and recognizing the possible sources of our convictions about both past and present, we can reduce the distortions that arise when memory functions as a pawn in the service of its masters.

The Update
FAKE NEWS: HOW BIAS IMPACTS MEMORY AND JUDGMENT

I began this chapter by discussing the manipulative practices of the Ministry of Truth in Orwell's *1984*. The totalitarian regime's chilling conclusion that past events "have no objective existence," surviving through malleable human memories that can be influenced for purposes of political control, seemed to me a compelling backdrop for thinking about the ways in which retrospective biases can shape individual memories. It never occurred to me back in 2001 that some of the issues raised by the workings of the fictional Ministry of Truth in 1984 would become central to political discussions fifteen years later. But concerns regarding the impact of "fake news" on the 2016 presidential election in the United States, and the emergence of "alternative facts" as a way of describing false claims made by members of Donald Trump's administration, brought discussions regarding the nature and even the existence of "truth" to the center of political life. Given a sharply divided electorate that often consumes political news from media silos that cater to and confirm preexisting beliefs, "truth" in today's political world is all too often the product of consistency biases that shape perception and memory.

A 2013 study of memory for true and false political events supports this idea. More than five thousand participants completed an online survey posted at Slate.com that probed whether people remembered three actual political events and five fabricated events. Consistent with previous studies of misattribution and suggestibility, 27 percent claimed to remember seeing the fabricated events on the news, and about 50 percent claimed some type of memory for the fabricated event. Bias, however, clearly played a role in shaping these false memories. For example, conservative participants were especially likely to report a false memory for a fabricated event that depicted President Barack Obama in a negative light (shaking hands with the president of Iran), whereas liberal participants were especially likely to report a false memory for a fabricated event that depicted President George W. Bush in a negative light (vacationing with a baseball player during Hurricane Katrina).

A study carried out just prior to the May 2018 referendum concerning abortion rights in Ireland provides additional evidence highlighting the close links between consistency bias, fake news, and false memories. The eighth amendment to the constitution of Ireland guaranteed the unborn a right to life, resulting in extremely restrictive abortion laws. The referendum was on whether to repeal the eighth amendment (the "yes" side) or preserve it (the "no" side). The "yes" side won a landslide victory over the "no" side. The week before the referendum, the Irish psychologist Gillian Murphy and her colleagues administered an online survey to more than three thousand adults, most of whom indicated that they would be voting in the referendum. The survey included photos and headlines of four true and two fake news stories pertaining to both the "yes" and "no" campaigns. Critically, there were two versions of each of the fake news stories, one that reflected negatively on the "yes" side and another that reflected negatively on the "no" side. For example, one of the fake news headlines — "The Together for Yes campaign (or Save the 8th campaign) was forced to destroy 25,000 campaign posters after evidence emerged that the posters were bought using funding received from American pro-choice (or pro-life) lobbyists" — was accompanied by a photo of the poster.

The researchers asked whether participants remembered the event described in the headline and then asked them to choose one of the following options:

1. I remember seeing/hearing this.
2. I don't remember seeing/hearing this but I remember it happening.
3. I don't remember this but I believe it happened.
4. I remember this differently.
5. I don't remember this.

Overall, 48 percent of the participants indicated that they remembered at least one of the two fake news stories by selecting Option 1 or 2; that percentage rose to 63 percent when Option 3 was included. (See The Update in Chapter 5 for my discussion of false memories versus false beliefs.) Among the 48 percent who claimed to remember a fake event, 37 percent chose Option 1, claiming a specific recollection, and the remaining 11 percent chose Option 2, indicating a more general memory.

Similar to the results from the Bush-Obama false memory study, bias played a crucial role: "yes" supporters were more likely than "no" supporters to report a false memory for fake news about the "no" side, whereas "no" supporters showed the opposite pattern. The researchers also obtained measures of overall cognitive ability (using a vocabulary test that is strongly positively correlated with overall IQ scores), and they found that biased false memories of fake news that depicted the opposite side in an unfavorable light were especially frequent among respondents with low cognitive ability.

Once again, we have evidence for the workings of an internal "Ministry of Truth" operating within individuals that colors memory to the point that we are more likely to falsely remember fake events when they fit our personal "party line" than when they don't. A study of Donald Trump and Hillary Clinton supporters in the 2016 presidential election has also pointed toward lazy thinking and low reasoning ability (as opposed to biased reasoning) as a key factor in susceptibility to fake news.

In addition to consistency bias, assessment of fake news stories is impacted by a "truth bias": when presented with ambiguous statements that might be true or might be false, people typically exhibit a moderate bias to judge them as true. Importantly, mere repetition of a statement often further bolsters a person's belief that it is true. This is known as the "illusory truth effect," which was initially established back in the 1970s but has recently been demonstrated when people make judgments about the veracity of real-life fake news stories posted on Facebook. In the latter study, a single previous exposure to a fake news story increased participants' judgments of how accurate it was, even when the story was implausible and fact-checkers flagged it as problematic. The only fake headlines that escaped this illusory truth effect were ones that promoted preposterous claims that could be quickly dismissed as false (e.g., "The Earth is a perfect square"), but more recent research indicates that even blatantly false statements can be subject to the illusory truth effect. Disturbingly, similar effects of repetition occur even for news stories that one knows for certain are fake. Other research has shown that following one or four exposures to a fake news headline, people judged that it was less unethical to share the news when they saw the headline again (compared to novel headlines), even though they were explicitly instructed that the headline was fake! People also indicated that they would be more likely to share repeated fake headlines than novel headlines.

One recent study examined the impact of repetition on both illusory truth and consistency bias. The researchers measured whether Democrats and Republicans responded differently after repeated exposure to claims made by Donald Trump. Participants made truth judgments about statements that, according to a fact-checking organization, varied in truth value on a six-point scale from "True" to "Pants on Fire." In light of the evidence we have considered regarding consistency bias and fake news, you might think that the illusory truth effect would be greater in Republicans than in Democrats. It wasn't. Repetition increased the rated truth value of Trump's statements to the same degree for both Republicans and Democrats. Moreover, this effect was present in both groups to the same degree, even for statements rated as "False" or "Pants on Fire" by fact-checkers. In this study, then, an illusory truth effect was evident even though a consistency bias was not.

Given that consistency bias and truth bias can play a role when people judge fake news items, it becomes an urgent matter to figure out how to counter the biasing influences of the internal "Ministry of Truth" that can lead us astray both when we attempt to reconstruct events from the past and when we assess the truth value of assertions in the present.

The Rise of Implicit Bias

On September 26, 2016, Clinton and Trump engaged in their first debate of the presidential campaign, which, with more than 80 million viewers tuned in, set a record as the most-watched debate in American history. The evening had its share of memorable moments, but one that stood out to me occurred when moderator Lester Holt asked Clinton about a recent remark she had made concerning the necessity of addressing implicit bias in police. Clinton responded, "Lester, I think implicit bias is a problem for everyone, not just police."

That moment was striking to a psychologist because we don't expect to hear concepts from the psychological literature discussed in a presidential debate. "Implicit bias" refers to the idea that people can be influenced by stereotypes that operate outside of conscious awareness. The concept grew out of two research literatures. The first concerns work on stereotype bias, discussed earlier in this chapter, which even by 2001 had produced evidence that this type of bias can occur automatically, outside of our awareness. The second concept concerns a distinction that the cognitive psychologist Peter Graf and I drew in 1985 between "explicit memory" (conscious recollection of past experiences) and "implicit memory" (nonconscious effects of past experience on subsequent behavior and thought). I haven't said much about implicit memory in this book because the seven sins refer mainly to misdeeds of explicit memory. In 1995, the social psychologists Anthony Greenwald and Mahzarin Banaji published an influential paper that extended the concept of implicit memory to what they called "implicit social cognition" (i.e., nonconscious effects of past experiences on subsequent social processing) and also made the case that stereotype biases can operate implicitly. A few years later, Greenwald and his colleagues reported a new task, the Implicit Association Test (IAT), which provided a novel measure of stereotypical biases. In 2017, Greenwald and Banaji described the initial IAT:

Subjects are asked to respond to four categories of stimuli with just two responses (usually two keys on a computer keyboard). In the first IAT, the four categories were flowers, insects, pleasant, and unpleasant, each represented by words. A surprisingly strong finding was that when one key was used for both flower names and pleasant-meaning words (and the other key for insect names and unpleasant-meaning words), responding averaged about 300 ms [milliseconds] faster than if one key was for insects and pleasant and the other for flowers and unpleasant.

The idea here is simple but ingenious: quicker responses to categories that fit together based on past experiences (e.g., flower names and pleasant words) compared with responses to categories that don't fit together (e.g., insect names and pleasant words) reflect the influence of stronger associations in memory that implicitly impact a person's performance. The finding that made the IAT relevant to social cognition and racial bias came from another experiment that found that white participants responded more quickly to pairings of white faces with pleasant words than to pairings of Black faces with pleasant words — even though, on an explicit measure of racial attitudes (e.g., rating on a numerical scale one's attitudes or feelings about a racial group), most of these participants did not express a preference for whites over Blacks. What began as a series of laboratory experiments spawned Project Implicit, a Harvard website where anyone can take an IAT regarding a number of topics (e.g., race, gender, sexual orientation). A large-scale 2002 study based on IAT data collected at the Project Implicit website from more than 100,000 white respondents and 17,000 Black respondents revealed that white participants showed a large implicit bias favoring whites over Blacks and a smaller explicit bias favoring whites. Black participants showed a much weaker implicit bias favoring whites despite showing an explicit bias favoring Blacks over whites.

Research using the IAT to examine implicit bias has exploded during the past two decades, more than 20 million people have taken an IAT at the Project Implicit website, and discussions of the implications of these findings have spread far beyond the bounds of social psychology labs to such domains of everyday life as policing and hiring practices — as well as to that 2016 presidential debate. This explosion has been accompanied by controversies regarding the reliability, validity, and interpretation of findings from the IAT that are still the subjects of intense debate.

However, the IAT is not the only task that reveals signs of implicit bias. Consider studies by the psychologist Joshua Correll and his colleagues concerning the "police officer's dilemma": whether or not to shoot a suspect who may or may not be armed. Correll's experiments use what he calls the first person shooter task (FPST), a video game in which participants see images of armed or unarmed young men, half white and half Black, and their goal is to shoot the targets armed with a gun while refraining from shooting the unarmed targets (who are holding a camera instead of a gun). The images are flashed to participants very quickly, and when participants pull the trigger, they typically do so in less than a second. In a series of studies, Correll and his colleagues found that participants were more likely (and quicker) to (1) shoot armed targets when the targets were Black than when they were white, (2) refrain from shooting an unarmed target when the targets were white than when they were Black, and (3) make the mistake of shooting unarmed targets when those targets were Black than when they were white. This same overall pattern was observed regardless of whether the *shooter* was Black or white.

Questions about implicit bias have special urgency for the police, especially in light of recent high-profile shootings of unarmed Blacks that have raised questions about the possible role of implicit bias. Correll and his colleagues addressed this issue by examining police performance in their FPST paradigm. They found that police officers from four different districts in Denver were overall more accurate in detecting the presence of a weapon and faster to make correct responses than were community members from the same districts. And in contrast to community members, police officers did not show a bias to shoot more Black than white targets. But like community members, the response times of police officers revealed an implicit bias: they were quicker to make shoot/no-shoot decisions regarding targets that fit racial stereotypes (unarmed white targets and armed Black targets) than those that did not (armed white targets and unarmed Black targets).

Can training to overcome implicit bias help with the kinds of racial biases revealed by the IAT and FPST? Social psychologists have been asking this question in research studies for the past twenty years, and training to counter implicit bias has become increasingly popular in various everyday settings, including in police departments, the corporate workplace, and academia. The potential importance of these efforts is underscored by recent evidence that people who perpetrate discrimination may be held less accountable when that discrimination is attributed to implicit bias than to explicit bias. As a result, discriminatory behaviors attributed to implicit bias may be especially difficult to stop.

Evidence for a significant and lasting influence of implicit bias training is, at best, patchy. In 2012, the social psychologist Patricia Devine, one of the pioneers in research on implicit bias, published a study in which ninety-one undergraduates took part in a twelve-week training program that used a suite of five strategies for reducing implicit racial bias, including imagining Black individuals who don't fit Black stereotypes, taking the perspective of a Black individual, and related approaches. Devine and her colleagues reported reductions in implicit bias, as assessed by the Black-white version of the IAT, at both four weeks and eight weeks after training. In a larger-scale 2014 effort, a group of more than twenty researchers led by the social psychologist Calvin Lai held a contest to evaluate the efficacy of eighteen interventions designed to reduce implicit racial bias. In studies based on a sample size of more than 17,000 participants, only half of the interventions reduced implicit bias on the IAT. The most effective interventions were those that exposed participants to examples that contradicted Black stereotypes, and the least effective ones required participants to think about values that emphasize equality or to experience empathy. Notably, none of the interventions reduced explicit racial preferences. In 2016, Lai and his colleagues performed additional experiments that confirmed that the nine interventions that were successful in reducing implicit bias in their previous work were also effective when they assessed implicit bias immediately after the intervention. But none of the interventions were effective when researchers assessed implicit bias after delays of just a few hours or days. A more recent meta-analysis examined attempts to change implicit biases on a variety of measures in nearly 500 different studies involving more than 87,000 participants. This analysis found some evidence that implicit biases can be changed, but the effects were often weak and short-term, and the observed changes in implicit bias did not predict changes in explicit measures or behavior.

These results raise serious questions about whether there can be a significant payoff from implicit bias training designed to impact everyday behaviors by police or in corporate or academic settings. But the lack of clear-cut evidence for robust and lasting training effects should not be entirely surprising if we view implicit bias as a result of experiences that are built up across a lifetime and maintain a strong hold at deep levels of memory. In the case of race, implicit bias likely reflects exposure to and retention of culturally widespread associations linking Black individuals with danger and threat based on information contained in sources such as media reports of crime and poverty in Black neighborhoods and television and movie depictions of Blacks as criminals. These negative cultural associations are likely offset to some extent in Black individuals by more positive personal interactions with other Blacks than are experienced by most whites.

Psychologists have made significant strides in addressing the nature and extent of implicit bias since 2001, and the field's database of experimental findings is much more robust now than it was then. But my conclusions regarding the prospects for eradicating bias are not much different than they were two decades ago: bias is so deeply embedded in human cognition that it is going to be a tough task to eliminate it altogether. Hopefully, however, with increasing awareness of the potentially pernicious effects of implicit bias, the cultural inputs that give rise to it will change over time. In fact, there is evidence that something along these lines is happening already. Using more than 4 million test results from the IAT gathered at the Project Implicit website between 2007 and 2016, Tessa Charlesworth and Mahzarin Banaji found that both explicit and implicit attitudes regarding race, skin tone, and sexual orientation showed decreasing evidence of bias across that decade. Explicit but not implicit attitudes showed reduced bias regarding age, disability, and body weight. Bias may not be easy to change, but neither is it entirely immutable.

7

The Sin of
Persistence

ON A SUNNY AFTERNOON in early October 1986, a jubilant
crowd of baseball fans cheered as the hometown California Angels
neared victory over the Boston Red Sox in the American League
Championship Series. In the ninth inning of the fifth game, the Angels held a seemingly insurmountable advantage: leading by a score
of 5–2, they needed only one more win to clinch the series. But the
Red Sox rallied, cutting the lead to 5–4 and putting a runner on first
base with two outs. Trying to end the game, the Angels manager,
Gene Mauch, summoned the ace reliever Donnie Moore from the
bullpen to face the journeyman outfielder Dave Henderson. Moore
quickly threw two strikes. Angels fans and players began to celebrate
as the seemingly overmatched Henderson barely fouled off a pitch
to avoid striking out. With the odds stacked heavily against him,
Henderson hammered Moore's next offering into deep left field for
a game-winning home run. Moore, his teammates, and the crowd
watched in disbelief as Henderson trotted around the bases. The Angels failed to bounce back, and the Red Sox advanced to the World
Series.

With the passing of time, Angels players and fans eventually recovered from the deflating loss. But Donnie Moore never did. He
was haunted, sometimes overwhelmed, by the memory of Henderson's home run. Though his teammates tried to remind him of all
the games he had saved during the season, Moore focused only on
the fateful pitch, blaming himself for the team's defeat. Fans and media helped to strengthen the vivid recollection by talking about the
incident incessantly. Unable to shake the memory, Moore sank into

an ever-deepening depression that undermined his marriage and career. In July 1989, Moore's descent concluded violently. "Tormented by the memory of one pitch," began a bulletin from the Associated Press, "and despondent over his failing career and marital troubles, former California Angels pitcher Donnie Moore shot his wife numerous times before killing himself, police said." Moore's agent, Dave Pinter, commented that "even when he was told that one pitch doesn't make a season, he couldn't get over it. That home run killed him."

Though Moore's downfall was probably not entirely attributable to this single incident, his demise nonetheless provides a dramatic example of memory's seventh and perhaps most debilitating sin: persistence. In contrast to transience, absent-mindedness, and blocking, which entail forgetting information or events you wish you could remember, persistence involves remembering those things that you wish you could forget. Sometimes persistence is no more than a mild irritant. We've all had the experience of a tune or a song that we can't get out of our heads. We may at first enjoy the experience, but as time goes on, we tire of mentally "hearing" the persisting melody and attempt to banish the intruder from consciousness. Sometimes these persistent memories can distract us from more important tasks. I recall feeling flustered as a high school student when a favorite Led Zeppelin song kept running through my head in the middle of an exam, making concentration on the test almost impossible. Laurie Gordon, an undergraduate in one of my Harvard seminars, recounted a similar annoyance and the steps she took to prevent its recurrence:

> I was able to bring in a double-sided review sheet for one of my finals. I found that I had extra room on the sheet, since there wasn't much information that would be useful to have during the exam. I decided to fill the extra space on the sheet with lyrics from 5 or so of my favorite songs, so that I wouldn't run into the situation I had experienced the day before, when I had had difficulty concen-

trating because of an annoying song running through my head. Instead, when I took the exam, I was able to block out this song by looking at the song lyrics that I had written on my review sheet.

Though irritating, the "tune running through the head" experience occurs relatively infrequently, most often does not have serious consequences, and can be managed effectively with techniques such as the one Gordon used. The type of persistence that overwhelmed Donnie Moore is far more troubling. Despite the extraordinary nature of Moore's story, it nevertheless illuminates the primary territory of persistence: disappointment, regret, failure, sadness, and trauma. Experiences that we remember intrusively, despite desperately wanting to banish them from our minds, are closely linked to, and sometimes threaten, our perceptions of who we are and who we would like to be.

HOT MEMORIES

Because persistence is strongly linked with our emotional lives, to understand the seventh sin we need to consider the relationship between emotion and memory. Everyday experience and laboratory studies reveal that emotionally charged incidents are better remembered than nonemotional events. The emotional boost begins at the moment a memory is born, when attention and elaboration strongly influence whether an experience will be subsequently remembered or forgotten. As bouts of absent-mindedness illustrate, when we fail to attend to or elaboratively encode incoming information, we stand little chance of remembering it later.

Experiments have shown that emotional information attracts attention quickly and automatically, illustrated nicely by experiments using a variant of the famous "Stroop effect." Print the word *yellow* in yellow marker, *red* in blue marker, and *green* in black marker, then try to name the color in which each of the words is printed. You will notice that you take longer to say "blue" and "black" than "yellow," because you can't help but analyze the meanings of *red* and *green*, which conflict with the colors you are trying to name. Something similar can happen when you use emotional words such as *sad* and *joy*: compared with neutral words like *wet*, naming the colors of positive and negative words takes longer. The emotional words seem to draw attention automatically, which gets in the way of naming the color. In the split second that it takes to read a word, its emotional significance is retrieved and evaluated, influencing how we name and encode it.

After this first-pass automatic evaluation, the significance of emotional information undergoes evaluation in relation to our current goals and concerns. Goals may be short-term, such as striking out a batter to end a baseball game, or long-term, such as performing well during the course of a baseball season to attain a higher future salary. When our actions prevent us from attaining our goals — as with Donnie Moore — we feel sadness, frustration, or disappointment. When they allow us to attain our goals — imagine that Moore had struck out Dave Henderson — we feel happiness and perhaps elation. When we relate a current experience to short- or long-term goals, we engage in a kind of reflection and analysis — elaborative encoding — that promotes subsequent memory for the experience.

Though memory for emotional events generally benefits from both automatic first-pass evaluation and later reflections, there's a cost. Consider a bystander in a bank as a robbery unfolds. Attempting to escape, the crook brandishes a gun; feeling a rush of fear, the bystander instantly focuses on the weapon. Consequently, the bystander can later recall the gun's features in great detail. But when police ask for a description of the robber, they can summon only a hazy memory of the robber's face — not enough information to help investigators. Psychologists call this phenomenon "weapon focus." The emotionally arousing object draws attention automatically, leaving few resources to help encode the rest of the scene. Experiments have shown that people usually remember well the central focus of an emotionally arousing incident, at the expense of poor memory for peripheral details.

The benefits of emotional arousal for subsequent memory extend to both positive and negative events: we remember more high and low moments from our lives than mundane ones. And positive experiences, just like negative experiences, tend to be remembered involuntarily and intrusively. Roughly 90 percent of college students who recorded emotional incidents in a diary reported that they later experienced at least some intrusive memories for both positive and negative events, with more intense emotions producing more frequent intrusive memories. The difference, of course, is that positive memories are usually welcome intruders — we enjoy basking in the glow of a recent business success, athletic accomplishment, or romantic encounter — whereas negative memories are decidedly not.

Psychologists have long debated whether positive experiences are better remembered than negative ones, or vice versa. Though little evidence in this regard has turned up so far, experiments conducted in my laboratory by the psychologist Kevin Ochsner revealed an intriguing qualitative difference between the two. He showed college students a series of positive, negative, and neutral photographs, such as a smiling baby, a disfigured face, and an ordinary building. On a later test, people recognized more of the positive and negative pictures than the neutral ones, and they recognized about the same number of positive and negative pictures. But when Ochsner probed the experimental participants more closely about why they claimed to recognize a particular picture, differences between positive and negative memories began to emerge. When people recognized positive pictures, they tended to say that the pictures just seemed familiar; when they recognized negative pictures, they reported detailed, specific recollections of what they thought and felt when they originally encountered the item. If we tend to remember negative events in greater detail than positive ones, then we may be at special risk for persistently retrieving painful particulars of those experiences we would like most to forget.

WHEN MEMORY HURTS

Our chances of becoming chronically plagued by persistence depend in part on what happens after an adverse experience. Over time, the sting associated with unpleasant events often fades. We've all endured difficult experiences — the death of a loved one, rejection by a lover, failure at work — that pain us mightily in the days and weeks after they occur. In the immediate aftermath, we may find ourselves reliving the painful incident to the point of distraction, but the raw hurt eventually dissipates. Some data suggest that negative emotions may actually fade faster than positive ones. Consider a study in which college students kept diaries of daily experiences, rated the pleasantness and other features of the events, and then tried to remember the experiences and associated emotions at various times ranging from three months to over four years after the incident occurred. Memory for unpleasant emotions faded faster than memory for pleasant emotions.

Reminders of difficult experiences can slow the normal fading of painful emotions over time. The great novelist Gabriel García Márquez began his novel *Love in the Time of Cholera* with a tribute to one: "It was inevitable: the scent of bitter almonds always reminded him of the fate of unrequited love." Continual reminding can strengthen recall of the disturbing specifics of what happened to the point that persistence becomes unbearable. Reporters, fans, and the media hounded Donnie Moore for months after Henderson's home run, making it impossible for him to find relief in the usual benefits conferred by the passing of time. His teammate Brian Downing blamed the media for reminding Moore unrelentingly. "You destroyed a man's life over one pitch," commented Downing ruefully after learning of Moore's suicide. "All you ever heard about, all you ever read about, was one pitch."

Reminders of unpleasant experiences can also induce us to engage in what psychologists call "counterfactual thinking" — generating alternative scenarios of what might have been or should have been. Anyone who has invested in the stock market is likely familiar with the power of counterfactual thinking. You track a favorite stock as its price steadily rises. Finally, you work up the nerve to invest, and in no time your worst fears are realized: the market begins a correction, and you lose 20 percent of your investment within a few days. As you helplessly watch the stock drop, you become overwhelmed with regret over your hasty action. "If only I had been more patient and waited for the market to tumble," you chide yourself as you relive the moments leading up to your decision to throw money after the stock. You wake up at night ruminating about your decision, imagining how happy you would have been had you decided to wait just one or two more days to invest. Such counterfactual thinking can easily lead to the kind of hindsight biases we considered in Chapter 6.

I experienced an unsettling episode of such counterfactual thinking during a trip to a midwinter conference in Florida. Scheduled to return to Boston on a Friday night, I heard a weather report warn of a massive storm that would surely result in my flight's cancellation. Should I leave the conference early and try to beat the storm to Boston, or relax and enjoy another day or two of Florida sunshine? After some hesitation, I opted to outrace the storm. The strategy almost worked: my flight was cleared to land in Boston, and it looked as if I would arrive home ahead of the blizzard. But conditions deteriorated rapidly, the pilot was unable to touch down, and we ended up making an emergency landing in Maine. Then I endured an eighteen-hour odyssey of waiting, another failed landing attempt, a diversion to JFK Airport in New York, and finally an overnight limousine ride to Boston with several other flustered passengers. "Why didn't I stay in the sunshine?" I kept thinking to myself as the situation fell apart. Reflecting back on the moment when I decided to try to outrace the storm, I imagined myself on the phone to the airline, making the now clearly wise decision to remain in Florida a little while longer.

Persistent counterfactual thinking can be far more serious when people feel that they could or should have acted to prevent a tragedy. Friends and relatives of people who commit suicide, for instance, are frequently plagued by persisting counterfactual thoughts about what they could or should have done to prevent a loved one from taking their own life. "Some survivors will blame themselves for not intervening," concludes the British suicide expert Mark Williams, "and endlessly ruminate on what they could have done to prevent it." Even after a loved one died from an untreatable illness, another researcher reported, grieving family members "found themselves repeatedly reviewing, going over in their minds, the events leading up to the death, often endlessly replaying the incident, as if by doing so they could undo or alter the events that had occurred." One widow paralyzed by persistent counterfactual thinking commented, "I go through that last week in the hospital again and again. It seems photographed on my mind." Consistent with these real-life examples, laboratory studies have revealed that negative experiences result in higher levels of subsequent counterfactual, "if only" kinds of thinking than do positive experiences.

Persisting memories and counterfactual thinking almost invariably accompany such overwhelming events as the death of a loved one. But responses to many kinds of disappointments and failures depend, at least in part, on previous experiences that shape the way we view ourselves: even relentless reminding of an unpleasant experience need not result in paralyzing counterfactual thinking or the kind of crippling persistence that undermined Donnie Moore. Consider the case of Jean Van de Velde. This previously unknown French golf professional captured international attention in July 1999 when he led the prestigious British Open in the tournament's final round. Standing on the eighteenth tee, Van de Velde held a commanding three-shot lead and seemed assured of victory, needing only to avoid a complete disaster to win. Instead, he collapsed: wild shots into the remote reaches of the rough and water led to a triple-bogey eight as millions of golf fans around the world watched incredulously. Van de Velde fell into a three-way tie for the lead and then lost the tournament in a playoff, completing the most stunning meltdown that professional golf had ever witnessed.

Recognizing the magnitude of the disaster, articles the next day in London newspapers proclaimed that the bitter memory of his collapse would torment Van de Velde for the rest of his life. But that's not what happened. Though shaken and disappointed in the hours and days after he lost the tournament, Van de Velde did not become a prisoner of persisting memory the way that Donnie Moore did. Nor did he endlessly engage in counterfactual thinking about what he could or should have done on the fateful eighteenth hole. Instead, he explained the rationale for some of the controversial decisions he had made — decisions that backfired — and placed the experience in a broader perspective, noting that golf is a game and was only one part of his life. Van de Velde also enjoyed the new fame he had achieved by contending in an event of international stature. "Maybe it's in my temperament," Van de Velde commented several weeks later when reporters asked how he managed to handle the situation so well and avoid endlessly reliving what had happened on the final hole. "I don't live in the past."

The contrasting fates of Donnie Moore and Jean Van de Velde remind us that long-lasting persistence is not an inevitable consequence of all disappointments: how we respond to adversity and whether we become plagued by persistence depend on how we evaluate and appraise what happens to us. Psychologists refer to the compilations of past experiences that influence current evaluations as "self-schemas." Built up over years and decades, self-schemas contain evaluative knowledge of our own characteristics. Consider whether the following words describe you: sad, optimistic, successful, lethargic. To make such judgments, you consult a self-schema that contains relevant information based on individual experiences and composite pictures from different stages of your life. Emotionally healthy people tend to endorse more positive than negative words, whereas depressed individuals endorse more negative than positive words. Depression is associated with a highly negative self-schema, resulting in a chronic perception of oneself as an inadequate or flawed individual.

The great Russian poet Alexander Pushkin captured some of the searing emotions associated with intrusive memories that reinforce a negative life script or self-schema in a poem titled "Remembrance":

> And in the idle darkness comes the bite
> Of all the burning serpents of remorse;

Dreams seethe; and fretful infelicities
Are swarming in my over-burdened soul
And Memory before my wakeful eyes
With noiseless hand unwinds her lengthy scroll.
Then, as with loathing I peruse the years,
I tremble, and I curse my natal day,
Wail bitterly, and bitterly shed tears,
But cannot wash the woeful script away.

A negative self-schema can easily lead to depression because it provides a rich network of knowledge that facilitates encoding and later retention of negative experiences. When depressed patients make judgments about whether such words as *failure* or *happy* describe them accurately, they later recall more of the negative words, but not more of the positive words, than healthy controls. The psychologist Patricia Deldin found that depressed and nondepressed individuals show different patterns of electrical brain activity during encoding of positive and negative information. Depressed patients, relative to healthy controls, showed larger electrical responses to negative than to positive words. These differences, which occur during the fleeting moments when a new memory is born, create conditions that favor persistent retrieval of negative experiences — which in turn can heighten depressed mood, contributing to a self-perpetuating and potentially vicious cycle.

We don't know whether Donnie Moore possessed an unusually negative self-schema that left him vulnerable to persistence, nor do we know whether Jean Van de Velde possessed an exceptionally positive self-schema that protected him from memory's seventh sin. But we do know that patients suffering from clinical depression are especially prone to persistence. Studies carried out by the University of London psychologist Chris Brewin and his associates reveal that depressed patients are much more prone to intrusive memories of negative experiences than are healthy controls. In one study, for instance, Brewin's group found that nearly all patients who became depressed as a result of a recent death, health problem, or incident of abuse or assault reported persistent and unwanted memories related to the precipitating event.

Brewin also examined intrusive memories in people who had recently received a cancer diagnosis. Some of these individuals sank into a severe depression, others became mildly depressed, and still others did not develop depression. The severely depressed patients reported many more intrusive memories — mainly related to illness, injury, and death — than did either the mildly depressed or nondepressed patients. This intensified persistence could be attributable to the negative mood that prevails in a severe depression. Laboratory studies have shown that current mood state influences the kinds of memories that people tend to retrieve: in happy moods, recollections of positive experiences spring to mind more readily than recollections of negative experiences; the opposite tends to occur in dark moods. The cancer patients' intrusive memories could also be related to negative self-schemas that predispose patients to developing depression in the first place: these patients may have a larger store of negative memories than patients who prove emotionally resilient in the face of a cancer diagnosis. Once again, conditions are in place for a self-perpetuating cycle in which negative self-schemas and moods create fertile ground for persistent retrieval of negative memories, which in turn amplifies the severity of depression.

The psychologist Susan Nolen-Hoeksema found that people with a "ruminative" style, who focus obsessively on their current negative moods and past negative events, are at special risk for becoming trapped in such destructive self-perpetuating cycles. Those with a ruminative style endure longer episodes of depression than individuals who do little ruminating. For instance, prior to the 1989 Loma Prieta earthquake that shook the Northern California Bay Area, Nolen-Hoeksema measured mood and tendencies toward rumination in a large group of college students. In the days and weeks following the destructive event, she assessed their moods and emotional responses. Students who exhibited a ruminative style before the earthquake were more likely to be depressed weeks afterward than students who had not shown signs of a ruminative style prior to the quake. More rumination after the earthquake was linked with longer and more severe depression. Nolen-Hoeksema observed something similar in caregivers of terminally ill patients, who are at great risk for depression. Caregivers who tended to ruminate on present and past negative events became more severely depressed during the course of a terminal illness than those who did not.

Nolen-Hoeksema's group linked rumination, depression, and memory even more strongly. College students who were experiencing depressed or nondepressed moods engaged in two types of tasks. The rumination task focused on students' current mood, energy level, and past events that influenced them to turn out the way they did. The distracting task drew attention away from the students' moods and concerns, requiring them to imagine the *Mona Lisa*'s face or clouds forming in the sky. Students were then asked to recall autobiographical incidents from their pasts. For students who were already experiencing a depressed mood, engaging in the rumination task led to recall of more negative autobiographical memories than did the distracting task.

Ruminative tendencies may explain some differences between the responses of men and women to depression. Nolen-Hoeksema monitored episodes of depression in women and men for a month. She found that women were more likely than men to ruminate over their depressed moods; men were more likely to engage in distracting activities that drew attention away from their negative moods, such as spending more time on work or hobbies. High levels of rumination contributed to longer-lasting and more severe depressive episodes in women than in men. Here again, the vicious cycle of rumination, memory, and depression was at work.

Women ruminated by asking questions about why they were depressed, thereby activating a wealth of negative memories: past experiences in which they felt inadequate or otherwise saw themselves in a negative light. These negative memories further deepened an already black mood, leading to more prolonged and painful depression. By fleeing into distracting activities, men escaped this downward spiral.

It's important to distinguish between ruminating about a painful experience and disclosing it to others. Rumination involves a kind of obsessive recycling of thoughts and memories regarding one's current mood or situation, which produces an even worse outcome. Disclosing difficult experiences to others, however, can have profoundly positive effects. The psychologist James Pennebaker and his coworkers at the University of Texas have carried out studies in which people disclose troubling experiences by writing or talking about them for several days. The resulting narratives that people create produce surprising benefits: more positive mood, enhanced immune system functions, fewer visits to the doctor, higher grade point averages, reduced absenteeism at work, and even higher rates of reemployment following job loss. Although the exact reasons for these benefits are still a matter of debate, the findings suggest that the act of converting turbulent emotions into narrative form influences important physiological systems.

The difference between generating useful narratives and endlessly ruminating is apparent in very severe or suicidal depression. Patients suffering from suicidal depression may have difficulty coming up with coherent narratives because they persistently recall and ruminate over what the British psychologist Mark Williams calls "overgeneral memories." Williams conducted experiments on autobiographical memory in suicidally depressed patients using a widely adopted word-cueing technique. Try to recall a specific incident from your life for each of the following words: *happy, sorry, angry, successful.* Most people have no difficulty coming up with detailed recollections of particular experiences. In response to *happy,* for instance, I recalled how pleased I felt when I watched my daughter Hannah score six points during a game in her fourth-grade basketball league. For *sorry,* I remembered how bad a professional acquaintance felt when she lost a set of slides I used to deliver a lecture at her university.

Williams noticed that severely depressed patients rarely generated memories of specific incidents in response to either positive or negative cues — even though, as we saw earlier, Kevin Ochsner's results suggest that the natural tendency is to remember negative events in great detail. Instead, they came up with summary descriptions, such as "when I do things wrong" in response to the cue *sorry,* or "my father" in response to *happy.* Williams notes that persistent retrieval of overgeneral memories can contribute to an eventual decision to commit suicide. An unpleasant event that turns out to be the final straw in a suicidal decline can stimulate recall and rumination about negative overgeneral memories, such as "I've always been a failure" or "Nobody's ever really liked me." A patient may be overwhelmed by persistent recall of such self-damaging descriptions, which dominate the patient's mind and lead to a decision to take their own life.

Studies of brain activity in depressed patients provide some clues concerning possible underlying bases of persistent overgeneral memories. Several studies have found that depressed patients show relatively reduced activity in parts of the left frontal lobe, mainly on the lateral surface (the dorsolateral frontal region), when they are either resting comfortably or performing cognitive tasks. Patients who suffer strokes to the left frontal lobe often become depressed, whereas patients with right frontal damage typically do not become depressed. The affected regions in the left frontal lobe may play a role in the generation of positive emotions.

From the standpoint of memory, neuroimaging studies suggest that similar regions in the left prefrontal cortex play a role in reflecting back on past experiences and retrieving specific aspects of what happened. In studies conducted by the Yale University psychologist Marcia Johnson and her group, the amount of activity in the left prefrontal cortex during retrieval was greatest when people recalled particular details of past episodes. If severely depressed patients have more trouble activating key regions of the left frontal lobe, they may be particularly vulnerable to persistent recall of overgeneral memories. A healthy individual might be able to counter retrieval of negative memories by recalling a specific positive experience. If, having had a paper rejected from a scientific journal, I am reminded of previous rejections and conclude that I am a lousy researcher, I still can generate specific memories of papers that journal reviewers accepted enthusiastically. Supported by these positive memories, I begin to feel better about my abilities and resolve to revise the rejected paper for publication elsewhere. But if I am depressed and thus unable to generate specific recollections, I could well become overwhelmed by intrusive overgeneral memories that match my despairing mood — "I've always had problems publishing in the top journals," "I feel like a failure again" — further increasing my sense of despair. A dysfunctional left frontal lobe might well contribute to this destructive cycle.

Persistence, then, thrives in an emotional climate of disappointment, sadness, and regret. But to witness the full force of the seventh sin, we need to turn our attention to the world of traumatic experiences.

TERROR IN THE PAST

In Sacai ... the ... earthquake was so terrible unto them, that many were bereft of their senses; and others by that horrible spectacle so much amazed, that they knew not what they did. Blasius, a Christian the reporter of the newes, was so affrighted for his part, that though it were two months after, hee was scarce his owne man, neither could hee drive the remembrance of it out of his minde. Many times, some years following, they will tremble afresh at the remembrance or conceipt of such a terrible object, even all their lives long, if mention be made of it.

In his classic seventeenth-century treatise, *The Anatomy of Melancholy,* the British writer Robert Burton described the devastating psychological consequences of an ancient earthquake. The experience of Blasius and others in Sacai has been replicated countless times across centuries and millennia: traumatic experiences almost invariably result in intrusive, persisting memories of a terrible event.

In the twentieth century, the damaging effects of traumatic experiences on memory and other mental functions were first recognized during World War I. Doctors began treating cases of "shell shock," in which soldiers exposed to life-threatening situations later become incapacitated by recurring nightmares and intrusive memories of their encounters with death. After the war, the British government established a committee to determine whether soldiers who had been executed for cowardice had in fact been suffering from shell shock. World War II produced another upsurge in cases of shell shock, but what we now call post-traumatic stress disorder became widely acknowledged and formally recognized by medical practitioners only after the conclusion of the Vietnam War. Hospitals and other organizations charged with caring for returning veterans became inundated with cases in which intrusive war memories and recurrent battle nightmares interfered with the ability of affected veterans to resume their lives at home and to reintegrate into society.

Persisting memories are a major consequence of just about any type of traumatic experience: war, violent assaults, rapes, sexual abuse, earthquakes and other natural disasters, torture and brutal imprisonment, motor vehicle accidents. Though such events may seem like relatively rare occurrences, epidemiological studies suggest that just over half of women and 60 percent of men will experience at least one traumatic event in their lives. The intrusive memories that result from such experiences usually take the form of vivid perceptual images, sometimes preserving in minute detail the very features of a trauma that survivors would most like to forget. Though intrusive recollections can occur in any of the senses, visual memories are by far the most common. The Oxford psychologist Anke Ehlers studied the perceptual qualities of intrusive memories in people who had been traumatized by sexual abuse or road traffic accidents. For both types of trauma, visual recollections predominated in nearly all survivors, with some remembering "single pictures" of the traumatic incident and a similar proportion recalling multi-image "film clips." Other senses still played some role: more than half of both sexual abuse and traffic accident survivors reported experiencing intrusive memories in the form of smells, sounds, or bodily sensations.

Post-traumatic stress disorder, or PTSD, is often associated with depression. Chris Brewin has directly compared intrusive memories in traumatized patients and in depressed patients who had not experienced a specific trauma. Patients with PTSD reported more frequent intrusive memories and flashbacks than depressed patients, but the qualities of the memories were generally similar in the two groups. Traumatized patients, however, reported more unusual dissociative experiences, in which they felt as though they were observers watching an event happen to someone else.

Studies of trauma survivors indicate that nearly all of them report having experienced troubling intrusive memories in the days and weeks after a trauma occurred. But, just as we saw with Jean Van de Velde, not everyone continues to be plagued by intrusive recollections months, years, or decades later. Those who continue to experience intrusive memories long after a traumatic event, and who as a result cannot return to normal functioning in their everyday lives, are likely to receive a diagnosis of post-traumatic stress disorder.

For some people, the force of a traumatic event is so compelling that they become "stuck" in the past. Studies of Vietnam veterans and victims of sexual abuse indicate that individuals who remain focused on the past for years after a traumatic event exhibit higher levels of psychological distress than those who focus on the present and future. High levels of psychological distress in turn stimulate even greater focus on the past, thus setting up a destructive self-perpetuating cycle of persistent remembering like that observed in cases of depression.

The likelihood of getting stuck in the past depends in part on how a person responds in the immediate aftermath of a trauma. Consider the terrible 1993 firestorms in Southern California that destroyed vast swaths of property, threatened lives, and forced scores of people to abandon their homes. Alison Holman and Roxane Silver of the University of California, Irvine, interviewed survivors of the firestorms in nearby Laguna Beach and the Malibu-Topanga area of Los Angeles within a few days of the disaster, and then followed up six months and one year later. Immediately after the fires, some survivors reported disturbances in their sense of orientation in time: they felt that time had stopped or that the present was no longer continuous with the past or the future. People who experienced high levels of such "temporal disintegration" immediately after the firestorms were especially likely to focus on and ruminate about the event six months later. A year after the firestorms, these same individuals experienced more distress than did people who were able to focus more on the present or future in the intervening months. Temporal disintegration in response to a trauma thus foreshadowed later troubles in people who remained stuck in the past, prisoners of persistent memories.

Long-term psychological trouble can also result from attempting to avoid thinking about a traumatic event in its immediate aftermath. The overwhelming pain of a traumatic experience and associated intrusive memories naturally leads people to want to avoid reminders of the incident and, if possible, to suppress trauma-related memories and thoughts. Consider the protagonist in Sarah Van Arsdale's 1995 novel *Toward Amnesia*. Libby has recently been abandoned by her lover and is trying to deal with persisting memories of their relationship. She devises a plan of psychological escape from memories that burden her continually. "It was on Memorial Day I decided to achieve amnesia," the novel begins. First trying to attain this goal by simply admonishing herself to forget — "I'd gotten through . . . by chanting that mantra or the other one: forget, forget, forget" — Libby eventually flees the ever-present reminders of her relationship, driving hundreds of miles to Canada in order to seek refuge from memory.

Though the prospect of forgetting may seem soothing after a disappointment or trauma, such attempts are likely to backfire. Consider a group that is at high risk for intrusive traumatic memories: emergency service personnel. Ambulance crews, firefighters, and disaster relief workers are frequently exposed to upsetting, sometimes overwhelming, events. In a study of ambulance workers, Anke Ehlers and her collaborators found that virtually all of them experienced some work-related intrusive memories. The most common sources of intrusive memories were accidents involving the loss of children or acquaintances, violent deaths, severe burns, or failed attempts to save a life. But despite the ubiquity of persisting traumatic memories in ambulance workers, just one in five of Ehlers's sample met the criteria for PTSD. These individuals often responded initially by trying to avoid remembering the trauma. They tended to interpret their traumatic recollections as an indication that they were going mad or otherwise unraveling. Instead of working through the traumatic event initially, they retreated into wishful thinking, sometimes trying to alter or undo the past in fantasies. Yet attempts to avoid distressing memories resulted in only more rumination and distress with the passing of time.

These observations fit nicely with pioneering laboratory studies conducted by the psychologist Daniel Wegner concerning paradoxical or ironic effects of attempting to suppress unwanted thoughts. In Wegner's experiments, people were instructed to try to avoid thinking about a particular topic — a neutral concept such as a white bear, or a personally meaningful one like an old flame. Wegner found that following a period of thought suppression, participants usually showed a "rebound effect": they later thought about the forbidden subject more often and intensely than they would have if they had never attempted to suppress thinking about it in the first place. "Although not thinking about painful thoughts may seem like a reasonable coping strategy to adopt," Wegner wrote, "trying to forget might not only prolong the misery, but make it worse." Wegner's ideas are backed up by other studies showing that after exposure to distressing films, people who are instructed to suppress thoughts related to the film later experience more film-related intrusive memories than those who do not try to suppress. Attempts to avoid thinking about a horrendous experience are common in trauma survivors but are more likely to amplify, rather than lessen, later problems with persisting memories.

One possible reason for this phenomenon is that reexperiencing a traumatic event in an otherwise safe context can take out some of the sting. Repetition of just about any stimulus or experience will result in what researchers call "habituation" — a reduced physiological response to the stimulus. If I play a loud sound for you at regular intervals and record physiological activity, at first you will show a strong response to the sound, followed by a gradual drop-off. The same goes for traumatic memories: repeated reexperiencing of a traumatic memory in a safe setting can dampen the initial physiological response to the trauma. Attempts to suppress memories of upsetting experiences prevent this normal process of habituation. Suppressed recollections thus retain an extra charge that eventually augments persistence.

Perhaps not surprisingly, then, therapeutic attempts to counter persistence in trauma survivors almost invariably focus on allowing patients to reexperience the traumatic event within the safe confines of the therapy setting. The approach that has proven most effective is imaginal exposure therapy: patients are repeatedly exposed to stimuli associated with their traumas, and they recall and reexperience vivid images of the incidents. In the early 1980s, the Boston psychologist Terrence Keane and his associates reported that exposure therapy reduced levels of anxiety and intrusive memories in Vietnam veterans, and others reported similar effects in survivors of sexual abuse. Later studies directly compared imaginal exposure therapy to other kinds of treatments that do not involve repeated reexperiencing of trauma, such as supportive counseling. Keane's group and another team led by the psychologist Edna Foa found that exposure therapy produced the greatest reductions in intrusive memories, flashbacks, and related symptoms of PTSD.

The psychiatrist Stevan Weine and his collaborators described a related approach to reducing persistence in people who have been traumatized by state-sponsored terrorism. Refugees who escaped the attempted genocide in Bosnia-Herzegovina during the early 1990s often experienced classic symptoms of PTSD, including overwhelming intrusive memories. Weine and his collaborators explored the effectiveness of what they called "testimony therapy," in which survivors retell and relive their traumatic experiences and try to relate them to the traumas suffered by others in their society. Weine's group gathered survivors' recollections into an oral history archive that was shared with other patients as part of the testimony therapy process. "Within this context, where the survivors explicitly understand that their remembrances are becoming part of a collective inquiry," observed Weine, "testimony can reduce individual suffering, even when survivors have not explicitly sought trauma treatment." Results indicated that testimony therapy does indeed produce reduced levels of intrusive memories in traumatized Bosnian refugees.

These findings fit well with James Pennebaker's studies concerning the beneficial effects of disclosing disappointments, losses, and other negative experiences. In the short term, persistence is a virtually inevitable consequence of difficult experiences. But for the long term, confronting, disclosing, and integrating those experiences we would most like to forget is the most effective counter to persistence.

THE ROOTS OF PERSISTENCE

To understand better why traumatic events produce such powerful persistence in the first place, it's helpful to consider the neural systems involved in remembering trauma. A key player in the brain's response to traumatic events is a small almond-shaped structure called the amygdala. Buried deep in the inner regions of the temporal lobe, the amygdala abuts the nearby hippocampus but performs quite different functions than its neighbor. Recall that when people sustain damage to the hippocampus and surrounding cortical areas, they almost invariably suffer a general impairment in forming and later retrieving new episodic memories of personal experiences. Damage to the amygdala does not result in this sort of global memory deficit: patients with amygdala damage can remember their recent experiences with little difficulty. The memories of patients with amygdala damage, however, do not benefit from the emotions that normally accompany an arousing experience and aid subsequent recollection. Consider what happens when healthy people view a slide sequence that begins mundanely — a mother walking her child to school — and later includes an emotionally arousing event: the child is hit by a car. When tested later, healthy people remember the arousing event better than the mundane ones. Patients with amygdala damage remember the mundane events normally but do not show improved memory for the emotionally arousing event.

Abnormal fear responses are a hallmark of amygdala damage: patients have great difficulty learning to fear situations that would normally scare the rest of us. Consider a rape victim who begins to experience fear and distress every time she drives near the park where she was assaulted. There is nothing inherently frightening about this particular park, but for the rape survivor it has become inextricably associated with trauma. Researchers have created experimental analogues of fear learning by using conditioning procedures that expose people or animals to normally innocuous stimuli that are associated with a fear-inducing event. The procedures are based on the famous conditioning experiments conducted in the early 1900s by the Russian physiologist Ivan Pavlov. Pavlov's dogs learned to salivate at the sound of a bell because it was previously associated with the enjoyable experience of gnawing on a piece of meat. Something similar happens with fear. Imagine that I show you a series of colored slides and that every time you see a blue slide, you also hear the jolting sound of a loud horn. It won't be too long before the appearance of a blue slide will induce an emotional response as you begin to dread the occurrence of the obnoxious sound. Researchers can measure this reaction by monitoring skin conductance responses, which provide a rough index of emotional arousal.

When patients with amygdala damage participated in this kind of conditioning procedure, they did not show any signs of fear or emotional arousal with repeated presentations of the blue slides. The psychologist Elizabeth Phelps videotaped one such patient who had just participated in a similar conditioning procedure. The patient knew perfectly well that whenever the blue slide appeared, a loud, unpleasant sound would begin to blare. "Blue slide, loud sound," she confidently announced to Dr. Phelps. Nonetheless, the patient showed no signs of fear learning — physiological arousal in response to the blue slide — at any time during the conditioning experiment.

These findings fit neatly with numerous studies in rats and other experimental animals showing that damage to the amygdala disrupts fear conditioning. When a normal rat receives an electric shock after hearing a particular tone, it will soon behave fearfully upon hearing the tone alone. The neuroscientist Joseph LeDoux, who has performed pioneering studies on fear conditioning, provides a vivid description of a terrified rat:

> After very few such pairings of the sound and the shock, the rat begins to act afraid when it hears the sound: it stops dead in its tracks and adopts the characteristic freezing posture — crouching down and remaining motionless, except for the rhythmic chest movements required for breathing. In addition, the rat's fur stands on end, its blood pressure and heart rate rise, and stress hormones are released into its bloodstream. These and other conditioned responses are expressed in essentially the same way in every rat.

LeDoux and others have discovered that selectively damaging specific regions within the amygdala eliminates these telltale signs of fear. LeDoux's group has further shown that memories created during fear conditioning in healthy animals are exceptionally durable — perhaps even indelible. Combined with the work on brain-damaged patients, these observations suggest that the amygdala plays a role in generating the kinds of persisting memories that haunt survivors of traumatic events.

As LeDoux points out, the amygdala is well positioned to guide evaluation of the personal significance of incoming information — the essence of emotional responding. He likens the amygdala to the hub of a wheel: it receives raw sensory information from the thalamus, a key subcortical switching station; more extensively processed perceptual information from higher-order areas in the cortex; and signals from the hippocampus about the general context of an event. Alerted by this converging information, the amygdala can flag the occurrence of a significant event.

The amygdala also has a powerful influence on hormonal systems that kick into high gear when we are confronted with a frightening or otherwise arousing event. The release of stress-related hormones, such as adrenaline and cortisol, mobilizes the brain and the body in the face of threat or other sources of stress, and also enhances memory for the experience (probably by influencing the activity of the hippocampus). When the amygdala is damaged, however, stress-related hormones no longer produce any memory enhancement. The amygdala thus regulates or modulates memory storage by turning on the hormones that allow us to respond to and remember vividly— but sometimes intrusively—threatening or traumatic events.

Neuroimaging techniques are beginning to provide new insights into the role of the amygdala and other brain structures in persistent memories of traumatic events. Several studies using PET scans and fMRI have shown that the amygdala is strongly activated by the presentation of aversive materials: pictures of mutilated bodies, film clips of traumatic events, even faces with angry or fearful expressions. These neuroimaging studies are particularly intriguing, because seeing a face with a fearful expression does not necessarily elicit an emotional response from the viewer. Experiments by the neuroscientist Paul Whalen and his collaborators revealed that even when fearful faces are presented so briefly that people do not consciously discern the expression—participants report that they see "expressionless" faces—the amygdala still shows greater activity for fearful faces than for happy ones. These and related results led Whalen to propose that the amygdala is turned on by events that signal a possible threat in the environment.

When the amygdala lights up during threatening or aversive events, the amount of activity predicts how well people later remember these experiences. Larry Cahill and James McGaugh at the University of California, Irvine, performed PET scans while people viewed film clips containing both neutral and upsetting episodes. Later, participants tried to recall episodes from the clips. The amount of activity in the amygdala was closely correlated with the number of upsetting episodes people recalled: the more amygdala activity during film clip viewing, the more aversive incidents later recalled. They found no such relationship for neutral incidents. (Interestingly, the amount of activity in the *hippocampus* correlated with subsequent recall of neutral, but not aversive, incidents.)

Neuroimaging studies have also shown that, consistent with studies of rats and other animals, the amygdala is strongly activated during fear conditioning. It is perhaps not surprising, then, that several imaging studies of trauma survivors, including Vietnam veterans and victims of sexual abuse, have documented amygdala activation when survivors recalled and relived traumatic events that they remember intrusively in their everyday lives. Imaging studies also reveal heightened activity during traumatic recollections in several other brain regions thought to play a role in fear and anxiety — one tucked deep down in the frontal lobe, another near the tip of the temporal lobe. These findings can help to explain why persistent recollections of trauma often preserve the intense fear and anxiety that prevailed during the original experience.

Consistent with animal studies implicating stress-related hormones in fear conditioning, studies of trauma survivors have also related these hormones to intrusive recollections. When stress-related hormones spring into action during an emotionally arousing experience, they stimulate the release of a class of chemical messengers known as catecholamines. Researchers have focused in particular on the role of norepinephrine, one of the major catecholamines. Several studies of Vietnam veterans and victims of sexual abuse have found that greater levels of norepinephrine (measured in urine samples) are associated with more frequent intrusive memories of traumatic experiences. Further, when traumatized patients were administered the drug yohimbine, which raises levels of norepinephrine in specific brain regions, nearly half of the patients experienced overwhelming visual flashbacks of a traumatic event, often accompanied by fear and even panic.

Yohimbine is available over the counter in pharmacies and health food stores, where it is marketed as an aphrodisiac, a remedy for male impotence, and a general energy booster. Several PTSD patients who purchased the drug experienced unexpected flashbacks and panic attacks. "I felt like I was going crazy," reflected one veteran who took yohimbine as an aphrodisiac and instead found himself overwhelmed by unwanted war flashbacks. "I kept thinking that my combat buddy was wounded. I kept thinking that I was a medic and that I had to save him."

Though its effects are most dramatic in patients suffering from PTSD, other studies have shown that giving normal volunteers yohimbine while they view emotionally arousing slides enhances later recall of the emotional events, probably by increasing levels of norepinephrine during encoding. Norepinephrine supplies a chemical spark that ignites intrusive recollections.

Understanding the chemical and hormonal bases of persistence also provides clues about how to counter it pharmacologically. If yohimbine and other substances that boost stress-related hormones and norepinephrine also heighten persistence, then it stands to reason that substances that lower stress-related hormones and norepinephrine should reduce persistence. This result is exactly what Larry Cahill and James McGaugh found in a study in which they administered a drug — the beta-blocker propranolol — that prevents the release of stress-related hormones. There were four groups of participants. After receiving either propranolol or a placebo, two of the groups watched a slide show depicting mundane events. Two other groups who had also received either propranolol or a placebo subsequently watched a slide show in which one slide of an emotionally arousing event was interposed among the mundane ones. Participants who had received propranolol remembered the mundane events about as well as participants who had received a placebo. But an important difference emerged: memory for the arousing events improved substantially in the placebo group, but not in the propranolol group. Propranolol effectively blocked the usual memory-enhancing effects of emotional arousal.

These results raise the intriguing possibility that beta-blockers such as propranolol could be administered to trauma survivors in order to reduce persisting memories. Beta-blockers might also be given ahead of time to emergency workers before they enter a disaster site, and thus thwart altogether the development of intrusive memories that would otherwise plague them later. These are exciting possibilities, because intrusive memories can be so crippling for long periods of time. And for emergency or disaster personnel who are repeatedly exposed to potential sources of persistence, preliminary administration of beta-blockers might make a highly stressful occupation more manageable.

But this strategy for countering persistence also poses risks. We've seen that attempts to avoid traumatic memories often backfire. Intrusive memories need to be acknowledged, confronted, and worked through in order for people to set them to rest for the long term. Unwelcome memories of trauma are symptoms of a disrupted psyche that requires attention before it can resume healthy functioning. Beta-blockers might make it easier for trauma survivors to face and incorporate traumatic recollections, and in that sense could facilitate long-term adaptation. Yet it is also possible that beta-blockers could work against the normal process of recovery: traumatic memories would not spring to mind with the kind of psychological force that demands attention and perhaps intervention. Prescription of beta-blockers could bring about an effective trade-off between short-term reductions in the sting of traumatic memories and long-term increases in persistence or related symptoms of a trauma that has not been adequately confronted.

For all its disruptive power, persistence serves a healthy function: events that we need to confront come to mind with a force that is hard to ignore. The seventh sin — just like the other six — is not merely an inconvenience or annoyance, but is instead a symptom of some of the greatest strengths of the human mind.

The Update
COUNTERING PERSISTENCE: A ROLE FOR RECONSOLIDATION?

When I finished the persistence chapter two decades ago, I was cautiously optimistic that beta-blockers might be useful weapons in the battle to mitigate the disturbing and sometimes disabling effects of intrusive traumatic memories, despite having some reservations about their long-term effectiveness. What I didn't know back then was that experimental findings regarding the neural basis of memory in rats that appeared just as I was completing the book would have significant implications for subsequent attempts to use beta-blockers such as propranolol to treat the debilitating effects of persistence.

The findings came from the NYU laboratory of the eminent neuroscientist Joseph LeDoux, whose pioneering research on the amygdala I discussed earlier in this chapter. Karim Nader, then a postdoctoral researcher with LeDoux and now a professor at McGill University, exposed rats to a neutral stimulus (a tone) together with a fear-inducing one (footshock). After a single pairing of these two stimuli, rats exhibited a freezing response when they heard the tone twenty-four hours later — evidence that they had established and retained a fear memory. Previous work had shown that injecting a particular drug (a protein synthesis inhibitor called anisomycin) shortly after the initial pairing of tone and shock into specific nuclei in the amygdala that are critical to the formation of fear memories prevented the consolidation (i.e., the initial storage) of this memory. In the experiment by Nader and his colleagues, the researchers instead injected the same protein synthesis inhibitor into the amygdala soon after presenting the reminder tone twenty-four hours later. You might think that injecting it at this point would have no effect because the fear memory had already been consolidated. Not so. In a subsequent test, the rats failed to exhibit freezing in response to the tone; they now exhibited amnesia for the tone-footshock pairing! Critically, the protein synthesis inhibitor had no effect on freezing unless the rat was cued to recall the fear memory just before the drug was administered. In other words, retrieving the initial fear memory put it into an unstable, or labile, state in which it became vulnerable to disruption by the protein synthesis inhibitor—a phenomenon that has come to be known as "reconsolidation."

This striking phenomenon was not entirely unprecedented, because something similar had been shown in experiments with rats conducted during the 1960s and 1970s using electric shocks. But the field had largely forgotten about the earlier experiments, and Nader's study used more precise and sophisticated techniques to induce and characterize reconsolidation. Still, the idea that when we retrieve a memory, we need to consolidate it all over again, and that the simple act of recalling a memory can render it vulnerable to disruption, is highly counterintuitive. The findings of Nader and his colleagues stimulated a virtual landslide of follow-up studies, so we now know a lot about the nature and characteristics of reconsolidation. Indeed, researchers have produced similar phenomena in humans. Reconsolidation effects have implications for memory sins, especially the sin of suggestibility, because they show that the act of retrieving memories can potentially change them by making them vulnerable to the incorporation of novel information or misinformation. But most important for this chapter, reconsolidation offers a potential avenue for countering persistence: if recalling an intrusive memory places that memory into an unstable state, then perhaps a drug like propranolol (which is also a protein synthesis inhibitor) could be administered during this unstable state in an attempt to effectively reengineer the memory and reduce its harmful psychological consequences.

Researchers have begun to test this possibility and so far have reported mixed results. Consider the case of a fifty-three-year-old woman who was the victim of an armed robbery while traveling in

South Africa and subsequently suffered from intrusive memories of the robbery, hyperarousal, and nightmares, leading to a diagnosis of PTSD. Two years after the robbery, the patient sought treatment and entered a pilot study conducted by the clinical psychologist Merel Kindt, using a therapeutic approach based on reconsolidation research. The first step was to reactivate the traumatic memory, which produced very strong responses in the patient:

> The reactivation focused on a hotspot memory of the robbery in which she awoke in their hotel cabin in Johannesburg. A burglar wearing a hat, plastic shoes, and dirty and extremely baggy trousers, stood next to her with a gun against her head. She turned her back to him, convinced that this was where her life ended. Although her partner was lying next to her, she could not talk and was overwhelmed by feelings of mental defeat and loneliness. During the reactivation, she was very distressed, cried, and felt the intense fear and disgust that she had experienced during the burglary.

Following reactivation, the patient received a dose of propranolol. When assessed one week and one month posttreatment, the patient's PTSD symptoms had dropped significantly, and she later traveled to Johannesburg again without experiencing a recurrence of intrusive memories or other symptoms of PTSD. In 2016, Kindt published a paper in which she described this patient as well as three other PTSD patients who received the same treatment. She reported significant posttreatment reductions in PTSD symptoms for two of the three other patients.

These preliminary results are encouraging, especially because they were observed following only a single treatment. However, a larger study of eighteen PTSD patients published in 2015 failed to find any effects of a single propranolol/reactivation treatment on PTSD symptoms (and also reported null effects for two other drugs). Moreover, as Kindt acknowledged, her results do not conclusively demonstrate that the reconsolidation-based treatment was responsible for the improvements she observed in three of the four patients because the study did not control for the possible influence of attention from a therapist, the patient's expectations of improvement, or other factors that might contribute to a placebo effect. To accomplish that objective, it would be necessary to conduct a double-blind, placebo-controlled, randomized clinical trial.

Researchers at McGill University and Harvard Medical School reported such a study in 2018. They tested sixty individuals who met the criteria for PTSD. Instead of only a single treatment session, all of the patients participated in one session per week for six weeks. During these sessions, half of the patients recalled the traumatic event just after receiving propranolol, and the other half just after receiving a placebo. Recalling the traumatic event after receiving propranolol produced significantly greater reduction in PTSD symptoms than did recalling the event after receiving a placebo. These results provide more compelling evidence for the therapeutic efficacy of combining propranolol and memory reactivation, but they do not conclusively show that interfering with reconsolidation produced the effect. As the researchers acknowledged, because propranolol was administered *before* the traumatic memory was reactivated, the beneficial effect might reflect impaired retrieval of the traumatic memory as opposed to interference with reconsolidation. Nonetheless, given the disabling nature of intrusive memories and other PTSD symptoms, any positive results from a controlled clinical trial are noteworthy and can provide a basis for future, more stringent tests of the reconsolidation hypothesis.

Related studies from the clinical psychologist Emily Holmes and her colleagues in Cambridge, England, targeted reconsolidation mechanisms without using any drugs by leveraging the video game *Tetris*, which involves visuospatial manipulation of colored geometric forms to create horizontal blocks. Healthy participants watched a trauma film containing scenes of violent death and serious injury; previous studies had shown that after watching this film, people experienced intrusive memories of its disturbing contents both in the lab and in everyday life. The next day, all of the participants came back to the lab. In the experimental group, memories of the film were reactivated by showing still clips from it, and the participants then played *Tetris* for twelve minutes. For the next week, they kept a diary in which they recorded any memories of the film that came to mind. The researchers hypothesized that the visuospatial processing demands of *Tetris* would interfere with reconsolidation of the visually salient and disturbing scenes of death and injury in the film, and thus reduce intrusive memories during the following week. In two experiments, they compared intrusive memories in this experimental group with control groups that watched the film and then (1) reactivated memories of the film but did not play *Tetris*, (2) played *Tetris* but did not reactivate memories of the film, or (3) neither reactivated memories of the film nor played *Tetris*. Intrusive memories of the film during the subsequent week were significantly reduced in the reactivation plus *Tetris* group, but not in any of the control groups. Importantly, when given a recognition test in the lab, participants in the reactivation plus *Tetris* group could still remember scenes from the trauma film about as well as participants in the control groups, indicating that the treatment had not wiped out their memories of the film. But it did interfere with the spontaneous and intrusive emergence of those memories, which is the hallmark of persistence.

In a more recent field study, Holmes's group gave the reactivation plus *Tetris* treatment to people who went to a hospital emergency room following a motor vehicle accident, cueing them to recall the worst parts of the accident prior to playing *Tetris*. Compared to a control group that had also been involved in a motor vehicle accident and then completed an activity log of what they did in the emergency room, people who received the reactivation plus *Tetris* treatment recorded fewer intrusive memories of the accident in a daily diary during the week following the accident. Applying a similar approach to patients with PTSD (patients recalled a specific intrusive memory, then played *Tetris*), the researchers documented a dramatic drop-off in subsequent intrusions of the targeted memory after the treatment, whereas non-targeted intrusive memories showed little change over the same period of time.

These reconsolidation-based treatment studies suggest that destabilizing a traumatic memory by recalling and interfering with it can help to reduce the negative psychological consequences of persistence. Exactly how, why, and how often this happens remains to be sorted out, but the perspective offered by reconsolidation research clearly has a role to play in the effort to counter the frequently crippling effects of persistence.

To Think or Not to Think: Implications for Persistence

Recall that in The Update in Chapter 3 on the sin of blocking, I discussed the research of Michael Anderson and his colleagues using the "think–no think" paradigm, where people study word pairs and are later presented with the first word of the pair and instructions either to recall the associated item (think) or to suppress it from conscious awareness (no think). Anderson's group and other researchers have provided evidence that not thinking about an associated target word inhibits later retrieval of the suppressed item in healthy individuals, whereas such inhibition effects are significantly smaller in anxious or depressed individuals. Evidence has also emerged in the past few years that people who suffer from PTSD and associated intrusive memories have a generally impaired ability to suppress memories. In a 2015 study, Anderson and his colleagues examined memory suppression using the think–no think procedure in patients with PTSD and controls who had been exposed to trauma but had not developed PTSD. They found that the patients with PTSD had more difficulty than the controls in achieving suppression-induced forgetting, and they further showed that those patients with the most severe PTSD symptoms had the largest impairments in memory suppression. In a related 2016 experiment, they found that among healthy individuals, those who showed impaired suppression-induced forgetting on the think–no think task reported more distress from intrusive memories after watching an emotionally upsetting film than those who showed greater memory-suppression abilities.

These results suggest that patients with PTSD could benefit from training aimed at increasing their memory-suppression abilities. Such an attempt might seem misguided in light of Daniel Wegner's well-known "white bear" effect (discussed earlier in this chapter), where not thinking about a designated item such as a white bear produces a rebound effect: after a delay, people are more likely to think about the white bear than if they hadn't tried to suppress it. However, Anderson and his colleagues have recently argued that there is not necessarily a conflict between Wegner's white bear effect and their demonstrations of memory suppression. In the white bear situation, to accomplish the task goal the person has to explicitly refer to the forbidden thought, so if a person thinks about what they should be doing to achieve the goal (i.e., don't think about a white bear), they undermine it. By contrast, in the think–no think procedure, the person sees a cue word and tries to avoid thinking about an *associated* word, but they can keep the task goal in mind by focusing on the cue word; they don't have to think about the associated word they are trying to suppress.

These ideas suggest that not all attempts at memory suppression will produce rebound effects and that targeting impaired memory-suppression abilities in individuals with PTSD could have beneficial consequences for countering the effects of persistence. Note also that this suggestion is compatible with the point I made earlier in this chapter that confronting and integrating disturbing experiences can be an effective counter to persistence. People with PTSD who are plagued by uncontrollable intrusive memories may not be able to engage in these productive ways of acknowledging and addressing upsetting past experiences. Reducing their impairments in memory control could help them feel less overwhelmed by their traumatic experiences so that they can work through and incorporate persisting experiences in a way that enhances their psychological well-being. Using memory suppression and memory reactivation to engage reconsolidation mechanisms might seem like very different ways of attempting to counter the effects of persistence, but both logic and evidence support continuing attempts to test the utility of both approaches.

8

The Seven Sins:
Vices or Virtues?

PEOPLE LOVE TO COMPLAIN about their memories. When I meet someone for the first time and the conversation turns to my research, I know what's coming next. "You should study me," my new acquaintance will almost invariably say with a shrug, especially if he or she is over age forty. Then follows a list of exasperating recent encounters with absent-mindedness or name blocking, and finally a sigh of relief when I offer assurances that these kinds of memory problems are common. The very pervasiveness of memory's imperfections, amply illustrated in the preceding pages, can easily lead to the conclusion that Mother Nature committed colossal blunders in burdening us with such a dysfunctional system. John Anderson, a cognitive psychologist at Carnegie Mellon University, summarizes the prevailing perception that memory's sins reflect poorly on its design: "Over the years we have participated in many talks with artificial intelligence researchers about the prospects of using human models to guide the development of artificial intelligence programs. Invariably, the remark is made, 'Well, of course, we would not want our system to have something so unreliable as human memory.'"

It is tempting to agree with this characterization, especially if you've just wasted valuable time looking for misplaced keys, read the statistics on wrongful imprisonment resulting from eyewitness misidentification, or woken up in the middle of the night persistently recalling a slipup at work. But along with Anderson, I believe that this view is misguided: it is a mistake to conceive of the seven sins as design flaws that expose memory as a fundamentally defective system. To the contrary, I suggest that the seven sins are by-products of otherwise adaptive features of memory, a price we pay for processes and functions that serve us well in many respects.

To support this suggestion, I rely on evidence and ideas from a variety of sources, including evolutionary biology and psychology. Evolutionary psychology has sparked heated debates. Proponents of this approach draw heavily on Darwin's ideas about natural selection in an attempt to explain cognition and behavior, claiming that the mind cannot be understood fully without adopting an evolutionary perspective. They contend that the mind consists of a collection of specialized abilities that arose to solve specific problems posed by the environment during the course of evolution, and that natural selection is the primary mechanism responsible for the mind's complex design. Evolutionary theorists contend further that much of the mind's structure is specified innately by intricate genetic programs. From this perspective, the task of psychology is to engage in what the cognitive psychologist and evolutionary theorist Steven Pinker calls "reverse-engineering":

> In forward-engineering, one designs a machine to do something; in reverse-engineering, one figures out what a machine was designed to do. Reverse-engineering is what the boffins at Sony do when a new product is announced by Panasonic, or vice versa. They buy one, bring it back to the lab, take a screwdriver to it, and try to figure out what all the parts are for and how they combine to make the device work.

Critics of the evolutionary approach, in contrast, express concern about several aspects of evolutionary theorizing. For example, they worry that evolutionary ideas too often rely on large doses of speculation — and too little on hard data. They question whether evolutionary theories can be adequately tested in a way that allows us to understand the origins of a particular ability, or whether attempts at reverse-engineering have succeeded. Some critics contend that evolutionary psychologists assign too much weight to innate genetic programs when attempting to explain the mind's abilities and complexities; others believe that the mind is better viewed as a general-purpose problem solver than as a collection of specialized abilities. And some critics wonder whether an evolutionary perspective really adds anything to the nonevolutionary theories that psychologists construct in their attempts to understand the working of the mind.

I'll return to some of these issues later in the chapter. Though I share the critics' concerns regarding the testability of evolutionary claims, I have drawn on evolutionary perspectives in earlier work and have found that an evolutionary orientation can serve as a rich source of suggestions and hypotheses. In previous chapters of this book, I have focused on lessons that experimental research has taught us about each of the seven sins. In this chapter, the spirit is more exploratory: I advance ideas about the origins of the seven sins that can help us to place them in a broader perspective, think thoughts that we might not otherwise consider, and appreciate why memory's vices can also be its virtues.

WHEN LESS IS MORE

To illustrate the general thrust of my proposal, consider the concept of "intelligent errors" that arises from experiments showing that animals sometimes make seemingly bizarre mistakes when they navigate their environments. For instance, if you train a rat to navigate a maze to find a food reward at the end and then place a pile of food halfway into the maze, the rat will run right past the pile of food as if it did not exist, continuing to the end, seeking its just reward! Why not stop at the halfway point and enjoy the reward there? The rat appears to be operating in this situation on the basis of "dead reckoning" — a method of navigating in which the animal keeps a literal record of where it has gone by constantly updating the speed, distance, and direction it has traveled. A similarly comical error occurs when a pup is taken from a gerbil nest containing several other pups and is placed in a nearby cup. The mother searches for her lost baby, and while she is away, the nest is displaced a short distance. When the mother and lost pup return, she uses dead reckoning to head straight for the nest's old location. Ignoring the screams and smells of the other pups just a short distance away, she searches for them at the old location.

Though the behaviors in these examples seem perverse, they reflect reliance on a type of navigation that serves each animal quite well in most situations. The system is adapted to aspects of the animal's environment but can get the animal into trouble when things change in unexpected ways. Fortunately, nests usually don't move in the real world that the animal inhabits; such confusing changes require the intervention of a cunning experimenter and tend not to occur in the wild.

Something similar occurs in the behavior known as imprinting. After hatching, a baby goose treats the first moving object it encounters as its mother. Because this object is almost always the mother, imprinting is an effective mechanism for ensuring that a newborn gosling follows its mother in order to receive proper feeding and care. But as shown by the student of animal behavior Konrad Lorenz, when a gosling first sees another moving object after hatching — a rolling red ball or a human (Lorenz used himself) — the animal imprints on that object instead. Consequently, a small flock of goslings often followed Lorenz. Imprinting depends on a specialized memory mechanism that is adapted to the regularities of the gosling's ordinary environment. Though usually adaptive, imprinting can cause problems for the gosling if the mother is not the first moving object it encounters. But in nature, this event is highly improbable.

I believe something similar is going on with memory's seven sins: mechanisms that serve us well much of the time occasionally get us into trouble. Of all the sins, it is perhaps easiest to see the positive side of persistence. René Descartes crystallized the issue several centuries ago. "The utility of all the passions consists in their strengthening thoughts which it is good that [the soul] preserve," he observed. "So too all the evil they can cause consists either in their strengthening and preserving those thoughts more than necessary or in their strengthening and preserving others it is not good to dwell upon." Although intrusive recollections of trauma can be disabling, it is critically important that emotionally arousing experiences, which sometimes occur in response to life-threatening dangers, persist over time. The amygdala and related structures contribute to the persistence of such experiences by modulating memory formation, sometimes resulting in memories we wish we could forget. But this system boosts the likelihood that we will recall easily and quickly information about threatening or traumatic events whose recollection may one day be crucial for survival. Remembering life-threatening events persistently — where the incident occurred, who or what was responsible for it — boosts our chances of avoiding future recurrences.

Transience — forgetting over time — also has an adaptive side. Forgetting can be frustrating, but it is often useful and even necessary to dismiss information that is no longer current, such as old phone numbers or where we parked the car yesterday. As the psychologists Robert and Elizabeth Bjork have pointed out, information that is unimportant or no longer needed will tend not to be retrieved and rehearsed, thereby losing out on the strengthening effects of postevent retrieval and becoming gradually less accessible over time.

John Anderson and his associates have taken this line of thinking even further, arguing that forgetting over time reflects an optimal adaptation to the structure of the environment. Anderson examined various situations involving information retrieval and analyzed how the history of using a particular bit of information predicts its current use. He observed a regularity that parallels the form of transience in human memory: the demand for a particular piece of information drops as greater periods of time pass since its last use. For example, the Anderson group has noted that in library systems, books that have been checked out recently or frequently in the past are more likely to be requested at a specific present moment than books that have been checked less recently or frequently. They observed something similar when they examined headlines in the *New York Times* for 730 days in 1986 and 1987, recording each time a particular word appeared. The likelihood that a particular word would appear on a specific day fell as a function of the time since it was last used. Anderson's group has found similar parallels in other situations, including the use of words in conversations with children and the likelihood of receiving an e-mail message from a correspondent as a function of the time elapsed since earlier messages.

A system that renders information less accessible over time is therefore highly functional, because when information has not been used for longer and longer periods of time, it becomes less and less likely that it will be needed in the future. On balance, the system would be better off setting aside such information — and transience leads to exactly that outcome. Anderson suggests that the general form of forgetting documented in numerous experiments — the rate of forgetting slows down over time — reflects a similar function in the environment that relates past and present use of information. According to Anderson, our memory systems have picked up on this regularity and in essence make a bet that when we haven't used information recently, we probably won't need it in the future. We win the bet more often than we lose it, but we are acutely aware of the losses — the frustrations of forgetting — and are never aware of the wins.

The basic idea here resembles what scientists who study animal behavior in natural environments call a "trade-off." Think about a squirrel that gingerly approaches a fractured cookie near a group of picnickers. The squirrel bravely grabs a bit of the cookie and retreats to a nearby tree before eating it. It returns several times and, on each occasion, grabs a cookie fragment, brings it back to the tree, and devours it. Though not the most efficient way to consume a cookie, this procedure allows the squirrel to reduce its exposure to possible predators. Researchers have indeed found that squirrels are more likely to haul big pieces of cookie to cover than small ones: big pieces take longer to eat than small ones, and thus place the squirrel at greater risk. There is a trade-off between maximizing the benefits of feeding and minimizing the costs of encountering a predator; the squirrel's behavior suggests that it is balancing the two. Similarly, in memory there is a trade-off between the benefit of reducing the accessibility of information that hasn't been used recently or frequently, and which probably won't be needed in the future, and the annoyance or other costs of forgetting.

Some of the same ideas involving frequency and recency of use also apply to blocking in semantic memory, as seen most clearly in tip-of-the-tongue states. Recall that people are most susceptible to blocking on names and other bits of information that have not been used recently. Recall also that blocking often results from a weakened connection between conceptual representations (things you know about a person or object) and phonological representations (the sound of a word or name). Tip-of-the-tongue states may thus reflect the principle articulated by Anderson's group: information that has not been used recently begins to lose out in memory because the odds are growing that it will not be needed. When a connection between conceptual and phonological representations has not been strengthened recently by using a word or a name, the link becomes ever more unreliable, and we become correspondingly susceptible to blocking.

Some types of blocking reflect the operation of inhibitory processes that render information inaccessible (see Chapter 3). Psychologists and neuroscientists have long recognized that inhibition is a fundamental feature of the nervous system: the brain relies on mechanisms that reduce activity as much as on mechanisms that intensify it. Think about what might result without the operation of inhibition: a memory system in which all the information that is potentially relevant to a cue invariably and rapidly springs to mind. Consider the following experiment. Try to recall an episode from your life that involves a table. What do you remember, and how long did it take to come up with the memory? You probably had little difficulty coming up with a specific incident — perhaps a conversation at the dinner table last night or a discussion at a conference table at the office this morning. Now imagine that the cue "table" brought forth all the memories that you have stored away involving a table. There are probably hundreds or thousands of such incidents. What if they all sprang to mind within seconds of considering the cue? A system that operated in this manner would likely result in mass confusion produced by an incessant coming to mind of numerous competing traces. It would be a bit like using an Internet search engine, typing in a word that has many matches in a worldwide database, and then sorting through the thousands of entries that the query elicits. We wouldn't want a memory system that produces this kind of data overload. Robert and Elizabeth Bjork have argued persuasively that the operation of inhibitory processes helps to protect us from such potential chaos.

The basic idea underlying the foregoing analyses of transience and blocking is that as far as memory is concerned, less is sometimes more. That same principle applies equally — if not more strongly — to absent-mindedness. Absent-minded errors occur in part because establishing a rich memory representation that can later be recollected voluntarily requires attentive, elaborate encoding. Events that receive minimal attention and elaboration as they are occurring also stand little chance of being recollected subsequently. But what if all events were registered in elaborate detail, regardless of the level or type of processing to which they were subjected? The result would be a potentially overwhelming clutter of useless details, as happened in the famous case of the mnemonist Shereshevski. Described by the Russian neuropsychologist Alexander Luria, who studied him for years, Shereshevski formed and retained highly detailed memories of virtually everything that happened to him — both the important and the trivial. Yet he was unable to function at an abstract level because he was inundated with unimportant details of his experiences — details that are best denied entry to the system in the first place. An elaboration-dependent system ensures that only those events that are important enough to warrant extensive encoding have a high likelihood of subsequent recollection. Events that do not attract attention and elaboration are likely to be less important and, hence, less likely to be needed for recall at a later time.

An elaboration-dependent system allows us to enjoy the considerable benefits of "operating on automatic," without having memory cluttered by unnecessary information about routine activities. As I discussed in Chapter 2, tasks that initially require considerable attention and effort, such as learning to drive a car, are eventually handled by automatic processes after sufficient practice, thereby freeing up resources for more important matters. It is surely infuriating when, operating on automatic, you put down a book or your wallet in an atypical location and later can't remember where you left it. But suppose that when you misplaced the object, you were mentally absorbed in thinking about ways to cut costs in your business and came up with a great idea that saved you lots of money. Operating on automatic led to an irritating incident of absent-minded forgetting, but because you were focusing attention on your business, you gained a lasting benefit. When we can perform routine tasks by relying on automatic processes, we are free to devote attention to more consequential matters. Because we rely on automatic processes frequently in our daily lives, the occasional absent-minded error seems a relatively small cost for such a large benefit.

The "less is more" principle also applies to two of the sins involving memory distortion: misattribution and suggestibility. I showed earlier that many instances of misattribution and suggestibility reflect poor memory for the source of an experience (see Chapters 4 and 5). When we don't recall exactly who told us a particular fact, where we saw a familiar face, or whether we actually witnessed an event or only heard about it later, the seeds of memory distortion are sown. If we don't recall the exact source of an experience — either because the details were not initially well encoded or because they've faded over time — we become quite vulnerable to the misattributions considered in Chapter 4 that are associated with source confusions and cryptomnesia (unintentional plagiarism). We may also be vulnerable to incorporating suggestions made after an event regarding the nature of specific details that we remember only vaguely.

Accepting inaccurate suggestions can have grave consequences for eyewitness testimony, as I showed in Chapter 5.

But what would be the consequences and costs of retaining the myriad of contextual details that define our numerous daily experiences? Assume, as I've argued, that memory is adapted to retain information that is most likely to be needed in the environment in which it operates. We seldom need to remember all the precise sensory and contextual details of our every experience. Would an adapted system routinely record all such details as a default option, or would it carefully record such details only when circumstances warn that they may later be needed? Our memories operate on the latter principle, and most of the time we are better off for it. We pay the price, however, when we are required to recollect detailed source information about an experience that did not elicit any special effort to encode source details.

Some types of misattribution occur when we fail to recollect specific details of an experience and at the same time recall the general sense of what happened. In the laboratory demonstrations of false recognition considered in Chapter 4, for instance, people incorrectly claimed that they previously heard the word *sweet* when in fact they had heard a group of semantically associated words, including *candy, sugar,* and *taste.* In related experimental procedures, people claim to have seen a picture of a particular car or teapot earlier in the experiment when they had actually seen pictures of physically similar but not identical cars and teapots. Misattribution occurs because participants in these experiments respond on the basis of memory for the general sense, or gist, of what they saw or heard.

However, the ability to remember the gist of what happened is also one of memory's strengths: we can benefit from an experience even when we do not recall all of its particulars. Indeed, studies conducted in my laboratory show that misattributions that result from remembering the gist are signs of a healthy memory system. For instance, after studying semantically associated words such as *candy, sugar,* and so forth, patients with amnesia caused by damage to the hippocampus and nearby structures in the temporal lobe remembered fewer of these words than did healthy control subjects — hardly a surprising result. But the amnesic patients were also less likely than the controls to make the mistake of falsely recognizing semantically related words such as *sweet,* which had not been presented in the original list. The same thing happened when amnesic patients studied pictures of cars, teapots, and other objects: compared to healthy controls, they later recognized fewer of the pictures they had actually seen, but they were also less likely to falsely recognize similar pictures they hadn't seen. Temporal lobe damage impairs patients' memories for both the particulars and the gist of what they have experienced, resulting in reduced true and false memories.

Memory for gist information is fundamental to such abilities as categorization and comprehension, allowing us to generalize across and organize our experiences. To develop a coherent category of "birds," for example, it's important to learn that a cardinal and an oriole are both members of the category despite superficial differences in their appearances. We need to notice and retain the recurring features that unite all birds, and to ignore the idiosyncratic details that differentiate between them. The cognitive psychologist James McClelland developed a theoretical model in which generalization results from retaining the gist of prior experiences. McClelland contends that generalization "is central to our ability to act intelligently." Yet in his model, McClelland also notes that "such generalization gives rise to distortions as an inherent by-product."

This idea receives striking experimental support from a study of false recognition in adults with a type of autistic disorder. Autism is associated with poor social skills, impaired communication abilities, and a highly rigid, literal style of processing information. But autistic children and adults can also show surprisingly good, and sometimes spectacular, rote memory abilities, as illustrated some years ago by Dustin Hoffman's character in the popular movie *Rain Man.* Despite his many limitations, Raymond Babbitt was a repository of obscure facts, spewing forth such nuggets as the name of the only major airline never to have suffered a crash (Qantas).

Scientists have described autistic patients who show exceptional memory for dates, names, or visual patterns. The neurologist David Beversdorf and his collaborators presented lists of semantically associated words to autistic adults and to a non-autistic control group. On a later test, the autistic subjects recognized just as many of the words they had studied earlier as the non-autistic subjects did. But the autistic group had fewer false alarms than the non-autistic group to semantically related words that they hadn't studied earlier. The autistic group thus discriminated between true and false memories more accurately than the cognitively intact subjects.

This pattern contrasts with that of the amnesic patients who showed reduced true memories and reduced false memories. The autistic adults were less likely than the controls to generalize from the words on the study list. They retained individual memories of the specific words they had studied, but not the semantic gist that misleads cognitively normal adults down the path of false recognition. A memory system that is not susceptible to gist-driven false recognition might free us from occasional bouts of misattribution. But it also might turn us into something like Raymond in *Rain Man*, burdened by a rote record of trivial facts while remaining insensitive to patterns and regularities in the environment that our memory systems normally exploit to our benefit. False recognition is, in part, a price we may pay for the benefit of generalization.

The sin of bias is also partly attributable to important strengths of our cognitive systems. Stereotypical biases often lead to unwarranted evaluations of individuals based on accumulated past experiences with groups, as we saw in Chapter 6. Though stereotypes can produce these undesirable consequences, they also make our cognitive lives more manageable by promoting generalizations that, on average, are reasonably accurate. The social psychologist Gordon Allport clearly saw this point back in the 1950s. He characterized stereotypes as consequences of ordinary processes of perception and memory, "[man's] normal and natural tendency to form generalizations, concepts, categories, whose content represents an oversimplification of his world of experience." Stereotypical biases constitute another price we pay for memory processes that generalize across past experiences.

We also saw that bias often results in memories that depict the self in an overly favorable light. Egocentric biases lead us to remember better grades than we actually achieved, or to exaggerate in memory our contributions at work or at home. Consistency and change biases can help to justify our involvement in a relationship, and hindsight biases make us seem wiser in retrospect than we actually were. On the face of it, these biases would appear to loosen our grasp on reality and thus represent a worrisome, even dangerous, tendency. After all, good mental health is usually associated with accurate perceptions of reality, whereas mental disorders and madness are associated with distorted perceptions of reality. But as the social psychologist Shelley Taylor has argued in her work on positive illusions, overly optimistic views of the self appear to promote mental health rather than undermine it. Far from functioning in an impaired or suboptimal manner, people who are most susceptible to positive illusions generally do well in many aspects of their lives. Depressed patients, in contrast, tend to lack the positive illusions that are characteristic of nondepressed individuals. Remembering the past in an overly positive manner may encourage us to meet new challenges by promoting an overly optimistic view of the future, whereas remembering the past more accurately or negatively can leave us discouraged. Clearly there must be limits to such effects, because wildly distorted optimistic biases would eventually lead to trouble. But as Taylor points out, positive illusions are generally mild and are important contributors to our sense of well-being. To the extent that memory bias promotes satisfaction with our lives, it can be considered an adaptive component of the cognitive system.

SEEKING THE SOURCES OF THE SEVEN SINS

Up to now, I've used the word *adaptive* in a quite general sense, but to explain the possible sources of the seven sins, I need to clarify what I mean when I say that a feature of memory is adaptive. Psychologists use the term *adaptation* in at least two ways. One comes from evolutionary theory and has a highly specific, technical meaning. An adaptation in this sense is a feature of a species that came into existence through the operation of natural selection because it increased the reproductive fitness of individuals. Darwin's argument for natural selection as the sole evolutionary mechanism to account for adaptive design rested on three fundamental observations. First, he observed that only a portion of each generation manages to reproduce. Second, he noted that offspring are not identical to their parents — some are taller, faster, or stronger than others. Variations like these that can be passed on to subsequent generations are considered heritable. Third, Darwin argued that some aspects of heritable variation raise the likelihood that their bearers will survive and reproduce. Features of an organism that result from natural selection are adaptations.

However, psychologists also often use the term *adaptation* in a looser manner — a colloquialism that refers to a feature of an organism that has generally beneficial consequences, whether or not it arose directly in response to natural selection during the course of evolution. Within the domain of memory, for instance, recalling telephone numbers and learning to use a computer provide examples of this looser sense of an adaptive feature. We can remember frequently used telephone numbers reasonably well, and in that sense memory can be considered adapted to the task. But telephones are such a recent invention that this ability could not have arisen during the course of evolution as an adaptation produced by natural selection. The same goes for the abilities needed to learn to use a computer or any other type of modern technology: our memory systems allow us to accomplish these tasks, but memory cannot have arisen as an adaptation for learning to operate modern technology.

The paleontologist Stephen Jay Gould used the term *exaptation* to refer to "features that now enhance fitness, but were not built by natural selection for their current role." Exaptations are, in effect, adaptations that are co-opted to perform functions other than the one for which they were originally selected. For instance, evolutionary biologists believe that the feathers of birds likely evolved initially as adaptations to perform such functions as thermal regulation or capturing prey, and were only later co-opted for the entirely different function of flight. In human cognition, the ability to read is an example of an exaptation. Because significant portions of the population have begun to read only during the past few centuries, reading is too new to be a product of natural selection. But reading draws on basic visual and cognitive abilities that likely arose as adaptations. Similarly, our abilities to remember telephone numbers and to use computers are not themselves evolutionary adaptations, but draw on features of memory that presumably originated as adaptations.

Gould and his colleague Richard Lewontin delineated a third type of evolutionary development called a "spandrel" — a special type of exaptation that is an unintended consequence or by-product of a particular feature. Whereas the exaptations discussed previously originated as adaptations and were later hijacked to perform a different function, spandrels had no adaptive function from the outset. The term *spandrel* is used in architecture to designate the leftover spaces between structural elements in a building. As an example, Gould and Lewontin described the four spandrels in the central dome of Venice's San Marco Basilica: spaces between arches and walls that were subsequently decorated with four evangelists and four biblical rivers. The spandrels were not designed for the specific purpose of housing these paintings, although they do so quite well. Similarly, people seeking shelter can sleep in the spaces between the pillars of a bridge, even though the pillars and spaces were not put there in order to provide shelter.

Determining whether particular features of the human mind are adaptations, exaptations, or spandrels is a difficult task that has turned into a kind of blood sport in contemporary psychology and biology. Evolutionary psychologists have sought to explain human cognition and behavior in terms of adaptations preserved by natural selection. "The mind is a system of organs of computation, designed by natural selection to solve the kinds of problems our ancestors faced in their foraging way of life," contends Steven Pinker, an enthusiastic advocate of the evolutionary perspective. The psychologist Leda Cosmides and the anthropologist John Tooby, pioneers of evolutionary psychology, argue in a similar spirit. "The human mind consists of a set of evolved information-processing mechanisms in the human nervous system," they assert. "These mechanisms, and the developmental programs that produce them, are adaptations, produced by natural selection over evolutionary time in ancestral environments."

In contrast, critics of evolutionary psychologists, including Stephen Jay Gould, have maintained that it is too easy to come up with after-the-fact explanations of mind and behavior that appeal to adaptations and natural selection — what have come to be known as "just so" stories. Gould held that many current features of the human mind are exaptations and spandrels — in addition to reading, other examples include writing and religious beliefs. He argued that exaptations and spandrels are such dominant influences in shaping the contemporary human mind that they constitute "a mountain to the adaptive molehill." Debates between advocates of these contrasting perspectives, exemplified by a 1997 exchange in the *New York Review of Books* between Pinker and Gould, are often quite contentious.

For evolutionary accounts of mind in general and memory in particular to amount to more than speculative exercises in post hoc storytelling, debates about the relative importance of adaptations, exaptations, and spandrels will have to be settled by empirical tests of hypotheses and predictions generated by alternative positions. Experimental psychologists such as myself tend to require hard evidence from controlled studies to decide between competing hypotheses. Although we do not have direct access to the evolutionary record of human cognition — there were no psychologists recording observations of our ancestors' behaviors in ancient environments — that doesn't preclude rigorous testing of evolutionary hypotheses.

The University of Texas psychologist David Buss and his associates have provided a helpful discussion of how such testing might proceed. They provide thirty examples in which predictions from an evolutionary perspective anchored by ideas of adaptation and natural selection led to empirical discoveries about human behavior or cognition. The cited examples include the nature of male sexual jealousy, patterns of spousal and same-sex homicide, relationship-specific sensitivity to betrayal, and mate guarding as a function of female reproductive value.

To test for evolutionary adaptations, psychologists and biologists rely on several types of evidence and considerations. One criterion is that of complex or special design: a feature of an organism is likely to be an adaptation if its internal structure is so complex as to minimize the possibility that the feature arose by chance or as an incidental by-product of something else. The vertebrate eye is a classic example of complex design. Intricate interdependencies among its many parts make it highly likely that the eye was designed by natural selection to accomplish the task of seeing, and highly unlikely that it developed by chance or as an incidental by-product. In the early nineteenth century, the theologian William Paley argued that such complex design reflects the presence of a designer with foresight. Invoking a comparison with a watchmaker, Paley noted that the intricate structure of a watch, like that of a living organism, reveals the presence of design that is devoted to specific functions and cannot be attributed to a fortuitous alignment of all the different parts in just the right arrangement. In his book *The Blind Watchmaker,* the biologist Richard Dawkins offered a Darwinian twist on Paley's watchmaker argument. A true watchmaker sets out with the goal of designing a watch, Dawkins observed, but natural selection is blind — it has no goal, purpose, or foresight.

Adaptations lead to differential reproductive success. It therefore follows that if a specific trait or feature has been favored by selection, it should be possible to find some evidence in the numbers of offspring produced by the trait's bearers. For instance, the hypothesis that women prefer to mate with tall men received support from the finding that tall men bear more offspring than short men. Physical stature in men may thus be, in part, an adaptation produced by selection.

The operation of natural selection may also be indicated when a trait turns up consistently in different species. Consider, for instance, the case of bodily symmetry. Humans and other organisms vary in the degree to which their bodies deviate from perfect left-right symmetry. In studies where raters judge attractiveness, greater bodily symmetry is generally associated with higher ratings. Further, symmetry produces advantages in sexual competition over asymmetry across a wide variety of nonhuman species, including insects, birds, and primates. Biologists have found that asymmetry is associated with the existence of genetic abnormalities and with exposure to negative environmental events, such as parasites and pollutants. Combining these observations with the sheer pervasiveness of selection for individuals with high symmetry across different species provides grounds for arguing that bodily symmetry is an adaptation produced by natural selection. Though this idea is not accepted by all researchers — a controversy exists concerning how symmetry and asymmetry come about — the findings point toward the operation of selective pressures.

An adaptation may also be signaled by the presence of what anthropologists call human universals: traits that are present in all recorded human cultures. For example, cross-cultural studies indicate that physical attractiveness is widely valued by both men and women (although more by men) and that people from different cultures tend to agree in their judgments of facial attractiveness. Aspects of facial attractiveness have, in turn, been associated with greater physical and mental health, raising the possibility that it may be an evolutionary adaptation.

The fact that a feature is a universal does not necessarily indicate that it arose as an adaptation. The anthropologists Donald Brown and Steven Gaulin both point out that universals can also arise from cultural traits that are ancient and highly useful, and therefore have spread through many societies. For example, the use of fire (particularly for cooking) is a human universal. However, we do not need to postulate that the use of fire reflects the operation of a shared adaptation. It's simpler to argue, as both Brown and Gaulin do, that people have long been exposed to fire and recognize its usefulness. But as Gaulin points out, if this type of cultural explanation can be ruled out, then the remaining universals can help to guide the search for psychological adaptations.

Conversely, if a trait is universally present across cultures with a single exception, that exception does not necessarily rule out the existence of an adaptation; there could be other cultural factors operating that help to explain the exception. On balance, then, while universals do not provide definitive evidence for (or against) adaptations, they can serve as helpful guideposts.

How about memory and the seven sins? Though we don't have a great deal of evidence on which to base strong claims about evolutionary origins, some relevant data come from studies of gender differences. Consider one evolutionary hypothesis about memory noted in the aforementioned article by Buss and his coworkers: women have more accurate memories for the spatial locations of objects than men do. The Canadian psychologists Marion Eals and Irwin Silverman noted that archaeological and paleontological data from the hunter-gatherer period, one of the important epochs during which human cognition evolved, suggest that men engaged primarily in hunting and women primarily foraged. Eals and Silverman hypothesized that these different activities placed different demands on spatial cognition and memory. Specifically, they suggested that successful foragers must locate food sources that are embedded within complex arrays of vegetation, and remember those locations for later visits. Natural selection, therefore, should have favored the development of superior memory for the spatial location of objects in women compared to men.

Eals and Silverman tested this hypothesis by showing men and women spatial arrays of objects. In one experiment, the objects appeared in a drawing; in another, they were dispersed on desks and tables in a room. In both experiments, women remembered the locations of objects more accurately than did men. But men outperformed women on other spatial tasks that, according to Eals and Silverman, tap spatial abilities that would have been required for successful hunting.

Some subsequent studies have replicated Eals and Silverman's results, whereas others have placed various qualifications and limitations on the findings. The question of whether spatial memory abilities in women are adaptations produced by selection for foraging skills is, accordingly, not yet settled. Nonetheless, these studies provide an example of how evolutionary hypotheses about the origins of memory can be formulated and tested.

A related type of evidence hinting at selection for sex differences in spatial memory abilities comes from research by the psychologist David Sherry at Western University in Ontario, who has studied memory in various bird species, including brown-headed cowbirds. When they breed, female cowbirds lay a single egg in another species' nest and then spend the rest of the day searching for other nests in which they can lay eggs during the coming days. Females must remember the locations of the nests, as the males do not help the females to locate nests. (In other cowbird species, both sexes play a role in such nest hunting.)

In earlier studies, Sherry and others demonstrated that the avian hippocampus plays a key role in allowing food-storing birds to remember where they have hidden food. A Clark's nutcracker, for instance, stores as many as thirty thousand seeds in five thousand locations during the fall, retrieving them the next spring. The bird accomplishes this daunting recall task with great success. Overall, the hippocampus is consistently larger in species that store and retrieve food than in those that do not. Further, after damage to the hippocampus, food-storing birds have great difficulty remembering the locations of their caches.

If the avian hippocampus is important for spatial memory, Sherry reasoned, then female brown-headed cowbirds ought to have a relatively larger hippocampus than male brown-headed cowbirds as a consequence of selection for spatial ability in the females related to finding and remembering nest locations. Measurements of hippocampal volume in relation to the overall size of cowbirds' brains revealed exactly that: the hippocampus is indeed relatively larger in females than in males. No such sex differences were found in two closely related species of birds that do not lay eggs in other birds' nests.

Studies of spatial abilities in other species show that the direction of sex differences can be reversed when selection pressures favor the development of spatial learning in males. Steven Gaulin examined two types of male rodents: a polygamous meadow vole that expands its home range during breeding season to increase mating opportunities, and a monogamous prairie vole that does not. Expanding its home range should produce selection for spatial abilities in the polygamous meadow vole. When Gaulin tested the two types of voles in laboratory maze learning tasks, he found evidence for superior spatial abilities in male compared with female meadow voles, and no sex difference among prairie voles. The hippocampus was also larger in male meadow voles than in females, but no difference existed in hippocampal size between male and female prairie voles.

The work of Gaulin and Sherry strongly supports the general idea that some features of memory are adaptations produced by natural selection. I'm not aware of any comparable evidence that speaks directly to the origins of the seven sins. Back in the 1980s, David Sherry and I coauthored a theoretical article arguing that some features of memory are adaptations produced by selection, whereas others are exaptations; we tried to identify characteristics of each. I take the same approach to the seven sins.

The most probable candidates for adaptations are persistence and transience. To the extent that persistence originated as a response to life-threatening situations that posed a direct threat to survival, animals and people who were able to remember those experiences persistently would surely be favored by natural selection. This ability seems so basic that if it did originate as an adaptation, we would expect many species to have neural machinery dedicated to preserving the memory of life-threatening experiences for long periods of time. As noted earlier, the universal presence of a particular feature across numerous cultures does not necessarily indicate that the feature is an adaptation, but it does provide one telltale sign of an adaptation. The neurobiologist Joseph LeDoux has noted that the amygdala and related structures are involved in long-lasting fear learning across diverse species, including humans, monkeys, cats, and rats. Likewise, we might also expect to observe links between persistence, the amygdala, and arousing or threatening experiences across diverse cultures and social groups. I am not aware of any evidence that addresses this issue directly, but cross-cultural studies examining neurobiological and cognitive aspects of persistence represent a promising avenue for future research. Consider also that, as discussed in Chapter 7, persistence results from a finely tuned interplay between the amygdala and stress-related hormones that modulates memory formation — an interdependent system that is suggestive of complex design.

The arguments of John Anderson and his group support the possibility that transience, too, could be an evolutionary adaptation. As mentioned earlier, Anderson's argument rests on the idea that properties of transience reflect properties of the environment in which memory operates. There is a catch here, however. If transience is an adaptation that arose through selection, then its properties should reflect those of the ancient environments in which our ancestors evolved. But how could we ever know about the relevant properties of environments during the hunter-gatherer period or other even earlier periods that may be relevant to human evolution? Not easily. Some anthropologists study contemporary foraging groups that remain culturally isolated, such as the Matsigenka indigenous people in southeastern Peru. If patterns of information retrieval in such groups could be examined, the results would help to determine whether transience reflects properties of environments more akin to ancestral environments than to modern Western societies. I am not aware of any such studies. However, the cognitive psychologist Lael Schooler, who has collaborated with Anderson on the idea that memory reflects environmental properties, has tried to get at the issue from a different but related angle.

Schooler drew on data collected by his collaborators Ramon Rhine and Juan Carlos Serio Silva concerning primate behavior in two separate environments that are similar in important respects to environments in which our hominid ancestors evolved: a tropical forest and a savanna. They studied the ranging behavior of howler monkeys living in a tropical forest on the volcanic island of Agaltepec in Mexico, and of baboons living in the savanna and open plains of Mikumi National Park in Tanzania. At both sites, the researchers observed the ranging behavior of troops of howlers and baboons over a period of several months as they moved from location to location. Schooler, Rhine, and Silva then analyzed the likelihood that a troop would return to a particular location as a function of the number of days that had passed since they were last there. The probability of returning to a particular location declined as time went on, and the form of the curve was similar to that observed for forgetting. As with the modern environments studied by Anderson and Schooler, the tropical forest of Agaltepec and the savanna of Mikumi appear to be environments in which it is an increasingly good bet to forget about information that hasn't been used for ever-longer periods of time. We don't know whether the similar patterns are based on independent mechanisms in modern humans and ranging primates, or whether they reflect a common evolutionary origin. Nonetheless, these observations encourage the view that transience is an adaptation to enduring properties of environments inhabited by both modern and ancient primates.

In her analysis of positive illusions, Shelley Taylor has suggested that overly optimistic biases may also be evolutionary adaptations. However, the psychologist Steven Heine and his collaborators have presented evidence that casts some doubt on this possibility. They suggest that biases to view the self in an overly positive manner are specific to certain cultures. For example, they cite anthropological, sociological, and psychological evidence that the Japanese tend to adopt a critical view of the self, rather than the positive bias commonly seen in studies of North Americans. If positive biases were evolutionary adaptations, we would expect to observe such biases across cultures. Although, as noted earlier, a single exception to a universal pattern does not rule out the possibility of an adaptation, this line of work suggests that cross-cultural studies of the various forms of memory bias could prove to be highly informative.

Bias is closely related to high-level cognitive operations and complex social interactions (see Chapter 6). These are precisely the kinds of processes that we would expect to vary considerably among cultures. Based on the work of Heine's group, I predict that the specific forms of memory biases will be found to vary considerably across cultures and that they are more likely the product of social and cultural norms than biological evolution produced by natural selection. It is still possible, however, that people in all cultures exhibit some type of bias during remembering, with the particular type or content of bias varying across cultures. Even if this is so, however, I hypothesize that bias is an incidental by-product of the fact that general knowledge and beliefs frequently guide acts of remembering.

I hypothesize that the remaining sins — blocking, absent-mindedness, misattribution, and suggestibility — are most likely evolutionary spandrels. Part of my reasoning is driven by plausibility considerations: it is difficult to imagine how or why natural selection would design a system that is especially prone to absent-minded errors, frequently blocks on names or words, or remembers events that never occurred. But we have already seen that each of these sins can be plausibly viewed as a by-product of useful features of memory that themselves arose as either adaptations or exaptations. Absent-minded errors, misattribution resulting from source memory confusion, and related effects of suggestibility are, I suggest, by-products of adaptations and exaptations that produced a memory system that does not routinely preserve all the details required to specify the exact source of an experience. Blocking may be an incidental by-product of effects related to recency and frequency of information retrieval that also give rise to transience. And gist-based false memories are by-products of categorization and generalization processes that are themselves vital to our cognitive function.

There is a difference, however, between these spandrels of memory and the architectural spandrels discussed by Gould and Lewontin. Architectural spandrels have benign consequences: they do not interfere with or undermine a building's structural or functional integrity. Not so for memory. The irritation of absent-minded errors, the momentary frustration of blocking, and the potentially shattering consequences of eyewitness misidentifications and false memories resulting from misattribution or suggestibility all have the power to disrupt our lives, temporarily or permanently. When suffering the consequences of these spandrels gone awry, it is difficult to appreciate or imagine that they are by-products of processes that, for the most part, keep our cognitive lives running smoothly. It may be helpful to think of these memory spandrels in relation to the squirrel that weighs the benefits of feeding against the possible costs of encountering a predator and returns to cover repeatedly with bits of cookie. The misbegotten spandrels represent the cost of a trade-off in memory that also has important, though less visible, benefits.

If my suggestions about the origins of the seven sins have merit, one thing we can count on is that the sins are not going to disappear any time soon. Recall the case of Binjimin Wilkomirski: he "remembered" childhood terrors experienced in a Nazi concentration camp when he actually appears to have lived safely in Switzerland during the war. The prospect of someone falsely recollecting that he endured one of the greatest horrors imaginable seems so bizarre that one is tempted to write off Wilkomirski as an inexplicable, onetime aberration. But if misattribution and suggestibility, the likely culprits in Wilkomirski's delusions, are truly evolutionary spandrels, then Wilkomirski should not be an isolated case. And he is not. Women and men who once believed that they had recovered memories of terrible childhood traumas, only to later retract them after ending psychotherapy, remind us that Wilkomirski's experience is far from unique. So, too, do the legions of self-proclaimed alien abductees who vividly remember impossible events such as sexual abuse at the hands of demonic — and elusive — alien captors. Suggestive proce- dures such as hypnosis are frequently implicated in such cases.

These types of false memories are nothing new. In Chapter 4, we considered the debate over false memories and déjà vu that raged in the 1890s. As early as 1881, the British psychologist James Sully devoted an entire chapter of his book *Illusions: A Psychological Study* to "illusions of memory," citing case after case of memory distortions that exemplify what I call misattribution and suggestibility. The his- torian Patrick Geary described an eleventh-century Bavarian monk named Arnold who "remembered" encountering a flying dragon on a journey he had made years earlier. Arnold's false memory was likely the product of imagination and suggestion. Misattribution and suggestibility have been with us for a long time and will surely con- tinue their mischief in the future.

The same applies to the other sins. Consider, for instance, tran- sience and persistence. People have been trying to overcome the limitations of transience for centuries. As I noted in Chapter 1, the invention of visual imagery mnemonics — a method of improving memory by encoding new information in the form of vivid visual images — dates back to the Greeks. Similarly, persistence has a long heritage. Recall Robert Burton's description of the terrified Blasius, a reporter who witnessed the ancient earthquake at Sacai and for years afterward could not "drive the remembrance of it out of his minde" (see Chapter 7). Post-traumatic stress disorder — where the effects of persistence are painfully magnified — has achieved recognition only relatively recently from psychologists and psychiatrists. Yet its symptoms have probably been around as long as people have experi- enced trauma. This idea is wonderfully illustrated by the psychiatrist Jonathan Shay's compelling book *Achilles in Vietnam,* which delineates parallels between the aftermath of combat trauma in Vietnam and in Homer's *Iliad*. Shay relates an incident where Achilles is overwhelmed by grief because he failed to cover for a fellow soldier who died, and feels "pierced by memory" as he intrusively remembers his fallen comrade.

Even though they often seem like our enemies, the seven sins are an integral part of the mind's heritage because they are so closely connected to features of memory that make it work well. The seemingly contradictory relationship between memory's sins and virtues captured the attention of Fanny Price, the heroine of Jane Austen's nineteenth-century novel *Mansfield Park*. Admiring a beautiful shrub-lined walkway that had emerged from a formerly rough patch of ground, Fanny recalled what the walkway had looked like years earlier and wondered whether she would lose this memory in the future. The moment inspired her to contemplate seemingly contradictory properties of memory:

> If any one faculty of our nature may be called *more* wonderful than the rest, I do think it is memory. There seems something more speakingly incomprehensible in the powers, the failures, the inequalities of memory, than in any other of our intelligences. The memory is sometimes so retentive, so serviceable, so obedient; at others, so bewildered and so weak; and at others again, so tyrannic, so beyond control! We are to be sure a miracle every way — but our powers of recollecting and of forgetting, do seem peculiarly past finding out.

Modern psychology and neuroscience have proven Fanny wrong on one point — that our powers of recollecting and forgetting are "peculiarly past finding out" — but her acute appreciation of memory's contrasting strengths and weaknesses could hardly be more apt. The seven sins are not merely nuisances to minimize or avoid. They also illuminate how memory draws on the past to inform the present, preserves elements of present experience for future reference, and allows us to revisit the past at will. Memory's vices are also its virtues, elements of a bridge across time that allows us to link the mind with the world.

The Update
ADAPTIVE MEMORY ERRORS: WHAT KIND OF EVIDENCE?

I consider the claim that ended the 2001 edition of this book to be the core of the seven sins framework for characterizing memory errors. The idea that memory's vices are also its virtues leads us away from the commonsense notion that memory is a fundamentally flawed capacity and that memory errors constitute damning proof in favor of this conclusion. I titled this book *The Seven Sins of Memory* in homage to the ancient seven deadly sins, but as I pointed out in the introduction, even the seven deadly sins can be seen as extensions of traits that serve adaptive functions. For this chapter, I drew on functional and evolutionary analyses of memory and cognition to make the case for the plausibility and utility of a "vices are also virtues" approach to conceiving the seven sins, but I didn't cite a lot of experimental evidence linking memory errors with adaptive processes or functions — mainly because there wasn't much evidence available in 2001. Two decades later, that situation has changed. There is now considerably more experimental evidence that directly connects several of the seven sins with these adaptive functions, as well as new theoretical proposals and integrative reviews regarding the adaptive functions of memory errors. Given the relative lack of hard evidence when I wrote the 2001 edition, I focus on some of the new findings here.

When discussing the adaptive value of transience in 2001, I talked a lot about the value of forgetting over time in ridding our minds of informational clutter that is no longer relevant, but I didn't say much about its role in promoting psychological well-being. In Chapter 7, however, I briefly alluded to what was then a recent finding from a study in which students kept diaries of their everyday experiences: their negative emotions faded faster over time than their positive emotions. The students still remembered the negative experiences, but the emotional sting associated with them dissipated more quickly than the warm glow associated with the positive experiences. That finding has since been replicated across many different populations and situations, and it is now known as the "fading affect bias" (FAB). The FAB doesn't always hold — for example, the evidence on persistence shows how traumatic events can produce crippling intrusive memories that retain their negative charge over time — but it is nonetheless present in many situations.

New evidence on the FAB highlights the fact that this form of transience is associated with adaptive functioning. For example, people who exhibit the mild form of depression known as dysphoria exhibit a much weaker FAB than do people who show low levels of dysphoria, and a reduced FAB is also seen in people who are characterized by high levels of anxiety. A weak FAB has been linked to eating disorders and to a condition known as alexithymia, where people have difficulty recognizing and describing their own emotions and experience a reduced positive affect. A recent study examined a possible connection between the FAB and the psychological characteristic known as Grit — the capacity to persevere and remain passionate about working toward long-term goals despite challenges and adversity. People characterized by relatively high levels of Grit showed a more robust FAB than did people characterized by lower levels of Grit. The authors suggest that a robust FAB may contribute to Grit by allowing people to recall mistakes and setbacks with less of the negative emotional charge that could prevent them from moving forward despite adversity. Although the exact nature of the relationship between the FAB and adaptive functioning remains to be determined (i.e., the FAB could be either a consequence or a cause of the psychological characteristics with which it is associated), it's clear that the type of transience conferred by the FAB is a sign of psychological well-being.

There is also new evidence suggesting a contribution to well-being from the form of memory blocking referred to as "memory suppression" or "retrieval inhibition." Recall from The Update in Chapter 7 the finding from research using the "think–no think" paradigm that individuals with PTSD exhibit impaired memory suppression compared with individuals who experienced trauma but did not develop PTSD. From an adaptive perspective, this finding implies that intact retrieval inhibition can contribute to psychological well-being after a traumatic experience. A related line of research has investigated whether similar impairments are observed in individuals with depression. Some studies have provided evidence for such impairments and others haven't, with the overall pattern of results suggesting that depressed individuals exhibit a modest deficit in the ability to suppress memories during the think–no think procedure. An fMRI study revealed that depressed and nondepressed individuals recruited different brain regions when engaging in memory suppression during think–no think, which could help to distinguish the neural bases of adaptive and nonadaptive retrieval inhibition. More research is needed to better understand how and when retrieval inhibition contributes to psychological well-being, but the evidence that it does is at least suggestive.

In The Update in Chapter 2, I discussed the recent surge of research into mind wandering and its negative impact on memory and learning, particularly in the classroom. But at the same time, new findings indicate that mind wandering has benefits as well as costs. For example, in a study where people occasionally engaged in mind wandering while performing a demanding cognitive task, their thoughts mostly focused on future events: they undertook a kind of autobiographical planning aimed at achieving personal goals. Autobiographical planning during mind wandering occurred most often in people with high working memory capacity, suggesting that they were able to deploy cognitive resources not needed for the main task in an adaptive manner. Related studies have examined whether mind wandering during a break from a demanding task can boost performance on a subsequent creative problem-solving task. The evidence so far is mixed, but related research suggests that individuals who report high levels of daydreaming in daily life or often intentionally engage in mind wandering during everyday tasks tend to perform at high levels on lab creativity tasks that require generating novel ideas.

Moving on from sins of omission to sins of commission, there is impressive new evidence for a "vices are also virtues" perspective on misattribution and suggestibility. Even by 2001, the Deese/Roediger-McDermott (DRM) paradigm for eliciting robust false recall and recognition of nonstudied semantic associates of previously studied words, which I discussed at length in Chapter 4 and again earlier in this chapter, had been used in both cognitive and neuroimaging studies of misattribution errors. And the interpretation of this false memory effect — that it reflects retention of semantic gist information regarding common features of list items — led me to highlight the critical benefits of a memory system that does a good job of retaining semantic gist information. Based on this perspective, it follows that brain regions that are important for the adaptive function of representing semantic information should also play a role in DRM false memories.

To investigate this possibility, I collaborated on a 2016 fMRI study with a team of researchers at University College London led by the cognitive neuroscientists Martin Chadwick and Demis Hassabis. We focused on a specific region located at the front of the left temporal lobe, the temporal pole (TP), which is known as a "semantic hub" of the brain because it plays a critical role in processing and representing the meaning of and relations between concepts. Abnormalities in the left TP have been linked to a devastating condition known as semantic dementia, in which patients exhibit severe impairments in comprehension and other aspects of semantic processing. Theoretical models of semantic cognition maintain that concepts are represented by a similarity-based code in the left TP: concepts that are close in meaning are represented by more similar neural codes or patterns in the left TP than concepts that are more distant in meaning.

Based on this idea, we predicted that DRM lists in which the neural representations of the nonstudied semantic lure words (e.g., *sweet*) and their associated study list items (e.g., *candy, sugar, tooth, taste*) in the left TP are highly similar would yield more false memories than DRM lists in which the neural representations of lure words and their associated list items are less similar. This is exactly what our study found — and, importantly, no other region of the brain showed this relationship. These findings support an adaptive perspective on DRM false memories because they reveal that the same left TP region that supports representation of semantic information and relations, a key adaptive process, is linked to false memories that result from that process.

Another source of evidence linking DRM false memories with adaptive processes comes from research reported over the past decade by Mark Howe and his colleagues at the City University of London. We know that exposure to a DRM list sets in motion semantic/associative processes that later result in false memories for the nonstudied lure. Howe and his colleagues asked whether such processes could also help people to solve a certain kind of associative problem. Consider the following three words and see if you can come up with another word that is associated with all of them: *walk, beauty, over.*

Did you think of *sleep*? The Remote Associates Test (RAT) consists of a series of word problems just like that one. For some RAT problems, the young adults in Howe's experiment first studied DRM lists that should prime the correct solution word (e.g., *bed, rest, awake, drowsy, tired, dream,* and so on, before solving for *sleep*); for other problems, there was no DRM priming. Howe and his colleagues found that exposure to a DRM list boosted solution rates on the subsequent RAT — but *only* when participants falsely recalled the lure word before taking the RAT. In a later study, Howe's group produced similar effects on an analogical reasoning task. For example, when young adults were asked to complete the analogy *"Hat is to head as sock is to _____,"* they were quicker to generate *foot* after they were exposed to a DRM list of words associated with *foot* (e.g., *shoe, hand, toe, walk*). Interestingly, this effect on reasoning was not observed when the lure word itself was actually presented in the study list! Only false memory priming led to quicker responses on the analogical reasoning task. Howe's group has also documented these and related effects in both young children and older adults, thus providing clear evidence that exposure to DRM lists and the resulting false memories can have beneficial effects on cognitive function.

Evidence for an adaptive perspective on memory errors isn't confined to the DRM paradigm. When discussing the sin of suggestibility, I talked at length about the corrupting influences of post-event misinformation on memory. But those errors may be a consequence of the normally adaptive process of memory updating, which I briefly mentioned earlier in this chapter in relation to transience. If I park in a different space in the same parking lot every day, I need to update my memory to the current space or waste time wandering around looking for my car. If I find out that a friend's relationship has broken up, I need to incorporate that new information into memory so that I don't ask an embarrassing question about the relationship based on outdated information. Our memories are flexible enough that we can update them with new information (and transience can make it easier to update an old memory), but this process also can result in updating with misinformation.

Research that I discussed in The Update in Chapter 7 concerning the phenomenon of reconsolidation is relevant here. Those studies show that reactivating a memory can put that memory into an unstable, or labile, state in which it is vulnerable to disruption. Many researchers who study reconsolidation believe that this reactivation-induced instability serves the function of memory updating because the reactivated memory is open to the incorporation of new information. But it can also lead to distortion. A nice example comes from an fMRI study in which people initially viewed a movie with several other observers and later completed a memory test on their own about events in the movie. A few days after that, while they were undergoing fMRI scanning, participants answered questions about the movie again. But this time, some of those questions were paired with answers that the participants believed (mistakenly) were given by people they had watched the movie with a few days earlier. The trick here was that a subset of the answers supposedly provided by others were wrong — pure fabrications. Participants made more errors when they answered questions that were paired with fabricated answers than those that were not, even though they had answered the same questions correctly the first time around. People were thus updating their memories incorrectly based on suggested misinformation and social influence. Many of these errors persisted on a final memory test, even though the participants were warned that the answers provided in the scanning session were randomly generated and shouldn't be trusted. The fMRI results revealed that these persistent memory errors were linked with greater activity in the medial temporal lobe — a brain region that plays a key role in memory formation and consolidation — at the time the fabricated answers were provided, compared with trials in which participants were not presented with fabricated responses, or trials in which participants later corrected their mistaken acceptance of a fabricated answer on a final test. Mechanisms that are normally used to update memory accurately were hijacked by fabricated post-event suggestions to produce a kind of false updating, highlighting that the same dynamic quality of memory that allows us to update it adaptively can also get us into trouble.

Episodic Recombination: Past, Present, and Future

In the 1980s, I directed the Unit for Memory Disorders at the University of Toronto, where I tested people with severe memory disorders resulting from various kinds of brain damage. The most intriguing patient I encountered during those years was a man known in the literature by the initials KC, who had sustained a head injury at age thirty in a motorcycle accident that damaged several parts of his brain important for memory, including the hippocampus and part of the frontal lobe. KC still had an IQ in the normal range and maintained mostly intact perceptual and linguistic abilities, but his capacity for episodic memory (remembering specific past personal experiences; see Chapter 1) was completely destroyed. (In contrast, KC had some preservation of semantic memory — knowledge of facts and concepts — although his semantic memory was not entirely intact.) When KC was asked to try to recall a particular event that had happened an hour, a day, a week, or a year earlier, he could not remember anything specific and would state that his mind was a blank.

One session with KC turned out to be particularly instructive. Endel Tulving, the great memory researcher who first advanced the distinction between episodic and semantic memory, and who was my colleague as well as my former PhD supervisor at Toronto, had taken an increasing interest in KC. Tulving and I sat across a testing table from KC when Tulving asked him a simple but revealing question: "What will you be doing tomorrow?" KC thought for a few seconds but couldn't come up with anything. Tulving then asked him to describe his state of mind when trying to think about tomorrow. "Blank, I guess," he responded. That was the same response he had given many times when asked to recall what he had been doing the day before.

This observation stunned us at the time because it suggested a close relationship between the ability to remember past experiences and the ability to imagine future experiences — a connection that had received almost no attention in the previous psychological literature. Tulving described that session with KC in a 1985 paper. I continued to think about the relationship between memory and imagining the future, and nearly initiated experimental work on the topic in the 1990s, but preoccupation with other lines of research in my laboratory led me to relegate it to the back burner.

That all changed in 2006, shortly after a new postdoctoral researcher, Donna Rose Addis, arrived in my lab. Addis had been doing fMRI studies examining episodic memories of everyday personal experiences. A few studies from other labs had appeared in the literature in the early 2000s suggesting similarities between remembering past experiences and imagining future ones. These studies piqued my interest in the topic again, so Addis and I began discussing ways to extend the methods she had used in her fMRI studies of memories for personal experiences to studying the mechanisms for imagining possible future experiences. We settled on a simple experimental procedure in which participants were given word cues in the scanner; they were instructed either to remember a past experience or imagine a future experience from a specified time period related to the word. For example, in response to the cue word *vacation* and an instruction to remember a related event from the past few years, a participant might recall a pleasant afternoon on the beach from their Cape Cod vacation last summer, and in response to the cue word *dog* and an instruction to imagine a related event that might happen in the next few years, a participant might imagine going to a local pet store next summer and picking out a puppy. We compared brain activity during these tasks with brain activity during control tasks that required visual and semantic processing but that did not require remembering or imagining a personal experience.

The results were striking: a network of brain regions associated with remembering past experiences in previous neuroimaging studies showed highly similar increases in activity when we asked people to remember past experiences and imagine future experiences. Other labs published fMRI findings consistent with ours, and both my lab and others also reported additional cognitive similarities between memory and future imagining. For instance, we found that older adults remembered fewer episodic details about their past experiences (e.g., details about what happened and where it happened) than did younger adults, and we found that they reported fewer episodic details than their younger counterparts when imagining future experiences.

What do these striking similarities between past and future events have to do with memory errors? A lot, I think. At the same time that we were publishing our fMRI results in 2007, Addis and I put forth an idea that we called the "constructive episodic simulation hypothesis," which maintains that the past-future similarities we and others observed reflect the key role that episodic memory plays in imagining future experiences. When people think ahead to what might happen to us in the future, it is important for us to use our episodic memories of past experiences to guide planning and future actions. But the future is rarely identical to the past, so when we imagine possible future experiences, we need to be able to recombine bits and pieces of past experiences into simulations of *novel* situations that might happen in the future. For example, if I am thinking about how to handle a delicate upcoming conversation with a colleague, I can draw on past experiences with that colleague and similar experiences with other people, then recombine details from those experiences into simulations of the upcoming encounter that I can run in my mind before finally deciding how to approach the conversation.

We hypothesized that this kind of episodic recombination is adaptive because it allows us to mentally "try out" different approaches to a novel future situation based on past experiences without having to engage in actual behaviors. Critically, however, we also hypothesized that this same capacity for flexibly recombining elements of episodic memory that makes the system adaptive for constructing novel simulations also contributes to errors and distortions that result from mistakenly combining elements of different episodes. In other words, certain kinds of misattribution errors where people mix up details from different episodes, such as source memory confusions and memory conjunction errors (see Chapter 4), may be a price we pay for a memory system that relies on episodic recombination processes to support an adaptive function: simulating future happenings based on past experiences.

A great deal of research in my lab during the past decade and more has provided new evidence that episodic memory does indeed play an important role in imagining future experiences, which lends support to the constructive episodic simulation hypothesis. But until recently, we didn't have experimental evidence directly linking memory errors with the flexible episodic recombination processes that we think play an important adaptive role in future simulation. Now, however, we do. One source of evidence is the work of the cognitive psychologist Stephen Dewhurst and his colleagues using the DRM paradigm. They found that when participants encoded DRM lists with reference to a future event — for example, imagining a future holiday and rating how relevant each list item would be to planning the holiday — subsequent false recall and false recognition of nonstudied associated lure words were both significantly higher than in other conditions that involved encoding study list words by thinking about the past or rating their pleasantness. In contrast, these encoding manipulations had no effect on true recall and true recognition of studied words. Dewhurst and his colleagues hypothesized that "the greater flexibility of future thinking may have enabled participants to think creatively about the possibility of encountering studied items in a hypothetical future event, thereby increasing the possibility of activating the critical lure." Translating to the language of the constructive episodic simulation hypothesis, flexible recombination processes that are adaptive for future planning might also contribute to memory errors.

Recent experiments from my laboratory led by Alexis Carpenter strengthen the link between flexible episodic recombination and memory errors in a slightly different context. Imagine that you are taking a morning stroll and you see an elderly man walking a black poodle. The next morning, you see an elderly woman walking the same black poodle. Even though you've never met the man or the woman, you can infer that they have some type of relationship (most likely, husband and wife) because you saw them walking the same dog. Psychologists call this "associative inference," and it is an adaptive process that involves the ability to recombine information from separate episodes. Could it also lead to memory errors? Carpenter's experiments employed an adapted version of a paradigm that others had used previously to study associative inference. Participants saw slides of scenes comprising a person, an object, and a background setting. They were told to try to infer the connection between different people shown in different background settings but paired with the same object, such as a man holding a toy in a room with a white couch and a boy holding the identical toy in a different room with a brown couch. On a subsequent test, participants sometimes made memory errors that were attributable to mixing up contextual details from related scenes, such as mistakenly recalling that the man was in a room with a brown couch instead of a white couch. Critically, people made more of these misattribution errors when they made *correct* inferences about the relationship between the people in the scenes than when they did not. That is, their memories for contextual details were more likely to be mistaken when they correctly inferred that the man and the boy were linked via the toy than when they did not make this associative inference. Once again, the same processes that underpin an adaptive process — in this case, associative inference — also produce memory errors. And the culprit here is the same type of episodic recombination process that we think people use when they imagine future experiences.

We've still got a lot to learn about how and why the virtues of memory sometimes turn into its vices. But we have a lot more evidence now than we did two decades ago to guide our theorizing, and from where I sit, the "vices are also virtues" approach has helped to paint a rich and expanding picture of how memory fits into the broader landscape of cognition, including the connections between memory errors and semantic representation, problem solving, imagining the future, and associative inference. As frustrating and even dangerous as the seven sins can be, they continue to provide valuable insight into the mind's inner workings and how its seeming weaknesses sometimes emerge from the same foundations as its strengths.

Notes

1   *"Yumiura"*: Kawabata (1999, quotation from p. 196).

2   *Wilkomirski*: Gourevitch (1999) provides a detailed history of the entire case. Although it cannot be treated as a factual account of the past, Wilkomirski's book is still fascinating to read in light of subsequent developments.

3   *high school memory test:* Offer et al. (2000).

4   *Brian Williams:* See Goldstein (2015).

5   *Dr. Christine Blasey Ford:* See Ducharme (2018). For an excellent analysis of Blasey Ford's testimony from the perspective of a memory researcher, see Hyman (2018a, 2018b).

   COVID-19 and memory problems: See Belluck (2020) for "brain fog" and examples of memory loss after COVID-19; for discussion by a neuroscientist of how COVID-19 could affect the brain to produce memory loss, see Tronson (2020).

6   *different ways that memory causes trouble:* Wilma Koutstaal and I addressed a number of issues related to this question in a chapter reviewing sources of inaccuracy and inaccessibility in memory (Koutstaal and Schacter, 1997b).

   the seven sins: An initial summary can be found in Schacter (1999b).

8   *"replication crisis":* For contrasting views, see Open Science Collaboration (2015) and Gilbert et al. (2016). In the Open Science Collaboration study, researchers attempted to replicate findings from one hundred studies published in the journal *Psychological Science,* which features mainly social psychology and cognitive psychology research. Although they reported frequent replication failures, replication success occurred more often for cognitive psychology studies than for social psychology studies. This book relies much more heavily on research from cognitive psychology than from social psychology, which may be part of the reason the findings reported in the 2001 edition have generally held up well over time.

10 *memory is a mainly reliable guide:* The question of whether memory is fundamentally reliable or unreliable continues to spark debate among researchers. For a recent discussion questioning claims of fundamental unreliability, see Brewin et al. (2020).

11 *Yo-Yo Ma:* Finkelstein (1999).

18 *"Memories are something":* Kawabata (1999, p. 194).

1. THE SIN OF TRANSIENCE

19   *memories of O. J. Simpson:* Schmolck et al. (2000).

21   *Ebbinghaus:* The experiments are described in Ebbinghaus (1885/1964); for historical background and modern perspectives, see Slamecka (1985).
Kansas State University diary study: Thompson et al. (1996).

22   *Thanksgiving memories:* Friedman and deWinstanley (1998).
work memories: Eldridge et al. (1994).

23   *recollections of when and where:* Bornstein and LeCompte (1995).
combination of transience and bias: Brewer (1996); Thompson et al. (1996).

24   *grand jury testimony:* My discussion of Clinton's testimony and all quotations from the grand jury session are drawn from the written transcript of Clinton's testimony on August 17, 1998 (Starr, 1998).

28   *transience in older adults:* Huppert and Kopelman (1989); Carlesimo et al. (1997). For a general discussion of memory loss in older adults, see Albert (1997).
In one study: Zelinski and Burnight (1997).

29   *variability of transience:* Davis et al. (2003).
Dutch study: Schmand et al. (1997).
Alzheimer brains: See Jack et al. (1998), Price and Morris (1999), and Small et al. (1999); for an accessible overview of scientific research and a view of Alzheimer's disease from the perspective of a family member, see Pierce (2000).

31   *Alzheimer memory test:* Buschke et al. (1999) and Killany et al. (2000) report success in using structural brain scans to predict which older adults will develop Alzheimer's disease.

32   *86 billion nerve cells:* von Bartheld et al. (2016).
HM: Scoville and Milner (1957) first described HM. For a readable summary of this landmark case, see Hilts (1995).

33   *functional magnetic resonance imaging, or fMRI:* For an overview of neuroimaging techniques, see Posner and Raichle (1994); for reviews of neuroimaging studies on memory, see Buckner (2000), Nyberg and Cabeza (2000), and Schacter and Wagner (1999).
a string of failures: For discussion of possible reasons why hippocampal activations are sometimes difficult to obtain, see Schacter and Wagner (1999).

34   *collaborative effort:* Wagner et al. (1998). Our study used a type of "reverse prediction": we first sorted subjects' performance on the recognition test according to whether they remembered or forgot an item, and then we determined which brain regions were more active for remembered than forgotten items. For a more general discussion of fMRI studies of encoding processes, see Wagner et al. (1999).

35   *elaboration based on previous knowledge:* Craik and Tulving (1975) report classic cognitive studies demonstrating the importance of elaborative encoding. See Schacter (1996, ch. 2) for further evidence and discussion.

36   *Stanford University study:* Brewer et al. (1998).
two articles on short-term forgetting: Brown (1958); Peterson and Peterson (1959).

Baddeley (1998) provides a nice overview of the development of this line of research.

37 *working memory:* Baddeley (1992, 1998).

38 *phonological loop:* Gathercole and Baddeley (1993).

39 *an intriguing patient:* Shallice and Warrington (1970). For a collection of similar cases, see Vallar and Shallice (1990).

    "a pimple on the face of cognition": Baddeley (1992, p. 21).

40 *phonological loop and language learning:* Baddeley et al. (1998); Gathercole and Baddeley (1993).

    neuroimaging of phonological loop: Paulesu et al. (1993).

42 *talking and thinking about experiences:* Thompson et al. (1996).

    Spanish vocabulary: Bahrick (1984). Bahrick (2000) summarizes numerous studies on long-term retention.

43 *neural connections:* Bailey and Chen (1989); for an excellent overview of relevant work, see Squire and Kandel (1999).

    reminders of lost experiences: For a review, see Koutstaal and Schacter (1997b).

    personal memory diary: Wagenaar (1986).

44 *memory improvement books:* Crook and Adderly (1998) and Lorayne and Lucas (1996) provide sensible tips.

45 *use of imagery mnemonics by older adults:* Stigsdotter-Neely and Backman (1993); Plude and Schwartz (1996); West and Crook (1992).

    Mega Memory: Trudeau (1997).

46 *Mega Memory and memory power audiotapes:* Rebok et al. (1997, p. 304).

47 *actors and memory:* Noice and Noice (1996, quotation from p. 8).

    active experiencing: Noice et al. (1999).

    ginkgo biloba: Experimental studies have been reported by several groups, including Kanowski et al. (1996) and Wesnes et al. (1997). Wong et al. (1998) provide a general review. A more recent meta-analysis by Laws et al. (2012) failed to find evidence of a positive effect of ginkgo biloba on memory.

48 *PS:* Crook and Adderly (1998).

    estrogen hormone replacement: See Drake et al. (2000) for the association between estrogen levels and verbal memory, Duka et al. (2000) for effects of estrogen replacement on memory for pairs of pictures, and Wolf et al. (1999) for effects on verbal memory. The relationship between estrogen levels and memory performance may be complex. For instance, Drake et al. (2000) found that high levels of estrogen were linked with high levels of verbal memory, whereas low levels of estrogen were associated with high levels of memory for visual shapes. Further, not all studies have found effects of estrogen replacement on memory; for discussion, see Duka et al. (2000).

49 *NMDA receptor:* Tang et al. (1999).

50 *Tim Tully and memory drugs:* Weiner (1999, p. 29).

51 *Wordsworth ode:* Hayden (1994, p. 144).

    AJ: For the initial case description, see Parker et al. (2006, quotation from p. 35).

53 *AJ published a book:* Price and Davis (2008).

2012 paper: LePort et al. (2012). The nine brain regions that showed volume differences between the HSAM and control groups were the uncinate fascicle; forceps major; parahippocampal gyrus; posterior insula; anterior putamen and caudate surrounding anterior limb of internal capsule; posterior pallidum; anterior and middle temporal gyrus; lingual gyrus; and intraparietal sulcus. The quotation is from p. 90.

fMRI study of HSAM: Santangelo et al. (2018). This study was conducted by a group of Italian researchers, with collaboration from James McGaugh. They scanned eight individuals with HSAM, who were identified according to the same criteria as in previous US samples, and compared them to twenty matched controls.

54   *the same kinds of mistakes:* Patihis et al. (2013).

2016 study: LePort et al. (2016).

the original 2006 case report: Parker et al. (2006, pp. 35, 38, 46).

frequently retrieve their past experiences: LePort et al. (2016) favor this idea.

55   *benefits have important implications:* Brown et al. (2014); Karpicke and Aue (2015).

2006 study: Roediger and Karpicke (2006). The effect I am referring to as "retrieval practice" is also known as the "testing effect."

specifically impact the rate of forgetting: See Sadeh and Pertzov (2019) and Slamecka and McElree (1983).

a reward can also impact transience selectively: Chowdhury et al. (2012); Murayama and Kuhbandner (2011); Wittmann et al. (2005).

56   *Elizabeth Warren boasted:* Warren referred to her 100,000 selfies in the Democratic debate on December 19, 2019. See Mueller (2019).

external reminders: Gilbert et al. (2019) report three experiments showing that a bias toward using external reminders persists even when people are offered financial incentives to adopt a better strategy. Risko and Gilbert (2016) provide an excellent overview of cognitive offloading.

57   *viewing photos:* See Koutstaal et al. (1999b) and Schacter et al. (1997b).

people took a museum tour: Henkel (2014). For a review of research on how taking photos impacts memory, see Henkel et al. (2021).

people toured a church: Tamir et al. (2018).

58   *photo impairment effect:* Soares and Storm (2018).

taking photos can enhance memory: Barasch et al. (2017).

participants exhibited worse memory: Sparrow et al. (2011).

subsequent research hasn't revealed similar costs: See Marsh and Rajaram (2019). Sparrow et al. (2011) also report that when people were asked a trivia question (e.g., "What country has a national flag that is not rectangular?"), they quickly started thinking about computers and Google as the source of the answer (Nepal). However, Camerer et al. (2018) report a large-scale attempt to replicate social science studies published in *Science* and *Nature* between 2010 and 2015 that failed to support this finding.

saved a pdf: Storm and Stone (2015).

laboratory of Hugo Spiers: Javadi et al. (2017).

59   *measures of hippocampal volume:* See, for example, Konishi and Bohbot (2013), Ma-

guire et al. (2000), and Woollett and Maguire (2011). But see Weisberg et al. (2019) for a failure to observe such an association.

have only just begun: The general topics of Internet effects on memory, and on off-loading memory to smartphones, the Internet, and related devices, have begun to elicit broad interest among cognitive psychologists. For wide-ranging and thoughtful integrative discussions, see Finley et al. (2018) and Marsh and Rajaram (2019); for discussion of cognitive offloading, see Risko and Gilbert (2016).

2. THE SIN OF ABSENT-MINDEDNESS

60   *National Memory Champion:* Levinson (1999).

62   *golf and amnesia:* Schacter (1983).
     bungled bank robbery: Tiffen (2009).

63   *divided attention and memory:* Baddeley et al. (1984) and Craik et al. (1996) both showed that divided attention during encoding reduces subsequent memory. Interestingly, they also found that divided attention during memory retrieval has little effect on performance, suggesting that some memory retrieval operations occur automatically and hence do not require much attention. Fernandes and Moscovitch (2000) delineated conditions under which divided attention at retrieval can influence memory performance.

64   *effects of divided attention on recollection and familiarity:* Jacoby (1991).
     "A day does not go by": Lew Lieberman, personal communication, April 15, 1999.

65   *divided attention and aging:* See Craik and Byrd (1982) and Jennings and Jacoby (1993).
     shift from effortful to automatic task execution: Anderson and Fincham (1994); Logan (1988).

66   *Samuel Butler on automatic actions:* Reason and Mycielska (1982, p. 146).
     frantically searching for glasses: Warren (1996).

67   *neuroimaging of divided attention:* Shallice et al. (1994).
     neuroimaging of automatic behavior: Raichle et al. (1994).

68   *neuroimaging of spaced versus massed repetition practice:* Wagner et al. (2000).

69   *change blindness:* Simons and Levin (1998); for a useful summary of studies on change blindness, see Simons (2000).

70   *door experiment:* Simons and Levin (1998).
     failing to notice a gorilla: Simons and Chabris (1999). Rees et al. (1999) report the brain imaging evidence concerning the effects of focusing attention on letter strings or line drawings.

71   *prospective memory:* Cockburn (1996). The edited volume that contains Cockburn's chapter (Brandimonte et al., 1996) also includes a variety of contributions that approach prospective memory from multiple perspectives.

72   *unreliability of memory versus person:* Winograd (1988).
     event-based versus time-based prospective memory: Einstein and McDaniel (1990).

73   *cue distinctiveness and prospective memory:* McDaniel and Einstein (1993).

74   *multitasking and prospective memory:* Marsh and Hicks (1998).

75 *PET scan study of prospective memory:* Okuda et al. (1998). The specific frontal regions that showed heightened activity during prospective memory included the surface of the right frontal lobe, the left frontal pole, and the inner (medial) regions of the frontal lobe.

76 *aging and event-based prospective memory:* Einstein et al. (1997).
   aging and time-based prospective memory: McDaniel and Einstein (1992). Maylor (1996) summarizes a number of relevant studies.

77 *converting time-based to event-based tasks:* Maylor (1990).
   medication schedules and aging: Gould et al. (1997); Park and Kidder (1996).

78 *"In leaving for":* Susan Whitbourne, personal communication, April 21, 1999.

79 *simulated study of air traffic control:* Vortac et al. (1995).

81 *use of external memory aids in schools:* Stepp (1996).
   survey of electronic memory aids: Petro et al. (1991).

82 *devoting resources to more important things:* Langer (1997, p. 89).

84 *July 5, 2001, column:* Parker (2001).
   Kari had not acted: Danielson (2001).
   "Fatal Distraction": Weingarten (2009).
   2018 report: National Safety Council (n.d.).

85 *2019 article:* Otterman (2019).
   2015 study: Hanson et al. (2015). This study assessed assignment of responsibility, blame, and controllability of outcome. All three measures were positively correlated. The study also assessed a variety of other features, including empathy for the forgetful parent, perception of the parent as perpetrator or victim, and assignment of legal punishment. Perhaps not surprisingly, less empathy and perception of the parent as a perpetrator predicted harsher legal punishment.

86 *Elepho eClip:* Baldwin (2019).
   have begun to develop: Messer (2017); Miller (2019).
   baby is on board: Rapson (2019).

87 *children aged six or younger:* Chuck (2019).
   faced stiff resistance: McKenzie (2018). This article brings together perspectives from memory researchers and a consideration of public policy issues. Regarding the fate of Congressman Tim Ryan's bill, see H.R. 3593 (116th): Hot Cars Act of 2019, GovTrack, n.d., https://www.govtrack.us/congress/bills/116/hr3593.
   zoning out: Feng et al. (2013); Sayette et al. (2009).

88 *hot topic in psychological research:* Smallwood and Schooler published several papers that ignited interest in mind wandering. See, for example, Smallwood and Schooler (2006). For a more recent update, see Smallwood and Schooler (2015).
   probed students' thoughts: Lindquist and McLean (2011).
   lectures by three Yale professors: Risko et al. (2012).

89 *distraction from media multitasking:* Wammes et al. (2019).
   frequent media multitasking and retrieval failure: Madore et al. (2020).
   embedding brief quizzes: Szpunar et al. (2013).
   quizzing enhances integration: Jing et al. (2016).

3. THE SIN OF BLOCKING

91   *"What's the name"*: DeLillo (1998, pp. 130–31).

92   *complaints about name blocking in elderly:* Martin (1986); Sunderland et al. (1986).
     objective data on name blocking in elderly: Burke et al. (1991).

93   *the Baker/baker paradox:* Cohen (1990).
     Mill's (1843) observation: Quoted in Semenza and Sgaramella (1993, pp. 265–66).

94   *blocking familiar names:* See Cohen (1990) and Semenza and Zettin (1989) for the basic ideas, and Brédart and Valentine (1998) for the experiment.
     Yuman Indians and Greek villages: Valentine et al. (1996, p. 17).

95   *visual, conceptual, and phonological representations:* For a general model, see Ellis and Young (1988).

96   *recall of names versus occupations:* Young et al. (1985) performed the diary study; Hanley and Cowell (1988) and Hay et al. (1991) provide experimental evidence.
     lexical level: Some models (e.g., Garrett, 1992; Levelt, 1989) split the lexical level into two types of nodes: "lemmas," which are connected to a word's syntactic features, and "lexemes," which are connected to a word's phonological features. Other theorists (e.g., Caramazza and Miozzo, 1997) argue against this distinction.
     network model: Burke et al. (1991).

97   *person identity node:* Young et al. (1985).

98   *cognitive slowing with age:* Salthouse (1996). Though researchers agree that retrieval of proper names declines significantly with advancing age, there is still some controversy about whether the magnitude of this decline is disproportionate to other age-related cognitive declines (Maylor, 1997).

99   *multiple versus specific labels:* Brédart (1993).

100 *name changes at different stages of life:* Valentine et al. (1996, p. 16).
     two or three blocks per month: Burke et al. (1991).
     LS: Semenza and Zettin (1989). Similar cases were described previously by McKenna and Warrington (1980) and Semenza and Zettin (1988).

101 *more retrieval blocks for people than places:* Hanley and Kay (1998).

102 *knowledge of occupations without name retrieval:* Hanley (1995) provides a detailed case study of this patient.
     injury to the left temporal pole: Damasio et al. (1996) provide evidence supporting this link, whereas Cappa et al. (1998) and Semenza et al. (1995) provide conflicting evidence.

103 *neuroimaging of name retrieval:* Damasio et al. (1996) and Tempini et al. (1998).
     John Prescott's block: Newton (1998).

104 *"on the brink of a sneeze"*: Brown and McNeill (1966, p. 326).
     tip-of-the-tongue expressions across languages: Schwartz (1999).

105 *ten definitions:* The definitions are drawn from Vigliocco et al. (1999). The answers are (1) javelin, (2) gingham, (3) paprika, (4) epitaph, (5) asbestos, (6) sextant, (7) cartilage, (8) cleaver, (9) protoplasm, (10) glucose.

106 The Mystery of Irma Vep: The play was reviewed by Canby (1998).

studies of Italian speakers: Caramazza and Miozzo (1997); Vigliocco et al. (1997).

107 *television theme songs:* Riefer et al. (1995).

"ugly sisters": Reason and Lucas (1984).

108 *evidence for the ugly sisters:* Jones (1989); Jones and Langford (1987).

evidence against the ugly sisters: Meyer and Bock (1992) and Perfect and Hanley (1992) carried out the more tightly controlled studies; Harley and Brown (1998) carried out experiments concerning the influence of "phonological neighbors."

109 *reducing TOTs:* Rastle and Burke (1996).

prolonging TOT states: Burke et al. (1991).

feeling "close" to the target: Reason and Lucas (1984).

110 *partial information, aging, and TOTs:* Burke et al. (1991) and Cohen and Faulkner (1986) found that older adults reported less partial information about the target and fewer blocking words, or "ugly sisters," than did younger adults. Brown and Nix (1996) also found less partial information in older than younger adults, but in addition observed that older adults produced more blockers than younger adults. Brown and Nix (1996, p. 88) suggested that this latter outcome might be attributable to the fact that the older adults in their studies exhibited higher verbal skills than the elderly adults in the earlier studies.

Ojai: Burke et al. (1991, p. 550).

removing attention from an ugly sister: See the excellent review by A. S. Brown (1991).

111 *Daisy Mae:* A. S. Brown (1991, p. 214).

thinking aloud and resolving TOTs: Read and Bruce (1982).

112 *initial letter cues:* Brennen et al. (1990); Hanley and Cowell (1988).

learning and reencoding names: Milders et al. (1998).

113 *"The enormity of the tragedy":* Drummie (1998).

forgetting traumatic events: I discuss the issue at some length in Schacter (1996, ch. 8).

114 *recalling lists of words:* The phenomenon, known as "part-list cueing," was first reported by Slamecka (1968). For another analysis, see Sloman et al. (1991).

inhibited recall of radish: Anderson and Spellman (1995). More recent research has called into question the inhibitory interpretation of retrieval-induced forgetting and suggest instead that context changes between the study phase and the retrieval practice phase of experiments that show retrieval-induced forgetting can better explain the observed effects. For discussion, see Jonker et al. (2015).

115 *impaired recall after seeing photos:* Koutstaal et al. (1999b).

eyewitness recall: Shaw et al. (1995).

questioned them selectively: Anderson (2001). Some of Anderson's ideas draw on the theoretical formulations outlined in Freyd (1996).

116 *memories of childhood sexual abuse:* For overviews of the controversy from various perspectives, see Brewin and Andrews (1998), Conway (1997), Freyd (1996), Kihlstrom (1995), Lindsay and Read (1994), Loftus (1993), Pendergrast (1995), Read and Lindsay (1997), Schacter (1996), and Schooler (1994).

family members versus nonfamily members: Freyd (1996).

117 *JR:* Schooler (1994).

directed forgetting, retrieval inhibition, and "release" from inhibition: Bjork and Bjork (1996). Some directed-forgetting effects are probably attributable to reduced encoding of to-be-forgotten items. See Basden et al. (1993) for discussion of different bases of directed forgetting in relation to different experimental procedures used to examine the phenomenon. Koutstaal and Schacter (1997c) review various experimental procedures for examining directed forgetting and consider the possible relationship of directed forgetting to remembering and forgetting of child abuse.

118 *repression and retrieval inhibition:* For discussion of different ways in which Freud used the concept of repression, see Erdelyi (1985) and Schacter (1996, ch. 9).
repressors, nonrepressors, and directed forgetting: Myers et al. (1998).
psychogenic amnesia: Schacter (1996, ch. 8).

119 *neuroimaging of psychogenic amnesia:* Markowitsch et al. (1997) report the study of NN; see Markowitsch (1999) for a more general discussion of similar cases. Fink et al. (1996) report data from healthy subjects.
cannot recollect personal pasts: For a review and discussion, see Kapur (1999).
PET scan study of PN: Costello et al. (1998).

121 *"most devastating moment":* @LarrySabato, November 9, 2011.

122 *"forgot the agency's name":* Lee (2017).
effects of stress on TOT states: James et al. (2018); Schmank and James (2019).

123 *resolving a TOT state after a delay:* Choi and Smith (2005); Kornell and Metcalfe (2006).

124 *Telemundo interview:* Democratic candidate Tom Steyer also failed to name AMLO in a Telemundo interview; candidate Pete Buttigieg did name him. See LeBlanc (2020).
fMRI study led by Anat Maril: Maril et al. (2001).

125 *fMRI study of TOTs in older adults:* Huijbers et al. (2017).
"think–no think" procedure: Anderson and Green (2001).

126 *failure to observe suppression effects:* Bulevich et al. (2006).
2012 review: Anderson and Huddleston (2012) provide a thorough review of the evidence from think–no think studies available at that time.
2020 meta-analysis: Stramaccia et al. (2020).
brain activity predicts impaired recall: Anderson et al. (2004).

127 *GABA effects on suppression:* Schmitz et al. (2017).

4. THE SIN OF MISATTRIBUTION

128 *Rossetti's "Sudden Light":* Quoted in Sno et al. (1992, p. 512), which explores déjà vu in literature and poetry. See Sno and Linszen (1990) for a broader perspective on déjà vu.
Louis and Dr. Arnaud: Berrios (1996, p. 219).

129 Diseases of Memory: Ribot (1882).
special 1893 issue: See Berrios (1996, pp. 217–19) for discussion of the *Révue Philosophique* debate.
David Copperfield: Quoted in Sno et al. (1992, p. 512).

130 *Canadian cognitive psychologist:* Whittlesea (1993).

131 *John Doe 2:* The story was reported by Hicks (1998).

132   *British ticket agent:* This case and others are reviewed in Ross et al. (1994).

    Donald Thomson: I describe this case more fully in Schacter (1996, ch. 4); see also Thomson (1988).

133   *mistaken eyewitness identifications:* Innocence Project (n.d.). For an excellent in-depth treatment of wrongful conviction, see Garrett (2011).

    innocent bystander: Ross et al. (1994).

    source misattributions: Brown et al. (1977); Davies (1988); Thomson (1988).

    eyewitnesses initially uncertain: See Wixted (2018), who makes this point based on the case analyses in Garrett (2011). For additional discussion of eyewitness confidence, see Wixted et al. (2015).

135   *memory binding:* For a general discussion of memory binding in relation to source memory, see Johnson and Chalfonte (1994).

    memory confusions: Goff and Roediger (1998).

    retired psychology professor: Lew Lieberman, personal communication, August 31, 1999.

    magnifying glass and lollipop: Henkel et al. (1998).

136   *memory conjunction error:* See Reinitz et al. (1994) and Rubin et al. (1999).

137   *conjunction errors and hippocampal damage:* Kroll et al. (1996).

    neuroimaging of hippocampus: Henke et al. (1999).

138   *frontal lobe damage:* Shimamura (1995) and Henkel et al. (1998).

    memory conjunction errors: Rubin et al. (1999).

    lineup practices that promote misidentification: Wells et al. (1998) report on experiments concerned with minimizing relative judgments. Wells et al. (2000) review research on improving the collection of eyewitness evidence and describe the deliberations and conclusions of the working group formed by Janet Reno. The working group's report is available at http://www.ojp.usdoj.gov/nij/pubs-sum/178240.htm. For a review of the controversy over simultaneous versus sequential lineups, and for more recent data that have helped to identify problems with the sequential procedure, see Gronlund et al. (2014) and Wilson et al. (2019).

139   *prominent group:* Wixted et al. (2016, p. 304).

140   New York Times *article:* Hilts (1996).

    Deese/Roediger-McDermott procedure: Deese (1959); Roediger and McDermott (1995).

141   *distinguish between true and false memories:* Our study is described in Schacter et al. (1996a).

142   *separating truth from deceit:* Halperin (1996).

143   *no reliable differences in electrical activity:* Our results are described in Johnson et al. (1997). In a related fMRI study, we found a similar pattern of results. There was some evidence of differences in brain activity during true and false recognition when previously studied words and nonpresented associates were tested in separate scans. But there was no evidence for such differences when the two types of items were mixed together (Schacter et al., 1997a). In these studies, subjects heard study lists comprised of semantic associates. In another fMRI experiment, we tried to provide subjects with richer sensory cues by showing them a videotape of a male and a fe-

male experimenter who took turns saying the words on the study list (Cabeza et al., 2001). With this procedure, both visual and auditory cues distinguished studied words from the semantic associates presented later on the recognition test alone. In this study, we obtained somewhat stronger evidence of differences in brain activity during true and false recognition. A region near the back of the temporal lobe (posterior parahippocampal gyrus) showed greater activity during true than false recognition, whereas hippocampal regions farther forward showed similar levels of activity during true and false recognition.

conditions that encourage people: Evidence of reduced false recognition in such conditions comes from experiments by Koutstaal et al. (1999a) and Mather et al. (1997).

144   *electrical recordings during memory conjunction errors:* Rubin et al. (1999).

differences in brain activity during recollection and familiarity: Düzel et al. (1997); Henson et al. (1999).

145   *individual differences in accurate/false recognition:* Curran et al. (2001).

semantic associates: Schacter et al. (1999) report the experimental data and introduce the idea of the distinctiveness heuristic.

146   *false recognition in elderly adults:* Norman and Schacter (1997), Schacter et al. (1999), and Tun et al. (1998) provide evidence that older adults are sometimes more susceptible to false recognition of semantic associates in the Deese/Roediger-McDermott procedure. Schacter et al. (1999) report that older adults can use the distinctiveness heuristic to reduce this false recognition effect. Koutstaal and Schacter (1997a) demonstrated even greater susceptibility to false recognition in elderly adults using a procedure in which participants studied pictures of objects from different categories (e.g., cars, shoes) and later falsely recognized new pictures from previously studied categories. However, Koutstaal et al. (1999a) found that elderly adults can use distinctive information to lower false recognition of novel pictures.

con artists and the elderly: Jacoby (1999).

148   *"seeing film stars everywhere":* Ward et al. (1999) report a detailed case study. This article was part of a special issue of the journal *Cognitive Neuropsychology* devoted to the subject of false memories that was also published in book form (Schacter, 1999a).

frontal lobe damage and false recognition: Rapcsak et al. (1999).

face recognition unit: See Young et al. (1985) and Ellis and Young (1988) for early ideas regarding face recognition units. For another analysis and review, see Breen et al. (2000).

149   *regions near the back of the brain:* Perrett et al. (1992) discuss evidence for face cells, and Kanwisher et al. (1997) and Tong et al. (2000) provide fMRI evidence linking the fusiform gyrus with face recognition.

150   *"victim of enemies":* Ellis et al. (1994, p. 134), an English translation of Courbon and Fail's 1927 paper. Ellis et al. also provide translations of two other classic French papers on delusional misidentifications.

IR: Box et al. (1999). Feinberg et al. (1999) also report a case of Fregoli delusion following a head injury that produced damage to the right frontal lobe as well as part of the left temporal and parietal lobes.

151   *plagiarism of Wallace biography:* Jack (1998).

152   *Nietzsche's unintentional plagiarism:* Taylor (1965, p. 1113).

153   *Daniels's unintentional plagiarism:* Daniels (1972, quotation from p. 124).

      catching ourselves in the act: "The Blue Danube" waltz incident is described in Reed
      (1988, p. 100). Skinner relates his experiences in an essay on intellectual function
      during old age (Skinner, 1983, p. 242).

154   *procedure for examining cryptomnesia:* Brown and Murphy (1989).

      priming: For a review of evidence and ideas concerning priming, see Schacter (1996,
      ch. 6), Schacter and Buckner (1998), and Wiggs and Martin (1998).

      paying attention to the source of ideas: Marsh et al. (1997).

155   *similarity between memory misattributions and social misattributions:* Jacoby et al.
      (1989b). Schachter and Singer (1962) report the famous experiments on the interpre-
      tation of adrenaline-induced arousal.

156   *experienced déjà vu at least once:* Brown (2004).

      a disturbing title: Long (2017).

      long-standing idea about déjà vu: Cleary et al. (2009, 2012).

157   *what is going to happen next:* Cleary and Claxton (2018).

158   *recognition of visual prototypes:* Slotnick and Schacter (2004).

159   *neural sensory reactivation:* For recent reviews of neuroimaging studies showing
      that sensory reactivation can distinguish true from false memories, see Kurkela and
      Dennis (2016) and Schacter et al. (in press).

      areas within the frontal lobe: The evidence is carefully reviewed by Kurkela and Den-
      nis (2016).

      not so fast: For a detailed discussion of the limitations of fMRI findings on true ver-
      sus false memories in legal settings and of other ways in which cognitive neurosci-
      ence could be useful in these settings, see Schacter and Loftus (2013). As a longtime
      admirer of Elizabeth Loftus and her research, it was a pleasure and an honor to
      collaborate with her in writing this article.

      brain activity and facial recognition: Rissman et al. (2010). In addition to showing
      that a pattern classifier could determine when people subjectively recognized a face
      as "old" or "new," Rissman et al. showed that the classifier could distinguish some-
      what between true and false recognition of faces in individual participants. However,
      this effect was present only for faces to which participants assigned low-confidence
      responses. Also, this discrimination was much weaker than the classifier's ability to
      discriminate between faces that were subjectively experienced as "old" versus "new."

160   *not just a flight of fancy:* For progress in using pattern classification techniques, see
      Rissman and Wagner (2012) and Poldrack (2018). For a nice example of acquiring
      data from individual participants, see Braga and Buckner (2017).

      brain activity associated with everyday experiences: For fMRI studies of everyday ex-
      periences, see Rissman et al. (2016) and St. Jacques et al. (2013).

      study of countermeasures: Uncapher et al. (2015).

5. THE SIN OF SUGGESTIBILITY

162   *study of El Al crash memories:* Crombag et al. (1996).

163   *Alan Alda:* The procedure I used in the show was based on experiments we had

recently performed in our laboratory, described in Schacter et al. (1997b). These experiments revealed that adults in their sixties are more likely than college students to confuse events seen only in photographs with those witnessed earlier on a videotape.

164   *Korean War memories:* Moss (2000, quotation from p. A22).

165   *laboratory studies of suggested memories:* For an overview of Loftus's pioneering studies, see Loftus et al. (1995). Higham (1998) describes the study of a staged robbery and his research student's false memory.

166   *British study of police questioning:* See Fisher (1995, p. 740).

       eyewitness in Missouri case: Wells and Bradfield (1998) discuss this case; the quotation is from p. 360.

167   *eyewitness confidence:* Since the publication of the first edition of *The Seven Sins of Memory* in 2001, there have been important advances and changes in our understanding of the relation between confidence and accuracy in memory that have clarified when confidence is more or less strongly related to accuracy. Under what Wixted and Wells (2017) call "pristine" conditions, in which fair lineups are used and suggestive influences are absent, confidence and accuracy are strongly related. But under "non-pristine" conditions, which involve feedback, unfair lineups, or misleading suggestions, confidence can become decoupled from accuracy. Wixted and Wells (2017) provide a useful synthesis of this research. For additional discussion on methodological and other issues regarding assessment of the relation between confidence and accuracy in memory, see Wixted et al. (2016, 2017). For discussion of how initially uncertain identifications can change into certain ones when "non-pristine" conditions are involved, see Wixted (2018).

       not set in stone: See Wells and Bradfield (1998) for discussion of evidence concerning the malleability of eyewitness confidence and for the experiment on the effects of confirming feedback. These effects have since been replicated many times. See Steblay et al. (2014) for a review and implications.

168   *suggestive procedures and Catch-22:* Wells and Bradfield (1998) discuss the Biggers criteria; the quotation is from p. 375.

169   *using hypnosis to question witnesses:* Kebbell and Wagstaff (1998) provide an informative discussion.

       Chowchilla case: See Reiser (1990) for an account of the use of hypnosis in this case.

       hypnosis and memory: For reviews of the scientific literature, see Kebbell and Wagstaff (1998) and Lynn and McConkey (1998).

170   *success of hypnosis:* Reiser (1990). Kebbell and Wagstaff (1998) discuss the idea of hypnosis as a "face-saving" device.

       Cognitive Interview: For a detailed description of the Cognitive Interview and a summary of the research on which it is based, see Fisher (1995) and Fisher and Geiselman (1992). Further ideas pertaining to the development, modification, and application of the Cognitive Interview are brought together in a special issue of the journal *Psychology, Crime and Law* (1999; vol. 5, nos. 1–2). The papers by Clifford and Gwyer (1999), Kebbell et al. (1999), and Memon and Higham (1999) are particularly relevant to the issues I have discussed. For a more recent review of evidence concerning the Cognitive Interview, see Memon et al. (2010).

171   *false confessions:* Munsterberg (1908).

172   *false confessions by Soviet prisoners:* Hinkle and Wolff (1956, quotation from p. 116). Gudjonsson (1992, ch. 6) provides an informative discussion of this and related observations.

Peter Reilly case and memory distrust syndrome: Gudjonsson and MacKeith (1988); see also Gudjonsson (1992, p. 228).

173   *Paul Ingram:* Wright (1994) provides a thorough description and analysis of the case; see also Ofshe (1992).

false confession by a seventeen-year-old: Gudjonsson et al. (1999) provide a detailed description of the case; the quotation is from p. 456.

174   *interrogative suggestibility:* See Gudjonsson (1984, 1992).

mock juries and false confessions: Kassin and Wrightsman (1981).

experimental study of false confessions: Kassin and Kiechel (1996).

176   *reality of recovered memories:* For summaries of relevant evidence, see Conway (1997), Lindsay and Read (1994), Loftus and Ketcham (1994), Pendergrast (1995), and Schacter (1996, ch. 9).

177   *"lost in the mall" study:* Loftus and Pickrell (1995).

implanted memories of childhood experiences: See Hyman et al. (1995) and Hyman and Billings (1998).

178   *visual imagery in suggested memories:* Hyman and Billings (1998) report data indicating a correlation between imagery vividness and production of false memories. Hyman and Pentland (1996) found that instructions to use visual imagery as an aid to recall resulted in a higher incidence of false memories. Using a different experimental procedure, Garry et al. (1996) found that requiring subjects to imagine unlikely incidents from childhood, such as finding money in a parking lot, heightened their confidence that the incidents had actually occurred. Goff and Roediger (1998) report similar findings using an experimental procedure in which people carried out some simple actions in the laboratory and only imagined others. Dewhurst and Conway (1994) provide experimental evidence that true memories of past events are often accompanied by vivid visual images.

dream interpretation: Mazzoni and Loftus (1998).

179   *implanted memories of an animal attack:* Porter et al. (1999). Pezdek (1997) describes a failure to implant memories of an enema.

our earliest memories: For data and general discussion, see Usher and Neisser (1993) and West and Bauer (1999). For possible links to brain function, see Nadel and Zola-Morgan (1984) and Schacter and Moscovitch (1984).

getting "in touch" with early memories: Malinoski and Lynn (1999).

180   *remembering events before first birthday:* Green (1999).

crib memories: Spanos et al. (1999). See also related work and similar findings by DuBreuil et al. (1998).

181   *"memories" for past lives and alien abductions:* See Spanos et al. (1993, 1994).

182   *surveys of psychotherapeutic practices:* Poole et al. (1995).

individual differences in creating false memories: See Hyman and Billings (1998) for

childhood memories, Winograd et al. (1998) for false recognition of semantic associates in college students, Clancy et al. (2000) for false recognition in adult women,
and Clancy et al. (2002) for false recognition in people who claim to recall alien
abductions.

184   *amicus brief: Commonwealth of Massachusetts v. Cheryl Amirault LeFave*, Massachusetts Supreme Judicial Court #SJC-7529. For a brief summary of the story of the
Amiraults, see Pollitt (1999). For summaries of preschool cases involving suggestive questioning and disputed memories, see the excellent books by Ceci and Bruck
(1995) and Nathan and Snedeker (1995).

186   *research fell far short:* See Bruck and Ceci (1999) for discussion of this point and
relevant research.

study of open-ended versus specific questions: Peterson and Bell (1996).

187   *the clown's actions:* This exchange is from an affidavit by Dr. Maggie Bruck, a copy
of which she kindly sent to me on October 25, 1999. She gave the affidavit during an
evidentiary hearing at which she testified.

188   *repeated questioning of young children:* For summaries of the research by Bruck and
Ceci, see Bruck et al. (1997) and Ceci (1995).

"Mr. Science" study: Poole and Lindsay (1995).

189   *single suggestive questions:* Rudy and Goodman (1991).

study based on McMartin techniques: Garven et al. (1998).

190   *forced generation of allegations:* Ackil and Zaragoza (1998, quotation from p. 1359).
All of the individuals convicted in the Wenatchee prosecutions were eventually set
free by the courts. For an overview, see Wikipedia, Wenatchee child abuse prosecutions, last modified January 13, 2021, 20:58, https://en.wikipedia.org/wiki/Wenatchee
_child_abuse_prosecutions.

191   *Amirault LeFave set free:* The final maneuvers in the Cheryl Amirault LeFave decision are chronicled in a series of articles published in the *Boston Globe* on October
22–23, 1999.

192   *rich false memories:* Loftus (2003). The 20 to 30 percent incidence of rich false memories in most studies using procedures similar to the "lost in the mall" study (Loftus
and Pickrell, 1995) was confirmed in a formal analysis by Scoboria et al. (2017).

false memory of committing a crime: Shaw and Porter (2015).

194   *critique of Shaw and Porter's study:* Wade et al. (2018). For background studies on the
distinction between false memories and false beliefs, see Lindsay et al. (2004) and
Scoboria et al. (2017).

seized public attention: For an excellent discussion of the psychology of false confessions and implications for criminal justice, see the authoritative white paper on
police-induced confessions by Kassin et al. (2010) and a more recent analysis by
Kassin (2017) that considers several of the high-profile cases.

196   *internalized false confessions:* Kassin et al. (2010) distinguish between "internalized
false confessions," where people come to mistakenly believe they committed a crime
in response to being presented with seemingly incontrovertible evidence of their
guilt; "compliant confessions," where suspects confess in order to escape a stressful

interrogation; and "voluntary confessions," where people confess in an attempt to achieve notoriety or satisfy other psychological needs. In some cases of voluntary confessions, people may be unable to distinguish fact from fantasy and thus in some sense believe that they committed a crime.

197   *False Memory Syndrome Foundation dissolved*: This announcement is posted on the organization's website, http://www.fmsfonline.org/, which, according to the announcement, "will continue to be available." Last accessed January 28, 2021.

   use of suggestive techniques: See Rabinowitz (2003) and Beck (2015) for in-depth analyses of psychological and social factors that produced these tragic daycare center cases. Pendergrast (2017) also provides an insightful discussion of the cases.

   study of board-certified psychotherapists: Patihis et al. (2014).

198   *continue to probe for memories*: Patihis and Pendergrast (2019).

6. THE SIN OF BIAS

199   *"Who controls the past"*: Orwell (1950/1984, p. 32).

   "Past events, it is argued": Orwell (1950/1984, p. 176). My treatment of Orwell's *1984* follows from the classic article on the totalitarian ego by Greenwald (1980), which draws on Orwell's novel to highlight some of the same points I make.

200   *study of Perot supporters*: Levine (1997).

201   *high school students' busing opinions*: Goethals and Reckman (1973). For excellent summaries of this and related research, see Dawes (1988) and Ross (1989).

   "implicit theory of stability": Ross (1989).

202   *recall of study skills*: Conway and Ross (1984).

   recall of emotional states during menstruation: McFarland et al. (1989).

203   *biased recall of dating college students*: McFarland and Ross (1987).

   recall biases in partners whose feelings had changed: Kirkpatrick and Hazan (1994) examined recall across a four-year interval; Scharfe and Bartholomew (1998) examined recall across an eight-month interval.

204   *study of Michigan couples*: Holmberg and Holmes (1994, quotation from p. 286).

   "I love you more today": See Sprecher (1999).

205   *wives' feelings about their marriages*: Karney and Coombs (2000).

   cognitive dissonance: The concept of cognitive dissonance derives from the classic work of Festinger (1957). For a review of relevant research, see Wood (2000).

206   *choices between art prints*: Lieberman et al. (2001) describe the experiment. For an alternative interpretation of these results, see Gawronski et al. (2007).

207   *Northwestern football fans*: Roese and Maniar (1997).

208   *students and the O. J. Simpson verdict*: Bryant and Brockway (1997).

   1980 presidential election: Leary (1982).

209   *deterministic and chance causes of British victory*: Wasserman et al. (1991). For an insightful review of research on hindsight bias, see Hawkins and Hastie (1990).

   subset of Northwestern fans: Roese and Maniar (1997).

   asked to make an independent diagnosis: Arkes et al. (1981).

   bias among jurors: See discussion by Hawkins and Hastie (1990, pp. 318–19). Hastie et al. (1999) report the dramatic effects of hindsight bias in an experimental simulation of a civil case that required mock jurors to assess the liability of a company for environmental damages.

211 *hindsight bias in recall of Jack and Barbara's encounter:* Carli (1999).

212 *egocentric bias among couples:* Ross and Sicoly (1979); Christensen et al. (1983). For laboratory evidence on enhanced recall of our own actions, see Engelkamp and Zimmer (1996).

213 *self-encoding and memory:* Symons and Johnson (1997) provide a thorough review.
positive illusions: The important review by Taylor and Brown (1988) makes the case for positive illusions and summarizes relevant evidence. Taylor (1989) provides an accessible treatment of the issue for the general reader.

214 *biased recall of introverted traits:* Sanitioso et al. (1990).
distorted recall of high school grades: Bahrick et al. (1996). As these authors note, it is possible that memory biases cause forgetting of actual grades. Alternatively, forgetting may occur for reasons unrelated to bias (decay of memory or other factors that produce transience), with bias operating later to fill in the resulting memory gaps. The authors provide arguments to support the latter interpretation.
divorce and memory biases: Gray and Silver (1990, quotation from p. 1188).

215 *exaggerated recall of anxiety:* Keuler and Safer (1998) provide data on recall of exam anxiety; Breckler (1994) examined recall in blood donors.
Mary Tyler Moore: The quotation originally appeared in a 1997 article in the *Ladies' Home Journal* (Gerosa, 1997) and was cited by Ross and Wilson (1999, p. 238).

216 *whistling Vivaldi:* Staples (1994) relates this incident in his autobiographical narrative; the quotation is from p. 202. I first heard the incident described in relation to stereotyping during a lecture by the social psychologist Claude Steele at Harvard in October 1997.
energy-saving devices: See Macrae et al. (1994) for evidence and discussion.

217 *stereotypes get us into trouble:* See Allport (1954, quotations from p. 21). In their excellent essay on stereotypes and prejudice, Banaji and Bhaskar (1999, p. 143) cite this line and note the prescience of Allport's views.
subliminal priming of stereotypes: Devine (1989).

218 *British study:* Lepore and Brown (1997).
nonexistent black criminals: The experiment is described briefly by Banaji and Bhaskar (1999, quotation from p. 151).
"false fame" error: Banaji and Greenwald (1995). Their work is based on earlier studies by Larry Jacoby's group (Jacoby et al., 1989a), which established the false fame error.

219 *guilt by association:* See Banaji and Bhaskar (1999) for a thoughtful discussion.
stereotype bias and cognitive effort: Macrae et al. (1994).

220 *Bob and Margie:* Spiro (1980) reports the experiment. For an excellent review of related work, see Alba and Hasher (1983).

221 *split-brain patients:* For summaries of this work, see Gazzaniga (1985, 1998).

222 *left-brain interpreter:* Gazzaniga (1985, 1998) has developed and elaborated the no-

tion of the interpreter. Phelps and Gazzaniga (1992) report the experiments showing false recognition of stereotype-consistent incidents by the left hemisphere; see also Metcalfe et al. (1995) for further experiments with similar results.

224   *object recognition study:* Koutstaal et al. (2001b) report these experiments.

225   *memory for true and false political events:* Frenda et al. (2013).

Irish referendum and fake news: Murphy et al. (2019). The finding that the impact of bias was most evident in supporters on both sides of the Irish referendum with low cognitive ability is particularly interesting because these individuals were not overall more susceptible to false memories (i.e., counting false memories that did and did not conform with one's bias) than individuals with higher cognitive ability, and there was no overall difference in cognitive ability between "yes" and "no" supporters. Instead, people with low cognitive ability were more driven by their preexisting biases when making memory judgments about fake events.

227   *susceptibility to fake news:* Pennycook and Rand (2019).

truth bias: For a comprehensive review that summarizes evidence regarding a truth bias, see Brashier and Marsh (2020). For an early incisive analysis of this issue, see Gilbert (1991). For an alternative perspective that emphasizes that people can exercise "epistemic vigilance" to avoid gullibility, see Mercier (2017).

illusory truth effect: For the initial demonstration of this effect, see Hasher et al. (1977). For the link between illusory truth and susceptibility to fake news, see Pennycook et al. (2018). For the evidence that even blatantly false statements can be subject to the illusory truth effect, see Fazio et al. (2019). For a review of mechanisms that produce the illusory truth effect, see Unkelbach et al. (2019).

sharing fake news: Effron and Raj (2020). Brashier and Schacter (2020) report that older adults shared the most fake news during the 2016 presidential campaign; it will be important to study the effects of repeated exposure on sharing fake news in this group.

228   *repeated exposure to statements by Trump:* Murray et al. (2020).

most-watched debate: Stelter (2016).

229   *explicit versus implicit memory:* The distinction was originally drawn by Graf and Schacter (1985). In Schacter (1987), I reviewed historical, empirical, and theoretical aspects of the distinction. Greenwald and Banaji (2017) specifically make the link between these two papers and their articulation of the concept of implicit social cognition.

implicit social cognition: Greenwald and Banaji (1995).

Implicit Association Test: Greenwald et al. (1998) first reported the IAT. Greenwald and Banaji (2017, p. 866) summarized the initial IAT procedure.

230   *relevance of IAT to social cognition and racial bias:* Greenwald et al. (1998).

study based on Project Implicit: See Nosek et al. (2002). Regarding the finding that Blacks showed a small implicit effect favoring whites, Project Implicit writes: "Results from this website consistently show that members of stigmatized groups (e.g., Black people, gay people, older people) tend to have more positive implicit attitudes toward their groups than do people who are not in the group, but that there is still a moderate preference for the more socially valued group. So gay people tend to show an implicit preference for straight people relative to gay people, but it is not as strong as the implicit preference shown by straight people. We think that this is because stigmatized group members develop negative associations about their group from their cultural environments, but also have some positive associations because of their own group membership and that of close others" (https://implicit.harvard.edu/implicit/faqs.html#faq10).

intense debate: For varying perspectives by psychological scientists on interpreting the IAT and thinking about implicit bias more generally, see Banaji and Greenwald (2013), De Houwer (2019), Eberhardt (2019), Gawronski (2019), Greenwald et al. (2015), Greenwald and Lai (2020), Jost et al. (2009), Schimmack (2019), and Tetlock and Mitchell (2009). For critiques and discussions in the popular press, see Bartlett (2017), Goldhill (2017), Mac Donald (2017), Mak (2018), and Nordell (2017).

231 *studies using the first person shooter task:* See Correll et al. (2002, 2007); for a review of this line of research, see Correll et al. (2014). For discussion of the implications of implicit bias for policing, see Eberhardt (2019) and Spencer et al. (2016).

examining police performance: Correll et al. (2007).

people who perpetrate discrimination: Daumeyer et al. (2019) report four experiments that support this idea.

232 *influence of implicit bias training:* See the intervention studies by Devine et al. (2012) and Lai et al. (2014, 2016), as well as the meta-analysis by Forscher et al. (2019).

233 *payoff from implicit bias training:* For a critical analysis, see Dobbin and Kalev (2018).

4 million test results: Charlesworth and Banaji (2019).

7. THE SIN OF PERSISTENCE

234 *Donnie Moore:* Louinn Lota, Associated Press bulletin, July 19, 1989.

preventing the recurrence of a persistent tune: Laurie Gordon, personal communication, December 13, 1999.

236 *Stroop effect:* MacLeod (1991) provides a thorough review of the voluminous literature on the Stroop effect. For a review of the research, see Williams et al. (1996). As Williams et al. note, the emotional Stroop effect is strongest in patients with emotional disorders and does not always occur in healthy adults.

237 *goals and evaluating emotional information:* See Lazarus (1991) for ideas about emotional appraisal and goals; see Ochsner and Schacter (2000) for the development of these ideas within the framework of cognitive neuroscience.

memory for the central focus: See Loftus et al. (1987) for "weapon focus" and Heuer and Reisberg (1992) for a general discussion.

238 *recording emotional incidents:* Rimé (1995, pp. 274–75).

recollection of pictures: Ochsner (2000).

239 *fading of unpleasant memories:* Walker et al. (1997).

reminders of difficult experiences: García Márquez (1994, p. 11).

"You destroyed a man's life": Quoted in Louinn Lota, Associated Press bulletin, July 19, 1989.

counterfactual thinking: For an informative review, see Roese (1997). For research concerning emotional influences on counterfactual thinking, see Roese and Hur (1997) and Zeelenberg et al. (1998).

240 *persistent counterfactual thinking:* See Williams (1997, quotation from p. 224). The quotations concerning persistence following an untreatable illness are from Parkes (1986, p. 93).

241 *counterfactual thinking after negative experiences:* Roese and Hur (1997).
      Jean Van de Velde: D'Amato (1999).

242 *self-schemas and depression:* For a review of the self-schema concept in relation to depression, see Segal (1988); for a review of related memory phenomena, see Mineka and Nugent (1995).
      Pushkin poem: The poem is reproduced in Washburn et al. (1998, p. 837).

243 *electrical brain activity:* The experiments are reported in Deldin et al. (2001).
      depression and intrusive memories: Brewin et al. (1996).

244 *intrusive memories in depressed cancer patients:* Brewin et al. (1998). For laboratory evidence concerning the effects of mood on memory, see Varner and Ellis (1998).
      rumination and depression: Nolen-Hoeksema (1991).

245 *rumination, depression, and memory:* Lyubormirsky et al. (1998).
      rumination differences between men and women: Nolen-Hoeksema (1991).

246 *disclosing difficult experiences:* Pennebaker (1997) provides a useful overview of research showing beneficial effects of disclosing emotional experiences.
      "overgeneral memories": See Williams (1997) for a review and discussion of relevant research; the quotations are from p. 170.

247 *brain activity in depressed patients:* Davidson et al. (1999) provide a cogent review of key developments.
      left prefrontal activity and recall of details: Nolde et al. (1998).

248 *"In Sacai":* Burton (1621/1989, p. 336).

249 *suffering from shell shock:* Bogacz (1989).
      epidemiological studies of trauma: The incidence estimates are discussed by Leskin et al. (1998, p. 984).
      senses involved in traumatic memories: See Ehlers and Steil (1995) and Ehlers and Clark (2000).

250 *intrusive memories in trauma versus depression:* Reynolds and Brewin (1999).
      PTSD diagnosis: For discussion, see Ehlers and Clark (2000) and Leskin et al. (1998).
      "stuck" in the past: Holman and Silver (1998).

251 *"It was on Memorial Day":* Van Arsdale (1995, pp. 3, 19).

252 *study of ambulance workers:* Clohessy and Ehlers (1999).
      ironic effects of thought suppression: For a review and theoretical account of the "rebound effect" in thought suppression, see Wegner (1994). Wegner and Gold (1995) studied thought suppression in relation to attempts to suppress memories of "old flames" from past relationships; the quotation is from p. 791. For a general review of thought suppression in relation to psychopathology, see Purdon (1999) and Koutstaal and Schacter (1997c).

253   *imaginal exposure therapy:* For an example of Keane's work, also referred to as "flooding" or "implosive" therapy, see Keane et al. (1989); for a comparison of procedures for treating PTSD, see Foa et al. (1991). Leskin et al. (1998) review the relevant research and provide treatment recommendations. For discussion of related approaches to treating PTSD, see Foa and Meadows (1997) and McNally (1999).

254   *"testimony therapy":* Weine et al. (1998, quotation from p. 1721).

255   *amygdala and emotional memory:* Cahill and McGaugh (1998) review the relevant research.

      abnormal fear responses: See Adolphs et al. (1994, 1999) and LeDoux (1996).

256   *videotape of patient:* Phelps et al. (1998) provide a detailed case study of this patient.

      fear conditioning in animals: LeDoux (1996) provides an engaging account of his own and others' work on fear conditioning in numerous species; the quotation is from pp. 141–42.

257   *hub of a wheel:* LeDoux (1996, p. 168).

      amygdala modulates memory storage: Cahill and McGaugh (1998).

      neuroimaging techniques: Whalen (1998) provides a cogent review. For Whalen's work on amygdala activation following brief presentations of fearful faces, see Whalen et al. (1998).

      amygdala activity and recall of upsetting episodes: Cahill et al. (1996). Alkire et al. (1998) found that hippocampal activity correlated with recall of neutral incidents.

258   *neuroimaging of fear conditioning:* See Whalen (1998) for a review. Rauch et al. (1996) and Shin et al. (1997) provide neuroimaging evidence of amygdala activity during traumatic recall in patients with PTSD, whereas Shin et al. (1999) failed to observe amygdala activation in such patients. Although the reasons for the discrepant findings are not entirely clear, Shin et al. (1999, p. 582) suggest that patients in their study may have experienced less fear during traumatic recall than did patients in the other studies.

      norepinephrine, yohimbine, and trauma: For an overview of the major findings, see Southwick et al. (1999a).

259   *yohimbine-induced flashbacks and panic attacks:* Southwick et al. (1999b, quotation from p. 443).

      yohimbine and emotionally arousing slides: O'Carroll et al. (1999b) report this experiment; another study with similar effects is summarized briefly by Southwick et al. (1999a, p. 1199).

260   *propranolol and memory:* Cahill et al. (1994) reported the initial findings that propranolol selectively impairs recall of emotional material. Van Stegeren et al. (1998) replicated the original results and extended them by showing that a beta-blocker (nadolol) that crosses the blood-brain barrier to a lesser extent than propranolol fails to impair emotional recall. However, O'Carroll et al. (1999a) used a slightly different experimental procedure than Cahill et al. (1994) and did not find that propranolol impairs emotional recall. Though the reasons for the different results are not known, subjects in O'Carroll et al. (1999a) showed different patterns of heart rate responses to the emotional materials than did subjects in Cahill et al. (1994) and van Stegeren

et al. (1998). These differences could be related to the varying effects of propranolol on memory (Larry Cahill, personal communication, March 23, 2000).

261 *tone-footshock experiments:* Nader et al. (2000).

262 *early experiments using electric shocks:* See Misanin et al. (1968) for the initial experiments. As a graduate student in the 1970s, I was aware of the early work by Misanin et al. and others and found it extremely interesting. However, an attempted extension to humans by Squire et al. (1976) using electroconvulsive therapy failed to show any amnesic effects of memory reactivation analogous to those seen in rats, which might have contributed to declining interest in the phenomenon during the 1980s and 1990s, at least from human memory researchers. For a comprehensive review and synthesis of reconsolidation research, see Dudai (2012) and Elsey et al. (2018).

similar phenomena in humans: For a recent review on reconsolidation that includes discussion of research in humans, see Lee et al. (2017). There is still debate as to whether the phenomena observed in rats and humans involve the same underlying mechanisms.

implications for memory sins: For discussion of these implications, see Hardt et al. (2010) and Schacter et al. (2011).

mixed results: For a review and discussion, see Lee et al. (2017) and Phelps and Hofmann (2019).

263 *victim of armed robbery:* Kindt and van Emmerik (2016, quotation from pp. 289–90).
a larger study: Wood et al. (2015).

264 *Researchers at McGill University:* Brunet et al. (2018).
targeting reconsolidation with Tetris: James et al. (2015).

265 Tetris *treatment in emergency room patients:* Iyduri et al. (2018).
Tetris *treatment for PTSD:* Kessler et al. (2018).

266 *memory suppression in PTSD:* Catarino et al. (2015).

267 *intrusive memories after watching an upsetting film:* Streb et al. (2016).
white bear effect and memory-suppression studies: Engen and Anderson (2018).

8. THE SEVEN SINS: VICES OR VIRTUES?

269 *"Over the years":* Anderson and Milson (1989, p. 703).

270 *proponents of evolutionary psychology:* For an introduction to evolutionary psychology from the perspective of its proponents, see Barkow et al. (1992), Buss et al. (1998), Cosmides and Tooby (1994), and Pinker (1997b). For critiques of various aspects of the evolutionary approach, see Coyne (2000), Gould (1991, 1997a, 1997b), and Sterelny and Griffiths (1999). The quotation concerning reverse engineering is from Pinker (1997b, p. 21).

evolutionary perspectives in earlier work: Sherry and Schacter (1987) provide an evolutionary account of multiple memory systems.

271 *"intelligent errors":* See Hauser (2000, pp. 80–84) and Gallistel (1990, p. 68). Note that at the time I wrote the 2001 edition, Marc Hauser was an evolutionary psychologist and faculty member in the Department of Psychology at Harvard University. In July 2011, Hauser resigned from Harvard in response to charges of scientific miscon-

duct brought by the university and subsequently left the field of psychology entirely. Several of Hauser's papers were retracted from scientific journals. The material that I cite comes from a book in which Hauser summarizes observations made by others and is unrelated to the problematic experimental papers from his own lab.

272 *behavior known as imprinting:* See Lorenz (1935/1970) for his pioneering observations. For a review and discussion of subsequent developments, see Shettleworth (1998).

"The utility of all the passions": Descartes (1649/1989, p. 59).

forgetting over time: Bjork and Bjork (1988).

adapting to the environment: Anderson and Schooler (1991, 2000).

274 *squirrel's cookie-eating behavior:* Krebs and Davies (1993, ch. 3). Students of animal behavior in natural environments (behavioral ecologists) have developed quantitative procedures for rigorously analyzing the costs and benefits involved in trade-offs. Memory researchers have yet to come up with such quantitative procedures, but it would be highly desirable to attempt to do so.

276 *inhibitory processes protect us from chaos:* See Bjork and Bjork (1988).

Shereshevski: See the classic account by Luria (1968).

279 *amnesic patients less likely to make false recognition error:* See Schacter et al. (1996b, 1998) for studies using the semantic associates paradigm. The study on categorized pictures is described by Koutstaal et al. (2001a). In a related vein, Koutstaal et al. (1999c) report that amnesic patients show reduced false recognition of novel visual shapes that are perceptually similar to previously studied shapes.

theoretical model: McClelland (1995, quotations from p. 84). Interestingly, amnesic patients are able to acquire new categorical knowledge in a manner similar to healthy control subjects (Knowlton and Squire, 1993). To the extent that learning new categories relies on memory for gist information, this finding would appear to conflict with the observation that amnesic patients show reduced false recognition of semantic associates, categorized pictures, and visual shapes, which also rely on memory for the gist. Possible reasons for the differences are considered by Koutstaal et al. (1999c).

rote memory in autism: Mottron et al. (1998); Waterhouse (1988).

280 *discrimination between true and false memories in autistic patients:* Beversdorf et al. (2000). It should be noted that other researchers using a Deese/Roediger-McDermott (DRM) semantic associates experimental paradigm similar to that of Beversdorf et al. have found individuals with Asperger's syndrome to be similarly susceptible to false recall and recognition as non-autistic individuals (Bowler et al., 2000; Kamio and Toichi, 2007). However, Kamio and Toichi also report evidence of reduced susceptibility to associative false memories in high-functioning autistic individuals. As Kamio and Toichi point out, differences across studies may reflect differences in patient populations and task details. Happe (1999) summarizes related evidence indicating that autistic patients are characterized by a cognitive style that focuses on local rather than global information processing, which she terms "weak central coherence" — that is, they tend to focus on specifics of a stimulus or situation at the expense of the big picture.

stereotypes as consequences of ordinary processes: Allport (1954, quotation from p. 27). Banaji and Bhaskar (1999, p. 141) discuss and quote Allport's ideas.

281 *positive illusions:* See Taylor (1989) and Taylor and Brown (1988) for discussion of relevant research.

282 *two uses of the term* adaptation: For detailed discussions concerning the nature of adaptation, see Reeve and Sherman (1993) and Williams (1992).

the term exaptation: See Gould (1991) for discussion and examples; the quotation is from p. 47.

283 *an evolutionary development called a "spandrel":* Gould and Lewontin (1979).

explaining cognition in terms of adaptations: Pinker (1997b, p. 21); Tooby and Cosmides (1992, p. 24).

284 *dominance of exaptations and spandrels:* Gould (1991, quotation from p. 59). For the exchange between Pinker and Gould, see Gould (1997a, 1997b) and Pinker (1997a).

testing evolutionary hypotheses: Buss et al. (1998). See p. 544 for the thirty predictions from an evolutionary perspective.

285 The Blind Watchmaker: Dawkins (1986). For the original watchmaker argument, see Paley (1802/1986).

286 *tall men bear more offspring:* Pawlowski et al. (2000).

bodily symmetry: For data and theory concerning bodily symmetry/asymmetry, see Møller and Swaddle (1997) and Thornhill and Møller (1997). For a critical analysis of their ideas, see Houle (1998).

cross-cultural analyses of facial attractiveness: Cunningham et al. (1995). For the relation between attractiveness and mental/physical health, see Shackelford and Larsen (1997, 1999).

universals can arise from cultural traits: D. E. Brown (1991) provides an extensive treatment of this topic; Gaulin (1997) also offers a thoughtful analysis.

287 *spatial memory in men and women:* Buss et al. (1998). For the hunter-gatherer hypothesis and related experimental data, see Eals and Silverman (1994) and Silverman and Eals (1992). McBurney et al. (1997) provide additional supportive data, whereas James and Kimura (1997) provide data from altered experimental conditions that did not produce gender differences in recall of object locations.

288 *spatial memory in birds:* See Sherry et al. (1993) for the studies of brown-headed cowbirds; see Sherry and Vaccarino (1989) for earlier work on memory and the hippocampus in food-storing birds. The finding that female brown-headed cowbirds have a relatively larger hippocampus than males is consistent with the hypothesis that this size difference is attributable to selection for spatial ability in the females, related to finding and remembering nest locations. However, variations in hippocampal size could also be produced by differences in experience: extensive use of the hippocampus for finding and remembering nest locations might increase its size. Although no direct evidence is available from brown-headed cowbirds (David Sherry, personal communication, July 11, 2000), Clayton (1996) found that when she prevented young marsh tits from storing food, their hippocampal size lagged behind that of controls that were allowed to store food. However, other studies have found

that comparable differences in experience produce no effects on hippocampal size in adults (Cristol, 1996). Thus, differences in hippocampal size related to food storing probably are not simple consequences of using the hippocampus. It does seem possible, though, that appropriate early experience may be necessary for differences in hippocampal size produced by selection to emerge. This issue has an interesting counterpart in human cognition: the back of the hippocampus in London taxi drivers, who have extensive experience with spatial navigation and memory, is relatively larger than that in control subjects (Maguire et al., 2000). This finding could reflect an increase in posterior hippocampal volume as a result of experience. Alternatively, it is possible that individuals who have relatively larger posterior hippocampi are skilled at spatial navigation, which in turn leads them to become taxi drivers. With respect to the latter possibility, Maguire et al. found that more experience driving taxis was associated with larger posterior hippocampal volume in the right hemisphere, suggesting a role for navigation experience. For a related discussion, see The Update in Chapter 1 concerning the impact of GPS reliance on navigation and memory.

289 *meadow voles:* Gaulin and Fitzgerald (1989); see also Hauser (2000, ch. 4) for a relevant discussion.

theoretical article on memory adaptations and exaptations: Sherry and Schacter (1987).

290 *function of amygdala across diverse species:* LeDoux (1996).

study of contemporary foraging groups: Yu and Shepard (1998).

291 *primate ranging behavior:* Schooler et al. (1999).

292 *cultural aspects of self-serving biases:* Heine et al. (1999).

294 *suggestive procedures and false memories:* See Pendergrast (1995) and Spanos et al. (1993, 1994).

misattribution and suggestibility: Sully (1881) presents numerous anecdotal examples; Geary (1994) describes Arnold's story in the context of an enlightening discussion of memory in eleventh-century Europe.

295 *Achilles overwhelmed by grief:* Shay (1994, quotation from p. 50).

Fanny Price's observation on memory: Austen (1816/1998, p. 143).

296 *new theoretical proposals and integrative reviews:* Nørby (2015, 2018) proposes an important role for forgetting in emotional regulation and maintaining psychological well-being, and also in facilitating cognitive functions such as abstraction. Fawcett and Hulbert (2020) provide a wide-ranging discussion of seven adaptive aspects of forgetting, which they term *serenity, stability, clarity, revision, abstraction, inspiration,* and *rediscovery.* Richards and Frankland (2017) provide a useful neurobiological perspective on adaptive aspects of transience and persistence in memory, and Klein (2019) assigns forgetting a key role in driving the evolution of memory systems. Several authors have proposed new functional/adaptive analyses of memory distortion, discussed later in this chapter, including Hardt et al. (2010), Howe (2011), Schacter and Addis (2007a, 2007b), and Schacter et al. (2011).

297 *fading affect bias (FAB):* Walker et al. (1997) provides the initial evidence for the FAB

and reviews previous related findings. For thorough reviews and discussion on the FAB, see Walker et al. (2003b) and Walker and Skowronski (2009). For evidence that the FAB doesn't always hold, see Ritchie et al. (2009).

the FAB and adaptive functioning: For the FAB and dysphoria, see Walker et al. (2003a); anxiety, see Walker et al. (2014); alexithymia, see Muir et al. (2017); eating disorders, see Ritchie et al. (2019); and Grit, see Walker et al. (2020). Duckworth (2016) details the concept of Grit. Sedikides and Skowronski (2020) discuss the FAB in the context of other positivity biases in memory. An intriguing question concerns whether the FAB is reduced in individuals with HSAM, such as Jill Price, whom I've characterized as exhibiting anti-transience (see The Update in Chapter 1). Although I know of no studies that have formally tested for the FAB in HSAM, certainly Jill's characterization of her own memory experiences as "non-stop, uncontrollable and totally exhausting" would be consistent with a reduced FAB if the negative affect associated with her memories of difficult or unpleasant events persists to an exaggerated degree over time. As Nørby (2015) points out in a related discussion, Jill has suffered from problems with anxiety and depression. However, significant depression has not been reported as a consistent feature of individuals with HSAM, though as Nørby notes, trends in this direction are evident in the paper by LePort et al. (2012).

298   *depressed individuals during think–no think:* For evidence and discussion, see Hertel and Gerstle (2003) and Joormann et al. (2005, 2009). For the fMRI study, see Sacchet et al. (2017).

mind wandering and autobiographical planning: For experimental evidence, see Baird et al. (2011).

mind wandering and creativity: Baird et al. (2012) report that high levels of mind wandering during a break from a demanding task were associated with higher levels of performance on a subsequent creative problem-solving test, but Smeekens and Kane (2016) failed to observe such effects. However, Smeekens and Kane did report a modest positive correlation between self-reported daydreaming and performance on a test of creative thinking. Agnoli et al. (2018) observed a positive correlation between self-reported *intentional* mind wandering and creativity (i.e., performance on a lab creativity task and also self-reported creative achievement), along with a negative correlation between self-reported *unintentional* mind wandering and creativity. Seli et al. (2016) argue that intentional mind wandering — deliberately deciding to disengage from a cognitive task to engage in mind wandering — should be distinguished from unintentional mind wandering, where people "drift away" from a cognitive task without an explicit intention to do so; they also summarize experimental evidence that intentional and unintentional mind wandering are dissociable. For a broader review and discussion of the costs and benefits of mind wandering, see Mooneyham and Schooler (2013), and for discussion of mind wandering and creativity, see Fox and Beaty (2019).

299   *fMRI study of left temporal pole:* Chadwick et al. (2016). Note that Demis Hassabis is also CEO of the artificial intelligence company DeepMind. To test the critical prediction of a link between left TP semantic representation and DRM false memories,

we scanned participants while they viewed a long list comprising sets of words from forty DRM lists (each set contained four list words and a semantically associated lure word). This procedure allowed us to measure neural patterns elicited by each set of DRM words and assess the degree of similarity between those patterns and the neural pattern elicited by the associated lure word using representational similarity analysis, which has been applied increasingly in fMRI studies of memory and cognition during the past decade. (For discussion of this method, see Kriegeskorte and Kievit, 2013.) Because participants saw the lure words on the study list, we obtained an estimate of false memory rates from a separate, previously published data set that contains the probability of false recall for each lure word on a large number of DRM lists. Putting these two together, we found that the degree of neural pattern similarity in the left TP between the lure word and its four associated list items in our participants predicted the probability of false recall of a lure word in this separate group of people.

semantic dementia: For a thorough review, see Landin-Romero et al. (2016).

theoretical models of semantic cognition: For a useful overview, see Patterson et al. (2007).

300 *false memories for the nonstudied lure:* Howe (2011).

analogical reasoning test: Howe et al. (2015).

301 *young children and older adults:* Howe et al. (2011).

updating with misinformation: The initial articulation of this idea comes from the work of Elizabeth Loftus. For an informative overview, see Loftus (2005). For discussion of the context of adaptive memory distortions, see Schacter et al. (2011).

reconsolidation and memory updating: See Dudai (2012), Hardt et al. (2010), Hupbach et al. (2011), and Lee et al. (2017). For related findings and discussion concerning memory reactivation and updating, see St. Jacques et al. (2013).

fMRI study of movie viewers: Edelson et al. (2011).

302 *KC:* For an overview of research with KC, see Rosenbaum et al. (2005). For the initial observation of his impaired future thinking, see Tulving (1985), and for an updated discussion of KC in the context of Tulving's thinking about episodic memory, see Tulving (2002). For the initial formulation of the distinction between episodic and semantic memory, see Tulving (1972). Sadly, KC passed away on March 27, 2014, a few months before his sixty-third birthday. His full name, which was made public some years ago, was Kent Cochrane.

303 *remembering the past and imagining the future:* Addis et al. (2007). Other similar fMRI evidence was reported by Szpunar et al. (2007) and Hassabis et al. (2007), and in an earlier PET scan study by Okuda et al. (2003). Early studies showing cognitive similarities between past and future experiences were reported by D'Argembeau and Van der Linden (2004, 2006) and Klein et al. (2002). For general reviews of research that links remembering the past and imagining the future, see Schacter et al. (2012, 2017).

304 *network of brain regions:* This network includes the medial temporal and frontal lobes, the posterior cingulate and retrosplenial cortex, and the lateral parietal and

temporal areas. In Schacter et al. (2007), we referred to these regions as the "core network," based on the few available studies at the time. Numerous fMRI studies of remembering past and imagining future experiences were subsequently published, and nearly a decade later, Benoit and Schacter (2015) confirmed the involvement of the core network in both functions based on a much larger sample of studies. The core network overlaps substantially with the well-known default mode network, which is associated with internally focused cognition. For a review, see Buckner et al. (2008) and Buckner and DiNicola (2019).

older adults remember fewer episodic details: For relevant evidence and ideas, see Addis et al. (2008), Gaesser et al. (2011), and Madore et al. (2014). For a recent review, see Schacter et al. (2018).

constructive episodic simulation hypothesis: Schacter and Addis (2007a, 2007b, 2020) and Schacter (2012) elaborate on the idea, provide additional background, and discuss relevant evidence. For related ideas, see Dudai and Carruthers (2005) and Suddendorf and Corballis (2007).

305   *"trying out" different approaches:* See the pioneering papers by Ingvar (1979, 1985) for a lucid articulation of this idea. For recent experimental evidence, see Jing et al. (2017).

306   *DRM lists and future imagining:* Dewhurst et al. (2016, quotation from p. 1083). Several studies by my collaborators and I have explored how future imagining and related adaptive processes may contribute to memory errors. In experiments led by Aleea Devitt, we linked flexible recombination processes used in an imagination task with autobiographical memory conjunction errors (Devitt et al., 2016) and memory biases to recall the past in an overly positive manner (Devitt and Schacter, 2018). In studies led by Preston Thakral, we have provided additional evidence that connects DRM false memories with episodic retrieval processes that support future imagining and related kinds of mental simulations. Thakral et al. (2019) found that when participants underwent an "episodic specificity induction" (i.e., brief training in recalling details of a recent experience based on an adapted version of the Cognitive Interview, discussed in Chapter 5) after studying a series of DRM lists and before a recall test on those lists, they were more likely to falsely recall a nonstudied associate lure word than following control inductions. However, earlier work in my lab led by Kevin Madore demonstrated that this same episodic specificity induction boosts the amount of episodic detail with which people imagine future experiences and remember past experiences. See Madore et al. (2014) for this initial study and Schacter and Madore (2016) for an overview of research showing a beneficial impact of an episodic specificity induction on memory, imagination, problem solving, and creativity.

associative inference, flexible recombination, and memory errors: Carpenter and Schacter (2017). A telling result of these experiments is that the increase in memory errors for correct associative inferences occurred only when contextual details (e.g., brown couch versus white couch) were probed *after* the associative inference test; there was no difference in memory errors for correct versus incorrect inferences when memory for contextual details was probed *before* the associative inference test. These results are critical, because the associative inference test engages flexible recombination processes that are needed to link the two scenes, which in turn provides a basis for making the correct inference that the people in those scenes are related. Carpenter and Schacter (2018) showed a similar effect in experiments focused on value details: flexible recombination processes involved in making a correct inference (versus an incorrect inference) about the relationship between a "high-value" item and a "low-value" item increased the subsequent likelihood that participants would misremember which item was high-value and which was low-value. For the basic work on associative inference that provided an impetus for the Carpenter and Schacter studies, see Zeithamova et al. (2010).

Bibliography

Ackil, J. K., and Zaragoza, M. S. 1998. Memorial consequences of forced confabulation: Age differences in susceptibility to false memories. *Developmental Psychology, 34,* 1358–72.

Addis, D. R., Wong, A. T., and Schacter, D. L. 2007. Remembering the past and imagining the future: Common and distinct neural substrates during event construction and elaboration. *Neuropsychologia, 45,* 1363–77.

Addis, D. R., Wong, A. T., and Schacter, D. L. 2008. Age-related changes in the episodic simulation of future events. *Psychological Science, 18,* 33–41.

Adolphs, R., Tranel, D., Damasio, H., and Damasio, A. 1994. Impaired recognition of emotion in facial expressions following bilateral damage to the human amygdala. *Nature, 372,* 669–72.

Adolphs, R., Tranel, D., Hamann, S., Yang, A. W., Calder, A. J., Phelps, E. A., Anderson, A., Lee, G. P., and Damasio, A. R. 1999. Recognition of facial expression in nine individuals with bilateral amygdala damage. *Neuropsychologia, 37,* 1111–17.

Agnoli, S., Vanucci, M., Pelagatti, C., and Corazza, G. E. 2018. Exploring the link between mind wandering, mindfulness, and creativity: A multidimensional approach. *Creativity Research Journal, 30,* 41–53.

Alba, J. W., and Hasher, L. 1983. Is memory schematic? *Psychological Bulletin, 93,* 203–31.

Albert, M. S. 1997. The ageing brain: Normal and abnormal memory. *Philosophical Transactions of the Royal Society of London B: Biological Sciences, 352,* 1703–9.

Alkire, M. T., Haier, R., Fallon, J. H., and Cahill, L. 1998. Hippocampal, but not amygdala, activity at encoding correlates with long-term, free recall of nonemotional information. *Proceedings of the National Academy of Sciences USA, 95,* 14506–10.

Allport, G. W. 1954. *The nature of prejudice.* Cambridge, Mass.: Addison-Wesley.

Anderson, J. R., and Milson, R. 1989. Human memory: An adaptive perspective. *Psychological Review, 96,* 703–19.

Anderson, J. R., and Schooler, L. J. 1991. Reflections of the environment in memory. *Psychological Science, 2,* 396–408.

Anderson, J. R., and Fincham, J. M. 1994. Acquisition of procedural skills from examples. *Journal of Experimental Psychology: Learning, Memory, and Cognition, 20,* 1322–40.

Anderson, J. R., and Schooler, L. J. 2000. The adaptive nature of memory. In E. Tulving and F. I. M. Craik (eds.), *The Oxford handbook of memory* (pp. 557–70). New York: Oxford University Press.

Anderson, M. C., and Spellman, B. A. 1995. On the status of inhibitory mechanisms in cognition: Memory retrieval as a model case. *Psychological Review, 102,* 68–100.

Anderson, M. C. 2001. Active forgetting: Evidence for functional inhibition as a source of memory failure. In J. J. Freyd and A. P. DePrince (eds.), *Trauma and cognitive science: A meeting of minds, science, and human experience* (pp. 185–210). New York: Haworth Press.

Anderson, M. C., and Green, C. 2001. Suppressing unwanted memories by executive control. *Nature, 410,* 366–69.

Anderson, M. C., Ochsner, K. N., Kulh, B., Cooper, J., Gabrieli, S. W., Glover, G. H., and Gabrieli, J. D. E. 2004. Neural systems underlying the suppression of unwanted memories. *Science, 303,* 232–35.

Anderson, M. C., and Huddleston, E. 2012. Toward a cognitive and biological model of motivated forgetting. In R. F. Belli (ed.), *True and false recovered memories: A reconciliation of the debate* (pp. 53–120). New York: Springer.

Arkes, H. R., Wortmann, R. L., Saville, P. D., and Harkness, A. R. 1981. Hindsight bias among physicians weighting the likelihood of diagnoses. *Journal of Applied Psychology, 66,* 252–54.

Austen, J. 1816/1998. *Mansfield Park.* New York: W. W. Norton.

Baddeley, A. D., Lewis, V., Eldridge, M., and Thomson, N. 1984. Attention and retrieval from long-term memory. *Journal of Experimental Psychology: General, 13,* 518–40.

Baddeley, A. D. 1992. Is working memory working? *Quarterly Journal of Experimental Psychology, 44A,* 1–31.

Baddeley, A. D. 1998. *Human memory: Theory and practice* (2d. ed.). Boston: Allyn and Bacon.

Baddeley, A. D., Gathercole, S., and Papagano, C. 1998. The phonological loop as a language learning device. *Psychological Review, 105,* 158–73.

Bahrick, H. P. 1984. Semantic memory content in permastore: 50 years of memory for Spanish learned in school. *Journal of Experimental Psychology: General, 113,* 1–29.

Bahrick, H. P., Hall, L. K., and Berger, S. A. 1996. Accuracy and distortion in memory for high school grades. *Psychological Science, 7,* 265–71.

Bahrick, H. P. 2000. Long-term maintenance of knowledge. In E. Tulving and F. I. M. Craik (eds.), *The Oxford handbook of memory* (pp. 347–62). New York: Oxford University Press.

Bailey, C. H., and Chen, M. 1989. Time course of structural changes at identified sensory neuron synapses during long-term sensitization in Aplysia. *Journal of Neuroscience, 9,* 1774–81.

Baird, B., Smallwood, J., and Schooler, J. W. 2011. Back to the future: Autobiographical planning and the functionality of mind-wandering. *Consciousness and Cognition, 20,* 1604–11.

Baird, B., Smallwood, J., Mrazek, M. D., Kam, J. W., Franklin, M. S., and Schooler, J. W. 2012. Inspired by distraction: Mind wandering facilitates creative incubation. *Psychological Science, 23,* 1117–22.

Baldwin, D. 2019, August 21. Life-saving car seat alarms that remind parents there's a baby in the back seat. Fatherly. https://www.fatherly.com/gear/best-car-seat-alarms/.

Banaji, M. R., and Greenwald, A. G. 1995. Implicit gender stereotyping in judgments of fame. *Journal of Personality and Social Psychology, 68*, 181–98.

Banaji, M. R., and Bhaskar, R. 1999. Implicit stereotypes and memory: The bounded rationality of social beliefs. In D. L. Schacter and E. Scarry (eds.), *Memory, brain, and belief*, 137–75. Cambridge, Mass.: Harvard University Press.

Banaji, M. R., and Greenwald, A. G. 2013. *Blindspot: Hidden biases of good people.* New York: Delacorte Press.

Barasch, A., Diehl, K., Silverman, J., and Zauberman, G. 2017. Photographic memory: The effects of volitional photo taking on memory for visual and auditory aspects of an experience. *Psychological Science, 28*, 1056–66.

Barkow, J., Cosmides, L., and Tooby, J. (eds.). 1992. *The adapted mind: Evolutionary psychology and the generation of culture.* New York: Oxford University Press.

Bartlett, T. 2017, January 5. Can we really measure implicit bias? Maybe not. *Chronicle of Higher Education.* https://www.chronicle.com/article/Can-We-Really-Measure-Implicit/238807.

Basden, B. H., Basden, D. R., and Gargano, G. J. 1993. Directed forgetting in implicit and explicit memory tests: A comparison of methods. *Journal of Experimental Psychology: Learning, Memory, and Cognition, 29*, 603–16.

Beck, R. 2015. *We believe the children: A moral panic in the 1980s.* New York: PublicAffairs.

Belluck, P. 2020, October 11. "I feel like I have dementia": Brain fog plagues Covid survivors. *New York Times.* https://www.nytimes.com/2020/10/11/health/covid-survivors.html.

Benoit, R. G., and Schacter, D. L. 2015. Specifying the core network supporting episodic simulation and episodic memory by activation likelihood estimation. *Neuropsychologia, 75*, 450–57.

Berrios, G. E. 1996. *The history of mental symptoms.* Cambridge: Cambridge University Press.

Beversdorf, D. Q., Smith, B. W., Crucian, G. P., Anderson, J. M., Keillor, J. M., Barrett, A. M., Hughes, J. D., Felopulos, G. J., Bauman, M. L., Nadeau, S. E., and Heilman, K. M. 2000. Increased discrimination of "false memories" in autistic spectrum disorder. *Proceedings of the National Academy of Sciences USA, 97*, 8734–37.

Bjork, E. L., and Bjork, R. A. 1996. Continuing influences of to-be-forgotten information. *Consciousness and Cognition, 5*, 176–96.

Bjork, R. A., and Bjork, E. L. 1988. On the adaptive aspects of retrieval failure in autobiographical memory. In M. M. Gruneberg, R E. Morris, and R. N. Sykes (eds.), *Practical aspects of memory: Current research and issues* (vol. 1, pp. 283–88). Chichester, England: John Wiley.

Bogacz, T. 1989. War neurosis and cultural change in England, 1914–22. *Journal of Contemporary History, 24*, 227–56.

Bornstein, B. H., and LeCompte, D. C. 1995. A comparison of item and source forgetting. *Psychonomic Bulletin and Review, 2*, 254–59.

Bowler, D. M., Gardiner, J. M., Grice, S., and Saavalaine, P. 2000. Memory illusions: False recall and recognition in adults with Asperger's syndrome. *Journal of Abnormal Psychology, 109*, 663–72.

Box, O., Laing, H., and Kopelman, M. 1999. The evolution of spontaneous confabulation, delusional misidentification and a related delusion in a case of severe head injury. *Neurocase, 5,* 251–62.

Braga, R. M., and Buckner, R. L. 2017. Parallel interdigitated distributed networks within the individual estimated by intrinsic functional connectivity. *Neuron, 95,* 457–71.

Brandimonte, M., Einstein, G. O., and McDaniel, M. (eds.). 1996. *Prospective memory: Theory and practice.* Mahwah, N.J.: Erlbaum Associates.

Brashier, N. M., and Marsh, E. J. 2020. Judging truth. *Annual Review of Psychology, 71,* 499–515.

Brashier, N. M., and Schacter, D. L. 2020. Aging in a fake news era. *Current Directions in Psychological Science, 29,* 316–23.

Breckler, S. J. 1994. Memory for the experiment of donating blood: Just how bad was it? *Basic and Applied Social Psychology, 15,* 467–88.

Brédart, S. 1993. Retrieval failures in face naming. *Memory, 1,* 351–66.

Brédart, S., and Valentine, T. 1998. Descriptiveness and proper name retrieval. *Memory, 6,* 199–206.

Breen, N., Caine, D., and Coltheart, M. 2000. Models of face recognition and delusional misidentification: A critical review. *Cognitive Neuropsychology, 17,* 55–71.

Brennen, T., Baguley, T., Bright, J., and Bruce, V. 1990. Resolving semantically induced tip-of-the-tongue states for proper nouns. *Memory and Cognition, 18,* 339–47.

Brewer, J. B., Zhao, Z., Glover, G. H., and Gabrieli, J. D. E. 1998. Making memories: Brain activity that predicts whether visual experiences will be remembered or forgotten. *Science, 281,* 1185–87.

Brewer, W. F. 1996. What is recollective memory? In D. C. Rubin (ed.), *Remembering our past: Studies in autobiographical memory* (pp. 19–66). New York: Cambridge University Press.

Brewin, C. R., Hunter, E., Carroll, F., and Tata, P. 1996. Intrusive memories in depression. *Psychological Medicine, 26,* 1271–76.

Brewin, C. R., and Andrews, B. 1998. Recovered memories of trauma: Phenomenology and cognitive mechanisms. *Clinical Psychology Review, 18,* 949–70.

Brewin, C. R., Watson, M., McCarthy, S., Hyman, P., and Dayson, D. 1998. Intrusive memories and depression in cancer patients. *Behaviour Research and Therapy, 36,* 1131–42.

Brewin, C. R., Andrews, B., and Mickes, L. 2020. Regaining consensus on the reliability of memory. *Current Directions in Psychological Science, 29,* 121–25.

Brown, A. S., and Murphy, D. R. 1989. Cryptomnesia: Delineating inadvertent plagiarism. *Journal of Experimental Psychology: Learning, Memory, and Cognition, 15,* 432–42.

Brown, A. S. 1991. A review of the tip-of-the-tongue experience. *Psychological Bulletin, 109,* 204–23.

Brown, A. S., and Nix, L. A. 1996. Age-related changes in the tip-of-the-tongue experience. *American Journal of Psychology, 109,* 79–91.

Brown, A. S. 2004. *The déjà vu experience.* New York: Psychology Press.

Brown, D. E. 1991. *Human universals.* Philadelphia: Temple University Press.

Brown, E., Deffenbacher, K., and Sturgill, W. 1977. Memory for faces and the circumstances of encounter. *Journal of Applied Psychology, 62,* 311–18.

Brown, J. 1958. Some tests of the decay theory of immediate memory. *Quarterly Journal of Experimental Psychology, 10,* 12–21.

Brown, P. C., Roediger, H. L., III, and McDaniel, M. A. 2014. *Make it stick: The science of successful learning.* Cambridge, Mass.: Harvard University Press.

Brown, R., and McNeill, D. 1966. The "tip-of-the-tongue" phenomenon. *Journal of Verbal Learning and Verbal Behavior, 5,* 325–37.

Bruck, M., Ceci, S. J., and Hembrooke, H. 1997. Children's reports of pleasant and unpleasant events. In D. Read and S. Lindsay (eds.), *Recollections of trauma: Scientific research and clinical practice,* 119–219. New York: Plenum Press.

Bruck, M., and Ceci, S. J. 1999. The suggestibility of children's memory. *Annual Review of Psychology,* 419–39.

Brunet, A., Saumier, D., Liu, A., Streiner, D. L., Tremblay, J., and Pitman, R. K. 2018. Reduction of PTSD symptoms with pre-reactivation propranolol therapy: A randomized controlled trial. *American Journal of Psychiatry, 5,* 427–33.

Bryant, E. B., and Brockway, J. H. 1997. Hindsight bias in reaction to the verdict in the O. J. Simpson criminal trial. *Basic and Applied Social Psychology, 19,* 225–41.

Buckner, R. L. 2000. Neuroimaging of memory. In M. S. Gazzaniga (ed.), *The new cognitive neurosciences* (2d. ed., pp. 817–28). Cambridge, Mass.: MIT Press.

Buckner, R. L., Andrews-Hanna, J. R., and Schacter, D. L. 2008. The brain's default network: Anatomy, function, and relevance to disease. In The year in cognitive neuroscience, special issue, *Annals of the New York Academy of Sciences, 1124,* 1–38.

Buckner, R. L., and DiNicola, L. 2019. The brain's default network: Updated anatomy, physiology and evolving insights. *Nature Reviews Neuroscience, 20,* 593–608.

Bulevich, J. B., Roediger, H. L., Balota, D. A., and Butler, A. C. 2006. Failures to find suppression of episodic memories in the think/no think paradigm. *Memory and Cognition, 34,* 1569–77.

Burke, D., MacKay, D. G., Worthley, J. S., and Wade, E. 1991. On the tip of the tongue: What causes word failure in young and older adults? *Journal of Memory and Language, 30,* 237–46.

Burton, R. 1621/1989. *The anatomy of melancholy.* (vol. 4). New York: Oxford University Press.

Buschke, H., Kulansky, G., Katz, M., Stewart, W. E, Sliwinski, M. J., Eckholdt, H. M., and Lipton, R. B. 1999. Screening for dementia with the Memory Impairment Screen. *Neurology, 52,* 231–38.

Buss, D. M., Haselton, M. G., Shackelford, T. K., Bleske, A. L., and Wakefield, J. C. 1998. Adaptations, exaptations, and spandrels. *American Psychologist, 53,* 533–48.

Cabeza, R., Rao, S., Wagner, A. D., Mayer, A., and Schacter, D. L. 2001. Can the hippocampal memory system distinguish true from false? An event-related fMRI study of veridical and illusory recognition memory. *Proceedings of the National Academy of Sciences USA, 98,* 4805–10.

Cahill, L., Prins, B., Weber, M., and McGaugh, J. L. 1994. β-Adrenergic activation and memory for emotional events. *Nature, 371,* 702–4.

Cahill, L., Haier, R. J., Fallon, J., Alkire, M. T., Tang, C., Keator, D., Wu, J., and McGaugh, J. L. 1996. Amygdala activity at encoding correlated with long-term, free recall of emotional information. *Proceedings of the National Academy of Sciences USA, 93,* 8016–21.

Cahill, L., and McGaugh, J. L. 1998. Mechanisms of emotional arousal and lasting declarative memory. *Trends in Neurosciences, 21,* 294–99.

Camerer, C. F., Dreber, A., Holzmeister, F., et al. 2018. Evaluating the replicability of social science experiments in *Nature* and *Science* between 2010 and 2015. *Nature Human Behavior, 2,* 637–44.

Canby, V. 1998, October 11. Theater: Highly intoxicating wit, served straight up. *New York Times,* p. 5.

Cappa, S. F., Frugoni, M., Pasquali, P., Perani, D., and Zorat, F. 1998. Category-specific naming impairment for artefacts: A new case. *Neurocase, 4,* 391–97.

Caramazza, A., and Miozzo, M. 1997. The relation between syntactic and phonological knowledge in lexical access: Evidence from the "tip-of-the-tongue" phenomenon. *Cognition, 64,* 309–43.

Carlesimo, G. A., Sabbadini, M., Fadda, L., and Caltagirone, C. 1997. Word-list forgetting in young and elderly subjects: Evidence for age-related decline in transferring information from transitory to permanent memory condition. *Cortex, 33,* 155–66.

Carli, L. L. 1999. Cognitive reconstruction, hindsight, and reactions to victims and perpetrators. *Personality and Social Psychology Bulletin, 25,* 966–79.

Carpenter, A. C., and Schacter, D. L. 2017. Flexible retrieval: When true inferences produce false memories. *Journal of Experimental Psychology: Learning, Memory, and Cognition, 43,* 335–49.

Carpenter, A. C., and Schacter, D. L. 2018. False memories, false preferences: Flexible retrieval mechanisms supporting successful inference bias novel decisions. *Journal of Experimental Psychology: General, 147,* 988–1004.

Catarino, A., Küpper, C. S., Werner-Seidler, A., Dalgleish, T., and Anderson, M. C. 2015. Failing to forget: Inhibitory-control deficits compromise memory suppression in post-traumatic stress disorder. *Psychological Science, 26,* 604–16.

Ceci, S. J. 1995. False beliefs: Some developmental and clinical considerations. In D. L. Schacter (ed.), *Memory distortion: How minds, brains, and societies reconstruct the past* (pp. 91–128). Cambridge, Mass.: Harvard University Press.

Ceci, S. J., and Bruck, M. 1995. *Jeopardy in the courtroom.* Washington, D.C.: American Psychological Association.

Chadwick, M. J., Anjum, R. S., Kumaran, D., Schacter, D. L., Spiers, H. J., and Hassabis, D. 2016. Semantic representations in the temporal pole predict false memories. *Proceedings of the National Academy of Sciences USA, 113,* 10180–85.

Charlesworth, T. E. S., and Banaji, M. R. 2019. Patterns of implicit and explicit attitudes: I. Long-term change and stability from 2007 to 2016. *Psychological Science, 30,* 174–92.

Choi, H., and Smith, S. M. 2005. Incubation and the resolution of tip-of-the-tongue states. *Journal of General Psychology, 132,* 365–76.

Chowdhury, R., Guitart-Masip, M., Bunzeck, N., Dolan, R. J., and Düzel, E. 2012. Dopamine modulates episodic memory persistence in old age. *Journal of Neuroscience, 32,* 14193–204.

Christensen, A., Sullaway, M., and King, C. E. 1983. Systematic error in behavioral reports of dyadic interaction: Egocentric bias and content effects. *Behavioral Assessment, 5,* 129–40.

Chuck, E. 2019, August 6. Technology to save kids in hot cars exists. So why isn't it in every vehicle? NBC News. https://www.nbcnews.com/news/us-news/technology-save-kids-hot-cars-exists-so-why-isn-t-n1038281.

Clancy, S. A., Schacter, D. L., McNally, R. J., and Pitman, R. K. 2000. False recognition in women reporting recovered memories of sexual abuse. *Psychological Science, 11,* 26–31.

Clancy, S. A., McNally, R. J., Schacter, D. L., Lenzenweger, M. F., and Pitman, R. K. 2002. Memory distortion in people reporting abduction by aliens. *Journal of Abnormal Psychology, 111,* 455–61.

Clayton, N. S. 1996. Development of food-storing and the hippocampus in juvenile marsh tits (*Parus palustris*). *Behavioural Brain Research, 74,* 153–59.

Cleary, A. M., Ryals, A. J., and Nomi, J. S. 2009. Can déjà vu result from similarity to a prior experience? Support for the similarity hypothesis of déjà vu. *Psychonomic Bulletin and Review, 16,* 1082–88.

Cleary, A. M., Brown, A. S., Sawyer, B. D., Nomi, J. S., Ajoku, A. C., and Ryals, A. J. 2012. Familiarity from the configuration of objects in 3-dimensional space and its relation to déjà vu: A virtual reality investigation. *Consciousness and Cognition, 21,* 969–75.

Cleary, A. M., and Claxton, A. B. 2018. Déjà vu: An illusion of prediction. *Psychological Science, 29,* 635–44.

Clifford, B. R., and Gwyer, P. 1999. The effects of the cognitive interview and other methods of context reinstatement on identification. *Psychology, Crime and Law, 5,* 61–80.

Clohessy, S., and Ehlers, A. 1999. PTSD symptoms, response to intrusive memories and coping in ambulance service workers. *British Journal of Clinical Psychology, 38,* 251–65.

Cockburn, J. 1996. Assessment and treatment of prospective memory deficits. In M. Brandimonte, G. O. Einstein, and M. McDaniel (eds.), *Prospective memory: Theory and practice* (pp. 327–50). Mahwah, N.J.: Erlbaum Associates.

Cohen, G., and Faulkner, D. 1986. Memory for proper names: Age differences in retrieval. *British Journal of Developmental Psychology, 4,* 187–97.

Cohen, G. 1990. Why is it difficult to put names to faces? *British Journal of Psychology, 81,* 287–97.

Conway, M., and Ross, M. 1984. Getting what you want by revising what you had. *Journal of Personality and Social Psychology, 39,* 406–15.

Conway, M. A. (ed.). 1997. *Recovered memories and false memories.* Oxford: Oxford University Press.

Correll, J., Park, B., Judd, C. M., and Wittenbrink, B. 2002. The police officer's dilemma: Using ethnicity to disambiguate potentially threatening individuals. *Journal of Personality and Social Psychology, 83,* 1314–29.

Correll, J., Park, B., Judd, C. M., Wittenbrink, B., Sadler, M. S., and Keesee, T. 2007. Across the thin blue line: Police officers and racial bias in the decision to shoot. *Journal of Personality and Social Psychology, 92,* 1006–23.

Correll, J., Hudson, S. M., Guillermo, S., and Ma, D. S. 2014. The police officer's dilemma: A decade of research on racial bias in the decision to shoot. *Social and Personality Psychology Compass, 8,* 201–13.

Cosmides, L., and Tooby, J. 1994. Beyond intuition and instinct blindness: Toward an evolutionarily rigorous cognitive science. *Cognition, 50,* 41–77.

Costello, A., Fletcher, P. C., Dolan, R. J., Frith, C. D., and Shallice, T. 1998. The origins of forgetting in a case of isolated retrograde amnesia following a haemorrhage: Evidence from functional imaging. *Neurocase, 4,* 437–46.

Courbon, P., and Fail, G. 1927. Syndrome d'illusion de Frégoli et schizophrénie. *Bulletin de la Société Clinique de Médecine Mentale.*

Coyne, J. A. 2000, April 3. Of vice and men: Review of R. Thornhill and C. Palmer, *A natural history of rape. New Republic,* 27–34.

Craik, F. I. M., and Tulving, E. 1975. Depth of processing and the retention of words in episodic memory. *Journal of Experimental Psychology: General, 104,* 268–94.

Craik, F. I. M., and Byrd, M. 1982. Aging and cognitive deficits: The role of attentional resources. In F. I. M. Craik and S. Trehub (eds.), *Aging and cognitive processes* (pp. 191–211). New York: Plenum Press.

Craik, F. I. M., Govoni, R., Naveh-Benjamin, M., and Anderson, N. D. 1996. The effects of divided attention on encoding and retrieval processes in human memory. *Journal of Experimental Psychology: General, 125,* 159–80.

Cristol, D. A. 1996. Food storing does not affect hippocampal volume in experienced adult willow tits. *Behavioural Brain Research, 81,* 233–36.

Crombag, H. F. M., Wagenaar, W. A., and Van Koppen, P. J. 1996. Crashing memories and the problem of "source monitoring." *Applied Cognitive Psychology, 10,* 95–104.

Crook, T. H., and Adderly, B. 1998. *The memory cure.* New York: Simon and Schuster.

Cunningham, M. R., Roberts, A. R., Barbee, A. P., Druen, P. B., and Wu, C. 1995. "Their ideas of beauty are, on the whole, the same as ours": Consistency and variability in the cross-cultural perception of female physical attractiveness. *Journal of Personality and Social Psychology, 68,* 261–79.

Curran, T., Schacter, D. L, Johnson, M. K., and Spinks, R. A. 2001. Brain potentials reflect behavioral differences in true and false recognition. *Journal of Cognitive Neuroscience, 13,* 201–16.

Damasio, H., Grabowski, T. J., Tranel, D., Hichwa, R. D., and Damasio, A. R. 1996. A neural basis for lexical retrieval. *Nature, 380,* 499–505.

D'Amato, G. 1999, August 12. Van de Velde still smiling after British Open fiasco. *Milwaukee Journal Sentinel,* p. 1.

Daniels, G. H. 1972. Acknowledgment. *Science, 175,* 124–25.

Danielson, D. 2001, December 10. "Not guilty" verdict still leaves Kari Engholm with questions about the future. RadioIowa. https://www.radioiowa.com/2001/12/10/not-guilty-verdict-still-leaves-kari-engholm-with-questions-about-the-future/.

D'Argembeau, A., and Van der Linden, M. 2004. Phenomenal characteristics associated with projecting oneself back into the past and forward into the future: Influence of valence and temporal distance. *Consciousness and Cognition, 13,* 844–58.

D'Argembeau, A., and Van der Linden, M. 2006. Individual differences in the phenomenology of mental time travel. *Consciousness and Cognition, 15*, 342–50.

Daumeyer, N. M., Onyeader, I. N., Brown, X., and Richeson, J. A. 2019. Consequences of
attributing discrimination to implicit vs. explicit bias. *Journal of Experimental Social
Psychology, 84*, 103812.

Davidson, R. J., Abercrombie, H., Nitschke, J. B., and Putnam, K. 1999. Regional brain
function, emotion and disorders of emotion. *Current Opinion in Neurobiology, 9*,
228–34.

Davies, G. 1988. Faces and places: Laboratory research on context and face recognition. In
G. M. Davies and D. M. Thomson (eds.), *Memory in context: Context in memory* (pp.
35–53). New York: John Wiley.

Davis, H. P., Small, S. A., Stern, Y., Mayeux, R., Feldstein, S. N., and Keller, F. R. 2003. Acquisition, recall, and forgetting of verbal information in long-term memory by young,
middle-aged, and elderly individuals. *Cortex, 39*, 1063–91.

Dawes, R. 1988. *Rational choice in an uncertain world*. San Diego: Harcourt, Brace, and
Jovanovich.

Dawkins, R. 1986. *The blind watchmaker*. New York: W. W. Norton.

Deese, J. 1959. On the prediction of occurrence of particular verbal intrusions in immediate recall. *Journal of Experimental Psychology, 58*, 17–22.

De Houwer, J. 2019. Implicit bias is behavior: A functional-cognitive perspective on implicit bias. *Perspectives on Psychological Science, 14*, 835–40.

Deldin, P. J., Deveney, C. M., Kim, A. S., Casas, B. R., and Best, J. L. 2001. A slow wave
investigation of working memory biases in mood disorders. *Journal of Abnormal Psychology, 110*, 267–81.

DeLillo, D. 1998. *Underworld*. London: Picador.

Descartes, R. 1649/1989. *The passions of the soul* (Voss, S., trans.). Indianapolis: Hackett.

Devine, P. G. 1989. Stereotypes and prejudices: Their automatic and controlled components. *Journal of Personality and Social Psychology, 56*, 5–18.

Devine, P. G., Forscher, P. S., Austin, A. J., and Cox, W. T. L. 2012. Long-term reduction
in implicit race bias: A prejudice habit-breaking intervention. *Journal of Experimental
Social Psychology, 48*, 1267–78.

Devitt, A. L., Monk-Fromont, E., Schacter, D. L., and Addis, D. R. 2016. Factors that influence the generation of autobiographical memory conjunction errors. *Memory, 24*,
204–22.

Devitt, A. L., and Schacter, D. L. 2018. An optimistic outlook creates a rosy past: The impact of episodic simulation on subsequent memory. *Psychological Science, 29*, 936–46.

Dewhurst, S. A., and Conway, M. A. 1994. Pictures, images, and recollective experience.
Journal of Experimental Psychology: Learning, Memory, and Cognition, 20, 1088–98.

Dewhurst, S. A., Anderson, R. J., Grace, L., and van Esch, L. 2016. Adaptive false memories: Imagining future scenarios increase false memories in the DRM paradigm. *Memory and Cognition, 44*, 1076–84.

Dobbin, F., and Kalev, A. 2018. Why doesn't diversity training work? The challenge for
industry and academia. *Anthropology Now, 10*, 48–55.

Drake, E. B., Henderson, V. W., Stanczyk, F. Z., McCleary, C. A., Brown, W. S., Smith, C. A., Rizzo, A. A., Murdock, G. A., and Buckwalter, J. G. 2000. Associations between circulating sex steroid hormones and cognition in normal elderly women. *Neurology*, 54, 599–603.

Drummie, G. 1998, March 20. Memory block possible — doctor. *Toronto Sun*, p. 44.

DuBreuil, S. C., Garry, M., and Loftus, E. F. 1998. Tales from the crib: Age regression and the creation of unlikely memories. In S. J. Lynn and K. M. McConkey (eds.), *Truth in memory* (pp. 137–62). New York: Guilford Press.

Ducharme, J. 2018, September 27. "Indelible in the hippocampus is the laughter." The science behind Christine Blasey Ford's testimony. *Time*. https://time.com/5408567/christine-blasey-ford-science-of-memory/.

Duckworth, A. L. 2016. *Grit: The power of passion and perseverance*. New York: Scribner.

Dudai, Y., and Carruthers, M. 2005. The Janus face of mnemosyne. *Nature*, 434, 823–24.

Dudai, Y. 2012. The restless engram: Consolidations never end. *Annual Review of Psychology*, 35, 227–47.

Duka, T., Tasker, R., and McGowan, J. F. 2000. The effects of 3-week estrogen hormone replacement on cognition in elderly healthy females. *Psychopharmacology*, 149, 129–39.

Düzel, E., Yonelinas, A. P., Mangun, G. R., Heinze, H. J., and Tulving, E. 1997. Event-related brain potential correlates of two states of conscious awareness in memory. *Proceedings of the National Academy of Sciences USA*, 94, 59731–38.

Eals, M., and Silverman, I., 1994. The hunter-gatherer theory of spatial sex-differences: Proximate factors mediating the female advantage in recall of object arrays. *Ethology and Sociobiology*, 15, 95–105.

Ebbinghaus, H. 1885/1964. *Memory: A contribution to experimental psychology*. New York: Dover.

Eberhardt, J. 2019. *Biased: Uncovering the hidden prejudice that shapes what we see, think, and do*. New York: Viking.

Edelson, M., Sharot, T., Dolan, R. J., and Dudai, Y. 2011. Following the crowd: Brain substrates of long-term memory conformity. *Science*, 333, 108–11.

Effron, D. A., and Raj, M. 2020. Misinformation and morality: Encountering false-news headlines makes them seem less unethical to publish and share. *Psychological Science*, 31, 75–87.

Ehlers, A., and Steil, R. 1995. Maintenance of intrusive memories in posttraumatic stress disorder: A cognitive approach. *Behavioural and Cognitive Psychotherapy*, 23, 217–49.

Ehlers, A., and Clarke, D. M. 2000. A cognitive model of posttraumatic stress disorder. *Behaviour Research and Therapy*, 38, 319–45.

Einstein, G. O., and McDaniel, M. A. 1990. Normal aging and prospective memory. *Journal of Experimental Psychology: Learning, Memory, and Cognition*, 16, 717–26.

Einstein, G. O., Smith, R. E., McDaniel, M. A., and Shaw, P. 1997. Aging and prospective memory: The influence of increased task demands at encoding and retrieval. *Psychology and Aging*, 12, 479–88.

Eldridge, M. A., Barnard, P. J., and Bekerian, D. A. 1994. Autobiographical memory and daily schemas at work. *Memory*, 2, 51–74.

Ellis, A. W., and Young, A. W. 1988. *Human cognitive neuropsychology.* Hove, England: Erlbaum Associates.

Ellis, H. D., Whitley, J., and Luauté, J. 1994. Delusional misidentification: The three original papers on the Capgras, Frégoli and intermetamorphosis delusions. *History of Psychiatry, 5,* 117–46.

Elsey, J. W. B., Van Ast, V. A., and Kindt, M. 2018. Human memory reconsolidation: A guiding framework and critical review of the evidence. *Psychological Bulletin, 144,* 797–848.

Engelkamp, J., and Zimmer, H. 1996. Organisation and recall in verbal tasks and in subject-performed tasks. *European Journal of Cognitive Psychology, 8,* 257–73.

Engen, H. G., and Anderson, M. C. 2018. Memory control: A fundamental mechanism of emotion regulation. *Trends in Cognitive Sciences, 22,* 982–85.

Erdelyi, M. H. 1985. *Psychoanalysis: Freud's cognitive psychology.* New York: W. H. Freeman.

Fawcett, J. M., and Hulbert, J. C. 2020. The many faces of forgetting: Toward a constructive view of forgetting in everyday life. *Journal of Applied Research in Memory and Cognition, 9,* 1–18.

Fazio, L. K., Rand, D. G., and Pennycook, G. 2019. Repetition increases perceived truth equally for plausible and implausible statements. *Psychonomic Bulletin and Review, 26,* 1705–10.

Feinberg, T. E., Eaton, L. A., Roane, D. M., and Giacino, J. T. 1999. Multiple Fregoli delusions after traumatic brain injury. *Cortex, 35,* 373–87.

Feng, S., D'Mello, S., and Graesser, A. C. 2013. Mind wandering while reading easy and difficult texts. *Psychonomic Bulletin and Review, 20,* 586–92.

Fernandes, M. A., and Moscovitch, M. 2000. Divided attention and memory: Evidence of substantial interference effects at encoding and retrieval. *Journal of Experimental Psychology: General, 129,* 155–76.

Festinger, L. 1957. *A theory of cognitive dissonance.* Stanford, Calif.: Stanford University Press.

Fink, J. R., Markowitsch, H. J., Reinkemeier, M., Bruckbauer, T., Kessler, J., and Heiss, W. 1996. Cerebral representation of one's own past: Neural networks involved in autobiographical memory. *Journal of Neuroscience, 16,* 4275–82.

Finkelstein, K. E. 1999, October 17. Yo-Yo Ma's lost Stradivarius is found after wild search. *New York Times,* p. 34.

Finley, J. R., Naaz, F., and Goh, F. W. 2018. *Memory and technology: How we use information in the brain and the world.* Switzerland: Springer.

Fisher, R. P., and Geiselman, R. E. 1992. *Memory-enhancing techniques for investigative interviewing: The Cognitive Interview.* Springfield, Ill.: Charles C. Thomas.

Fisher, R. P. 1995. Interviewing victims and witnesses of crime. *Psychology, Public Policy, and Law, 1,* 732–64.

Foa, E. B., Rothbaum, B. O., Riggs, D., and Murdock, T. 1991. Treatment of post-traumatic stress disorder in rape victims: A comparison between cognitive-behavioral procedures and counseling. *Journal of Consulting and Clinical Psychology, 59,* 715–23.

Foa, E. B., and Meadows, E. A. 1997. Psychosocial treatments for posttraumatic stress disorder: A critical review. *Annual Review of Psychology, 48,* 449–80.

Forscher, P. S., Lai, C. K., Axt, J. R., Ebersole, C. R., Herman, M., Devine, P. G., and Nosek, B. A. 2019. A meta-analysis of procedures to change implicit measures. *Psychological Bulletin, 117,* 522–59.

Fox, K. C. R., and Beaty, R. E. 2019. Mind-wandering as creative thinking: Neural, psychological, and theoretical considerations. *Current Opinion in Behavioral Sciences, 27,* 123–30.

Frenda, S. J., Knowles, E. D., Saletan, W., and Loftus, E. F. 2013. False memories of fabricated political events. *Journal of Experimental Social Psychology, 49,* 280–86.

Freyd, J. J. 1996. *Betrayal trauma: The logic of forgetting childhood abuse.* Cambridge, Mass.: Harvard University Press.

Friedman, W. J., and deWinstanley, P. A. 1998. Changes in the subjective properties of autobiographical memories with the passage of time. *Memory, 6,* 367–81.

Gaesser, B., Sacchetti, D. C., Addis, D. R., and Schacter, D. L. 2011. Characterizing age-related changes in remembering the past and imagining the future. *Psychology and Aging, 26,* 80–84.

Gallistel, C. R. 1990. *The organization of learning.* Cambridge, Mass.: MIT Press.

García Márquez, G. 1994. *Love in the time of cholera.* New York: Penguin.

Garrett, B. L. 2011. *Convicting the innocent: Where criminal prosecutions go wrong.* Cambridge, Mass.: Harvard University Press.

Garrett, M. F. 1992. Disorders of lexical selection. *Cognition, 42,* 143–80.

Garry, M., Manning, C., Loftus, E. F., and Sherman, S. J. 1996. Imagination inflation: Imagining a childhood event inflates confidence that it occurred. *Psychonomic Bulletin and Review, 3,* 208–14.

Garven, S., Wood, J. M., Malpass, R. S., and Shaw, J. S. 1998. More than suggestion: The effect of interviewing techniques from the McMartin Preschool case. *Journal of Applied Psychology, 83,* 347–59.

Gathercole, S. E., and Baddeley, A. D. 1993. *Working memory and language.* East Sussex, England: Erlbaum Associates.

Gaulin, S. J. C., and Fitzgerald, R. W. 1989. Sexual selection for spatial-learning ability. *Animal Behaviour, 37,* 322–31.

Gaulin, S. J. C. 1997. Cross-cultural patterns and the search for evolved psychological mechanisms. In G. R. Bock and G. Cardew (eds.), *Characterizing human psychological adaptations* (pp. 195–207). Chichester, England: John Wiley.

Gawronski, B., Bodenhausen, G. V., and Becker, A. P. 2007. I like it, because I like myself: Associative self-anchoring and post-decisional change of implicit evaluations. *Journal of Experimental Social Psychology, 43,* 221–32.

Gawronski, B. 2019. Six lessons for a cogent science of implicit bias and its criticisms. *Perspectives on Psychological Science, 14,* 574–95.

Gazzaniga, M. S. 1985. *The social brain.* New York: Basic Books.

Gazzaniga, M. S. 1998. The split brain revisited. *Scientific American, 279,* 50–55.

Geary, P. J. 1994. *Phantoms of remembrance.* Princeton, N.J.: Princeton University Press.

Gerosa, M. 1997, Fall. Moore than ever. *Ladies' Home Journal*, 79–83.

Gilbert, D. T. 1991. How mental systems believe. *American Psychologist, 46,* 107–19.

Gilbert, D. T., King, G., Pettigrew, S., and Wilson, T. D. 2016. Comment on "Estimating the reproducibility of psychological science." *Science, 351,* 1037a.

Gilbert, S. J., Bird, A., Carpenter, J. M., Fleming, S. M., Sachdeva, C., and Tsai, P.-C. 2019. Optimal use of reminders: Metacognition, effort, and cognitive offloading. *Journal of Experimental Psychology: General.* http://dx.doi.org/10.1037/xge0000652.

Goethals, G. R., and Reckman, R. F. 1973. The perception of consistency in attitudes. *Journal of Experimental Social Psychology, 9,* 491–501.

Goff, L. M., and Roediger, H. L., III. 1998. Imagination inflation for action events: Repeated imaginings lead to illusory recollections. *Memory and Cognition, 26,* 20–33.

Goldhill, O. 2017, December 3. The world is relying on a flawed psychological test to fight racism. Quartz. https://qz.com/1144504/the-world-is-relying-on-a-flawed-psychological-test-to-fight-racism/.

Goldstein, J. 2015, February 6. Is it possible to "misremember" getting shot out of the sky? A scientific exploration. ThinkProgress. https://thinkprogress.org/is-it-possible-to-misremember-getting-shot-out-of-the-sky-a-scientific-exploration-4114022f1b10/.

Gould, O. N., McDonald-Miszczak, L., and King, B. 1997. Metacognition and medication adherence: How do older adults remember? *Experimental Aging Research, 23,* 315–42.

Gould, S. J., and Lewontin, R. C. 1979. The spandrels of San Marco and the Panglossian paradigm: A critique of the adaptationist programme. *Proceedings of the Royal Society of London B: Biological Sciences, 205,* 581–98.

Gould, S. J. 1991. Exaptation: A crucial tool for evolutionary psychology. *Journal of Social Issues, 47,* 43–65.

Gould, S. J. 1997a. Darwinian fundamentalism. *New York Review of Books, 44,* 34–37.

Gould, S. J. 1997b. Evolution: The pleasures of pluralism. *New York Review of Books, 44* 47–52.

Gourevitch, P. 1999, June 14. The memory thief. *The New Yorker,* 48–68.

Graf, P., and Schacter, D. L. 1985. Implicit and explicit memory for new associations in normal and amnesic subjects. *Journal of Experimental Psychology: Learning, Memory, and Cognition, 11,* 501–18.

Gray, J. D., and Silver, R. C. 1990. Opposite sides of the same coin: Former spouses' divergent perspectives in coping with their divorce. *Journal of Personality and Social Psychology, 59,* 1180–91.

Green, J. P. 1999. Hypnosis, context effects, and the recall of early autobiographical memories. *International Journal of Clinical and Experimental Hypnosis, 47,* 284–300.

Greenwald, A. G. 1980. The totalitarian ego: Fabrication and revision of personal history. *American Psychologist, 35,* 603–18.

Greenwald, A. G., and Banaji, M. R. 1995. Implicit social cognition: Attitudes, self-esteem, and stereotypes. *Psychological Review, 102,* 4–27.

Greenwald, A. G., McGhee, D. E., and Schwartz, J. L. K. 1998. Measuring individual differences in implicit cognition: The Implicit Association Test. *Journal of Personality and Social Psychology, 74,* 1464–80.

Greenwald, A. G., Banaji, M. R., and Nosek, B. A. 2015. Statistically small effects of the Implicit Association Test can have societally large effects. *Journal of Personality and Social Psychology, 108,* 553–61.

Greenwald, A. G., and Banaji, M. R. 2017. The implicit revolution: Reconceiving the relation between conscious and unconscious. *American Psychologist, 72,* 861–71.

Greenwald, A. G., and Lai, C. K. 2020. Implicit social cognition. *Annual Review of Psychology, 71,* 419–45.

Grisham, J. 2006. *The innocent man: Murder and injustice in a small town.* New York: Random House.

Gronlund, S. D., Wixted, J. T., and Mickes, L. 2014. Evaluating eyewitness identification procedures using receiver operating characteristic analysis. *Current Directions in Psychological Science, 23,* 3–10.

Gudjonsson, G. H. 1984. A new scale of interrogative suggestibility. *Personality and Individual Differences, 5,* 303–14.

Gudjonsson, G. H., and MacKeith, J. A. C. 1988. Retracted confessions: Legal, psychological and psychiatric aspects. *Medical Science Law, 28,* 187–94.

Gudjonsson, G. H. 1992. *The psychology of interrogations, confessions and testimony.* New York: John Wiley.

Gudjonsson, G. H., Kopelman, M. D., and MacKeith, J. A. C. 1999. Unreliable admissions to homicide: A case of misdiagnosis of amnesia and misuse of abreaction technique. *British Journal of Psychiatry, 174,* 455–59.

Halperin, J. L. 1996. *The truth machine.* Dallas: Ivy Press.

Hanley, J. R., and Cowell, E. S. 1988. The effects of different types of retrieval cues on the recall of names of famous faces. *Memory and Cognition, 16,* 545–55.

Hanley, J. R. 1995. Are names difficult to recall because they are unique? A case study of a patient with anomia. *Quarterly Journal of Experimental Psychology, 48A,* 487–506.

Hanley, J. R., and Kay, J. 1998. Proper name anomia and anomia for the names of people: Functionally dissociable impairments? *Cortex, 34,* 155–58.

Hanson, B. L., Terrance, C. A., and Plumm, K. M. 2015. Parent as both perpetrator and victim: Blame and punishment in a case of child neglect. *Applied Psychology in Criminal Justice, 11,* 162–84.

Happe, F. 1999. Autism: Cognitive deficit or cognitive style? *Trends in Cognitive Sciences, 3,* 216–22.

Hardt, O., Einarsson, E. O., and Nader, K. 2010. A bridge over troubled water: Reconsolidation as a link between cognitive and neuroscientific memory research traditions. *Annual Review of Psychology, 61,* 141–67.

Harley, T. A., and Brown, H. E. 1998. What causes the tip-of-the-tongue state? Evidence for lexical neighborhood effects in speech production. *British Journal of Psychology, 89,* 151–74.

Hasher, L., Goldstein, D., and Toppino, T. 1977. Frequency and the conference of referential validity. *Journal of Verbal Learning and Verbal Behavior, 16,* 107–12.

Hassabis, D., Kumaran, D., and Maguire, E. A. 2007. Using imagination to understand the neural basis of episodic memory. *Journal of Neuroscience, 27,* 14365–74.

Hastie, R., Schkade, D. A., and Payne, J. W. 1999. Juror judgments in civil cases: Hindsight effects on judgments of liability for punitive damages. *Law and Human Behavior, 23,* 597–614.

Hauser, M. D. 2000. *Wild minds: What animals really think.* New York: Henry Holt.

Hawkins, S. A., and Hastie, R. 1990. Hindsight: Biased judgments of past events after the outcomes are known. *Psychological Bulletin, 107,* 311–27.

Hay, D. C., Young, A. W., and Ellis, A. W. 1991. Routes through the face recognition system. *Quarterly Journal of Experimental Psychology, 43A,* 761–91.

Hayden, J. O. (ed.). 1994. *William Wordsworth: Selected poems.* London: Penguin Books.

Heine, S. J., Lehman, D. R., Markus, H. R., and Kitayama, S. 1999. Is there a universal need for positive self-regard? *Psychological Review, 106,* 766–94.

Henke, K., Weber, B., Kneifel, S., Wieser, H. G., and Buck, A. 1999. Human hippocampus associates information in memory. *Proceedings of the National Academy of Sciences USA, 96,* 5884–89.

Henkel, L. A., Johnson, M. K., and DeLeonardis, D. M. 1998. Aging and source monitoring: Cognitive processes and neuropsychological correlates. *Journal of Experimental Psychology: General, 127,* 251–68.

Henkel, L. A. 2014. Point-and-shoot memories: The influence of taking photos on memory for a museum tour. *Psychological Science, 25,* 396–402.

Henkel, L. A., Nash, R. A., and Paton, J. A. 2021. "Say cheese!" How taking photos can shape memory and cognition. In S. Lane and P. Atchley (eds.), *Human capacity in the attention economy* (pp. 103–33). Washington, D.C.: American Psychological Association.

Henson, R. N. A., Rugg, M. D., Shallice, T., Josephs, O., and Dolan, R. J. 1999. Recollection and familiarity in recognition memory: An event-related functional magnetic resonance imaging study. *Journal of Neuroscience, 19,* 3962–72.

Hertel, P. T., and Gerstle, M. 2003. Depressive deficits in forgetting. *Psychological Science, 14,* 573–78.

Heuer, F., and Reisberg, D. 1992. Emotion, arousal, and memory for detail. In S.-A. Christianson (ed.), *The handbook of emotion and memory: Research and theory* (pp. 151–80). Hillsdale, N.J.: Erlbaum Associates.

Hicks, V. L. 1998, June 14. Experts explain John Doe 2 "sightings": Bombing suspect may have been figment of witnesses' imaginations. *Boston Globe,* p. A14.

Higharn, P. A. 1998. Believing details known to have been suggested. *British Journal of Psychology, 89,* 265–83.

Hilts, P. 1995. *Memory's ghost: The strange tale of Mr. M and the nature of memory.* New York: Simon and Schuster.

Hilts, P. J. 1996, July 2. In research scans, telltale signs sort false memories from true. *New York Times,* p. C3.

Hinkle, L. E., and Wolff, H. G. 1956. Communist interrogation and indoctrination of "enemies of the states." *Archives of Neurology and Psychiatry, 76,* 115–74.

Holman, E. A., and Silver, R. C. 1998. Getting "stuck" in the past: Temporal orientation and coping with trauma. *Journal of Personality and Social Psychology, 74,* 1146–63.

Holmberg, D., and Holmes, J. G. 1994. Reconstruction of relationship memories: A mental models approach. In N. Schwarz and S. Sudman (eds.), *Autobiographical memory and the validity of retrospective reports* (pp. 267–88). New York: Springer-Verlag.

Houle, D. 1998. Review of A. P. Møller and J. P. Swaddle, *Asymmetry, developmental stability, and evolution* (1997). *Evolution, 52,* 1872–76.

Howe, M. L. 2011. The adaptive nature of memory and its illusions. *Current Directions in Psychological Science, 20,* 312–15.

Howe, M. L., Garner, S. R., Charlesworth, M., and Knott, L. 2011. A brighter side to memory illusions: False memories prime children's and adults' insight-based problem solving. *Journal of Experimental Child Psychology, 108,* 383–93.

Howe, M. L., Garner, S. R., Threadgold, E., and Ball, L. J. 2015. Priming analogical reasoning with false memories. *Memory and Cognition, 43,* 879–95.

Huijbers, W., Papp, K. V., LaPoint, M., Wigman, S. E., Dagley, A., Hedden, T., Rentz, D. M., Schultz, A. P., and Sperling, R. A. 2017. Age-related increases in tip-of-the-tongue are distinct from decreases in remembering names: A functional MRI study. *Cerebral Cortex, 27,* 4339–49.

Hupbach, A., Gomez, R., and Nadel, L. 2011. Episodic memory updating: The role of context familiarity. *Psychonomic Bulletin and Review, 18,* 787–97.

Huppert, E. A., and Kopelman, M. D. 1989. Rates of forgetting in normal ageing: A comparison with dementia. *Neuropsychologia, 27,* 849–60.

Hyman, I. E., Husband, T. H., and Billings, F. J. 1995. False memories of childhood experiences. *Applied Cognitive Psychology, 9,* 181–97.

Hyman, I. E., Jr., and Pentland, J. 1996. The role of mental imagery in the creation of false childhood memories. *Journal of Memory and Language, 35,* 101–17.

Hyman, I. E., and Billings, F. J. 1998. Individual differences and the creation of false childhood memories. *Memory, 6,* 1–20.

Hyman, I. E. 2018a, September 24. A Supreme Court nominee, a sexual assault, and memory. *Psychology Today.* https://www.psychologytoday.com/us/blog/mental-mishaps/201809/supreme-court-nominee-sexual-assault-and-memory.

Hyman, I. E. 2018b, September 30. Is the Kavanaugh sexual assault accusation a false memory? *Psychology Today.* https://www.psychologytoday.com/us/blog/mental-mishaps/201809/is-the-kavanaugh-sexual-assault-accusation-false-memory.

Ingvar, D. H. 1979. Hyperfrontal distribution of the cerebral grey matter flow in resting wakefulness: On the functional anatomy of the conscious state. *Acta Neurologica Scandinavica, 60,* 12–25.

Ingvar, D. H. 1985. "Memory of the future": An essay on the temporal organization of conscious awareness. *Human Neurobiology, 4,* 127–36.

Innocence Project. n.d. DNA exonerations in the United States. https://innocenceproject.org/dna-exonerations-in-the-united-states/.

Iyduri, L., Blackwell, S. E., Meiser-Stedman, R., Watson, P. C., Bonsall, M. B., Geddes, J. R., Nobre, A. C., and Holmes, E. A. 2018. Preventing intrusive memories after trauma via a brief intervention training involving Tetris computer game play in the emergency department: A proof-of-concept randomized controlled trial. *Molecular Psychiatry, 23,* 674–82.

Jack, C. R., Petersen, R. C., Xu, Y., O'Brien, P. C., Smith, G. E., Ivnik, R. J., Tangalos, E. G., and Kokmen, E. 1998. Rate of medial temporal lobe atrophy in typical aging and Alzheimer's disease. *Neurology, 51,* 993–99.

Jack, D. 1998, July 11. Between the lines of writer's fall from literary pinnacle. *Scotsman,* p. 3.

Jacoby, L. L., Kelley, C. M., Brown, J., and Jasechko, J. 1989a. Becoming famous overnight: Limits on the ability to avoid unconscious influences of the past. *Journal of Personality and Social Psychology, 56,* 326–38.

Jacoby, L. L., Kelley, C. M., and Dywan, J. 1989b. Memory attributions. In H. L. Roediger III and F. I. M. Craik (eds.), *Varieties of memory and consciousness: Essays in honour of Endel Tulving* (pp. 391–422). Hillsdale, N.J.: Erlbaum Associates.

Jacoby, L. L. 1991. A process dissociation framework: Separating automatic from intentional uses of memory. *Journal of Memory and Language, 30,* 513–41.

Jacoby, L. L. 1999. Ironic effects of repetition: Measuring age-related differences in memory. *Journal of Experimental Psychology: Learning, Memory, and Cognition, 25,* 3–22.

James, E. L., Bonsall, M. B., Hoppitt, L., Tunbridge, E. N., Geddes, J. R., Milton, A. L., and Holmes, E. A. 2015. Computer game play reduces intrusive memories of experimental trauma via reconsolidation-update mechanisms. *Psychological Science, 26,* 1201–15.

James, L. E., Schmank, C. J., Castro, N., and Buchanan, T. W. 2018. Tip of the tongue states increase under evaluative observation. *Journal of Psycholinguistic Research, 47,* 169–78.

James, T. W., and Kimura, D. 1997. Sex differences in remembering the locations of objects in an array: Location-shifts versus locations-exchanges. *Evolution and Human Behavior, 18,* 155–63.

Javadi, A.-H., Emo, B., Howard, L. R., Zisch, F. E., Yu, Y., Knight, R., Silva, J. P., and Spiers, H. J. 2017. Hippocampal and prefrontal processing of network topology to simulate the future. *Nature Communications, 8,* 14652. https://doi.org/10.1038/ncomms14652.

Jennings, J. M., and Jacoby, L. L. 1993. Automatic versus intentional uses of memory: Aging, attention, and control. *Psychology and Aging, 8,* 283–93.

Jing, H. G., Szpunar, K. K., and Schacter, D. L. 2016. Interpolated testing influences focused attention and improves integration of information during a video-recorded lecture. *Journal of Experimental Psychology: Applied, 22,* 305–18.

Jing, H. G., Madore, K. P., and Schacter, D. L. 2017. Preparing for what might happen: An episodic specificity induction impacts the generation of alternative future events. *Cognition, 169,* 118–28.

Johnson, M. K., and Chalfonte, B. L. 1994. Binding of complex memories: The role of reactivation and the hippocampus. In D. L. Schacter and E. Tulving (eds.), *Memory systems 1994* (pp. 311–50). Cambridge, Mass.: MIT Press.

Johnson, M. K., Nolde, S. E, Mather, M., Kounios, J., Schacter, D. L., and Curran, T. 1997. The similarity of brain activity associated with true and false recognition memory depends on test format. *Psychological Science, 8,* 250–57.

Jones, G. V., and Langford, S. 1987. Phonological blocking and the tip of the tongue state. *Cognition, 26,* 115–22.

Jones, G. V. 1989. Back to Woodworth: Role of interlopers in the tip-of-the-tongue phenomenon. *Memory and Cognition, 27,* 69–76.

Jonker, T. R., Seli, P., and MacLeod, C. M. 2015. Retrieval-induced forgetting and context. *Current Directions in Psychological Science, 24,* 273–78.

Joormann, J., Hertel, P. T., Brozovich, F., and Gotlib, I. H. 2005. Remembering the good, forgetting the bad: Intentional forgetting of emotional material in depression. *Journal of Abnormal Psychology, 114,* 640–48.

Joormann, J., Hertel, P. T., LeMoult, J., and Gotlib, I. H. 2009. Training forgetting of negative material in depression. *Journal of Abnormal Psychology, 118,* 34–43.

Jost, J. T., Rudman, L. A., Blair, I. V., Carney, D. R., Dasgupta, N., Glaser, J., and Hardin, C. D. 2009. The existence of implicit bias is beyond reasonable doubt: A refutation of ideological and methodological objections and executive summary of ten studies that no manager should ignore. *Research in Organizational Behavior, 29,* 39–69.

Kamio, Y., and Toichi, M. 2007. Memory illusion in high-functioning autism and Asperger's disorder. *Journal of Autism and Developmental Disorders, 37,* 867–76.

Kanowski, S., Hermann, W. M., Stephan, K., Wierich, W., and Horr, R. 1996. Proof of efficacy of the Ginkgo biloba special extract EGb 761 in outpatients suffering from mild to moderate primary degenerative dementia of the Alzheimer type or multi-infarct dementia. *Pharmacopsychiatry, 29,* 47–56.

Kanwisher, N., McDermott, J., and Chun, M. M. 1997. The fusiform face area: A module in human extrastriate cortex specialized for face perception. *Journal of Neuroscience, 17,* 4302–11.

Kapur, N. 1999. Syndromes of retrograde amnesia: A conceptual and empirical synthesis. *Psychological Bulletin, 125,* 800–825.

Karney, B. R., and Coombs, R. H. 2000. Memory bias in long-term close relationships: Consistency or improvement? *Personality and Social Psychology Bulletin, 26,* 959–70.

Karpicke, J. D., and Aue, W. R. 2015. The testing effect is alive and well with complex materials. *Educational Psychology Review, 27,* 317–26.

Kassin, S. M., and Wrightsman, L. S. 1981. Coerced confessions, judicial instruction, and mock juror verdicts. *Journal of Applied Social Psychology, 11,* 489–506.

Kassin, S. M., and Kiechel, K. L. 1996. The social psychology of false confessions: Compliance, internalization, and confabulation. *Psychological Science, 7,* 125–28.

Kassin, S. M., Drizin, S. A., Grisso, T., Gudjonsson, G. H., Leo, R. A., and Redlich, A. D. 2010. Police-induced confessions: Risk factors and recommendations. *Law and Human Behavior, 34,* 3–38.

Kassin, S. M. 2017. False confessions: How can psychology so basic be so counterintuitive? *American Psychologist, 72,* 951–64.

Kawabata, Y. 1999. Yumiura. In *First snow on Fuji* (pp. 187–99). Washington, D.C.: Counterpoint.

Keane, T. M., Fairbank, J. A., Caddell, J. M., and Zimering, R. T. 1989. Implosive (flooding) therapy reduces symptoms of PTSD in Vietnam combat veterans. *Behavior Therapy, 20,* 245–60.

Kebbell, M. R., and Wagstaff, G. F. 1998. Hypnotic interviewing: The best way to interview eyewitnesses? *Behavioral Sciences and the Law, 16,* 115–29.

Kebbell, M. R., Milne, R., and Wagstaff, G. F. 1999. The Cognitive Interview: A survey of its forensic effectiveness. *Psychology, Crime and Law, 5,* 101–15.

Kessler, H., Holmes, E. A., Blackwell, S. E., Schmidt, A. C., Schweer, J. M., Bücker, A., Herpetz, S., Axmacher, N., and Kehyayan, A. 2018. Reducing intrusive memories of trauma using a visuospatial interference intervention with inpatients with post-traumatic stress disorder (PTSD). *Journal of Consulting and Clinical Psychology, 86,* 1076–90.

Keuler, D. J., and Safer, M. A. 1998. Memory bias in the assessment and recall of pre-exam anxiety: How anxious was I? *Applied Cognitive Psychology, 12,* S127–37.

Kihlstrom, J. F. 1995. The trauma-memory argument. *Consciousness and Cognition, 4,* 63–67.

Killany, R. R., Gomez-Isla, T., Moss, M., Kikinis, R., Sandor, T., Tanzi, R., Jones, K., Hyman, B. T., and Albert, M. S. 2000. Use of structural magnetic resonance imaging to predict who will get Alzheimer's disease. *Annals of Neurology, 47,* 430–39.

Kindt, M., and van Emmerik, A. 2016. New avenues for treating emotional memory disorders: Towards a reconsolidation intervention for posttraumatic stress disorder. *Therapeutic Advances in Psychopharmacology, 6,* 283–95.

Kirkpatrick, L. A., and Hazan, C. 1994. Attachment styles and close relationships: A four-year prospective study. *Personal Relationships, 1,* 123–42.

Klein, S. B., Loftus, J., and Kihlstrom, J. F. 2002. Memory and temporal experience: The effects of episodic memory loss on an amnesic patient's ability to remember the past and imagine the future. *Social Cognition, 20,* 353–79.

Klein, S. B. 2019. An essay on the ontological foundations and psychological realization of forgetting. *Psychology of Consciousness: Theory, Research, and Practice, 6,* 292–305.

Knowlton, B. J., and Squire, L. R. 1993. The learning of categories: Parallel brain systems for item memory and category level knowledge. *Science, 262,* 1747–49.

Konishi, K., and Bohbot, V. D. 2013. Spatial navigation strategies correlate with gray matter of the hippocampus of healthy older adults tested in a virtual maze. *Frontiers in Aging Neuroscience, 5.* https://doi.org/10.3389/fnagi.2013.00001.

Kornell, N., and Metcalfe, J. 2006. "Blockers" do not block recall during tip-of-the-tongue states. *Metacognition and Learning, 1,* 248–61.

Koutstaal, W., and Schacter, D. L. 1997a. Gist-based false recognition of pictures in older and younger adults. *Journal of Memory and Language, 37,* 555–83.

Koutstaal, W., and Schacter, D. L. 1997b. Inaccuracy and inaccessibility in memory retrieval: Contributions from cognitive psychology and cognitive neuropsychology. In P. S. Appelbaum, L. Uyehara, and M. Elin (eds.), *Trauma and memory: Clinical and legal controversies* (pp. 93–137). New York: Oxford University Press.

Koutstaal, W., and Schacter, D. L. 1997c. Intentional forgetting and voluntary thought suppression: Two potential methods for coping with childhood trauma. In L. J. Dickstein, M. B. Riba, and J. M. Oldham (eds.), *Review of psychiatry* (vol. 16, pp. 79–121). Washington, D.C.: American Psychiatric Press.

Koutstaal, W., Schacter, D. L., Galluccio, L., and Stofer, K. A. 1999a. Reducing gist-based false recognition in older adults: Encoding and retrieval manipulations. *Psychology and Aging, 14,* 220–37.

Koutstaal, W., Schacter, D. L., Johnson, M. K, and Galluccio, L. 1999b. Facilitation and impairment of event memory produced by photograph review. *Memory and Cognition,* *27,* 478–93.

Koutstaal, W., Schacter, D. L., Verfaellie, M., Brenner, C. J., and Jackson, E. M. 1999c. Perceptually based false recognition of novel objects in amnesia: Effects of category size and similarity to category prototypes. *Cognitive Neuropsychology, 16,* 317–41.

Koutstaal, W., Verfaellie, M., and Schacter, D. L. 2001a. Recognizing identical vs. similar categorically related common objects: Further evidence for degraded gist-representations in amnesia. *Neuropsychology, 15,* 268–89.

Koutstaal, W., Wagner, A. D., Rotte, M., Maril, A., Buckner, R. L., and Schacter, D. L. 2001b. Perceptual specificity in visual object priming: fMRI evidence for a laterality difference in fusiform cortex. *Neuropsychologia, 39,* 184–99.

Krebs, J. R., and Davies, N. B. 1993. *An introduction to behavioural ecology* (3d. ed.). Oxford: Blackwell Scientific.

Kriegeskorte N., and Kievit, R. A. 2013. Representational geometry: Integrating cognition, computation, and the brain. *Trends in Cognitive Sciences, 17,* 401–12.

Kroll, N. E. A., Knight, R. T., Metcalfe, J., Wolf, E. S., and Tulving, E. 1996. Cohesion failure as a source of memory illusions. *Journal of Memory and Language, 35,* 176–96.

Kurkela, K. A., and Dennis, N. A. 2016. Event-related fMRI studies of false memory: An activation likelihood estimation meta-analysis. *Neuropsychologia, 81,* 149–67.

Lai, C. K., Marini, M., Lehr, S. A., et al. 2014. Reducing implicit racial preferences: I. A comparative investigation of 17 interventions. *Journal of Experimental Psychology: General, 143,* 1765–85.

Lai, C. K., Skinner, A. L., Cooley, E., et al. 2016. Reducing implicit racial preferences: II. Intervention effectiveness across time. *Journal of Experimental Psychology: General, 145,* 1001–16.

Landin-Romero, R., Tan, R., Hodges, J. R., and Kumfor, F. 2016. An update on semantic dementia: genetics, imaging, and pathology. *Alzheimer's Research and Therapy, 8,* article number 52. https://alzres.biomedcentral.com/articles/10.1186/s13195-016-0219-5.

Langer, E. J. 1997. *The power of mindful learning.* Reading, Mass.: Addison-Wesley.

Laws, K. R., Sweetnam, H., and Kondel, T. K. 2012. Is *Ginkgo biloba* a cognitive enhancer in healthy individuals? A meta-analysis. *Human Psychopharmacology: Clinical and Experimental, 27,* 527–632.

Lazarus, R. S. 1991. *Emotion and adaptation.* New York: Oxford University Press.

Leary, M. R. 1982. Hindsight distortion and the 1980 presidential election. *Personality and Social Psychology Bulletin, 8,* 257–63.

LeBlanc, P. 2020, February 15. Klobuchar and Steyer couldn't name Mexico's president while campaigning in Nevada. CNN. https://www.cnn.com/2020/02/15/politics/klobuchar-steyer-mexican-president-telemundo-interview/index.html.

LeDoux, J. E. 1996. *The emotional brain.* New York: Simon and Schuster.

Lee, J. C. L., Nader, K., and Schiller, D. 2017. An update on memory reconsolidation updating. *Trends in Cognitive Sciences, 21,* 531–45.

Lee, T. 2017, January 18. Rick Perry is Trump's pick to run Energy. He once forgot the agency's name. Vox. https://www.vox.com/2015/6/4/8731957/rick-perry-oops.

Lepore, L., and Brown, R. 1997. Category and stereotype activation: Is prejudice inevitable? *Journal of Personality and Social Psychology, 72,* 275–87.

LePort, A. K. R., Mattfield, A. T., Dickinson-Anson, H., Fallon, J. H., Stark, C. E. L., Kruggel, F., Cahill, L., and McGaugh, J. L. 2012. Behavioral and neuroanatomical investigation of Highly Superior Autobiographical Memory (HSAM). *Neurobiology of Learning and Memory, 98,* 78–92.

LePort, A. K. R., Stark, S. M., McGaugh, J. L., and Stark, C. E. L. 2016. Highly Superior Autobiographical Memory: Quality and quantity of retention over time. *Frontiers in Psychology.* https://doi.org/10.3389/fpsyg.2015.02017.

Leskin, G. A., Kaloupek, D. G., and Keane, T. M. 1998. Treatment for traumatic memories: Review and recommendations. *Clinical Psychology Review, 18,* 983–1002.

Levelt, W. 1989. *Speaking: From intention to articulation.* Cambridge, Mass.: MIT Press.

Levine, L. J. 1997. Reconstructing memory for emotions. *Journal of Experimental Psychology: General, 126,* 165–77.

Levinson, A. 1999, February 22. Two-time memory champion still lives by Post-its. *San Antonio Express-News,* p. 5A.

Lieberman, M. D., Ochsner, K. N., Gilbert, D. T., and Schacter, D. L. 2001. Do amnesics exhibit cognitive dissonance reduction? The role of explicit memory and attention in attitude change. *Psychological Science, 12,* 135–40.

Lindquist, S. L., and McLean, J. P. 2011. Daydreaming and its correlates in an educational environment. *Learning and Individual Differences, 21,* 158–67.

Lindsay, D. S., and Read, J. D. 1994. Psychotherapy and memories of childhood sexual abuse: A cognitive perspective. *Applied Cognitive Psychology, 8,* 281–338.

Lindsay, D. S., Hagen, L., Read, J. D., Wade, K. A., and Garry, M. 2004. True photographs and false memories. *Psychological Science, 15,* 149–54.

Loftus, E. F., Loftus, G., and Messo, J. 1987. Some facts about "weapon focus." *Law and Human Behavior, 11,* 55–62.

Loftus, E. F. 1993. The reality of repressed memories. *American Psychologist, 48,* 518–37.

Loftus, E. F., and Ketcham, K. 1994. *The myth of repressed memory: False memories and allegations of sexual abuse.* New York: St. Martin's Press.

Loftus, E. F., and Pickrell, J. E. 1995. The formation of false memories. *Psychiatric Annals, 25,* 720–25.

Loftus, E. F., Feldman, J., and Dashiell, R. 1995. The reality of illusory memories. In D. L. Schacter (ed.), *Memory distortion: How minds, brains, and societies reconstruct the past* (pp. 47–68). Cambridge, Mass.: Harvard University Press.

Loftus, E. F. 2003. Make-believe memories. *American Psychologist, 58,* 867–73.

Loftus, E. F. 2005. Planting misinformation in the human mind: A 30-year investigation of the malleability of memory. *Learning and Memory, 12,* 361–66.

Logan, G. D. 1988. Toward an instance theory of automatization. *Psychological Review, 95,* 492–527.

Long, P. 2017, May 29. My déjà vu is so extreme I can't tell what's real anymore. *Mosaic.* https://mosaicscience.com/story/my-deja-vu-so-extreme-i-cant-tell-whats-real-anymore/.

Lorayne, H., and Lucas, J. 1996. *The memory book.* New York: Ballantine Books.

Lorenz, K. 1935/1970. Companions as factors in the bird's environment. In R. Martin (ed.), *Studies in animal and human behavior* (vol. 1, pp. 101–258). London: Methuen.

Luria, A. R. 1968. *The mind of a mnemonist: A little book about a vast memory* (Solotaroff, L., trans.). New York: Basic Books.

Lynn, S. J., and McConkey, K. M. (eds.). 1998. *Truth in memory.* New York: Guilford Press.

Lyubormirsky, S., Caldwell, N. D., and Nolen-Hoeksema, S. 1998. Effects of ruminative and distracting responses to depressed mood on retrieval of autobiographical memories. *Journal of Personality and Social Psychology, 75,* 166–77.

Mac Donald, H. 2017, October 9. The false "science" of implicit bias. *Wall Street Journal.* https://www.wsj.com/articles/the-false-science-of-implicit-bias-1507590908.

MacLeod, C. M. 1991. Half a century of research on the Stroop effect: An integrative review. *Psychological Bulletin, 109,* 163–203.

Macrae, C. N., Milne, A. B., and Bodenhausen, G. V. 1994. Stereotypes as energy-saving devices: A peek inside the cognitive toolbox. *Journal of Personality and Social Psychology, 66,* 37–47.

Madore, K. P., Gaesser, B., and Schacter, D. L. 2014. Constructive episodic simulation: Dissociable effects of a specificity induction on remembering, imagining, and describing in young and older adults. *Journal of Experimental Psychology: Learning, Memory, and Cognition, 40,* 609–22.

Madore, K. P., Khazenzon, A. M., Backes, C. W., Jiang, J., Uncapher, M. R., Norcia, A. M., and Wagner, A. D. 2020. Memory failure predicted by attention lapsing and media multitasking. *Nature.* https://doi.org/10.1038/s41586-020-2870-z.

Maguire, E. A., Gadian, D. G., Johnsrude, I. S., Good, C. D., Ashburner, J., Frackowiak, R. S. J., and Frith, C. D. 2000. Navigation-related structural change in the hippocampi of taxi drivers. *Proceedings of the National Academy of Sciences USA, 97,* 4398–403.

Mak, A. 2018, April 20. What can Starbucks accomplish? *Slate.* https://slate.com/technology/2018/04/does-implicit-bias-training-work-starbucks-racial-bias-plan-will-probably-fail.html.

Malinoski, P. T., and Lynn, S. J. 1999. The plasticity of early memory reports: Social pressure, hypnotizability, compliance, and interrogative suggestibility. *International Journal of Clinical and Experimental Hypnosis, 47,* 320–45.

Maril, A., Wagner, A. D., and Schacter, D. L. 2001. On the tip of the tongue: An event-related fMRI study of retrieval failure and cognitive conflict. *Neuron, 31,* 653–60.

Markowitsch, H. J., Fink, G. R., Thone, A. I. M., Kessler, J., and Heiss, W.-D. 1997. Persistent psychogenic amnesia with a PET-proven organic basis. *Cognitive Neuropsychiatry, 2,* 135–58.

Markowitsch, H. J. 1999. Functional neuroimaging correlates of functional amnesia. *Memory, 5/6,* 561–83.

Marsh, E. J., and Rajaram, S. 2019. The digital expression of the mind: Implications of Internet usage for memory and cognition. *Journal of Applied Research in Memory and Cognition, 8,* 1–14.

Marsh, R. L., Landau, J. D., and Hicks, J. L. 1997. Contributions of inadequate source monitoring to unconscious plagiarism during idea generation. *Journal of Experimental Psychology: Learning, Memory, and Cognition, 23,* 886–97.

Marsh, R. L., and Hicks, J. L. 1998. Event-based prospective memory and executive control of working memory. *Journal of Experimental Psychology: Learning, Memory, and Cognition, 24*, 336–49.

Martin, M. 1986. Aging and patterns of change in everyday memory and cognition. *Human Learning, 5*, 63–74.

Mather, M., Henkel, L. A., and Johnson, M. K. 1997. Evaluating characteristics of false memories: Remember/know judgments and memory characteristics questionnaire compared. *Memory and Cognition, 25*, 826–37.

Maylor, E. A. 1990. Age and prospective memory. *Quarterly Journal of Experimental Psychology, 42A*, 471–93.

Maylor, E. A. 1996. Does prospective memory decline with age? In M. Brandimonte, G. O. Einstein, and M. A. McDaniel (eds.), *Prospective memory: Theory and applications* (pp. 173–98). Mahwah, N.J.: Erlbaum Associates.

Maylor, E. A. 1997. Proper name retrieval in old age: Converging evidence against disproportionate impairment. *Aging, Neuropsychology, and Cognition, 4*, 211–26.

Mazzoni, G. A., and Loftus, E. F. 1998. Dream interpretation can change beliefs about the past. *Psychotherapy, 35*, 177–87.

McBurney, D. H., Gaulin, S. J. C., Devineni, T., and Adams, C. 1997. Superior spatial memory of women: Stronger evidence for the gathering hypothesis. *Evolution and Human Behavior, 18*, 165–74.

McClelland, J. L. 1995. Constructive memory and memory distortions: A parallel-distributed processing approach. In D. L. Schacter (ed.), *Memory distortion: How minds, brains, and societies reconstruct the past* (pp. 69–90). Cambridge, Mass.: Harvard University Press.

McDaniel, M. A., and Einstein, G. O. 1992. Aging and prospective memory: Basic findings and practical applications. *Advances in Learning and Behavioral Disabilities, 7*, 87–105.

McDaniel, M. A., and Einstein, G. O. 1993. The importance of cue familiarity and cue distinctiveness in prospective memory. *Memory, 1*, 23–41.

McFarland, C., and Ross, M. 1987. The relation between current impressions and memories of self and dating partners. *Personality and Social Psychology Bulletin, 13*, 228–38.

McFarland, C., Ross, M., and DeCourville, N. 1989. Women's theories of menstruation and biases in recall of menstrual symptoms. *Journal of Personality and Social Psychology, 57*, 522–31.

McKenna, P., and Warrington, E. K. 1980. Testing for nominal dysphasia. *Journal of Neurology, Neurosurgery, and Psychiatry, 42*, 781–88.

McKenzie, V. 2018, August 21. Memory's surprising role in child death trials. The Crime Report. https://thecrimereport.org/2018/08/21/when-forgetting-kills-a-child/.

McNally, R. J. 1999. Research on eye movement desensitization and reprocessing (EMDR) as treatment for PTSD. *PTSD Research Quarterly, 10*, 1–7.

Memon, A., and Higham, P. A. 1999. A review of the Cognitive Interview. *Psychology, Crime and Law, 5*, 177–96.

Memon, A., Meissner, C. A., and Fraser, J. 2010. The Cognitive Interview: A meta-analytic review and study space analysis of the past 25 years. *Psychology, Public Policy, and Law, 16*, 340–72.

Mercier, H. 2017. How gullible are we? A review of the evidence from psychology and social science. *Review of General Psychology, 21,* 103–22.

Messer, S. 2017, June 14. How 4 technologies designed to prevent hot car deaths work. ABC News. https://abcnews.go.com/US/technologies-designed-prevent-hot-car-deaths-work/story?id=47991074.

Metcalfe, J., Funnell, M., and Gazzaniga, M. S. 1995. Right-hemisphere memory superiority: Studies of a split-brain patient. *Psychological Science, 6,* 157–64.

Meyer, A. S., and Bock, K. 1992. The tip-of-the-tongue phenomenon: Blocking or partial activation? *Memory and Cognition, 20,* 715–26.

Milders, M., Deelman, B., and Berg, I. 1998. Rehabilitation of memory for people's names. *Memory, 6,* 21–36.

Mill, J. S. 1843. *A system of logic.* London: Longman.

Miller, S. S. 2019, August 9. High-tech alarms go off when kids are left in hot cars. Mashable. https://mashable.com/article/car-seat-alarms-prevent-hot-car-death/.

Mineka, S., and Nugent, K. 1995. Mood-congruent memory biases in anxiety and depression. In D. L. Schacter (ed.), *Memory distortion: How minds, brains, and societies reconstruct the past* (pp. 173–96). Cambridge, Mass.: Harvard University Press.

Misanin, J. R., Miller, R. R., and Lewis, D. J. 1968. Retrograde amnesia produced by electroconvulsive shock after reactivation of a consolidated memory trace. *Science, 160,* 203–4.

Møller, A. P., and Swaddle, J. P. 1997. *Asymmetry, developmental stability and evolution.* New York: Oxford University Press.

Mooneyham, B. W., and Schooler, J. W. 2013. The costs and benefits of mind-wandering: A review. *Canadian Journal of Experimental Psychology, 67,* 11–18.

Moss, M. 2000, May 31. The story behind a soldier's story. *New York Times,* p. A1.

Mottron, L., Belleville, S., Stip, E., and Morasse, K. 1998. Atypical memory performance in an autistic savant. *Memory, 6,* 593–607.

Mueller, E. 2019, December 19. Elizabeth Warren wants you to know that she takes selfies. Politico. https://www.politico.com/news/2019/12/19/elizabeth-warren-selfies-debate-088552.

Muir, K., Madill, A., and Brown, C. 2017. Individual differences in emotional processing and autobiographical memory: Interoceptive awareness and alexithymia in the fading affect bias. *Cognition and Emotion, 31,* 1392–404.

Munsterberg, H. 1908. *On the witness stand: Essays on psychology and crime.* New York: Clark, Boardman, Doubleday.

Murayama, K., and Kuhbandner, C. 2011. Money enhances memory consolidation — but only for boring material. *Cognition, 119,* 120–24.

Murphy, G., Loftus, E. F., Grady, R. H., Levine, L. J., and Greene, C. M. 2019. False memories for fake news during Ireland's abortion referendum. *Psychological Science, 30,* 1449–59.

Murray, S., Stanley, M., McPhetres, J., Pennycook, G., and Seli, P. 2020. "I've said it before and I will say it again . . .": Repeating statements made by Donald Trump increases perceived truthfulness for individuals across the political spectrum. PsyArXiv Preprints. https://psyarxiv.com/9evzc/.

Myers, L. B., Brewin, C. R., and Power, M. J. 1998. Repressive coping and the directed forgetting of emotional material. *Journal of Abnormal Psychology, 107,* 141–48.

Nadel, L., and Zola-Morgan, S. 1984. Infantile amnesia: A neuro-biological perspective. In M. Moscovitch (ed.), *Infant memory* (pp. 145–72). New York: Plenum Press.

Nader, K., Schafe, G. E., and LeDoux, J. E. 2000. Fear memories require protein synthesis in the amygdala for reconsolidation after retrieval. *Nature, 406,* 722–26.

Nathan, D., and Snedeker, M. 1995. *Satan's silence: Ritual abuse and the making of a modern American witch hunt.* New York: Basic Books.

National Safety Council. n.d. Record number of children died in hot cars in 2018. https://www.nsc.org/road-safety/safety-topics/child-passenger-safety/kids-hot-cars.

Newton, P. 1998, January 30. Prescott forgets name of the game. *Times* (London).

Noice, H., and Noice, T. 1996. Two approaches to learning a theatrical script. *Memory, 4,* 1–18.

Noice, H., Noice, T., Perrig-Chiello, P., and Perrig, W. 1999. Improving memory in older adults by instructing them in professional actors' learning strategies. *Applied Cognitive Psychology, 13,* 315–28.

Nolde, S. F., Johnson, M. K., and D'Esposito, M. 1998. Left prefrontal activation during episodic remembering: an event-related fMRI study. *NeuroReport, 9,* 3509–14.

Nolen-Hoeksema, S. 1991. Responses to depression and their effects on the duration of depressive episodes. *Journal of Abnormal Psychology, 100,* 569–82.

Nørby, S. 2015. Why forget? On the adaptive value of memory loss. *Perspectives on Psychological Science, 10,* 551–78.

Nørby, S. 2018. Forgetting and emotional regulation in mental health, anxiety and depression. *Memory, 26,* 342–63.

Nordell, J. 2017, May 7. Is this how discrimination ends? *Atlantic.* https://www.theatlantic.com/science/archive/2017/05/unconscious-bias-training/525405/.

Norman, K. A., and Schacter, D. L. 1997. False recognition in young and older adults: Exploring the characteristics of illusory memories. *Memory and Cognition, 25,* 838–48.

Nosek, B. A., Banaji, M. R., and Greenwald, A. G. 2002. Harvesting implicit group attitudes and beliefs from a demonstration website. *Group Dynamics: Theory, Research, and Practice, 6,* 101–15.

Nyberg, L., and Cabeza, R. 2000. Brain imaging of memory. In E. Tulving and F. I. M. Craik (eds.), *The Oxford handbook of memory* (pp. 501–19). New York: Oxford University Press.

O'Carroll, R. E., Drysdale, E., Cahill, L., Shajahan, P., and Ebmeier, K. P. 1999a. Memory for emotional material: A comparison of central versus peripheral beta blockade. *Journal of Psychopharmacology, 13,* 32–39.

O'Carroll, R. E., Drysdale, E., Cahill, L., Shajahan, P., and Ebmeier, K. P. 1999b. Stimulation of the noradrenergic system enhances and blockade reduces memory for emotional material in man. *Psychological Medicine, 29,* 1083–88.

Ochsner, K. N. 2000. Are affective events richly recollected or simply familiar? The experience and process of recognizing feelings past. *Journal of Experimental Psychology: General, 129,* 242–61.

Ochsner, K. N., and Schacter, D. L. 2000. Constructing the emotional past: A social-cognitive-neuroscience approach to emotion and memory. In J. Borod (ed.), *The neuropsychology of emotion* (pp. 163–93). New York: Oxford University Press.

Offer, D., Kaiz, M., Howard, K. I., and Bennett, E. S. 2000. The altering of reporting experiences. *Journal of the American Academy of Child and Adolescent Psychiatry, 39,* 735–42.

Ofshe, R. J. 1992. Inadvertent hypnosis during interrogation: False confession due to dissociative state; mis-identified multiple personality and the satanic cult hypothesis. *International Journal of Clinical and Experimental Hypnosis, 40,* 125–56.

Okuda, J., Fujii, T., Yamadori, A., Kawashima, R., Tsukiura, T., Fukatsu, R., Suzuki, K., Ito, M., and Fukuda, H. 1998. Participation of the prefrontal cortices in prospective memory: Evidence from a PET study in humans. *Neuroscience Letters, 253,* 127–30.

Okuda, J., Fujii, T., Ohtake, H., Tsukiura, T., Tanji, K., Suzuki, K., Kawashima, R., Fukuda, H., Itoh, M., and Yamadori, A. 2003. Thinking of the future and the past: The roles of the frontal pole and the medial temporal lobes. *NeuroImage, 19,* 1369–80.

Open Science Collaboration. 2015. Estimating the reproducibility of psychological science. *Science, 349,* aac4716.

Orwell, G. 1950/1984. *1984.* New York: Signet Classic.

Otterman, S. 2019, August 1. He left his twins in a hot car and they died. Accident or crime? *New York Times.* https://www.nytimes.com/2019/08/01/nyregion/children-left-to-die-in-hot-cars-accident-or-murder.html.

Paley, W. 1802/1986. *Natural theology.* Charlottesville, Va.: Lincoln Rembrandt.

Park, D. C., and Kidder, D. P. 1996. Prospective memory and medication adherence. In M. Brandimonte, G. O. Einstein, and M. A. McDaniel (eds.), *Prospective memory: Theory and applications* (pp. 369–90). Mahwah, N.J.: Erlbaum Associates.

Parker, E. S., Cahill, L., and McGaugh, J. L. 2006. A case of unusual autobiographical remembering. *Neurocase, 12,* 35–49.

Parker, K. 2001, July 5. Leaving the baby in the hot car. *Orlando Sentinel.* https://helenair.com/news/opinion/leaving-the-baby-in-the-hot-car/article_8f6a1254-13b9-5ad6-8151-2dc5cdee44d3.html.

Parkes, C. M. 1986. *Bereavement: Studies of grief in adult life.* London: Tavistock.

Patihis, L., Frenda, S. J., LePort, A. K. E., Petersen, N., Nichols, R. M., Stark, C. E. L., McGaugh, J. L., and Loftus, E. F. 2013. False memories in highly superior autobiographical memory individuals. *Proceedings of the National Academy of Sciences USA, 110,* 20947–52.

Patihis, L., Ho, L. Y., Tingen, I. W., Lillienfeld, S. O., and Loftus, E. F. 2014. Are the "memory wars" over? A scientist-practitioner gap in beliefs about repressed memory. *Psychological Science, 25,* 519–30.

Patihis, L., and Pendergrast, M. H. 2019. Reports of recovered memories of abuse in therapy in a large age-representative U.S. national sample: Therapy type and decade comparisons. *Clinical Psychological Science, 7,* 3–21.

Patterson K., Nestor P. J., and Rogers T. T. 2007. Where do you know what you know? The representation of semantic knowledge in the human brain. *Nature Reviews Neuroscience, 8,* 976–87.

Paulesu, E., Frith, C. D., and Frackowiak, R. S. J. 1993. The neural correlates of the verbal component of working memory. *Nature, 362,* 342–45.

Pawlowski, B., Dunbar, R. I. M., and Lipowicz, A. 2000. Tall men have more reproductive success. *Nature, 403,* 156.

Pendergrast, M. 1995. *Victims of memory: Incest accusations and shattered lives.* Hinesburg, Vt.: Upper Access.

Pendergrast, M. 2017. *The repressed memory epidemic: How it happened and what we need to learn from it.* New York: Springer.

Pennebaker, J. W. 1997. Writing about emotional experiences as a therapeutic process. *Psychological Science, 8,* 162–66.

Pennycook, G., Cannon, T. D., and Rand, D. G. 2018. Prior exposure increases perceived accuracy of fake news. *Journal of Experimental Psychology: General, 147,* 1865–80.

Pennycook, G., and Rand, D. G. 2019. Lazy, not biased: Susceptibility to partisan fake news is better explained by lack of reasoning than by motivated reasoning. *Cognition, 188,* 39–50.

Perfect, T. J., and Hanley, J. R. 1992. The tip-of-the-tongue phenomenon: Do experimenter-presented interlopers have any effect? *Cognition, 45,* 55–75.

Perrett, D. I., Hietanen, J. K., Oram, M. W., and Benson, P. J. 1992. Organization and functions of cells responsive to faces in the temporal cortex. *Philosophical Transactions of the Royal Society of London B: Biological Sciences, 335,* 23–30.

Peterson, C., and Bell, M. 1996. Children's memory for traumatic injury. *Child Development, 67,* 3045–70.

Peterson, L. R., and Peterson, M. J. 1959. Short-term retention of individual verbal items. *Journal of Experimental Psychology, 58,* 193–98.

Petro, S. J., Herrmann, D., Burrows, D., and Moore, C. M. 1991. Usefulness of commercial memory aids as a function of age. *International Journal of Aging and Human Development, 33,* 295–309.

Pezdek, K. 1997. Memory for pictures: A life-span study of the role of visual detail. *Child Development, 58,* 807–15.

Phelps, E. A., and Gazzaniga, M. S. 1992. Hemispheric differences in mnemonic processing: The effects of left hemisphere interpretation. *Neuropsychologia, 30,* 293–97.

Phelps, E. A., LaBar, K. S., Anderson, A. K., O'Connor, K. J., Fulbright, R. K., and Spencer, D. D. 1998. Specifying the contributions of the human amygdala to emotional memory: A case study. *Neurocase, 4,* 527–40.

Phelps, E. A., and Hoffman, S. G. 2019. Memory editing from science fiction to clinical practice. *Nature, 572,* 43–50.

Pierce, C. P. 2000. *Hard to forget: An Alzheimer's story.* New York: Random House.

Pinker, S. 1997a. Evolutionary psychology: An exchange. *New York Review of Books, 44,* 55–58.

Pinker, S. 1997b. *How the mind works.* New York: W. W. Norton.

Plude, D. J., and Schwartz, L. K. 1996. Compact disc–interactive memory training with the elderly. *Educational Gerontology, 22,* 507–21.

Poldrack, R. A. 2018. *The new mind readers: What neuroimaging can and cannot reveal about our thoughts.* Princeton, N.J.: Princeton University Press.

Pollitt, K. 1999, October 18. "Finality" or justice? *The Nation*, 10.

Poole, D. A., and Lindsay, D. S. 1995. Interviewing preschoolers: Effects of nonsuggestive techniques, parental coaching, and learning questions on reports of nonexperienced events. *Journal of Experimental Child Psychology*, 60, 129–54.

Poole, D. A., Lindsay, D. S., Memon, A., and Bull, R. 1995. Psychotherapy and the recovery of memories of childhood sexual abuse: U.S. and British practitioners' opinions, practices, and experiences. *Journal of Consulting and Clinical Psychology*, 63, 426–87.

Porter, S., Yuille, J. C., and Lehman, D. R. 1999. The nature of real, implanted, and fabricated memories for emotional childhood events: Implications for the recovered memory debate. *Law and Human Behavior*, 23, 317–37.

Posner, M. I., and Raichle, M. E. 1994. *Images of the mind*. New York: Scientific American Library.

Price, J. L., and Morris, J. C. 1999. Tangles and plaques in nondemented aging and "preclinical" Alzheimer's disease. *Annals of Neurology*, 45, 358–68.

Price, J. L., and Davis, B. 2008. *The woman who can't forget: The extraordinary story of living with the most remarkable memory known to science*. New York: Free Press.

Purdon, C. 1999. Thought suppression and psychopathology. *Behaviour Research and Therapy*, 37, 1029–54.

Rabinowitz, D. 2003. *No crueler tyrannies: Accusation, false witness, and other terrors of our times*. New York: Free Press.

Raichle, M. E., Fiez, J. A., Videen, T. O., MacLeod, A. M., Pardo, J. V., Fox, P. T., and Petersen, S. E. 1994. Practice-related changes in human brain functional anatomy during nonmotor learning. *Cerebral Cortex*, 4, 8–26.

Rapcsak, S. Z., Reminger, S. L., Glisky, E. L., Kasniak, A. W., and Comer, J. F. 1999. Neuropsychological mechanisms of false facial recognition following frontal lobe damage. *Cognitive Neuropsychology*, 16, 267–92.

Rapson, J. 2019, August 22. 4th grader invents device so parents won't forget their baby in the car. For Every Mom. https://foreverymom.com/family-parenting/4th-grader-invents-device-so-parents-wont-forget-their-baby-in-the-car-sophie-rapson/?fbclid=IwAR0gWoJMac764mDYymfYFC4lG1TlxcLuiDdb8wvi92GyOnwii-UMbeTvBoY.

Rastle, K. G., and Burke, D. M. 1996. Priming the tip of the tongue: Effect of prior processing on word retrieval in young and older adults. *Journal of Memory and Language*, 35, 586–605.

Rauch, S. L., van der Kolk, B. A., Fisler, R. E., Alpert, N. M., Orr, S. P., Savage, C. R., Fishman, A. J., Jenike, M. A., and Pitman, R. K. 1996. A symptom provocation study of posttraumatic stress disorder using positron emission tomography and script-driven imagery. *Archives of General Psychiatry*, 35, 380–87.

Read, J. D., and Bruce, D. 1982. Longitudinal tracking of difficult memory retrievals. *Cognitive Psychology*, 14, 280–300.

Read, J. D., and Lindsay, D. S. (eds.). 1997. *Recollections of trauma: Scientific research and clinical practice*. New York: Plenum Press.

Reason, J. T., and Mycielska, K. 1982. *Absent-minded? The psychology of mental lapses and everyday errors*. Englewood Cliffs, N.J.: Prentice-Hall.

Reason, J. T., and Lucas, D. 1984. Using cognitive diaries to investigate naturally occurring memory blocks. In J. E. Harris and P. E. Morris (eds.), *Everyday memory, actions and absentmindedness* (pp. 53–69). Orlando, Fla.: Academic Press.

Rebok, G. W., Rasmusson, D. X., Bylsma, F. W., and Brandt, J. 1997. Memory improvement tapes: How effective for elderly adults? *Aging, Neuropsychology, and Cognition, 4,* 304–11.

Reed, G. 1988. *The psychology of anomalous experience* (rev. ed.). Buffalo, N.Y.: Prometheus Books.

Rees, G., Russell, C., Frith, C. D., and Driver, J. 1999. Inattentional blindness versus inattentional amnesia for fixated but ignored words. *Science, 286,* 2504–7.

Reeve, H. K., and Sherman, P. W. 1993. Adaptation and the goals of evolutionary research. *Quarterly Review of Biology, 68,* 1–32.

Reinitz, M. T., Morrissey, J., and Demb, J. 1994. The role of attention in face encoding. *Journal of Experimental Psychology: Learning, Memory, and Cognition, 20,* 161–68.

Reiser, M. 1990. Investigative hypnosis. In D. C. Raskin (ed.), *Psychological methods in criminal investigation and evidence* (pp. 151–90). New York: Springer.

Reynolds, M., and Brewin, C. R. 1999. Intrusive memories in depression and post-traumatic stress disorder. *Behaviour Research and Therapy, 37,* 201–15.

Ribot, T. 1882. *Diseases of memory.* New York: Appleton-Century-Crofts.

Richards, B. A., and Frankland, P. W. 2017. The persistence and transience of memory. *Neuron, 94,* 1071–84.

Riefer, D. M., Kevari, M. K., and Kramer, D. L. F. 1995. Name that tune: Eliciting the tip-of-the-tongue experience using auditory stimuli. *Psychological Reports, 77,* 1379–90.

Rimé, B. 1995. Mental rumination, social sharing, and the recovery from emotional exposure. In J. W. Pennebaker (ed.), *Emotion, disclosure, and health* (pp. 271–91). Washington, D.C.: American Psychological Association.

Risko, E. F., Anderson, N., Sarwal, A., Engelhardt, M., and Kingstone, A. 2012. Everyday attention: Variation in mind wandering and memory in a lecture. *Applied Cognitive Psychology, 26,* 234–42

Risko, E. F., and Gilbert, S. J. 2016. Cognitive offloading. *Trends in Cognitive Sciences, 20,* 676–88.

Rissman, J., Greely, H. T., and Wagner, A. D. 2010. Detecting individual memories through the neural decoding of memory states and past experience. *Proceedings of the National Academy of Sciences USA, 107,* 9849–54.

Rissman, J., and Wagner, A. D. 2012. Distributed representations in memory: Insights from functional brain imaging. *Annual Review of Psychology, 63,* 101–28.

Rissman, J., Chow, T. E., Reggente, N., and Wagner, A. D. 2016. Decoding fMRI signatures of real-world autobiographical memory retrieval. *Journal of Cognitive Neuroscience, 28,* 604–20.

Ritchie, T. D., Skowronski, J. J., Hartnett, J. L., Wells, B. M., and Walker, W. R. 2009. The fading affect bias in the context of emotion activation level, mood, and personal theories of emotion change. *Memory, 17,* 428–44.

Ritchie, T. D., Kitsch, K. S., Dromey, M., and Skowronski, J. J. 2019. Individuals who report eating disorder symptoms also exhibit a disrupted fading affecting bias in autobiographical memory. *Memory, 27,* 239–49.

Roediger, H. L., III, and McDermott, K. B. 1995. Creating false memories: Remembering words not presented in lists. *Journal of Experimental Psychology: Learning, Memory, and Cognition, 21,* 803–14.

Roediger, H. L., III, and Karpicke, J. D. 2006. Test-enhanced learning: Taking memory tests improves long-term retention. *Psychological Science, 17,* 249–55.

Roese, N. J. 1997. Counterfactual thinking. *Psychological Bulletin, 121,* 133–48.

Roese, N. J., and Hur, T. 1997. Affective determinants of counterfactual thinking. *Social Cognition, 15,* 274–90.

Roese, N. J., and Maniar, S. D. 1997. Perceptions of purple: Counterfactual and hindsight judgments at Northwestern Wildcats football games. *Personality and Social Psychology Bulletin, 23,* 1245–53.

Rosenbaum, R. S., Kohler, S., Schacter, D. L., Moscovitch, M., Westmacott, R., Black, S. E., Gao, F., and Tulving, E. 2005. The case of K.C.: Contributions of a memory-impaired person to memory theory. *Neuropsychologia, 43,* 989–1021.

Ross, D. F., Ceci, S. I., Dunning, D., and Toglia, M. P. 1994. Unconscious transference and mistaken identity: When a witness misidentifies a familiar but innocent person. *Journal of Applied Psychology, 79,* 918–30.

Ross, M., and Sicoly, R. 1979. Egocentric biases in availability and attribution. *Journal of Personality and Social Psychology, 37,* 322–36.

Ross, M. 1989. Relation of implicit theories to the construction of personal histories. *Psychological Review, 96,* 341–57.

Ross, M., and Wilson, A. E. 1999. Constructing and appraising past selves. In D. L. Schacter and E. Scarry (eds.), *Memory, brain, and belief.* Cambridge, Mass.: Harvard University Press.

Rubin, S. R., Van Petten, C., Glisky, E. L., and Newberg, W. M. 1999. Memory conjunction errors in younger and older adults: Event-related potential and neuropsychological data. *Cognitive Neuropsychology, 16,* 459–88.

Rudy, L., and Goodman, G. S. 1991. Effects of participation on children's reports: Implications for children's testimony. *Developmental Psychology, 27,* 527–38.

Sacchet, M. D., Levy, B. J., Hamilton, J. P., Makismovskiy, A., Hertel, P. T., Joormann, J., Anderson, M. C., Wagner, A. D., and Gotlib, I. H. 2017. Cognitive and neural consequences of memory suppression in major depressive disorder. *Cognitive, Affective, and Behavioral Neuroscience, 17,* 77–93.

Sadeh, T., and Pertzov, Y. 2019. Scale-invariant characteristics of forgetting: Toward a unifying account of hippocampal forgetting across short and long timescales. *Journal of Cognitive Neuroscience, 32,* 1–17.

St. Jacques, P. L., Olm, C., and Schacter, D. L. 2013. Neural mechanisms of reactivation-induced updating that enhance and distort memory. *Proceedings of the National Academy of Sciences USA, 110,* 19671–78.

Salthouse, T. A. 1996. The processing-speed theory of adult age differences in cognition. *Psychological Review, 103,* 403–28.

Sanitioso, R., Kunda, Z., and Fong, G. T. 1990. Motivated recruitment of autobiographical memories. *Journal of Personality and Social Psychology, 59,* 229–41.

Santangelo, V., Cavallina, C., Colucci, C., Santori, A., Macri, S., McGaugh, J. L., and Campolongo, P. 2018. Enhanced brain activity associated with memory access in highly superior autobiographical memory. *Proceedings of the National Academy of Sciences USA, 115,* 7795–800.

Sayette, M. A., Reichel, E. D., and Schooler, J. W. 2009. Lost in the sauce: The effects of alcohol on mind wandering. *Psychological Science, 20,* 747–52.

Schachter, S., and Singer, J. 1962. Cognitive, social, and physiological determinants of emotional learning. *Psychological Review, 69,* 379–99.

Schacter, D. L. 1983. Amnesia observed: Remembering and forgetting in a natural environment. *Journal of Abnormal Psychology, 92,* 236–42.

Schacter, D. L, and Moscovitch, M. 1984. Infants, amnesics, and dissociable memory systems. In M. Moscovitch (ed.), *Infant memory* (pp. 173–216). New York: Plenum Press.

Schacter, D. L. 1987. Implicit memory: History and current status. *Journal of Experimental Psychology: Learning, Memory, and Cognition, 13,* 501–18.

Schacter, D. L. 1996. *Searching for memory: The brain, the mind, and the past.* New York: Basic Books.

Schacter, D. L., Reiman, E., Curran, T., Yun, L. S., Bandy, D., McDermott, K. B., and Roediger, H. L., III. 1996a. Neuroanatomical correlates of veridical and illusory recognition memory: Evidence from positron emission tomography. *Neuron, 17,* 267–74.

Schacter, D. L., Verfaellie, M., and Pradere, D. 1996b. The neuropsychology of memory illusions: False recall and recognition in amnesic patients. *Journal of Memory and Language, 35,* 319–34.

Schacter, D. L., Buckner, R. L., Koutstaal, W., Dale, A. M., and Rosen, B. R. 1997a. Late onset of anterior prefrontal activity during retrieval of veridical and illusory memories: An event-related fMRI study. *NeuroImage, 6,* 259–69.

Schacter, D. L., Koutstaal, W., Johnson, M. K., Gross, M. S., and Angell, K. A. 1997b. False recollection induced by photographs: A comparison of older and younger adults. *Psychology and Aging, 12,* 203–15.

Schacter, D. L., and Buckner, R. L. 1998. Priming and the brain. *Neuron, 20,* 185–95.

Schacter, D. L., Verfaellie, M., Anes, M. D., and Racine, C. 1998. When true recognition suppresses false recognition: Evidence from amnesic patients. *Journal of Cognitive Neuroscience, 10,* 668–79.

Schacter, D. L. (ed.). 1999a. *The cognitive neuropsychology of false memories.* Hove, England: Psychology Press.

Schacter, D. L. 1999b. The seven sins of memory: Insights from psychology and cognitive neuroscience. *American Psychologist, 54,* 182–203.

Schacter, D. L., Israel, L., and Racine, C. 1999. Suppressing false recognition: The distinctiveness heuristic. *Journal of Memory and Language, 40,* 1–24.

Schacter, D. L., and Wagner, A. D. 1999. Medial temporal lobe activations in fMRI and PET studies of episodic encoding and retrieval. *Hippocampus, 9,* 7–24.

Schacter, D. L., and Addis, D. R. 2007a. Constructive memory: The ghosts of past and future. *Nature, 445,* 27.

Schacter, D. L., and Addis, D. R. 2007b. The cognitive neuroscience of constructive memory: Remembering the past and imagining the future. *Philosophical Transactions of the Royal Society B: Biological Sciences, 362,* 773–86.

Schacter, D. L., Addis, D. R., and Buckner, R. L. 2007. Remembering the past to imagine the future: The prospective brain. *Nature Reviews Neuroscience, 8,* 657–61.

Schacter, D. L., Guerin, S. A., and St. Jacques, P. L. 2011. Memory distortion: An adaptive perspective. *Trends in Cognitive Sciences, 15,* 467–74.

Schacter, D. L. 2012. Adaptive constructive processes and the future of memory. *American Psychologist, 67,* 603–13.

Schacter, D. L., Addis, D. R., Hassabis, D., Martin, V. C., Spreng, R. N., and Szpunar, K. K. 2012. The future of memory: Remembering, imagining, and the brain. *Neuron, 76,* 677–94.

Schacter, D. L., and Loftus, E. F. 2013. Memory and law: What can cognitive neuroscience contribute? *Nature Neuroscience, 16,* 119–23.

Schacter, D. L., and Madore, K. P. 2016. Remembering the past and imagining the future: Identifying and enhancing the contribution of episodic memory. *Memory Studies, 9,* 245–55.

Schacter, D. L., Benoit, R. G., and Szpunar, K. K. 2017. Episodic future thinking: Mechanisms and functions. *Current Opinion in Behavioral Sciences, 17,* 41–50.

Schacter, D. L., Devitt, A. L., and Addis, D. R. 2018. Episodic future thinking and cognitive aging. In *Oxford research encyclopedia of psychology.* Oxford University Press. https://oxfordre.com/view/10.1093/acrefore/9780190236557.001.0001/acrefore-9780190236557-e-380.

Schacter, D. L., and Addis, D. R. 2020. Memory and imagination: Perspectives on constructive episodic simulation. In A. Abraham (ed.), *The Cambridge handbook of the imagination* (pp. 111–31). Cambridge: Cambridge University Press.

Schacter, D. L., Carpenter, A. C., Devitt, A. L., and Thakral, P. P. (in press). Memory errors and distortion. In M. J. Kahana and A. D. Wagner (eds.), *The Oxford handbook of human memory.* New York: Oxford University Press.

Scharfe, E., and Bartholomew, K. 1998. Do you remember? Recollections of adult attachment patterns. *Personal Relationships, 5,* 219–34.

Schimmack, U. 2019. The Implicit Association Test: A method in search of a construct. *Perspectives on Psychological Science.* https://doi.org/10.1177/1745691619863798.

Schmand, B., Smit, J., Lindeboom, J., Smits, C., Hooijer, C., Jonker, C., and Deelman, B. 1997. Low education is a genuine risk factor for accelerated memory decline and dementia. *Journal of Clinical Epidemiology, 50,* 1025–33.

Schmank, C. J., and James, L. E. 2019. Adults of all ages experience increased tip-of-the-tongue states under ostensible evaluative observation. *Aging, Neuropsychology, and Cognition.* https://doi.org/10.1080/13825585.2019.1641177.

Schmitz, T. W., Correia, M. M., Ferreira, C. S., Prescot, A. P., and Anderson, M. C. 2017. Hippocampal GABA enables inhibitory control over unwanted thoughts. *Nature Communications, 8,* 1311. https://doi.org/10.1038/s41467-017-00956-z.

Schmolck, H., Buffalo, E. A., and Squire, L. R. 2000. Memory distortions develop over time: Recollections of the O. J. Simpson trial verdict after 15 and 32 months. *Psychological Science, 11,* 39–45.

Schooler, J. W. 1994. Seeking the core: The issues and evidence surrounding recovered accounts of sexual trauma. *Consciousness and Cognition, 3,* 452–69.

Schooler, L., Rhine, R., and Silva, J. C. S. 1999. *Does human memory reflect the environment of early hominids?* Paper presented at the Annual Meeting of the Psychonomic Society, Los Angeles, Calif.

Schwartz, B. L. 1999. Sparkling at the end of the tongue: The etiology of tip-of-the-tongue phenomenology. *Psychonomic Bulletin and Review, 6,* 379–93.

Scoboria, A., Wade, K. A., Lindsay, D. S., Azad, T., Strange, D., Ost, J., and Hyman, I. E. 2017. A mega-analysis of memory reports from eight peer-reviewed false memory implantation studies. *Memory, 25,* 146–63.

Scoville, W. B., and Milner, B. 1957. Loss of recent memory after bilateral hippocampal lesions. *Journal of Neurology, Neurosurgery, and Psychiatry, 20,* 11–21.

Sedikides, C., and Skowronski, J. J. 2020. In human memory, good can be stronger than bad. *Current Directions in Psychological Science, 29,* 86–91.

Segal, Z. V. 1988. Appraisal of the self-schema construct in cognitive models of depression. *Psychological Bulletin, 103,* 147–62.

Seli, P., Risko, E. F., Smilek, D., and Schacter, D. L. 2016. Mind-wandering with and without intention. *Trends in Cognitive Sciences, 20,* 605–17.

Semenza, C., and Zettin, M. 1988. Generating proper names: A case of selective inability. *Cognitive Neuropsychology, 5,* 711–21.

Semenza, C., and Zettin, M. 1989. Evidence from aphasia for the role of proper names as pure referring expressions. *Nature, 342,* 678–79.

Semenza, C., and Sgaramella, T. M. 1993. Production of proper names: A clinical case study of the effects of phonemic cueing. *Memory, 1,* 265–80.

Semenza, C., Mondini, S., and Zettin, M. 1995. The anatomical basis of proper name processing: A critical review. *Neurocase, 1,* 183–88.

Shackelford, T. K., and Larsen, R. J. 1997. Facial asymmetry as an indicator of psychological, emotional, and physiological distress. *Journal of Personality and Social Psychology, 72,* 456–66.

Shackelford, T. K., and Larsen, R. J. 1999. Facial attractiveness and physical health. *Evolution and Human Behavior, 20,* 71–76.

Shallice, T., and Warrington, E. K. 1970. The independence of the verbal memory stores: A neuropsychological study. *Quarterly Journal of Experimental Psychology, 22,* 261–73.

Shallice, T., Fletcher, P., Frith, C. D., Grasby, P., Frackowiak, R. S. J., and Dolan, R. J. 1994. Brain regions associated with acquisition and retrieval of verbal episodic memory. *Nature, 368,* 633–35.

Shaw, J., and Porter, S. 2015. Constructing rich false memories of committing crime. *Psychological Science, 26,* 291–301.

Shaw, J. S., Bjork, R. A., and Handal, A. 1995. Retrieval-induced forgetting in an eyewitness memory paradigm. *Psychonomic Bulletin and Review, 2,* 249–53.

Shay, J. 1994. *Achilles in Vietnam: Combat trauma and the undoing of character.* New York: Atheneum.

Sherry, D. F., and Schacter, D. L. 1987. The evolution of multiple memory systems. *Psychological Review, 94,* 439–54.

Sherry, D. F., and Vaccarino, A. L. 1989. Hippocampus and memory for food caches in black-capped chickadees. *Behavioral Neuroscience, 103,* 308–18.

Sherry, D. F., Forbes, M. R. L., Khurgel, M., and Ivy, G. O. 1993. Females have a larger hippocampus than males in the brood-parasitic brown-headed cowbird. *Proceedings of the National Academy of Sciences USA, 90,* 7839–43.

Shettleworth, S. J. 1998. *Cognition, evolution, and behavior.* New York: Oxford University Press.

Shimamura, A. P. 1995. Memory and frontal lobe function. In M. Gazzaniga (ed.), *The cognitive neurosciences* (pp. 803–13). Cambridge, Mass.: MIT Press.

Shin, L. M., Kosslyn, S. M., McNally, R. J., Alpert, N. M., Thompson, W. L., Rauch, S. L., Macklin, M. L., and Pitman, R. K. 1997. Visual imagery and perception in posttraumatic stress disorder: A positron emission tomographic investigation. *Archives of General Psychiatry, 54,* 233–41.

Shin, L. M., McNally, R. J., Kosslyn, S. M., Thompson, W. L., Rauch, S. L., Alpert, N. M., Metzger, L. J., Lasko, N. B., Orr, S. P., and Pitman, R. K. 1999. Regional cerebral blood flow during script-driven imagery in childhood sexual abuse-related PTSD: A PET investigation. *American Journal of Psychiatry, 156,* 575–84.

Silverman, I., and Eals, M. 1992. Sex differences in spatial abilities: Evolutionary theory and data. In J. Barkow, L. Cosmides, and J. Tooby (eds.), *The adapted mind: Evolutionary psychology and the generation of culture* (pp. 487–503). New York: Oxford University Press.

Simons, D. J., and Levin, D. T. 1998. Failure to detect changes to people during a real-world interaction. *Psychonomic Bulletin and Review, 4,* 501–6.

Simons, D. J., and Chabris, C. F. 1999. Gorillas in our midst: Sustained inattentional blindness for dynamic events. *Perception, 28,* 1059–74.

Simons, D. J. 2000. Current approaches to change blindness. *Visual Cognition, 7,* 1–15.

Skinner, B. F. 1983. Intellectual self-management in old age. *American Psychologist, 38,* 239–44.

Slamecka, N. J. 1968. An examination of trace storage in free recall. *Journal of Experimental Psychology, 76,* 504–13.

Slamecka, N. J., and McElree, B. 1983. Normal forgetting of verbal lists as a function of their degree of learning. *Journal of Experimental Psychology: Learning, Memory, and Cognition, 9,* 384–97.

Slamecka, N. J. 1985. Ebbinghaus: Some associations. *Journal of Experimental Psychology: Learning, Memory, and Cognition, 11,* 414–35.

Sloman, S. A., Bower, G. H., and Rohrer, D. 1991. Congruency effects in part-list cueing inhibition. *Journal of Experimental Psychology: Learning, Memory, and Cognition, 17,* 974–82.

Slotnick, S. D., and Schacter, D. L. 2004. A sensory signature that distinguishes true from false memories. *Nature Neuroscience, 7,* 664–72.

Small, S. A., Perera, G. M., DeLaPaz, R., Mayeux, R., and Stern, Y. 1999. Differential regional dysfunction of the hippocampal formation among elderly with memory decline and Alzheimer's disease. *Annals of Neurology, 45,* 466–72.

Smallwood, J., and Schooler, J. W. 2006. The restless mind. *Psychological Bulletin, 132,* 946–58.

Smallwood, J., and Schooler, J. W. 2015. The science of mind wandering: Empirically navigating the stream of consciousness. *Annual Review of Psychology, 66,* 487–518.

Smeekens, B. A., and Kane, M. J. 2016. Working memory capacity, mind wandering, and creative cognition: An individual-differences investigation into the benefits of controlled versus spontaneous thought. *Psychology of Aesthetics, Creativity, and the Arts, 10,* 389–415.

Sno, H. N., and Linszen, D. H. 1990. The déjà vu experience: Remembrance of things past? *American Journal of Psychiatry, 147,* 1587–95.

Sno, H. N., Linszen, D. H., and De Jonghe, F. 1992. Art imitates life: Déjà vu in experiences in prose and poetry. *British Journal of Psychiatry, 160,* 511–18.

Soares, J. S., and Storm, B. C. 2018. Forget in a flash: A further investigation of the photo-taking-impairment effect. *Journal of Applied Research in Memory and Cognition, 7,* 154–60.

Southwick, S. M., Bremner, J. D., Rasmusson, A., Morgan, C. A., Arnsten, A., and Charney, D. S. 1999a. Role of norepinephrine in the pathophysiology and treatment of posttraumatic stress disorder. *Biological Psychiatry, 46,* 1192–204.

Southwick, S. M., Morgan, C. A., Charney, D. S., and High, J. R. 1999b. Yohimbine use in a natural setting: Effects on posttraumatic stress disorder. *Biological Psychiatry, 46,* 442–44.

Spanos, N. P., Cross, P. A., Dickson, K., and DuBreuil, S. C. 1993. Close encounters: An examination of UFO experiences. *Journal of Abnormal Psychology, 102,* 624–32.

Spanos, N. P., Burgess, C. A., and Burgess, M. F. 1994. Past-life identities, UFO abductions, and satanic ritual abuse: The social construction of memories. *International Journal of Clinical and Experimental Hypnosis, 42,* 433–46.

Spanos, N. P., Burgess, C. A., Burgess, M. F., Samuels, C., and Blois, W. O. 1999. Creating false memories of infancy with hypnotic and non-hypnotic procedures. *Applied Cognitive Psychology, 13,* 201–18.

Sparrow, B., Liu, J., and Wegner, D. M. 2011. Google effects on memory: Cognitive consequences of having information at our fingertips. *Science, 333,* 776–78.

Spencer, K. B., Charbonneau, A. K., and Glaser, J. 2016. Implicit bias and policing. *Social and Personality Compass, 10,* 50–63.

Spiro, R. J. 1980. Accommodative reconstruction in prose recall. *Journal of Verbal Learning and Verbal Behavior, 19,* 84–95.

Sprecher, S. 1999. "I love you more today than yesterday": Romantic partners' perceptions of changes in love and related affect over time. *Journal of Personality and Social Psychology, 76,* 46–53.

Squire, L. R., Slater, P. C., and Chace, P. M. 1976. Reactivation of recent or remote memory before electroconvulsive therapy does not produce retrograde amnesia. *Behavioral Biology, 18,* 335–43.

Staples, B. 1994. *Parallel time.* New York: Pantheon Books.

Starr, K. 1998. *The Starr evidence: The complete text of the grand jury testimony of President Clinton and Monica Lewinsky.* New York: HarperCollins.

Steblay, N. M., Wells, G. L., and Douglass, A. L. 2014. The eyewitness post identification feedback effect 15 years later: Theoretical and policy implications. *Psychology, Public Policy, and Law, 20,* 1–18.

Stelter, B. 2016, September 27. Debate breaks record as most-watched in U.S. history. CNN Business. https://money.cnn.com/2016/09/27/media/debate-ratings-record-viewership/.

Stepp, D. R. 1996, October 7. Going by the book to cure forgetfulness; planners work wonders, teachers say. *Atlanta Journal and Constitution,* p. B1.

Sterelny, K., and Griffiths, P. E. 1999. *Sex and death: An introduction to philosophy of biology.* Chicago: University of Chicago Press.

Stigsdotter-Neely, A., and Backman, L. 1993. Long-term maintenance of gains from memory training in older adults: Two 3-year follow-up studies. *Journal of Gerontology, 48,* 233–37.

Storm, B. C., and Stone, S. M. 2015. Saving-enhanced memory: The benefits of saving on the learning and remembering of new information. *Psychological Science, 26,* 182–88.

Stramaccia, D. F., Meyer, A.-K., Rischer, K. M., Fawcett, J. M., and Benoit, R. G. 2020. Memory suppression and its deficiency in psychological disorders: A focused meta-analysis. *Journal of Experimental Psychology: General.* https://doi.org/10.1037/xge0000971.

Streb, M., Mecklinger, A., Anderson, M. C., Lass-Hennemann, J., and Michael, T. 2016. Memory control ability modulates intrusive memories after analogue trauma. *Journal of Affective Disorders, 192,* 134–42.

Suddendorf, T., and Corballis, M. C. 2007. The evolution of foresight: What is mental time travel and is it unique to humans? *Behavioral and Brain Sciences, 30,* 299–313.

Sully, J. W. 1881. *Illusions: A psychological study.* New York: D. Appleton.

Sunderland, A., Watts, K., Baddeley, A., and Harris, J. E. 1986. Subjective memory assessment and test performance in elderly adults. *Journal of Gerontology, 41,* 376–84.

Symons, C. S., and Johnson, B. T. 1997. The self-reference effect in memory: A meta-analysis. *Psychological Bulletin, 121,* 371–94.

Szpunar, K. K., Watson, J. M., and McDermott, K. B. 2007. Neural substrates of envisioning the future. *Proceedings of the National Academy of Sciences USA, 104,* 642–47.

Szpunar, K. K., Khan, N. Y., and Schacter, D. L. 2013. Interpolated memory tests reduce mind wandering and improve learning of online lectures. *Proceedings of the National Academy of Sciences USA, 110,* 6313–17.

Tamir, D. I., Templeton, E. M., Ward, A. F., and Zaki, J. 2018. Media usage diminishes memory for experiences. *Journal of Experimental Social Psychology, 76,* 161–68.

Tang, Y. P., Shimizu, E., Dube, G. R., Rampon, C., Kerchner, G. A., Zhuo, M., Liu, G., and Tsien, J. Z. 1999. Genetic enhancement of learning and memory in mice. *Nature, 401,* 63–69.

Taylor, F. K. 1965. Cryptomnesia and plagiarism. *British Journal of Psychiatry, 111,* 1111–18.

Taylor, S. E., and Brown, J. D. 1988. Illusion and well-being: A social psychological perspective on mental health. *Psychological Bulletin, 103,* 193–210.

Taylor, S. E. 1989. *Positive illusions.* New York: Basic Books.

Tempini, M. L, Price, C. J., Josephs, O., Vandenbergh, R., Cappa, S. F., Kapur, N., and Frackowiak, R. S. J. 1998. The neural systems sustaining face and proper-name processing. *Brain, 121,* 2103–18.

Tetlock, P., and Mitchell, G. 2009. Implicit bias and accountability systems: What must organizations do to prevent discrimination? *Research in Organizational Behavior, 29,* 3–38.

Thakral, P. P., Madore, K. P., Devitt, A. L., and Schacter, D. L. 2019. Adaptive constructive processes: An episodic specificity induction impacts false recall in the Deese-Roediger-McDermott paradigm. *Journal of Experimental Psychology: General, 148,* 1480–93.

Thompson, C. P., Skowronski, J., Larsen, S. F., and Betz, A. 1996. *Autobiographical memory: Remembering what and remembering when.* Mahwah, N.J.: Erlbaum Associates.

Thomson, D. M. 1988. Context and false recognition. In G. M. Davies and D. M. Thomson (eds.), *Memory in context: Context in memory* (pp. 285–304). Chichester, England: John Wiley.

Thornhill, R., and Møller, A. P. 1997. Developmental stability, disease and medicine. *Biological Reviews of the Cambridge Philosophical Society, 72,* 497–548.

Tiffen, R. 2009, June 17. Barefaced robbery … by mistake. *New Zealand Herald.* https://www.nzherald.co.nz/nz/barefaced-robbery-by-mistake/PY45WO2U IXIBEWNFFENHUZCUXU/.

Tong, F., Nakayama, K., Moscovitch, M., Weinrib, O., and Kanwisher, N. 2000. Response properties of the human fusiform face area. *Cognitive Neuropsychology, 17,* 257–79.

Tooby, J., and Cosmides, L. 1992. The psychological foundations of culture. In J. Barkow, L. Cosmides, and J. Tooby (eds.), *The adapted mind* (pp. 19–136). New York: Oxford University Press.

Tronson, N. C. 2020, August 7. How Covid-19 might increase the risk of memory loss and cognitive decline. *Discover.* https://www.discovermagazine.com/health/how-covid-19 -might-increase-risk-of-memory-loss-and-cognitive-decline.

Trudeau, K. 1997. *Mega Memory.* New York: William Morrow.

Tulving, E. 1972. Episodic and semantic memory. In E. Tulving and W. Donaldson (eds.), *Organization of memory* (pp. 381–403). New York: Academic Press.

Tulving, E. 1985. Memory and consciousness. *Canadian Psychology, 26,* 1–12.

Tulving, E. 2002. Episodic memory: From mind to brain. *Annual Review of Psychology, 53,* 1–25.

Tun, P. A., Wingfield, A., Rosen, M. J., and Blanchard, L. 1998. Response latencies for false memories: Gist-based processes in normal aging. *Psychology and Aging, 13,* 230–41.

Uncapher, M. R., Boyd-Meredith, J. T., Chow, T. E., Rissman, J., and Wagner, A. D. 2015. Goal-directed modulation of neural memory patterns: Implications for fMRI-based memory detection. *Journal of Neuroscience, 35,* 8531–45.

Unkelbach, C., Koch, A., Silva, R. R., and Garcia-Marques, T. 2019. Truth by repetition: Explanations and implications. *Current Directions in Psychological Science, 28,* 257–63.

Usher, J. A., and Neisser, U. 1993. Childhood amnesia and the beginnings of memory for four early life events. *Journal of Experimental Psychology: General, 122,* 155–65.

Valentine, T., Brennen, T., and Brédart, S. 1996. *The cognitive psychology of proper names: On the importance of being Ernest.* London: Routledge.

Vallar, G., and Shallice, T. 1990. *Neuropsychological impairments of short-term memory*. Cambridge: Cambridge University Press.

Van Arsdale, S. 1995. *Toward amnesia*. New York: Riverhead Books.

van Stegeren, A. H., Everaerd, W., Cahill, L., McGaugh, J. L., and Gooren, L. J. G. 1998. Memory for emotional events: Differential effects of centrally versus peripherally acting β-blocking agents. *Psychopharmacology, 138*, 305–10.

Varner, L. J., and Ellis, H. C. 1998. Cognitive activity and physiological arousal: Processes that mediate mood-congruent memory. *Memory and Cognition, 26*, 939–50.

Vigliocco, G., Antonini, T., and Garrett, M. F. 1997. Grammatical gender is on the tip of Italian tongues. *Psychological Science, 8*, 314–17.

Vigliocco, G., Vinson, D. P., Martin, R. C., and Garrett, M. F. 1999. Is "count" and "mass" information available when the noun is not? An investigation of tip of the tongue states and anomia. *Journal of Memory and Language, 40*, 534–58.

von Bartheld, C. S., Bahney, J., and Herculano-Houzel, S. 2016. The search for true numbers of neurons and glial cells in the human brain: A review of 150 years of cell counting. *Journal of Comparative Neurology, 524*, 3865–95.

Vortac, O. U., Edwards, M. B., and Manning, C. A. 1995. Functions of external cues in prospective memory. *Memory, 3*, 201–19.

Wade, K. A., Garry, M., and Pezdek, K. 2018. Deconstructing rich false memories of committing crime: Commentary on Shaw and Porter (2015). *Psychological Science, 29*, 471–76.

Wagenaar, W. A. 1986. My memory: A study of autobiographical memory over six years. *Cognitive Psychology, 18*, 225–52.

Wagner, A. D., Schacter, D. L., Rotte, M., Koutstaal, W., Maril, A., Dale, A. M., Rosen, B. R., and Buckner, R. L. 1998. Building memories: Remembering and forgetting of verbal experiences as predicted by brain activity. *Science, 281*, 1188–91.

Wagner, A. D., Koutstaal, W., and Schacter, D. L. 1999. When encoding yields remembering: Insights from event-related neuroimaging. *Proceedings of the Royal Society of London B: Biological Sciences, 354*, 1307–24.

Wagner, A. D., Maril, A., and Schacter, D. L. 2000. Interactions between forms of memory: When priming hinders new learning. *Journal of Cognitive Neuroscience, 12*, 52–60.

Walker, W. R., Vogl, R., and Thompson, C. R. 1997. Autobiographical memory: Unpleasantness fades faster than pleasantness over time. *Applied Cognitive Psychology, 11*, 399–413.

Walker, W. R., Skowronski, J. J., Gibbons, J. A., Vogl, R. J., and Thompson, C. P. 2003a. On the emotions that accompany autobiographical memories: Dysphoria disrupts the fading affect bias. *Cognition and Emotion, 17*, 703–24.

Walker, W. R., Skowronski, J. J., and Thompson, C. P. 2003b. Life is pleasant . . . and memory helps to keep it that way! *Review of General Psychology, 7*, 203–10.

Walker, W. R., and Skowronski, J. J. 2009. The fading affect bias: But what the hell is it for? *Applied Cognitive Psychology, 23*, 1122–36.

Walker, W. R., Yancu, C. N., and Skowronski, J. J. 2014. Trait anxiety reduces affective fading for positive and negative autobiographical memories. *Advances in Cognitive Psychology, 10*, 81–89.

Walker, W. R., Alexander, H., and Aune, K. 2020. Higher levels of Grit are associated with a stronger fading affect bias. *Psychological Reports, 123,* 124–40.

Wammes, J. D., Ralph, B. C. W., Mills, C., Bosch, N., Duncan, T. L., and Smilek, D. 2019. Disengagement during lectures: Media multitasking and mind wandering in university classrooms. *Computers and Education, 132,* 76–89.

Ward, J., Parkin, A. J., Powell, G., Squires, E. J., Townshend, J., and Bradley, V. 1999. False recognition of unfamiliar people: "Seeing film stars everywhere." *Cognitive Neuropsychology, 16,* 293–315.

Warren, C. K. 1996, August 9. The forgetfulness epidemic that is a plague to many of us. *St. Louis Post-Dispatch,* p. E9.

Washburn, K., Major, J. S., and Fadiman, C. (eds.). 1998. *World poetry: An anthology of verse from antiquity to our time.* New York: W. W. Norton.

Wasserman, D., Lempert, R. O., and Hastie, R. 1991. Hindsight and causality. *Personality and Social Psychology Bulletin, 17,* 30–35.

Waterhouse, L. 1988. Extraordinary visual memory and pattern perception in an autistic boy. In L. K. Obler and D. Fein (eds.), *The exceptional brain: Neuropsychology of talent and special abilities* (pp. 325–40). New York: Guilford Press.

Wegner, D. M. 1994. Ironic processes of mental control. *Psychological Review, 101,* 34–52.

Wegner, D. M., and Gold, D. B. 1995. Fanning old flames: Emotional and cognitive effects of suppressing thoughts of a past relationship. *Journal of Personality and Social Psychology, 68,* 782–92.

Weine, S. M., Kulenovic, A. D., Pavkovic, I., and Gibbons, R. 1998. Testimony psychotherapy in Bosnian refugees: A pilot study. *American Journal of Psychiatry, 155,* 1720–26.

Weiner, J. 1999. *Time, love, memory: A great biologist and his search for the origins of behavior.* New York: Alfred A. Knopf.

Weingarten, G. 2009, March 8. Fatal distraction: Forgetting a child in the backseat of a car is a horrifying mistake. Is it a crime? *Washington Post Magazine.* https://www.washingtonpost.com/lifestyle/magazine/fatal-distraction-forgetting-a-child-in-thebackseat-of-a-car-is-a-horrifying-mistake-is-it-a-crime/2014/06/16/8aeofe3a-f580-11e3-a3a5-42be35962a52_story.html?noredirect=on.

Weisberg, S. M., Newcombe, N. S., and Chatterjee, A. 2019. Everyday taxi drivers: Do better navigators have larger hippocampi? *Cortex, 115,* 280–93.

Wells, G. L., and Bradfield, A. L. 1998. Good, you identified the suspect: Feedback to eyewitnesses distorts their reports of the witnessing experience. *Journal of Applied Psychology, 83,* 360–76.

Wells, G. L., Small, M., Penrod, S., Malpass, R. S., Fulero, S. M., and Brimacombe, C. A. E. 1998. Eyewitness identification procedures: Recommendations for lineups and photospreads. *Law and Human Behavior, 22,* 603–47.

Wells, G. L., Malpass, R. S., Lindsay, R. C. L., Fisher, R. P., Turtle, J. W., and Fulero, S. M. 2000. From the lab to the police station: A successful application of eyewitness research. *American Psychologist, 55,* 581–98.

Wesnes, K. A., Faleni, R. A., Hefting, N. R., Hoogsteen, G., Houben, J. J. G., Jenkins, E., Jonkman, J. H. G., Leonard, J., Petrini, O., and van Lier, J. J. 1997. The cognitive, subjective, and physical effects of a *Ginkgo biloba/Panax ginseng* combination in healthy volunteers with neurasthenic complaints. *Psychopharmacology Bulletin, 33,* 677–83.

West, R. L., and Crook, T. H. 1992. Video training of imagery for mature adults. *Applied Cognitive Psychology, 6,* 307–20.

West, T. A., and Bauer, P. J. 1999. Assumptions of infantile amnesia: Are there differences between early and later memories? *Memory, 7,* 257–78.

Whalen, P. J. 1998. Fear, vigilance, and ambiguity: Initial neuroimaging studies of the human amygdala. *Current Directions in Psychological Science, 7,* 177–88.

Whalen, P. J., Rauch, S. L., Etcoff, N. L., McInerney, S. C., Lee, M. B., and Jenike, M. A. 1998. Masked presentations of emotional facial expressions modulate amygdala activity without explicit knowledge. *Journal of Neuroscience, 18,* 411–18.

Whittlesea, B. W. A. 1993. Illusions of familiarity. *Journal of Experimental Psychology: Learning, Memory, and Cognition, 19,* 1235–53.

Wiggs, C. L., and Martin, A. 1998. Properties and mechanisms of perceptual priming. *Current Opinion in Neurobiology, 8,* 227–33.

Williams, G. C. 1992. *Natural selection: Domains, levels, and challenges.* New York: Oxford University Press.

Williams, J. M. G., Mathews, A., and MacLeod, C. 1996. The emotional Stroop task and psychopathology. *Psychological Bulletin, 120,* 3–24.

Williams, M. 1997. *Cry of pain.* London: Penguin Books.

Wilson, B. M., Donnelly, K., Christenfeld, N., and Wixted, J. T. 2019. Making sense of sequential lineups: An experimental and theoretical analysis of position effects. *Journal of Memory and Language, 104,* 108–25.

Winograd, E. 1988. Some observations on prospective remembering. In M. M. Gruneberg, P. E. Morris, and R. N. Sykes (eds.), *Practical aspects of memory: Current research and issues* (vol. 1, pp. 348–53). New York: Cambridge University Press.

Winograd, E., Peluso, J. P., and Glover, T. A. 1998. Individual differences in susceptibility to memory illusions. *Applied Cognitive Psychology, 12,* S5–27.

Wittmann, B. C., Schott, B. H., Guderian, S., Frey, J. U., Heinze, H.-J., and Düzel, E. 2005. Reward-related fMRI activation of dopaminergic midbrain is associated with enhanced hippocampus-dependent long-term memory formation. *Neuron, 45,* 459–67.

Wixted, J. T., Mickes, L., Clark, S. E., Gronlund, S. D., and Roediger, H. L. 2015. Initial eyewitness confidence reliably predicts eyewitness identification accuracy. *American Psychologist, 70,* 515–26.

Wixted, J. T., Mickes, L., Clark, S. E., Dunn, J. C., and Wells, W. 2016. Estimating the reliability of eyewitness identifications from police lineups. *Proceedings of the National Academy of Sciences USA, 113,* 304–9.

Wixted, J. T., and Wells, G. L. 2017. The relationship between eyewitness confidence and identification accuracy: A new synthesis. *Psychological Science in the Public Interest, 18,* 10–65.

Wixted, J. T. 2018. Time to exonerate eyewitness memory. *Forensic Science International, 292,* e13–15.

Wolf, O. T., Kudielka, B. M., Hellhammer, D. H., Torber, S., McEwen, B. S., and Kirschbaum,

C. 1999. Two weeks of transdermal estradiol treatment in postmenopausal elderly women and its effect on memory and mood: Verbal memory changes are associated with the treatment induced estradiol levels. *Psychoneuroendocrinology, 24,* 727–41.

Wong, A. H. C., Smith, M., and Boon, H. S. 1998. Herbal remedies in psychiatric practice. *Archives of General Psychiatry, 55,* 1033–44.

Wood, N. E., Rosasco, M. L., Suris, A. M., Spring, J. D., Marin, M. F., Lasko, N. B., Goetz, J. M., Fischer, A. M., Orr, S. P., and Pitman, R. K. 2015. Pharmacological blockade of memory reconsolidation in posttraumatic stress disorder: Three negative psychophysiological studies. *Psychiatry Research, 225,* 31–39.

Wood, W. 2000. Attitude change: Persuasion and social influence. *Annual Review of Psychology, 51,* 539–70.

Woollett, K., and Maguire, E. A. 2011. Acquiring "the Knowledge" of London's layout drives structural brain changes. *Current Biology, 21,* 2109–14.

Wright, L. 1994. *Remembering Satan: A case of recovered memory and the shattering of an American family.* New York: Alfred A. Knopf.

Young, A. W., Hay, D. C., and Ellis, A. W. 1985. The faces that launched a thousand slips: Everyday difficulties and errors in recognizing people. *British Journal of Psychology, 76,* 495–523.

Yu, D. W., and Shepard, G. H. 1998. Is beauty in the eye of the beholder? *Nature, 396,* 321–22.

Zeelenberg, M., van Dijk, W. W., van der Pligt, J., Manstead, A. S. R., van Empelen, P., and Reinderman, D. 1998. Emotional reactions to the outcomes of decisions: The role of counterfactual thought in the experience of regret and disappointment. *Organizational Behavior and Human Decision Processes, 75,* 117–41.

Zeithamova, D., and Preston, A. R. 2010. Flexible memories: Differential roles for medial temporal lobe and prefrontal cortex in cross-episode binding. *Journal of Neuroscience, 30,* 14676–84.

Zelinski, E. M., and Burnight, K. P. 1997. Sixteen-year longitudinal and time lag changes in memory and cognition in older adults. *Psychology and Aging, 12,* 503–13.

Index

Page numbers in *italics* refer to illustrations.